fig.3

fig.6

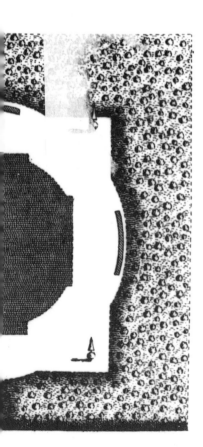

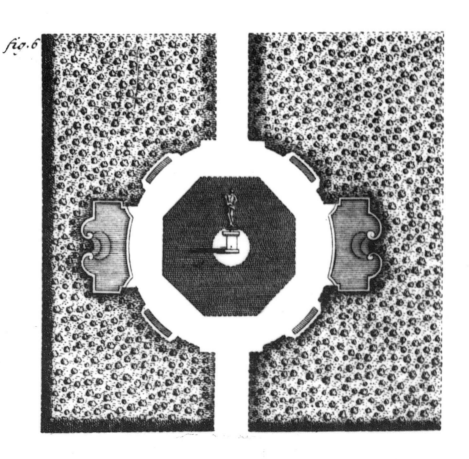

10   13 *Fathom*

M.V.^dr Guchi seul.

THE PLANTERS OF THE ENGLISH
LANDSCAPE GARDEN

11·4·95		04 00
7·6·95		0 0
		13
22 APR 1996		
27 AUG 1996		
29 NOV 1996		
11 MAR 1997		
15 SEP 1997		
-4 MAR 1998		
27 OCT 2003		

THE PLANTERS OF THE ENGLISH LANDSCAPE GARDEN:

BOTANY, TREES, AND THE *GEORGICS*

DOUGLAS CHAMBERS

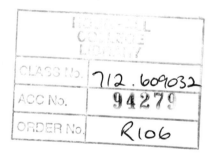
PUBLISHED FOR
THE PAUL MELLON CENTRE FOR STUDIES
IN BRITISH ART
BY
YALE UNIVERSITY PRESS
NEW HAVEN AND LONDON 1993

Designed by Faith Glasgow
Set in Linotron Bembo by Best-set Typesetter Ltd., Hong Kong
Printed in Hong Kong through World Print Ltd.

Library of Congress Cataloging-in-Publication Data

Chambers, Douglas.
The planters of the English landscape garden: botany, trees, and
the Georgics / Douglas Chambers.
p.   cm. — (Studies in British art)
Includes index.
ISBN 0-300-05464-5
1. Gardens, English—History.   2. Gardeners—England—History.
3. Gardens—England—History.   4. Plants, Ornamental—England—
History.   5. Ornamental trees—England—History.   I. Title.
II. Series.
SB457.6.C47   1993
712′.0942—dc20
92-35695
CIP

CONTENTS

ACKNOWLEDGMENTS

Garden history is still a relatively new field. Until recently no one was, by training, a garden historian and few were historians of botany. As a novice in both disciplines, I am grateful to many people for generous assistance and thoughtful advice, and especially to Alan Armstrong, Alan Bewell, Edward Chaney, George Clarke, Brian Corman, Gina Douglas, Joe Ewen, Peter Goodchild, Alan Harding, Edward Harwood, Clyde Janes, Mark Laird, Richard Landon, Todd Longstaffe-Gowan, Robert MacCubbin, Michael McCarthy, Desmond Neill, Steve Parks, Allen Paterson, Craig Patterson, Diana Patterson, Robert Williams, Chris Ridgway, Peter Stevens, John Wing, and Jan Woudstra. I am also indebted to the helpful staff at the following libraries: the British Library, the Beinecke Library, the Essex County Record Office, the Hertfordshire County Record Office, the Houghton Library, the West Sussex Record Office, the West Yorkshire Archives, and the Sutro Library. I want especially to thank the staff of the Trinity College Library and the Fisher Library in the University of Toronto. Without the unfailing assistance of John Glover, the Faculty of Arts photographer at the University of Toronto, the illustrations to this book could never have been compiled.

Earlier versions of chapters 5 and 2 appeared in *Garden History* and the *University of Toronto Quarterly* respectively. The appendix previously appeared in *Garden History Society Newsletter* 29 (Summer, 1990), pp. 11–12. Because the *Newsletter* has a limited circulation, I have chosen to reprint the article here.

In citing early quotations I have changed '&' to 'and' and silently corrected punctuation where (as is often the case in Peter Collinson, for example) the reading would be ambiguous or incomprehensible. Where names in the eighteenth century were commonly misspelled (i.e. spelled in a way that is not standard today), I have not put '*sic*' after them nor have I noted such common eighteenth-century usage as 'it's' for the possessive. Only where the original seems to me incomprehensible to a modern reader have I put a correction in square brackets. In the eighteenth century, three spellings were common for one of Pliny's Villas: Laurentum, Laurentium, and Laurentinum. To avoid confusion, I have chosen the last: the one most commonly used. In all cases where no page number is given in the original printed text, I have given the signature number but not invented a leaf number. 'BL' refers to the British Library. All other libraries are identified in full.

Prioribus
Hortulanis agricolisque

Nor have we herein forgot to take Notice of the Gardens of those worthy Patriots of Horticulture, where many of the Trees here treated of, are now in a flourishing Condition, or grown to a considerable Magnitude; to which Persons (as we have before said) the Nation as well as we are indebted for introducing many new Species of Trees among us, the Advantage of which would be no difficult Matter to set forth, were it necessary.

Society of Gardeners, *Catalogus Plantarum* (London, 1730), sig. [cv].

1

THE PATRIOTS OF HORTICULTURE: AN INTRODUCTION

The history of English gardens and landscapes, at least since its effective beginning in the 1950s, has been largely the preserve of literary and art historians. In the process, much of the most important pioneering work done on gardeners, botany, and planting has frequently been marginalised or neglected in the attempt both to chart a great tradition of patrons and designers and to establish the dominant mythologies that sustained that tradition.

What follows is not a comprehensive account of the development of the English landscape garden in the late seventeenth and early eighteenth centuries. Much of that history has already been written. Studies of such major designers as George London, Sir John Vanbrugh, Charles Bridgeman, and William Kent, have made clear how the shift from French and Dutch conceptions to what we think of as the English style came about. At the same time, a great deal of attention has been given to the theorists of gardening and their literary sources and influences. Alexander Pope and James Thomson, for example, receive considerable attention in John Dixon Hunt's *The Figure in the Landscape*, but Joseph Spence appears there not as an important gardener but only as a recorder of Pope's *dicta*, and William Shenstone, another important maker of landscape, enters only as an audience for Thomson.[1]

What has been overlooked is not the place of artists, architects, and poets but that of botanists, nurserymen, and gardeners in the creation of these new landscapes. How did the Virgilian concept of *ingentia rura* come to be translated by them into the newly appropriated landscape? How, moreover, was the botanical revolution of the early eighteenth century, inspired by similar Virgilian ideals, instrumental in the creation of these landscape gardens?

If European art history has suffered from the split between iconographers on the one hand and historians of technique on the other, its step-sister garden history, in its much shorter career, has been equally bedevilled. The distinction between the history of gardening and the history of gardens has been more at the cost of the former than the latter, but both have suffered. The danger now, however, is that instead recent sociological and historical scholarship will introduce into garden history a prolepsis as distorting as the intellectually gentrified account it replaces. The history of landscape is, it seems, particularly susceptible to theory and generalisation, but the more closely one looks at the evidence, the more difficult it is to find theoretical solutions.

Although it would be convenient, for example, to see the rise of the landscape garden as a Whig attempt to 'launder' commercial wealth in the myth of landed property, Pope's portrait of Timon's villa in the 'Epistle to Burlington' suggests that this kind of 'laundering' was largely unsuccessful, both in execution (its uncongenial and old-fashioned symmetry) and in adopting the modes and mores of traditional establishment values. The landed establishment, in the voice of Pope, remained unimpressed. In the 'Epistle to Burlington' Pope not only contrasts the turbulence of public life with the continuing patterns of agriculture but allows 'laughing Ceres,' in the name of agriculture and right nature, to repossess a landscape falsely appropriated by commerce.

And yet Pope's addressee was Lord Burlington, himself a Whig and of a family whose fortunes dated only from the middle of the seventeenth century. Burlington, nonetheless, had captured the high ground of Palladianism and become the arbiter of taste, certainly so far as landscape and architecture were concerned. In so doing, he was like many men of both political parties who were increasingly disenchanted with what looked like tyrannical greed in Sir Robert Walpole's government.[2] In 1727, moreover, Leonard Welsted solicited the support of Walpole himself for a translation of Horace on just the basis of a restored antiquity that was thought to be the prerogative of the circle of the Tory leader, Edward Harley, Earl of Oxford.[3]

In fact many of the interesting and pioneering landscape gardens were created by men of traditional landed connections and conservative, even Tory, impulses. But that this was not simply so is reflected in the obvious examples of such Whig improvers as Lord Cobham at Stowe, the Duke of Argyll (himself a government minister) at Whitton, and Henry Hoare at Stourhead. That Hoare married the daughter of a Tory peer and in turn married his daughters to Tory peers is indicative of the dangers of easy political generalisation. It may be possible to suggest that, in a period of social revolution in which a rising commercial class assumes the power (and the mantle) of traditional landed interest, those who represent that previously unquestioned interest are called upon to reexamine the nature and meaning of landowning and to redefine its purpose.[4]

It is a cliché that in times of such social change there is a rise in the desire and need for a myth to sustain what are thought of as traditional values. What may have occurred then in the early eighteenth century was a reaction against the new capitalism and its appropriation of the countryside, a reaction that looked back to a myth of acceptable agrarianism in which man worked not as the exploiter of but the co-operator with nature. In such a situation, Virgil's *Georgics* supplied a myth of right husbandry that could also be reconciled with a sacred landscape. In such a context too, John Evelyn's *Sylva* was particularly potent. It offered a way for use to 'sanctify expense': tree-planting both as profitable husbandry and the re-creation of sacred or Edenic landscape.

Such certainly was the case at Cassiobury, the first landscape garden consciously to create extensive woodland. Evelyn's *Sylva* and Marvell's 'Upon Appleton House' are both prophetic of 'the extensive way of rural gardening' celebrated by Stephen Switzer in the second decade of the eighteenth century. Marvell's poem, moreover, connected such gardening with the tradition of the country house ideal, a tradition that stretched back to Jonson's celebration of the Sidneys' Penshurst and was to become a central Tory myth in the early eighteenth century.

Jonathan Swift's scepticism about this ideal, expressed in his various poems about country-house life, is the more striking in contrast to its fervent espousal among the many Tories and disaffected Whigs who were his friends and correspondents. 'I have no very strong Faith in you pretenders to retirement,' he wrote in 1723 to Pope, who was then staying at Lord Peterborough's in

Parson's Green near London.[5] That he himself was a botanical experimenter in his garden ('Naboth's Vineyard') in Dublin, however, indicates both his infection with the germ of botanical improvement and that he was less sceptical about the possibilities of horticulture in a postlapsarian world than his poems and correspondence might suggest.[6]

In the general reaction against Calvinism, a host of late seventeenth-century writers, buoyed up by Cambridge Platonism, were keen to unite the ideal of stoic retirement to the tradition of the country-house ideal.[7] That many of their estates, like that of Swift's patron, Sir William Temple, in Surrey or those of Pope's circle in Twickenham, were small and virtually suburban did not diminish the potency of the ideal. The irony implicit in this ideal was, after all, apparent in Horace's second epode (*Beatus ille*) where such a retreat is the fond dream of an urban moneylender. No late seventeenth-century reader, moreover, needed to be reminded that Paradise had been lost. In his famous and popular painting, *The Shepherds of Arcadia*, Poussin suggests that the ideal of arcadian retreat was the more potent and meaningful precisely because of our living in an imperfect world where death was very much present. And John Evelyn was in no doubt that the gardener's labour created a restored arcadia. Writing to Sir Thomas Browne in 1660, he described his proposed *Elysium Britannicum* in just those terms:

> The Modell, Sir, which I propose, and which I perceive you have seene, will abundantly testifie my abhorrency of those painted and formall projections of our Cockney Gardens and little plotts, which appear like Gardens of past-board and March-pane, and smell more of paynt, then of flowers and verdure: Our drift is a noble, princely and universall Elysium, capable of all the amoenities, that can naturally be introduced into Gardens of Pleasure, and such is my stand in competition with all the august designes and stories of this nature either of antient or modern tymes; Yet so, as to become usefull, and significant to the least pretences and faculties: We do endeavour to shew, how the aire and genius of Gardens worke upon humane Spirits towards virtue and Sanctitie, I meane in a remote preparatory and instrumentall working: How Caves, Grotts, Mounds and other like irregular ornmaments of Gardens do contribute to contemplative and Philosophical Enthusiasms: How Elysium, Antrum, Newmus, Paradisus, Hortus, and Lucus signifie all of them Rem Sacrum et divinam.[8]

Evelyn's 'usefull' also suggests how Horace's *Ars Poetica* offered another text—*utile dulci*—whereby the pleasure of this ideal might be reconciled to moral and economic use. And Virgil's *Georgics*, first made widely popular in Dryden's 1697 translation, provided (in Book II) both a model for silviculture and an encouragement to the sort of botanical experimentation already taking place. As Swift wrote to Pope: 'I suppose Virgil and Horace are equally read by Whigs and Tories.'[9] Out of this union of ancient philosophical ideals, the sudden expansion of botany, and practical silviculture came the remaking of the English landscape and the creation of the English landscape garden.

It is now a truism that we escape from reading history through the spectacles of our own cultural assumptions only insofar as we struggle to see more clearly without them. Part of that struggle involves attempting to see the evidence before us unmediated by our own assumptions and vocabulary. If it is not helpful to think of English society in the late seventeenth and early eighteenth centuries as an *ancien régime*, for example, neither is it helpful to think of it as a 'banana republic.'[10]

This understanding also involves attempting to recover a sense of the society in question as it understood and 'translated' itself to itself: its cultural assumptions. Although the word 'Augustan' has conventionally been used to identify the nature of the dominant culture in the early eighteenth century, the botanic science that originally constituted part of what that word meant has largely been edited out in favour of literary, aesthetic, or political readings. What the revitalised social history of *annales* offers us is not only a larger 'text' in which to read that history but many 'vocabularies' in which to pursue it.

It is as impossible for the twentieth-century reader to recover totally the nature of Restoration and early eighteenth-century society as to enter fully into the life of Shakespeare's Globe. It has long been a cliché, however, that to understand Shakespeare's printed text we need to know a great deal more about the physical, social, and intellectual circumstances of his audience. The printed text in and of itself has become almost as elusive as the biblical text before the advent of higher criticism in the nineteenth century. One of the basic questions for the garden historian must concern the mythology available to and believed in by the men who actually made the gardens: in many cases men dismissed by those who would be their champions as too illiterate to understand this mythology.

Our struggle to understand involves looking at society as widely as possible, not restricting ourselves to the documentation and assumptions of one class or to one kind of literature. In garden history, estate account books, journals, and the letters of stewards and gardeners may tell us as much about the way a garden 'means' as the stated intentions of its owner or designer. But the two need not be at odds. Indeed, if there was one field in which the celebrated divorce between polite and popular culture in post-Restoration England was not apparent, it was gardening.

An influential owner such as Lord Petre was a designer in the new extensive manner inspired by Virgil and Pliny, but he was as much a plantsman and propagator as any nurseryman of his day. Moreover he translated landscape's painterly origins back into his own estate by 'painting in planting to show the Contrast of Light and Shades.'[11] These were the very colour effects on which contemporary nurserymen prided themselves, and they were just the ones that interested Joseph Spence, a classicist and aesthetician whose accounts of tree-planting are among the most interesting of the period. Stephen Switzer, who described himself as a seedsman, was nonetheless one of the great exponents of Virgilian principles of landscape-making, and ordinary gardeners, such as Peter Aram at Newby Hall or John MacClary at Rousham, were plainly familiar with the aesthetic and philosophical aspects of garden design.

The Society of Gardeners who put together the *Catalogus Plantarum* in 1730 were in no doubt of the horticultural alliance among aristocracy, gentry, clergy, and ordinary gardeners in creating what they saw as a revolution in gardens that was as significant as the political Revolution of 1688. The dedication of the *Catalogus* is to the Earl of Pembroke, but the list of 'Patriots of Horticulture' concludes with the highest praise for Charles Dubois, a gardener of Mitcham.[12]

The word 'patriots' invokes a controversy that continued to vex Augustan society until well into the eighteenth century: the true nature of English polity. In attaching patriotism to the promotion of botany and horticulture, however, the preface to the *Catalogus* subverts political division by translating patriotism into an apparently neutral field. Inspired as it is by having translated the language of the *Georgics* into the nursery and the garden-landscape, the

Catalogus offers to gardeners and nurserymen in turn a new English vocabulary. It does so, moreover, in an idiom of translation that Pope had already employed in the preface to his 1715 translation of the *Iliad*:

> Our Author's Work is a wild Paradise, where if we see not all the Beauties so distinctly as in an order'd Garden, it is only because the number of them is infinitely greater. 'Tis like a copious Nursery which contains the Seeds and first Productions of every kind, out of which those who follow'd him have but selected some particular Plants, each according to his Fancy, to cultivate and beautify.[13]

What the *Catalogus* celebrates is not the revolution in garden design (a subject, it suggests, frequently canvassed by those who know little about plants), but rather 'tracing out the various Operations of vegetative Nature thro' her many intricate Mazes, where by discovering her various Footsteps, the business of Gardening is reduced to a much greater Certainty.'[14]

The language of that celebration is as Virgilian as Switzer's invocation of *ingentia rura* (extensive landscape) or Tempe. It translates Virgil's insistence, that the gardener know the causes of things (*rerum naturae causas*), into the practice of early eighteenth-century England. Moreover it invokes Virgil's celebration of national superiority and his insistence (in Book II of the *Georgics*) upon improving native stocks in the context of what may be discovered from foreign plants:

> These generous Encouragers have inspirited ingenious Gardeners to make the Study of Vegetation their Business, and to improve the Cultivation not only of those Trees, Plants and Flowers of our own Growth, but also to procure and naturalize foreign Ones of many different Climates to our own; and they have by great Pains, Industry, and artful Management, happily succeeded in many Things, not only to their own Satisfaction, but also to that of their Employers; and may, we hope without Arrogancy, be said, to be able not only to vie with, but to out-do most of the same Profession in Europe.[15]

In the words of Pope's *Essay on Man*, the universe is a landscape garden: a mighty maze, but not without a plan. In the frontispiece of that poem [Fig. 1] his persona sits like a sardonic Democritus contemplating the ruins of antiquity. But the frontispiece also invokes a work of art: John Wooton's *Classical Landscape with a Temple* [Fig. 2], a canvas probably painted for Pope at the same time. If, as Pope believed, 'all gardening is like landscape [painting], just like a landscape hung up,'[16] trees were not only the medium but the palette of that new landscape.

★　　★　　★　　★　　★

Between the middle of the seventeenth and the middle of the eighteenth centuries, the English landscape underwent a transformation that had its origins in this reinterpretation of classical concepts of arcadia. At the beginning of the 1650s, Andrew Marvell wrote the classic garden poem, 'Upon Appleton House', and John Evelyn began to consider garden-making as a serious philosophic exercise. By 1751 the major revolution, not only in garden design but in attitudes to the natural world, was complete. In that year died Henry Frederick, Prince of Wales, and Lord Bolingbroke, both of them representative of a patriotism that saw gardening as a chief metaphor of liberty. In that year too, Warburton's magisterial edition of Pope's *Works* and John Boyle's edition of

1. Frontispiece to Pope's *Essay on Man* (1748). The Trustees of the British Library.

2. John Wooton, *Classical Landscape with a Temple*. By kind permission of J. J. Eyston. Mapledurham House. Photograph: Courtauld Institute of Art.

Pliny's *Letters* canonised an Augustan tradition that saw the reinterpretation of classical antiquity as intimately connected with the recreation of its landscapes.

No classical work, however, was so influential as Virgil's *Georgics*. By the middle of the seventeenth century pastoral, as represented primarily by Virgil's *Eclogues*, had been trivialised and devalued by the artifice of royalist propaganda.[17] Marvell's radical examination of its terminology and referents in 'Upon Appleton House' is in effect the necessary corollary of his appropriation of a georgic landscape into his poem. When he steps out of Lord Fairfax's arcadian (and already comic) garden into the 'abbyss' of the hayfield, he steps into a different kind of text, one where the *Georgics* not the *Eclogues* are literally foregrounded. Behind him lies the literary artifice of pastoral romance as enshrined in Sidney's *Arcadia*, travestied by what Milton deplored as the 'masking scenes' of Stuart policy and debased in the mawkish sentimentality of the deposed abbess's diction in his own poem. Before him lies a landscape in which the fate that 'worthily translates' Lord Fairfax's daughter into the fruitful world of marriage also encourages us to see that 'Thessalian Tempe's seat' (from *Georgics* II) must be translated into the social and natural world that we know.

If it is true that 'few Latin poems draw so extensively, or so creatively, from their inherited tradition'[18] as the *Georgics*, it is equally true that few have had the extensive cultural impact that this poem, especially its second book, had in Restoration and Augustan England. Taking his cue from the Augustan theme of rural withdrawal, in *Georgics* II.492–512, Dr. Johnson wrote in *The Rambler* in 1751: 'There is, indeed, scarce any writer who has not celebrated the happiness of rural privacy.'[19] Rural withdrawal is only one of the many themes from the *Georgics* whose resonances are to be heard in this period. Out of that book came not only the vision of re-created arcadia but the inspiration for a renovated science.

Only recently have a few studies begun to suggest the importance to garden history not only of plants but of ordinary gardeners.[20] But the horticultural and the philosophical aspects of garden history share the *Georgics* as a primary work of reference. The text *divini gloria ruris* (from *Georgics* I.168), cited repeatedly by the aestheticians of the new landscape, depends upon the careful fore-thought and labour of a husbandman who is both gardener and farmer. And the man who would be blessed, both in his thoughts and in his fields, must know *rerum naturae causas* (II.490), the philosophical as well as the practical causes of things.

Throughout the first half of the eighteenth century, much garden design and writing began with a reaction against the artificialities of both Dutch and French garden design. In so doing its celebration was of a landscape that aspired towards the condition of an ideal farm, such a farm as Pliny describes in his two famous letters on Tusculum and Laurentinum, Horace in the second epode and the sixth satire of the second book of his *Satires*, and Virgil in lines 458–540 of *Georgics* II. Another much-cited tag from the *Georgics*, *laudato ingentia rura, exiguum colito* (praise a large farm but cultivate a small one), became the hallmark of the *ferme ornée*. That most Augustan invention represented the unity of beauty with profit and use with pleasure that was within the means of a man of modest income: the smallholding of a man of philo-sophical mind.

Even when the estate in question was considerably larger than what would usually be meant by a farm, the rhetoric of spiritualised and regenerated landscape was invoked. In effect, farm and garden came to be looked at

3. James Gardiner. *Rapin of Gardens. A Latin Poem* (1706). Illustration to Book II, 'Of Trees'.

through the spectacles of Virgilian texts, and the result was a sort of redefined countryside: a *rus in rure*.

At least from the second edition of Evelyn's *Sylva* (1670) onwards, the text of the *Georgics* came to be foregrounded in the debate about agriculture, horticulture, and *patria*. It appears there in Evelyn's use of the translation of René Rapin's *Of Gardens* by his son. Rapin's work itself was in large measure a translation of the *Georgics* and remained popular in the early eighteenth century in the 1706 translation by James Gardiner [Fig. 3]. But of course the *Georgics* is present also in the political and spiritual arguments for tree-planting that became increasingly apparent in the later editions of *Sylva*. And even in

4. Wenceslas Hollar, 'Bey Albury' (1645). View of the Grotto. Thomas Fisher Library, University of Toronto.

Evelyn's contemporary design for the garden at Albury in Surrey for Henry Howard [Fig. 4], his conscious re-creation of the landscape of Virgil's tomb showed the potency of that Augustan tradition of retirement and meditation long before what is usually thought of as Augustanism in England.[21]

This *Georgic* theme of withdrawal from the corruption of courts to the simplicity of rural life is also central to Shaftesbury's *The Moralists*. Writing in praise of William Shenstone's *ferme ornée*, The Leasowes, in 1768, George Mason identified Milton's depiction of Christ (in *Paradise Regained*) within a 'woody scene' with Shaftesbury's celebration of 'these sacred silvan scenes... such as of old gave rise to temples, and favoured the religion of the ancient world.'[22]

One of Shenstone's earlier monuments at The Leasowes was to his friend, the poet James Thomson. In that Thomson's long poem, *The Seasons*, was one of the major works to translate the themes of the *Georgics* into English verse, it is only natural that Shenstone's inscription should have been another passage from Virgil. And it is also appropriate that Thomson should have been translated into the very landscape that he celebrated in Virgilian terms.

Of early eighteenth-century poems engaged in imitating the *Georgics*, Thomson's was only the most extensive. The poet Thomas Tickell (himself a writer on gardens) encouraged such imitation in a lecture at Oxford in 1711, but by then it was already in place. Dryden's translation of 1697 led the way,[23] [Fig. 5] and John Philips's *Cyder* (1708) provides an early example of English domestication, in this case of Virgil's praise of the vine in Book II. Pope's 'Epistle to Burlington' (1731), Shenstone's *Miscellaneous Poems* (1737), Akenside's *The Pleasures of the Imagination* (1744), and Dyer's *The Fleece* (1757) are only some of the more obvious examples of this poetic interchange.

In *The Pleasures of the Imagination*, for example, Akenside canvases three of the themes from *Georgics* II that had revolutionised attitudes to landscape: the alliance of science and imagination in understanding nature (*rerum cognoscere causas*); the invocation of an arcadian Tempe of the golden age as opposed to 'Pow'rs purple robes' (*procul discordibus armis*); and the alignment of true patriotism with solitary and philosophic withdrawal first to 'the windings of an ancient wood' and thence in to 'a solitary prospect, wide and wild,' 'the primeval seat of man' in the golden age (*Speluncaque, vivique lacus*).

Pope and Shenstone are also instances of how this imitation included translating the *Georgics* into the landscape. In his advice to a wide range of gardeners, but chiefly in his participation in Lord Bathurst's gardening enterprises, Pope had opportunity to anglicise Virgil's ideal landscapes. At his arcadian *ferme ornée* Shenstone's first act was to create 'Virgil's Grove'.

Certainly there was no doubt in the mind of Stephen Switzer, the author of *Ichnographia Rustica* (1718) that the *Georgics* were to be the chief source for the making of 'rural or extensive gardens.' The very phrase is a translation of Virgil's *ingentia rura*. Switzer, who described himself as a seedsman, was nonetheless both a designer and a plantsman of some skill. So too was John Martyn, the autodidact who became the second Professor of Botany at Cambridge and whose 1742 translation of the first two books of the *Georgics* was known as the *Flora Virgiliana*.

What Martyn represents is a great company of gardener-designers whose labours in the early eighteenth century represented the putting into practice of Virgilian dictates. From the late 1660s onwards, botanists (as natural philosophers) felt increasingly excluded from the largely mathematical deliberations of the Royal Society. They were certainly not excluded from the world of classical studies, however. In the sixteenth century, Marlowe's Dr. Faustus could be depicted as satanic for wanting a book that showed him the names of all the trees, plants, and herbs in the world. But even Marlowe's picture of Virgil was the bogey of the middle ages: the ancient necromancer who could in one night drive a tunnel through a mountain. By the seventeenth century, Evelyn could use just such a tunnel in a garden to invoke a Virgilian arcadia. By the eighteenth, Virgil's commendation of the search for nature's causes had become a founding text for the newly re-established science of botany.

The search for nature's causes that lay behind the gradual elaboration of Linnaean taxonomy in the early eighteenth century was one in which gardeners of all kinds participated.[24] And the fascination with the possibilities of grafting, evident everywhere in the period between Evelyn and Lord Petre, was one to which Virgil's somewhat disingenuous precepts (*aliena ex arbore* in *Georgics* II.73–83) gave rise. [Fig. 6]

Trees were, in fact, the chief instruments in the making of extensive landscape. If the country was, in Pope's phrase, to be 'called in', the manipulation

5. Dryden, *The Works of Virgil* (1697). Illustration to *Georgics* II, 310 by Francis Cleyn. Thomas Fisher Library, University of Toronto.

6. Illustration of grafting by Francis Cleyn for John Ogilby, *The Works of Virgil* (1654). Thomas Fisher Library, University of Toronto.

To George London of his Ma:ᵗⁱᵉˢ Royall Garden in Sᵗ James's Park Gent.

Geo:2 L 310

Aut rurfum enodes trunci finditur in solidum Planta immitintur; nec Exit ad cælum ramis Miraturque novas frondes. *refecantur; et altè cuneus via; deinde feraces longum tempus, et ingens felicibus arbor, et non fua poma.*

Houoratiffimo Dñ. Domino Ordinis Balnei, Comiti Car

Richardo Vaughan Equiti heriæ, et Baroni Vaughan

Plane et Saue

Tabula merito votiua, &

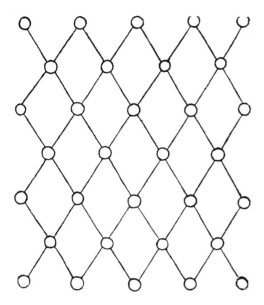

Quid Quincunce speciosius, qui, in quam cunqz partem spectaueris, rectus est. Quintilian://

7. Plan of a Quincunx from Sir Thomas Browne. *The Garden of Cyrus* (1658). Thomas Fisher Library, University of Toronto.

8. Plan of an Ideal Rural Garden (Riskins) from Stephen Switzer *Ichnographia Rustica* (1742). Trinity College Library, Toronto.

of that perspective could only be achieved by plantations on a very large scale. And yet these plantations, as Evelyn pointed out in *Sylva*, were to be not only aesthetic but spiritual, philosophic, and practical as well. Indeed, in his notes for *Elysium Britannicum*, he remarks on the combination of utility, beauty, and retirement in many gardens before his time. These included both the royal gardens of Charles V of Spain and the 'Fruit Gardens and Orchards of Kent' that the antiquary William Camden says were dedicated by one Richard Harris 'to the public good and for 30 parishes thereabout.'[25]

None of this was new. Ralph Austen could write of *The Spiritual Use of an Orchard* (1653) and Sir Thomas Browne could recommend planting one according to the mystical mathematics of the ancient world [Fig. 7] in *The*

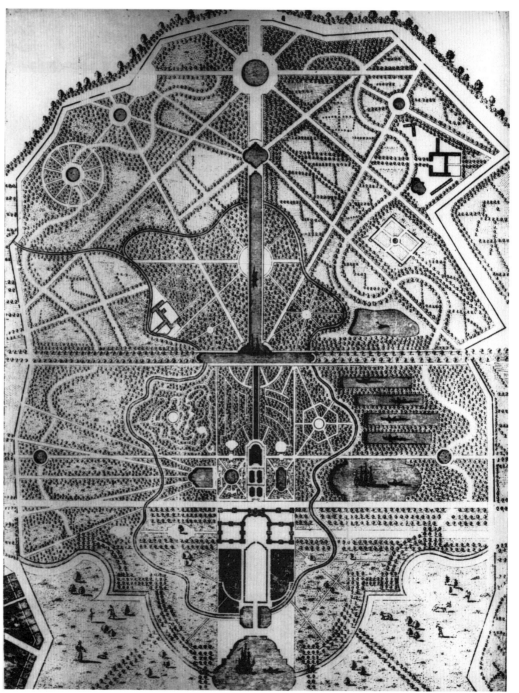

Garden of Cyrus (1658).[26] What was new was the scale of the enterprise and the belief that (in a phrase associated with William Kent) 'all nature was a garden.' What was also new was a classicised spirituality in which the sacredness of ancient groves could be seen as an aspect of the divinity of a redeemed nature. Evelyn himself, in drafting the notes for *Elysium Britannicum*, made a memorandum: 'How the *Elysium* of the Antients might be prov'd to be these *British Islands.*'[27]

That men such as John MacClary at Rousham or William Fisher at Studley Royal should have been not simply planters of trees but designers of landscape is reflected at the other end of the social scale in the botanical and horticultural experimentation of such patriot 'improvers' as the Duke of Argyll, Lord Petre, and the Dukes of Richmond and Newcastle. Here Virgil's concerns with agricultural improvement, botanical experimentation, philosophic speculation, rural retirement, and arcadian landscape come together in the recreation of an Augustan ideal.

Nowhere was this ideal more consciously the model, however, than in the creation of the *ferme ornée*. In *Ichnographia Rustica* Stephen Switzer celebrates Lord Bathurst's early creation of such a garden at Riskins in 1705–12 [Fig. 8]. It may well be, indeed, that some aspects of the *ferme ornée* were in John Evelyn's mind when he laid out the gardens at Warley Place in Essex as early as 1650. Certainly by the 1730s 'Worlies' was recognised as a *ferme ornée* and must have been known as such by Lord Petre's cousin, Philip Southcote, who grew up nearby at Witham. There Southcote seems to have made early experiments with the sort of planting that a few years later (after 1735) he was to make at Wooburn Farm in Surrey.

Whatever its origins (and Lord Petre's Thorndon must have had some influence) Wooburn Farm became known as the model of the *ferme ornée*, an enactment of the classical ideal of a working farm as a philosophical retreat. Southcote was by no means consciously indebted to antiquity, but his most famous imitators were. His near neighbour, Joseph Spence, was an ardent classicist who as Professor of Poetry at Oxford lectured on the *Aeneid* and elaborated an idea of *belle nature* that was based on Virgil's depiction of ideal nature in the *Georgics*. What was covert in the gardens of Southcote and Spence, however, was overt in Shenstone's The Leasowes, where no less than eleven monuments on the peripheral walk employed texts from Virgil and where Virgil's Grove, his earliest creation, was the culminating experience of the garden.

2

THE TRANSLATION OF ANTIQUITY: PLINY AND VIRGIL

All gardening is in some sense an act of translation. Even at its most basic it involves the literal translation or physical movement of plants from one place to another. But there is also a figurative translation involved: the translation of an idea or a text or a picture or even of a garden elsewhere. In each case a text of some kind is translated on to the landscape. As with all translations the enterprise is open to argument and debate as to which version more accurately represents the original text or its intention. As Annabel Patterson has observed: 'Any translation is an act of interpretation, and no one any longer doubts that all translation is culturally determined.'[1]

Nowhere was this more the case than in England between the middle of the seventeenth and the middle of the eighteenth centuries. Not only was this the great period of garden-building, or 'place-making' as it was called, but it was also the period in which the classical civilisation of Greece and Rome was rediscovered and made the basis of the national style. In architecture it took the form of celebrating the first of the English classicists, Inigo Jones, and thereby his translation of Palladio, who had in turn translated the works of the Roman architect Vitruvius. If Palladian architecture brought in its wake the gardens of Roman antiquity, it also encouraged and was sustained by the new attention to classical scholarship and the great spate of editions of classical texts and translations that appeared throughout this period.

In 1751, the year in which Capability Brown set out from Stowe to make his career, John Boyle, the fifth Earl of Cork and Orrery, published his edition of the letters of Pliny the Younger. Among these letters were two that had an enormous impact on the development of the English landscape garden: one describing Pliny's villa at Laurentinum and the other his villa at Tusculum. Indeed, as early as 1731, Boyle already thought of his estate (Marston in Somerset) in terms of Pliny's ideal of rural retirement:

> I remember he concludes one of his Epistles (the description of his Villa) by telling his Friend whose name I have forgot, 'That he hoped Laurentinum amidst a thousand Beauties and Recommendations already mentioned might still have one Glory superior to them all, the honour of his Company.' The Latin may be more concise, but it is to this purpose, and I could make you the same compliment, when I am settled at Marston.[2]

In the 1720s these two letters had opened a controversy over the nature of ancient gardens that was more than 'merely academic.' It was a debate about the nature of nature and about the classical ideal of it. On one side was the

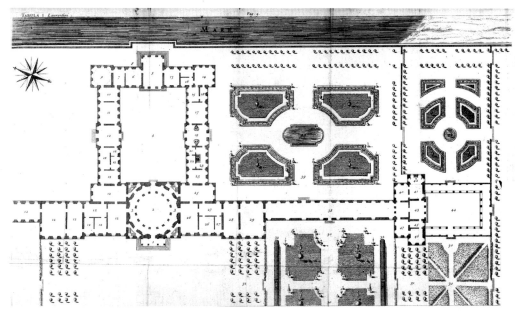

9. Laurentinum from Jean-Francois Félibien *Les Plans et les descriptions de deux des plus belles maisons de campagne de Plinie le consul* (London, 1707), pp. 11, 8.

French scholar, Jean François Félibien, who in 1706 had translated these two letters and reprinted, with commentary, the plates from Scamozzi's earlier imaginative reconstruction of Pliny's villas [Fig. 9]. Félibien recognised that everything in Pliny's description of the gardens, apart from the list of components, was rather vague. His claim that, in the absence of evidence from Pliny, everything in his design had been kept simple would, however, surprise a modern reader. Perhaps the clue to Félibien's idea of simplicity is his remark that in these gardens '*on n'y trouvera rien de contraire à la maniere de se loger, qui a été presque tout temps en usage en Italie.*' His claim that this is '*fort differente . . . de celle que nous pratiquons en France,*' is, however, belied by his reconstructed plan of Laurentinum, complete with *broderie* parterres.[3]

The French manner of extensive landscape gardening had been influential in England in the late seventeenth and very early eighteenth centuries, chiefly through the practice of the firm of London and Wise. By the third decade, however, it was certainly open to question if not to attack. In the van of this revision was the most eminent Palladian of the time, Richard Boyle, Third Earl of Burlington, whose villa and garden at Chiswick were begun in 1719, the same year in which his friend, Alexander Pope, began to create his equally influential garden at Twickenham only a few miles away.

Among Burlington's circle was Robert Castell, who in 1728 published *The Villas of the Ancients Illustrated*, a work dedicated to Lord Burlington and subscribed to by some of the more interesting makers of landscape gardens in the early eighteenth century: the Duke of Norfolk, who made Worksop with Lord Petre's assistance, the Earl of Pembroke, who created the naturalised garden at Wilton and the Palladian Bridge there, and John Aislabie, who created Studley Royal. Castell's work was a large and handsome folio volume that outstripped the earlier little work of Félibien and gave a very different emphasis to the translation of Pliny's description [Figs. 10, 11].

Where Pliny in describing the garden at Tusculum used the phrase *ruris imitatio* to describe part of the garden, Félibien had thought this incidental to the overall symmetry of the scheme. He translated Pliny as recommending careless and rustic touches by the planting of casual groups of trees here and there. Castell's translation gives the passage quite a different emphasis. The word *urbanissimo* is taken not to modify the earlier passages about box cut into

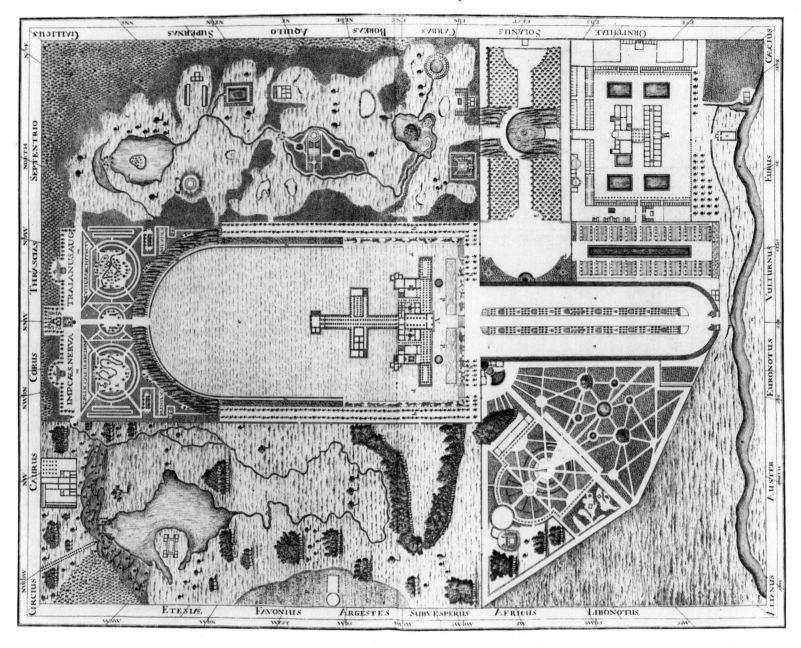

10. Robert Castell, Tusculum from *The Villas of the Ancients Illustrated* (1728). Thomas Fisher Library, University of Toronto.

letters and figures but to mean 'a most elegant Taste' and to refer to 'a sudden Imitation of the Country [which] seems accidentally introduced in the Middle.'

Castell's notes, moreover, make it perfectly clear that, whereas Pliny's garden included what he called 'a Scene of Regularities' as well as a simple lawn, its chief effect was in the combination of these with a wilder landscape that 'afforded at least all the Pleasures that could be enjoy'd in the most regular [i.e. symmetrical] Gardens.'[4] Reflecting Lord Burlington's own practice, Castell retained many of the symmetrical elements of Pliny's description, but offered a reconstruction of his gardens altogether more incidental in its composition, a garden on a large scale but very much the sum of its various parts.

One of the sources of Castell's argument must also have been the famous series of engravings made in 1713 of the imperial summer residence at Jehol in Manchuria. These engravings, made by the Italian Jesuit, Father Matteo Ripa, from earlier Chinese woodblocks [Fig. 12], caused an enormous stir when they

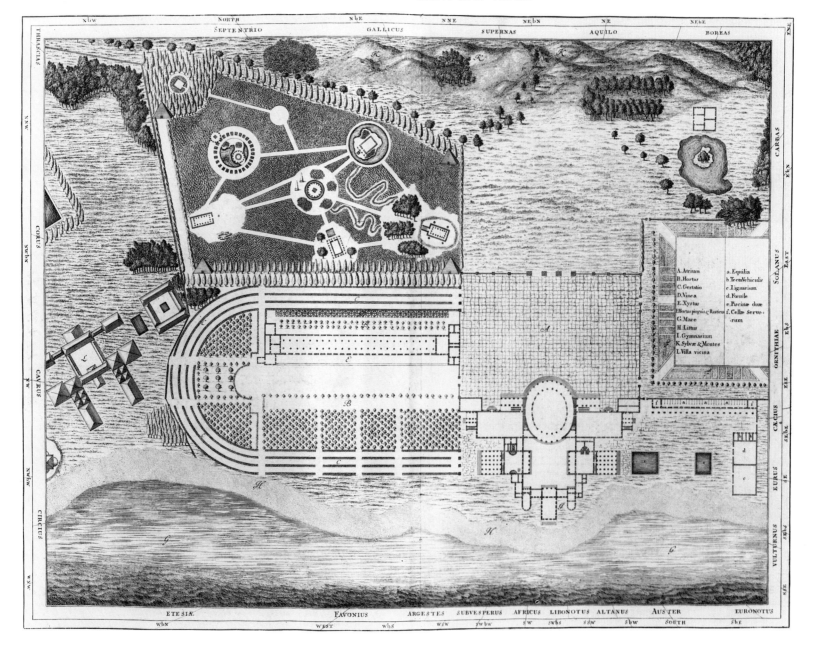

11. Robert Castell, Laurentinum from *The Villas of the Ancients Illustrated* (1728). Thomas Fisher Library, University of Toronto.

were brought back to Europe. They confirmed ideas already adumbrated by Sir William Temple about the informality of oriental gardens and reinforced the arguments already espoused by Addison, Pope, and Lord Burlington.

Only eight sets of these engravings are known to exist, and one of them was presented to Lord Burlington in 1724. No two sets are identical, but all of them contain a hand-written transliteration of the original Chinese titles of the plates and a brief translation into Italian. All of them also illustrate a landscape both man-made and natural, where a great range of *Casino di recreazioni* indicates a peripatetic approach to gardens, one in which dining, resting, and walking (as well as inscriptions on natural formations) constitute the experience of an extensive garden. 'Many rivers and winds that sigh through the pine trees,' is Ripa's translation of plate 13, which illustrates the garden houses where the emperor conducted his business with his European servants.[5]

These plates must have served to underline an interpretation of Pliny's descriptions already congenial to Burlington's circle and to influence not only

12. Matteo Ripa, View of part of the Imperial Summer Palace at Jehol, Manchuria (c. 1713). Collection Centre Canadien d'architecture/Canadian Centre for Architecture, Montreal.

13. Vignette of Laurentinum from John [Boyle] Earl of Orrery, *The Letters of Pliny the Younger* (1751). Thomas Fisher Library, University of Toronto.

Kent's designs at Chiswick but Castell's translations. Here was the landscape not only of Pliny but Claude, a place where the extensive experience of nature in a landscape, surrounded by wind, water, and natural vegetation, was also part of the everyday life of the court.

That John Boyle was aware of this argument is not in doubt. Writing of Pliny's villas in his edition of the letters, he observed: 'it is impossible to rebuild them, even upon paper.'[6] Richard Boyle was his cousin and the man from whom he was to inherit the earldom of Cork in 1753. Castell's *Villas of the Ancients Illustrated*, moreover, was in his father's library, and in the notes to his own edition of Pliny he cites Félibien. But his 'Observations' (as he called them) went beyond literary or even archeological annotation. Boyle recognised that by 1751 the quest for a landscape arcadia based on the writings of the ancients had transformed the gardens of England. And the example he chose to cite was his cousin's estate, a villa 'with as true elegance, as *Greece* or *Italy* could ever celebrate, and at no greater distance from *London* than *Cheswick*.'[7] [Fig. 13]

The argument about the interpretation of classical antiquity was not confined to Burlington's circle. Boyle's father, the fourth Earl, had in fact been a central disputant in the famous debate about *The Epistles of Phalaris*, a debate between modernity and the classical past upon which Swift based his *Battle of the Books*, published in 1704. A central figure in this controversy was Swift's patron at the

16

time of the book's composition, Sir William Temple, himself an influential author on garden matters. Indeed, there is a sense in which the revolution in garden design in the early eighteenth century was a re-enactment of the battle of the books, an enormous piece of textual analysis in which the landscape garden was the final translation of texts by Pliny, Horace, and Virgil.

In his *Upon the Gardens of Epicurus* (1685) Temple had first urged the 'Chinese' idea of garden beauty as being 'without any order or disposition of parts.'[8] Moreover, he included in his own garden, Moor Park in Surrey, an irregular serpentining garden that invoked this principle. [Fig. 14] It was this *sharawadgi*, as Temple called it, that Castell referred to when he described 'the present Manner of Designing in China' as one where 'tho' the Parts are disposed with the greatest Art, the Irregularity is still preserved.' And it was this that he found in Pliny and that he took to be the meaning of *Imitatio Ruris*,

> where, under the Form of a beautiful Country, *Hills, Rocks, Cascades, Rivulets, Woods, Buildings*, etc. were possibly thrown into such an agreeable Disorder, as to have pleased the Eye from several Views, like so many beautiful Landskips [i.e. landscape paintings]; and at the same time have afforded at least all the Pleasures that could be enjoy'd in the most regular Gardens.[9]

By 1728 'the most regular gardens' were already outmoded, and Castell could write in the confidence that Burlington himself was beginning to conceive of his garden in a more naturalistic manner. [Figs. 15, 16] By 1751 this passage might also have been a description both of John Boyle's estate, Caledon, in Ireland and of Marston, his house in Somerset. When he wrote that he would 'make Pliny an Englishman,' he meant something more than verbal translation. Marston (and later Caledon) were to be the Augustan ideals of rural retirement. In 1743, when he wrote to thank a correspondent for a gift of books, he wrote in the persona of 'a plain Somersetshire Farmer.'[10] At Marston, as he wrote to his kinswoman Lady Elizabeth Spelman two years

14. Todd Longstaffe-Gowan, Reconstruction Plan after Kip of Part of the Garden at Moor Park, Surrey, Showing Parterres and 'Sharawdagi'.

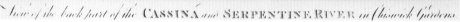

15. 'View of the Back Part of the Cassina and Serpentine River in Chiswick Gardens,' from *The Modern Universal British Traveller* (London, 1779).

16. 'Chiswick Seen from the Garden,' c. 1755.

later, he could live free from the 'constant Malice reigning in the great World which we Haymakers know nothing of.'

This myth of rural withdrawal is also present in Boyle's *The First Ode of the First Book of Horace Imitated* which, like his Pliny, he published in 1751. There, though in terms that mix the pastoral with the georgic, he praises the man who 'shares a Landlord's Pride, and Tenant's Toil,' and reserves for his poetic persona an arcadian retreat:

> Far from the feeble Glance of vulgar Eye,
> To pleasing Shades, and cooling Grottoes fly; . . .
> Be rural Pastimes, harmless Sports my Theme,
> The smiling Shepherdess, the limpid Stream![11]

18

This also is the burden of *Georgics* II, where the poet's prayer that the muses may teach him the causes of things (*me vero primum dulces ante omnia Musae*) is contained within the celebration of the ideal world of the farmer in the golden age. In his note on this line the famous Renaissance rhetorician, Peter Ramus, compared the description of Tempe to a passage in Pliny and remarked that Tempe was no more than a synecdoche for all ideal places.[12]

At Caledon, a sort of *ferme ornée*, Boyle created a grove of Diana in a ford by the river at some distance from the house, and a hermitage 'all neat plain, humble, proper and rural' where he spoke of reading with pleasure *The Castle of Indolence*, by the landscape poet James Thomson. 'The hermit,' he wrote, 'lives in a garden on a beautifull island, surrounded by a noble river, and thickened by a wood of thirty year's growth...cut into natural winding walks.'[13]

At Marston, with the help of the landscape designer and engineer, Stephen Switzer, he had continued the improvement of the estate begun by his father [Fig. 17]. As early as 1737, only six years after succeeding to the estate, Boyle

17. Todd Longstaffe-Gowan, Reconstruction Plan of Marston Bigot (c. 1750).

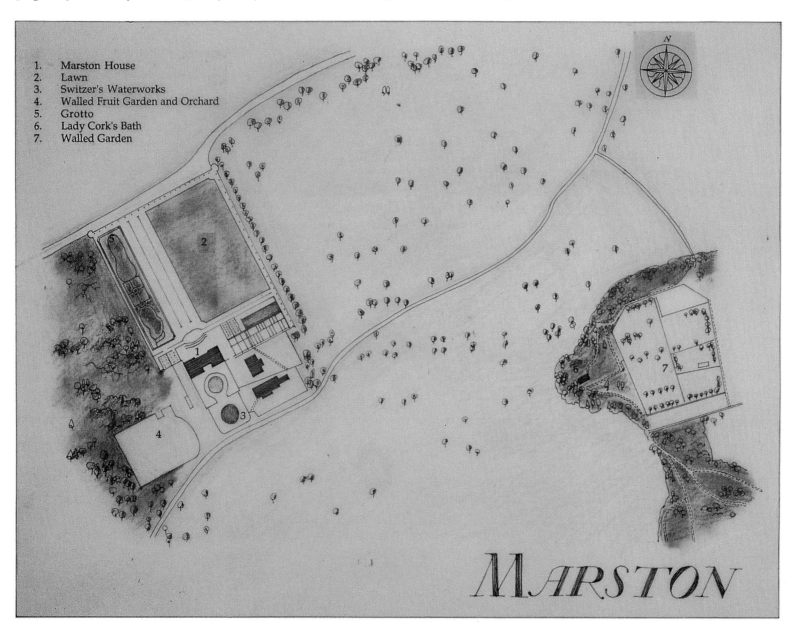

1. Marston House
2. Lawn
3. Switzer's Waterworks
4. Walled Fruit Garden and Orchard
5. Grotto
6. Lady Cork's Bath
7. Walled Garden

MARSTON

18. Lake and Temples, Stourhead.

19. Temple of Apollo, Stourhead.

was able to make the Horatian invitation to Swift: 'come away with Me to Marston: there You shall enjoy *Otium cum dignitate*.'[14] This was an offer he was to press in similar terms on Pope in 1742: 'You should come into a warm house, see an agreeable situation, and live void of noise and disturbance.'[15]

Marston was imbued with the same literary and classical ideals as its near neighbour, Stourhead. Created in the 1740s by Henry Hoare, whose daughter Boyle's eldest son was to marry, Stourhead's landscape garden was an imaginative recreation of Aeneas's descent into the underworld [Figs. 18, 19, 20]. At Marston, Boyle wrote of his nightly rambles in the landscape among the ghosts of his ancestors as being like 'Aeneas descent to the Elysian Feilds.'[16] When, in the early 1730s, Boyle had to leave Marston to deal with his Irish estates, he wrote of his regret at leaving 'Marston and the Muses' and his desire to be 'in the sweet Silence of its sacred Grove.'[17] By 1749 his work was well on the way to maturity. Writing from Ireland after an absence of three and a half years, Boyle conjured up in his imagination a classical elysium at Marston in which trees were the chief component: 'I hope to find my hamadryads there in perfect health, and their shady habitations making a great progress towards the arch of Heaven.'[18]

20. Lake from Grotto, Stourhead.

21. Palladian Bridge, Stowe. A copy of the bridge at Wilton.

Boyle's image of his retired life, both at Marston and at Caledon, was informed by a classical ideal. His description of his reasons for admiring Pliny might be a description of what he hoped for in himself: 'his way of thinking, open, humane and noble. His Friendships sincere and well-chosen: his Fortune easy and well managed; and his whole Life a Scene of Virtue and honourable Acts.'[19] Such certainly was the life that Boyle sought for himself, a life in which, as he also says of Pliny, 'the chief point, the retirement, was particularly studied.'[20] By 1756 Boyle could refer to himself as 'the greatest example of solitude and retirement in England,'[21] but even Lady Orrery, who herself helped with the transcription of Pliny, thought in such terms. In the midst of the furor about the Pretender's invasion in 1744 she could write: 'no man who is burthened with a Crown can enjoy the peace and tranquility . . . that my dear Lord and I do, amidst our Walkes, our Children, and our books in our Country retreat.'[22]

Pliny's letters also suggested to Boyle the sort of garden landscape in which such a retirement might best be achieved, one of a 'diversity of prospects' in which the foaming of the sea, and the intermingled cottages among distant woods, composed perhaps of ever-greens, and forming a kind of winter-garden, must be a great entertainment to the eye, and must give infinite delight to a speculative mind, which is always happy in beholding a variety in the works of nature.[23]

Certainly Boyle himself seemed never to tire of writing about this georgic topography and of longing for it when he was away in London. Indeed it was just such a variety of 'the finest Prospects that the eye could wish' that Boyle offered to tempt the painter, Richard Wilson, to come to visit Marston in 1752.[24] The 'prospects' he referred to, however, were not to be found in untouched natural scenery but in the landscape gardens of Stourhead, Wilton, and Longleat. What this indicates is the prevalence of the neoclassical aesthetic that Boyle espoused. The Palladian Bridge built by the seventh Earl of Pembroke at Wilton in 1736, [Fig. 21] like the topography of the *Aeneid* translated into the landscape of Stourhead, indicate the widespread potency of this neoclassical arcadianism in the early eighteenth century. In 1737, responding ecstatically to the poem *Leonidas* by the poet Richard Glover, Boyle wrote of the author: 'Where has he dwelt? certainly either on the Hill of Parnassus with the tuneful Apollo, or in the Shades of Stowe with my Lord Cobham.'[25]

In 1737 'my Lord Cobham' was also about to engage in a major act of translation at Stowe, whereby the regular garden of Vanbrugh and Bridgeman was to have added to it the landscape of the Elysian Fields. Such an overt act of classical translation went far beyond what had been done at Stowe previously: an emblematic anthology of temples, statues and mottos. Under the direction chiefly of William Kent, a neoclassical topography was created that provided a large-scale 'reading' of antiquity. This 'reading', moreover, required the peripatetic modern figure in this landscape to translate the ancient text into the modern world. The intelligent visitor would see, in other words, how the Temple of Ancient Virtue on one side of the 'River Styx' there was answered by the Temple of British Worthies on the other as each met the reflection of the other in the river. [Fig. 22]

Kent's inspiration in all this may have been Claude,[26] but Claude's source was Virgil. And it was Virgil, and chiefly Virgil's *Georgics*, that was the central text being translated into the English landscape of the early eighteenth century. If John Boyle thought that his cousin's Chiswick had translated Pliny into England, he was encouraged to do so because Virgil, as a Roman Augustan, first described himself as leading 'in triumph from Greek Helicon to my native land the Muses.'[27]

Virgil's agrarian mythology in the *Georgics* was especially attractive to the English Augustans, for whom, as for the Roman Augustans, the celebration of agriculture was a primary myth. Saturnus, the exile who came to Italy to establish agriculture, was the antecedent of Aeneas but he was also, by descent, the antecedent of the golden English agricultural myth. What is distinctive about Virgil's myth of the golden age is that it can recur. If for Virgil it was returning in the Italy of Augustus, for the English Virgilians it was recurring in post–Restoration England, a country, like Virgil's Italy, recently liberated from the scars of civil war.

Whether as a celebration of rural life, as an inspiration to didactic poetry on all aspects of husbandry, or as the source of poems about gardens, Virgil's poem was a potent mythical force. Probably the most popular eighteenth century poem, James Thomson's *The Seasons* (published between 1726 and

1744), was derived from the *Georgics*, and translates Virgil's themes in contemporary terms. Indeed the climax of Thomson's 'Autumn' [Fig. 23] was taken from the famous lines in Virgil's Book II about discovering the causes of things (ll. 490–92). For Thomson, the twin themes of country retirement and the fortunate farmer (both from the end of *Georgics* II) are allied with an affirmation of the 'vital scale' of nature, the 'great chain of being' that was a Christianised version of Virgil's providential universe. Throughout the period in which many of the greatest landscape gardens of the early eighteenth century were being created, Thomson was publishing and revising this major georgic poem. Indeed, in the 1744 edition he added to it a description of Hagley, the garden of his patron, the patriot boy, Lord Lyttelton.

Patriotism itself was the major theme of Thomson's 'masque' *Alfred*, first published after his death in 1751. Taking as its hero a figure associated with ancient Saxon liberties, Thomson's poem (adapted by David Mallet) deployed a myth that was also being used in contemporary landscapes: 'Alfred's Tower' at Stourhead [Fig. 24] and 'Alfred's Hall' at Cirencester. Moreover, the prologue was written by John Boyle. In the year of the death of both Lord Bolingbroke and Henry Frederick, the gardener Prince of Wales, Boyle's denunciation of tyranny must have seemed especially relevant to contemporary Whig politics. Indeed, the revisions in it requested by Garrick (who was to speak the part) bring it even closer to the world of spies and government censors who had been especially attentive to Boyle's own correspondence:

> When Danish fury, with wide-wasting hand
> Had spread pale fear, and ravag'd o'er the land
> This prince arising bade confusion cease,
> Bade order shine, and blest his isle with peace;
> Taught liberal arts to humanize the mind,
> And heaven-born science to sweet freedom join'd.[28]

This georgic combination of science and liberty (botany and true patriotism) was also in *The Seasons*. But that poem's adaptation of motifs from the *Georgics* was, of course, preceded by a host of poets who had adapted or 'metaphrased' Virgil's work, among them Pope.[29] In 'Windsor Forest', for example, Pope looks back to Virgil through an earlier adaptation, Denham's 'Cooper's Hill', a poem in which there is a continuous act of translation of Virgil's landscape into England. John Chalker writes of Pope's using 'the Virgilian interpretation of experience and the *Georgic* pattern of contrast and digression in "an abstracted manner" to formalise his response to the subject matter—topographical and political—of the poem.'[30]

In 'Windsor Forest' and in such later poems as the *Essay on Man*, Pope also picks up the Virgilian theme (from *Georgics* II) of *rerum cognoscere causas*, in his words 'to follow Nature, and regard its end' ('Windsor Forest', l. 252). But even Virgil's lines, widely cited as an inspiration to scientific discovery in the eighteenth century, were themselves translated from Lucretius's earlier poem, *De Rerum Natura* (3.1072)[31] and from Aristotle's *Posterior Analytics* (2.645a5). Indeed, many of the famous passages from the *Georgics* were similarly translated from earlier classical works: Hesiod's *Works and Days*, Varro's *De Re Rustica*, and Cato the Elder's *On Agriculture*. Even Virgil's famous and much-cited advice in Book II, about praising a large farm but cultivating a small one (l. 412) came from Hesiod (*Works and Days*, 643) by way of Columella's *De Re Rustica* (3.1.8).

Varro's treatise seems also to have been the source of the idyllic description

22. The Temple of the British Worthies and the Elysian Fields, Stowe.

23. Tardieu after William Kent, Title-page for Thomson's *Autumn* (1744). Thomas Fisher Library, Toronto.

24. Alfred's Tower, Stourhead.

of country life (*O fortunatos nimium*) with which Book II concludes, a passage cited again and again in early eighteenth-century celebrations of rural life. Far more potent than Horace's equally famous *beatus ille*, it offered praise of the country life apparently without Horace's ironic detachment.[32] Even the concept of 'the genius [or spirit] of the place,' so central to Pope's theory of landscape gardening, is present not only in Pliny's concern with the situation of a villa but in Virgil's concern (in Book I of the *Georgics*, lines 50ff.) about the suitability of climate and soil. And the hamadryads that John Boyle hoped to find on his return to Marston were the spiritual and literary progeny of the fauns and dryads who dance together at the beginning of Book I of the *Georgics*.

Virgil's poem was also the source of René Rapin's *Of Gardens*, a work first translated into English in 1673 by John Evelyn, the son of the diarist, and again in 1706 by James Gardiner. John Ogilby's edition of Virgil's *Works* (first published in folio in 1654 and reissued in 1684) also indicated the centrality of georgic mythology to gardening even in the book's illustrations. One of the plates (see figure 6) shows different sorts of grafting[33] taking place in a very Italianate garden in which there are plots planted with trees, a fountain in the midst, and a temple at the far end. But Ogilby recognised that the *Georgics* were about a horticulture that was at one with agriculture. His notes are largely agricultural, and their botanical bent reflects Virgil's insistence (in the second *Georgic*) that the husbandman know the causes of things.

This concern with botany, as we shall see later, coincided with the enormously increased importation of botanical specimens and the need to accommodate them both taxonomically and philosophically to what was already known. Virgil had seen scientific understanding as an alternative to rural retirement, and the exoticism of foreign flora and fauna as separate from the simplicity of Italian agriculture. By the early eighteenth century all these elements had become part of the English Augustan myth.

If Virgil in the second *Georgic* had extended the farmer's sphere of concern from cultivated trees to all trees, even wild ones, he now offered a text to the followers of Evelyn for extending the province of both agriculture and horticulture to include the new exotics. Under cultivation trees will change their character, thereby raising questions about the relation of art and nature, a question that is both practical and a part of natural philosophy.

Here then was a *rus* that was not escapism but a place where honest toil was both a moral and an intellectual reward. It was also the place of a new kind of heroism, the heroic struggle between man and nature that, in Milton's phrase, was 'not less but more heroic' than the subjects of ancient epic. Whatever Virgil had meant in his praise of rural life, it came in the late seventeenth century to be associated with the Edenic golden age in which, as in *Paradise Lost* (1667), Adam and Eve worked in a garden where labour was no pain. For Milton's contemporary, Thomas Farnaby, Virgil's *O fortunatos nimium* was a celebration of a rustic world in which justice may once again be found and the golden age restored. In his edition the famous text, *Laudato ingentia rura* was printed in bold type. Here the existence of country people not only surpassed all other conditions of life (especially urban life) but is equal with that of the philosopher.[34]

This countryside was not, however, the countryside of pastoral escapism, the sort of thing that Shakespeare gently mocked in *As You Like It*. Two years after *Paradise Lost* and four after the publication of John Evelyn's influential work, *Sylva*, John Worlidge published his *Systema Agriculturae* [Fig. 25] and

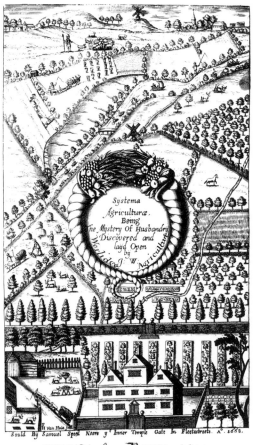

25. Title-page from John Worlidge, *Systema Agriculturae* (1668).

dedicated it 'to the *Gentry* and *Yeomanry of England*' with an invocation of that most influential of Virgilian texts in the making of the landscape garden: *Laudato ingentia rura/Exiguum colito.*

On the title-page he quotes Virgil's *O fortunatos nimium* and his preface is concerned, by citing both ancient and modern writers on agriculture, to assert in very Virgilian terms that a country life 'far excels the City life, and is much to be preferred before it.' Like Virgil's contented farmer, Worlidge's lives 'remote and free from envy, malice, calumny, covetousness and ambition.' His life is not without toil but it offers also 'the best opportunities to the Insatiable humane Spirit, to Contemplate and Meditate on, and to penetrate into, and discover the obscure, and hitherto occult Mysteries and secrets of Nature.' Much, indeed, of what Worlidge catalogues in the poem explaining his frontispiece might have come from the *Georgics*.[35]

Throughout the first half of the eighteenth century this Virgilian myth continued to inspire both agriculture and horticulture. An edition of both the *Pastorals* and the *Georgics* published by James Hamilton in 1742 was dedicated to Thomas Hope of Rankeilor, President of the 'Society for Improving in the Knowledge of AGRICULTURE in *North-Britain*,' i.e. Scotland. Hamilton, who hoped to make enough from his publication 'to betake myself to a Farm . . . [and] to shew a Specimen of good Husbandry,' entitled his edition: *Virgils Pastorals . . . as also His Georgicks With Such Notes and Reflexions as make him appear like an excellent farmer.* 'Improvement,' in other words, came to mean both improved farming methods and the laying out of estates as landscape gardens.

Castell's *Villas of the Ancients Illustrated* also included the villas of the Roman agricultural writers Varro and Columella, and Castell was concerned to insist that even Pliny's villa at Tusculum was in part a working farm: 'This *Tuscan Villa*, not less than that of *Laurentinum*, would deserve the Censure of *Varro*, had we not (for what has been before observed concerning the large Estate he had here) Reason to believe there was a Farm-House not far removed from the other, and all other Necessaries of Life.'[36]

Here the georgic insistence on the intimate relation between labour and pleasure becomes part of the Augustan myth: Lord Bolingbroke turns Dawley Park into Dawley Farm. This too, surely, is what Pope meant in the 'Epistle to Burlington' when he said: ''Tis use alone that sanctifies expense.' Although it is difficult to see what 'use' Pope had in mind in his own garden at Twickenham (apart, possibly, from the growing of vegetables in one part of it), it is plain that a number of 'improvers' did think in these terms. The Earl of Islay, for example, created a garden at Whitton (figure 63), not far from Twickenham, where botanical experimentation and transplantation were central to the enterprise. And Islay, who had large estates in Scotland, was also an active member of the Scottish agricultural society to whose president Hamilton dedicated his edition of Virgil.

Even at a competition for prize auriculas in 1732, the Reverend William Harper identified his congregation of 'Gardeners and Florists' with 'the well-meaning Husband-man or Artificer,' the archetypal English 'Plowman at his *Hallelujahs*,' whose origin was in the spiritualised readings of the *Georgics* in the Middle Ages. For Harper, in this case inspired by Plutarch, 'the Gardener, when digging, and the Husbandman, when plowing his Ground' were both singing hymns to God, a providential God such as the one Virgil also celebrates in his Book I.[37] Harper's extensive praise of botany, moreover, was part of a widespread contemporary recognition of botany as essential to husbandry.

Virgil's recommendation that the husbandman seek out the causes of things was fulfilled not only in the burgeoning of botanical importation and experimentation in the early eighteenth century but in the final triumph of the Linnean system of botanical classification after 1753. As if in testimony to Virgil's blessing on botany, the 1742 edition of the *Georgics* by John Martyn, the Professor of Botany at Cambridge, was called a *Flora Virgiliana*.

For William Benson, another early eighteenth-century editor and translator of the *Georgics*, Virgil's poem represented 'the utmost height of poetical Invention.' Virgil, he said, had united 'all the Arts and Sciences, and all the Beauties of Poetry with such subjects as Plowing, Planting, Breeding of Cattle, raising Insects [bees] and the like.' Benson published each of the first two books of the *Georgics* separately in 1724 and 1725, in each case under the title *Virgil's Husbandry, or an Essay on the Georgics*. In the light of his contemporary creation of a landscape garden at Wilbury, it is interesting that Benson chose only those books of the *Georgics* that deal with plants. He was certainly in no doubt about the translation of his subject into England: 'I am certain that the Husbandry of *England* in general is *Virgilian* . . . there is more of *Virgil's* Husbandry put in Practice in *England* at this Instant than in *Italy* itself.'[38]

In this belief he had already been preceded by the poets. John Philips's poem *Cyder* (1708) was a translation of one aspect of Virgilian husbandry (vintage) into English. Dedicated to his patron, the Tory Prime Minister, Lord Harley, Philips's poem might also have suggested political connections between the polity of Augustan Rome and that of early eighteenth-century England.

Although Benson's preface to his edition of the second book deplored the idleness of 'finding Faults in the Labours of other People,' his preface to the first book (published subsequently) was largely occupied with attacking Dryden's earlier translation of 1697. Dryden is generally credited with making the georgic mode popular, but if Virgil's *Georgics* in the eighteenth century came to be thought of as elegant versifying of a mean subject, it may well be that Dryden, abetted by Addison's preface, was to blame. Certainly Benson thought so. As an example of Dryden's failure to understand Virgil's sense in many places, he gives the famous line from Book I: *Si te digna manet divini Gloria Ruris*. 'The real Sence of which Line is, *If you have a due value for Husbandry as the most glorious of all Employments*; but Mr *Dryden* has translated this line . . .

—*If Ploughman hope*
The promis'd Blessing of a bounteous Crop.'[39]

Certainly 'bounteous Crop' seems a poor rendering of a phrase that came to resonate in much writing about gardens in the early eighteenth century. From Stephen Switzer in 1715 to William Shenstone, writing in the 1750s, *divini gloria ruris* was a central text in the creation of the landscape garden. Benson also accuses Dryden of imitating neither Virgil's prosody nor his sense: 'Mr. *Dryden*'s Translation makes a most solid, polite, chaste, religious Writer, trifling, unmannerly, fulsome and profane.'[40] But his most trenchant criticism is of Dryden's ignorance of his subject, and he gives as an example Virgil's description of cross-ploughing (I.139ff.) which Dryden totally misconstrues in his translation.

The messianic aspect of the *Georgics*, their celebration of a coming golden age, was one that had long been identified by Christian apologists as referring to the birth of Christ. Benson, however, translated Virgil's messianism in strictly political terms. For him, as for Virgil, agriculture (and thereby improvement generally) was part of the world of both myth and politics. In that context it made perfect sense that the *Georgics'* messianism was prophetic of the Whig settlement in England. Virgil, after all, wrote in the wake of the Roman civil war. Why should his celebration of the ensuing Roman constitution not also be relevant to a country like England that had come through two political revolutions in order to arrive at its constitution?[41]

If Benson thought the *Georgics* superior to the *Aeneid* because the latter had been written by Virgil 'merely to please his Prince' (Augustus), it was only natural that, as an opponent of royal privilege, he should have welcomed Virgil's apparent prophecy of English parliamentary democracy. Here again, as in the translation of Pliny's villas, the British were more legitimately the heirs of the Romans than the French: 'And this very Constitution, which *Virgil* plann'd for his own Country, almost two thousand Years since, is the Constitution of the happiest People upon Earth [i.e the British] at this instant.'[42]

Although Benson associated himself with Tory peers in supporting the appointment of the architect John James as master carpenter at St. Paul's, Benson's own politics were primarily Whig. The son of a 'city knight' and therefore associated with the rising Whig middle class, he further identified himself with Whig interests by writing a pamphlet on limiting the powers of the Crown while Queen Anne was still on the throne. For this he was rewarded, after the Whigs came to power in 1714, with the position of Surveyor General, a position in which he replaced the aged Christopher Wren in spite of the opposition of Vanbrugh and Hawksmoor to his appointment.

Palladianism, with its appeal to a classical Roman past and chaste English traditions of good taste (as opposed to the vulgarity of Vanbrugh's and Hawksmoor's baroque) offered a vocabulary of protest and creation. It combined the pure and neat language of architecture with a landscape liberated from the symmetrical restrictions of either elaborate French parterres or the clipped artificial shrubbery of Dutch topiary.

Benson was, in Christopher Hussey's phrase, 'one of the first of the *dilettanti* Palladians.' He was a patron of Colen Campbell, whose *Vitruvius Britannicus* (1725) set the seal on the new Palladianism.[43] Moreover his house, Wilbury, built as early as 1710, echoed Amesbury by Inigo Jones's follower, John Webb, and heralded a whole group of villas that established Palladianism as the national style. Like Chiswick more than a decade later, for example, Wilbury was impracticable as a country mansion but suitable for occasional residence.

More a patron of the arts and a generous benefactor than a creator in his own right,[44] Benson in his claim to the post of Surveyor General was at least in part substantiated by his skill in engineering. He designed the fountains for the Hanoverian palace at Herrenhausen in Germany and it is possible that he also created the water-works at Ebberston in Yorkshire. Benson's family came originally from Yorkshire and he may have been related to Robert Benson (Lord Bingley) the creator of Bramham Park, another contemporary estate in which water-works were prominent.

In the laying out of Wilbury Benson may also have been advised by John James, whose appointment to St. Paul's he was supporting at this time. In 1712 James published his translation of Dezallier d'Argenville's *La Théorie et la Pratique du Jardinage* (1709) [Fig. 26], a work that, in explaining the 'ha-ha', did more than any other to popularise that 'calling in of the country' that was the hallmark of the new landscape garden. Certainly Wilbury had many of the French features that were also evident at Bramham: [Fig. 27]

26. 'Designs of Wood of Forrest Trees' from A. J. Dézallier D'Argenville, *The Theory and Practice of Gardening* tr. John James (1712).

27. An Avenue at Bramham.

With little doubt the slope south from the house was originally laid out and framed in semi-formal lines such as the other Benson employed on a much larger scale at Bramham. On the north side from the front door a vista through tall beeches runs up the hill to a column; thence at right angles a similar avenue is aligned on a charming octagon temple of rough-cast brick, with a dome, a wooden cornice and stone rusticated columns.[45]

Here the French landscape design, however, was congruent with Palladian architecture. As at Bramham, what is most interesting is the way in which 'French' appropriation of the countryside served to translate Virgil's *ingentia rura* into the English landscape. At Bramham plantations of trees carry the eye out far beyond the bounds of what previously would have been accepted as the garden. At Wilbury avenues and stands of beech, which Christopher Hussey thought 'prophetic on a modest scale of Bridgeman's work at Stowe,'[46] also call in the country.

Benson's sister married Henry Hoare, the banker who created Stourhead from 1743 onwards. More than any other garden of the early eighteenth century, Stourhead represents the translation of a classical text into an English landscape, in this case the landscape of Aeneas's descent into the underworld in Virgil's epic.[47] It is hard to imagine a better example of how, by the mid-eighteenth century the world of classical antiquity had enabled English 'improvers' to call in the landscape and thereby transform the idea of nature.

One hundred years before the publication of Boyle's edition of the *Letters of Pliny*, in 1651 in the poem 'Upon Appleton House', Andrew Marvell left the enclosed garden near the house and stepped down into the landscape of the estate. In so doing, he stepped down into what he called 'the Abbyss . . . / Of that unfathomable Grass,'[48] but his journey took him ultimately to 'sanctuary in the wood.' There the trees, in contrast to the false architecture of the ruined convent earlier in the poem, offered him 'a green, yet growing ark' of salvation and their 'arching boughs' together with 'the columns of the temple green' created a new kind of spiritualised nature.

Marvell's step into the landscape beyond the garden and eventually to the woods reflects a momentous stage in English attitudes to landscape. The wood of error that Spenser had inherited from Dante and a long tradition of medieval ballad and romance began to be replaced by a notion of redeemed nature in which man had a place.[49] It may well have been that this new attitude to the landscape beyond the garden resulted in part from the blowing up of fortified houses and castles captured by the Parliamentarians in the Civil War (called 'slighting'). Certainly it was no longer possible to think of the garden as part of defensible space near the house, a *hortus conclusus* in the language of medieval gardens. Marvell himself alludes to this in his play with military language in the description of those gardens, a military language grown comic in the fragrant volleys of the flowers. Whatever the reasons, nearly a century before William Kent is said to have 'leaped the fence [and seen] that all nature was a garden,'[50] Marvell's poem enacted a similar moment of recognition: that there was a necessary treaty between the world of art and the world of nature.[51] As a result of this change in the seventeenth century, nature and art, gardens and landscape required new definitions.

The basis of these redefinitions lay within a theological controversy of the seventeenth century: whether nature after the Fall was altogether deformed (as traditional Augustinian theology had claimed) or whether its various parts all in their way showed forth divine providence. Usually traced to the publication in 1635 of George Hakewill's *Apology for the Power and Providence of God*, the claim that even fallen nature was redeemed can be traced back even further to the conventional argument that God gave us two books to read from, one the book of the Scriptures, the other the book of nature. In the late seventeenth century this attitude to the book of nature was given additional support by the writings of the Cambridge Platonists for whom, in the words of Ralph Cudworth, its most powerful apologist, the world was an 'intellectual system' not a deformed ruin. In reaction to the Calvinist stress on damnation that had shadowed the middle years of the century, Cambridge Platonism provided a way of spiritualising nature, of seeing in it, in Addison's later words, 'the works of an Almighty hand.'

By the middle of the eighteenth century such an affirmation of the divine plan manifest in natural creation was almost a truism. Pope's *Essay on Man* (published in 1733–34) had given it a wide currency. But its relevance to the making of gardens is, perhaps, nowhere more tellingly stated than in a letter from the Earl of Bute, the effective founder of the botanic gardens at Kew, to the botanist Peter Collinson in March of 1745:

> What Infinite obligations all Lovers of Planting have to your good nature. I can't really express how much it delights me, to see so generous an ardour for increasing the knowledge of Nature, a knowledge that infallibly brings a Good Man to that of His Great Maker; So easy that its rather an amusement, so sweet that far from bringing care or trouble with it (as most other kinds do) wonderfully calms the mind, subduing the fiercer passions, softens the heart and leaves the soul at Liberty to exert its greatest power, in thankfull acknowledgement to that bountifull hand who for Mans sole use and pleasure, has lavished Myriads of beautys over the whole Creation.[52]

Thomas Burnet's *Sacred Theory of the Earth*, first published in Latin in 1681, sought to reassert the older notion of the original perfection of the world, but it served largely to elicit further support for the opposite case. In the library of John Boyle's father at Marston were copies of Burnet's work in English and

Latin, but he also owned Hakewill's *Apology*, Cudworth's *True Intellectual System*, and John Keill's critical *Examen* of Bishop Burnet's *Sacred Theory*. Charles Boyle also owned the major philosophical works of one of the pre-eminent writers to emerge from this controversy, the botanist John Ray. Ray's *The Wisdom of God Manifested in the Works of Creation* (1691) affirmed what many of the English poets had already celebrated, the spirituality of nature and of trees in particular.

'How easily doth Nature teach the Soul,' Thomas Traherne wrote in his poem 'Ease', probably written like most of his poems in the 1670s. Even atoms, Traherne believed, 'another Glory in the Soul Express.' His picture of 'Christendom' was of a city of green lanes where the inhabitants sat out of doors 'beneath the lofty Trees.' He was able, even in Teddington, to write of himself as standing 'like Adam, in the midst of Eden.'[53] Milton's Paradise, a 'woody theatre of stateliest view,' was to provide the inspiration for many such woody theatres in the early eighteenth century, and his celebration of 'hedgerow elms' and 'twilight groves'[54] found repeated echo both in later poetry and in the landscape it inspired.

Groves, Traherne believed, 'represent a kinde of heaven on earth, and exhibit a profe unto thee of som divine power present.' This certainly was consonant with Sir Thomas Browne's earlier celebration of trees in *The Garden of Cyrus* (1658), a work largely concerned with tree-planting. Browne's affirmation there of the connection between groves of trees 'and the *Exedra* of the Ancients, wherein men discoursed, walked and exercised,'[55] was echoed not only by the Restoration poets, Waller and Cowley, but by the most famous garden writer of the period, John Evelyn.

3

A GROVE OF VENERABLE OAKS: JOHN EVELYN AND HIS CONTEMPORARIES

In 1664, only eight years after the publication of *The Garden of Cyrus*, John Evelyn published what was to be the most influential book on trees for over a century, his *Sylva, or a Discourse of Forest-Trees*. Many years later, in a letter to the Countess of Sunderland, he gave an account of its origins:

> When many years ago I came from rambling abroad, observed a little there, and a great deal more since I came home than gave me much satisfaction, and (as events have proved) scarce worth one's pursuit, I cast about how I should employ the time which hangs on most young men's hands, to the best advantage; and when books and severer studies grew tedious, and other impertinence would be pressing, by what innocent diversions I might some-time relieve myself without compliance to recreation I took no felicity in, because they did not contribute to any improvement of the mind. This set me upon planting of trees, [Fig. 28] and brought forth my *Sylva*, which book, infinitely beyond my expectation, is now also calling for a fourth impression, and has been the occasion of propagating many millions of useful timber-trees throughout this nation.[1]

Commissioned by the Royal Society, its purpose was largely to restore the nation's defenses by encouraging the replantation of woodlands devastated during the Civil War. As Evelyn says in his dedication to Charles II, 'no *Jewel* in your Majesties resplendent Crown can render you so much *Lustre* and *Glory* as your regards to *Navigation*; so, nor can anything impeach your *Navigation*, and the *Reputation* of *That*, whiles you continue thus careful of your *Woods* and *Forests*.'[2]

Christopher Hussey singles out Evelyn's work as one of the chief influences in the remaking of the gardens of Restoration England, remarking at the same time that the nature of Evelyn's book was 'economic and the book is technical with no aesthetic aspects.'[3] This description is not entirely accurate, however, for Evelyn overtly unites patriotic duty and sound investment in his argument for raising trees: an argument from Horace's *utile dulci* that had been common-place earlier in the century.[4] In the letter to Lady Sunderland, he says: 'I confess I had an inclination to the employment upon a public account, as well as being suitable to my rural genius, born as I was at Wotton, among the woods.'[5] Moreover, although the first edition of 1664 deals almost exclusively with the technicalities of tree-planting, the second edition of 1670 is not so restricted. It contains for the first time (as chapter 35) 'An Historical Account of the Sacrednesse and Use of Standing Groves'—a chapter that was to reach its final form as Book IV of the fourth edition of 1706.

28. The Plan of Sayes Court, John Evelyn's garden at Deptford. The Trustees of the Will of Major Peter George Evelyn.

Because *Dendrologia* (as this fourth book came to be called)[6] was not included in the first edition, it has largely been overlooked by readers familiar only with the first edition or its reprints. And yet *Dendrologia* is a classic philosophical and aesthetic justification for one of the major shifts in the late seventeenth and early eighteenth centuries—the shift from the contained traditional garden (often identified as Dutch) to large open estates in the French manner whose chief effects were dependent upon trees.

Before the end of the seventeenth century, the impact of reforestation was already observable in England. Many houses recorded in the engravings of Kip and Knyff show the effect of tree-planting on a vast scale. At Badminton, for example, vast tree-lined vistas led the estate out into the surrounding countryside.[7] [Fig. 29] Long before Vanbrugh, Bridgeman, or Kent, this estate had, without the help of that other French importation, the ha-ha, leapt the garden wall by means of trees and brought the countryside in.

Evelyn was himself concerned with silviculture long before the publication of *Sylva*. In 1653, only four years after his purchase of Warley Place in Essex, he noted in his *Diary*: 'I went to Warley to see my Woods.'[8] Two decades later he was involved in the afforestation of the estate of the Lord Chancellor, Lord Arlington, at Euston in Suffolk. There the author of *Sylva* recommended in 1671 (the year after the first publication of 'The Sacrednesse and Use of Standing Groves') the planting of 'firs, Elmes, limes, etc. up his [Lord Arlington's] parke, and in all other places and Avenues.' Evelyn also persuaded Lord Arlington 'to bring his Park so neere, as to "comprehend" his house with in it'—a recommendation that Arlington seems to have accepted. On a return visit in July 1677 Evelyn 'found things exceedingly improvd.' Writing of the house, he refers to its 'front into the Park' where a walk of trees 'reaches to the Parke Pale which is 9 miles in Compas, and the best for riding and meeting the game that ever I saw.'[9]

It is now widely recognised that William Kent's so-called revolution in garden design—'he leaped the fence and saw all nature was a garden' in Horace Walpole's phrase—was a good deal less revolutionary than Walpole claimed. Certainly sixty years before Kent began his work at Stowe and Rousham, Evelyn recommended to Lord Arlington at Euston just that bringing in of the landscape for which Kent was to get the honour. In a witty poem on the translation of Lucretius's *De Rerum Natura* published by Evelyn in 1656, Edmund Waller chose to celebrate the Roman poet in terms that were apposite to Evelyn's landscape practice. Nature was, he says, previously

suppos'd
By moderate wits to be enclos'd,

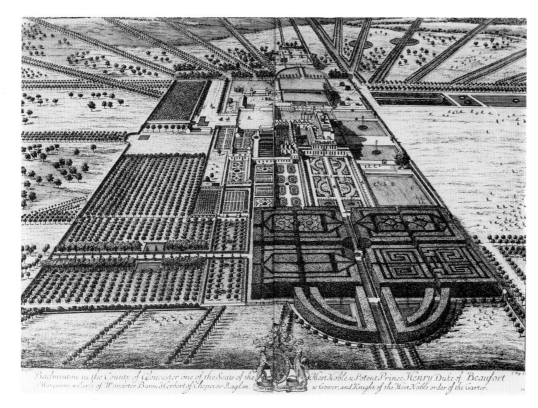

29. Badminton, from Leonard Knyff and John Kip. *Nouveau Theatre de la Grande Bretagne* (1708).

Till his free Muse threw down the Pale
And did at once dispark them all.[10]

This breaking the bounds of the enclosed garden, celebrated only five years earlier by Marvell in 'Upon Appleton House,' was plainly what Evelyn had in mind at Euston. Indeed it has not been recognised sufficiently how early garden designers sought to destroy the boundary between garden and park. Evelyn quotes the royal gardener, André Mollet, as saying: 'The middle Ally should go out of the Garden Walk, out of sight into the Park.'[11] Like Marvell, Evelyn sought to make trees part of the experience of the garden by bringing them to "comprehend" the house.

In that Kent himself worked at Euston in the 1740s and was in turn succeeded there by Capability Brown in the 1760s, there is an interesting arboreal succession stretching over more than a century. For 'Evelyn's method of bringing the park to "comprehend" the house [involved planting] avenues on its east and west axes,'[12] i.e. he achieved his effect with trees. And even though Kent cleared both avenues from the slopes near the house, he left a large part of one avenue and 'proposed a vista much broader than Evelyn's avenue... where wooded belts were to extend laterally to give height and shelter.'[13]

Kent's plan at Euston was more conservative than much of his practice: the views eastward and westward were symmetrical. But his plantations of woods were a loose mixture of hardwoods and conifers to the east and unmixed plantings to the west, clumped in a manner that was to become Capability Brown's hallmark. And similar to Brown's later practice, the parkland unobstructed by garden reached to the windows of the house, enclosing it with forest trees. Kent, as a mediator between Evelyn's original plan and Brown's final modification of it, both respected (more than was his usual practice) the precedent set by Evelyn and passed on to Brown what Evelyn had begun with his plantations.

Evelyn's repertoire of trees at Euston (fir, elm, lime, and ash) [Fig. 30] was more limited than what would have been the case by the second quarter of the eighteenth century. Limes were, nonetheless, a relatively new introduction, still (in the 1664 edition of *Sylva*) described as commonly imported from Flanders and Holland.[14] Evelyn, moreover, continued to interest himself in exotic trees. In a letter to William London 'at Barbados' in 1681, he writes of his longstanding curiosity about 'your culture of trees and plants,' and expresses his admiration of the *Hortus Malabaricus* a twelve-volume work, dealing in Part with Indian trees, that began to appear in 1678.[15] Three years later, in a letter to the Royal Society about damage to his trees in the winter of 1683–84, he refers to his cork trees (the cork oak not usually thought to have been introduced until 1699) and to his 'pine, which bears the greater cone': probably the white pine or *Pinus strobus*, which is said not to have been generally introduced until 1705.[16]

Throughout the last quarter of the seventeenth century, Evelyn continued to interest himself in the introduction of new trees. Although he thought John Smith's *England's Improvement Reviv'd* (1670), 'industriously perform'd,'[17] its practical recommendations for tree-planting suggested no new species. In a letter of 1699 from Maryland, published in the *Philosophical Transactions of the Royal Society*, however, a Mr. Hugh Jones catalogued a number of American trees that were plainly of interest to Evelyn who marked the relevant passage in his copy of the *Transactions*. Jones's account was both aesthetic and practical. It included both a 'Tulip-Bearing-Laurel' for its beauty and the tulip tree

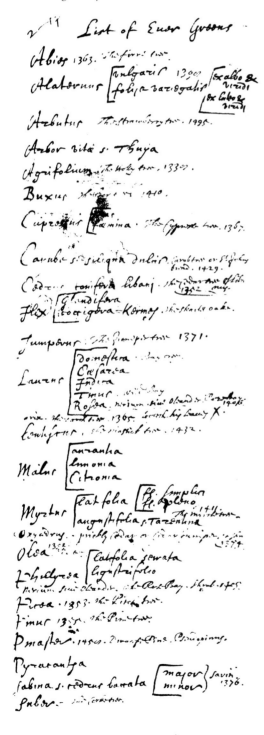

30. John Evelyn, List of Trees and Shrubs, Manuscript Notes for *Sylva*. The Trustees of the Will of Major Peter George Evelyn.

31. Cornelius Johnson, 'The Family of Arthur Capel' National Portrait Gallery, London.

32. Anonymous 19th-century copy of a 1649 drawing of the garden at Hadham Hall, Herts. Hertfordshire Record Office.

(*Liriodendron*), which Jones recommended for making a 'good White Plank.' Evelyn seems especially to have been interested in Jones's list of oaks: 'The Red, White, Black, Chesnut, Water, Spanish and Line [i.e. Live],' some of which were not introduced widely until the early eighteenth century.[18]

In terms of the history of gardening, however, Evelyn's most interesting silvicultural contacts were with the Capel family. Arthur and Henry Capel were the sons of Baron Capel of Hadham, himself a gardener of distinction and a royalist who had been executed in 1648 for his part in the Second Civil War. Baron Capel's garden at Hadham in Hertforshire, created in the 1630s, has been described as among 'the most advanced gardens of the period.'[19] Like Sir John Danvers' garden in Chelsea, Lucy Harrington's Moor Park, and the Earl of Pembroke's Wilton, it reflected the spread of the Italian style that (in the last especially) first suggested 'calling in the country.'

The gardens of Hadham Hall, neglected during the 1650s, disappeared at the Restoration when Lord Capel's son, Arthur (1632–83), became the first Earl of Essex of the seventh creation and moved to nearby Cassiobury. Fortunately, however, a record of that garden survives both in the painting by Cornelius Johnson of the family sitting in the Banqueting Hall that Capel had added to the house (c. 1639) [Fig. 31] and in an anonymous drawing of 1648 which shows the garden looking back towards the house.[20] [Fig.32] The garden was probably a *giardino d'amore* in the popular Caroline neo-Platonic mode, for the Italianate statues that stood in (at least) the four corners of the garden were cupids. These were subsequently moved to Cassiobury when Hadham was reduced to a farmhouse, residence for Moses Cook, the chief gardener.

After the execution of Lord Capel, his land was sequestered by the Parliamentary Commissioners, and Capel's brother, William, acted as steward and guardian of his nephew, the future Earl. There is correspondence between William and the commissioners about the woods at Hadham and elsewhere on the Capel estates. As steward, William seems to have argued successfully that it would be 'a losse to the Common wealth to have so many trees rooted up,'[21] as was common practice with seized royalist land. As the dedication to Evelyn's *Sylva* suggests, trees were especially associated with the royalist cause, not least

Charles I., in Honour of the Inftallation of our late Sovereign CHARLES II. caufed fome *Emblematic Medals* to be ftamp'd, with the *Royal Oak* under a Princes Coronet, overfpreading fub-nafcent Trees and young Suckers.

SERIS. FACTVRA. NEPOTIBVS. VMBRAM.

Reverfe

The *Legend* on the Table of the *Medal*, within the Garter of the Order.

CAROL. M. B. REGIS. FILIVS. CAROL. PRINC. INAVGVRATVR. XXII. MAII. MDCXXXIIX.

33. Medal in Honour of Charles II's Installation as Prince of Wales, 1638. John Evelyn, *Numismata. A Discourse of Medals Antient and Modern* (1697).

the oak which had been identified with Charles II from the time of his installation as Prince of Wales in 1638 [Fig. 33]. Charles II is described in *Sylva* '*as having* once *your* Temple, *and* Court *too under that* Holy-Oak *which you Consecrated with your Presence.*'[22] Perhaps for both these reasons, as much as for his taste for French gardens, Capel's son, Arthur, created at Cassiobury a garden dependent almost entirely upon trees.

Cassiobury first came into Capel hands through the marriage of Essex's grandfather to the daughter of Sir Charles Moryson.[23] In the 1640s, rather confusingly, it was tenanted by the previous Earl of Essex, Robert Devereux, who was the last of that family. During that period the house was repaired, but further work on it was not undertaken until about 1668 when the Earl of Essex decided to move there and to add to the old house a series of state rooms designed by Hugh May. It is these, including the library, that Evelyn describes in his visit there in 1680.[24]

The building of the house took some time. In January 1677 May wrote to Lord Essex about the 'Frontispeece' or tympanum on the east side of the house. This had been designed by the painter Lely who, nearly twenty years earlier, painted a portrait of Essex in which the bust of his 'martyred' father has an honoured place and groves have replaced an Italian garden as a landscape feature. [Fig. 34] This May describes as 'the most proper for a Countrey Scituation—Representing Diana and the Countrey Nymphs; with a figure representing the Rivers.'[25] It seems that the garden was well in hand by this time, however, for May subsequently refers to setting up iron railings and bringing in gravel. In the Cassiobury accounts for 1679–80 there are frequent entries for lime-burning (for mortar) as well as for bringing in stone. In 1680 John White was paid £2.19.0 'for Iron Worke about the new building,' and John Baldwyn £7.12.0 'for carrying gravell into the woodwalkes.'[26]

Evelyn had previously been to the house and garden of Essex's brother,

34. Sir Peter Lely, 'Arthur Capel, 1st Earl of Essex' (c. 1658). National Portrait Gallery, London.

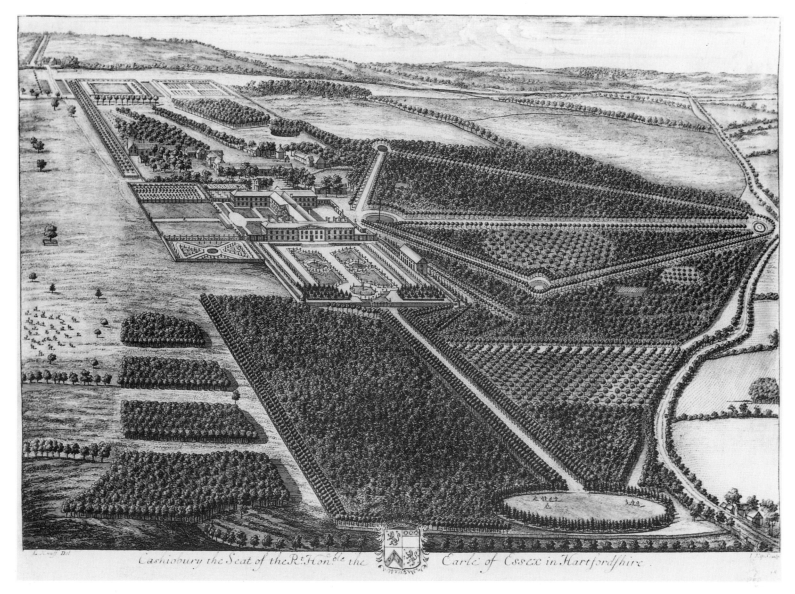

Cassiobury the Seat of the R.t Hon.ble the — Earle of Essex in Hartfordshire.

35. Cassiobury, from Leonard Knyff and John Kip, *Britannia Illustrata* (1707).

Henry, at Kew,[27] but Cassiobury (near Watford) was a country house on a far larger scale and with a far greater garden. [Fig. 35] The gardens that Essex inherited there had been laid out by the Morysons in a conventional enclosed sixteenth-century style.[28] What Essex, with the assistance of his gardener Moses Cook, did at Cassiobury was to go beyond the still-enclosed parterre gardens near the house and extend the pleasure grounds to the Hemel Hempstead road that bounded the estate on the northwest. This they did with a series of radiating 'wood walks' through woodland, terminating in the east with a crow's-foot and roundel and in the south with a large circular bowling green: a radical departure from previous English practice both in scale and materials.[29]

In creating such a landscape garden out of woodland, Essex and Cook not only anticipated the recommendations of Addison and Pope and Stephen Switzer[30] but the practice of such forest gardens as Bathurst's Cirencester, Bingley's Bramham, and even Charles Hamilton's Painshill. Cassiobury was not a hunting lodge (like Ashdown House, Berkshire or Westwood Park, Worcestershire) but a sort of *forêt ornée*, a garden created out of and through productive woodland that also anticipated the *fermes ornées* of Philip Southcote

36. The former Wood Walks at Cassiobury.

37. (below left) One of the surviving oaks at Cassiobury.

38. (below right) An avenue on the site of the Wood Walks at Cassiobury.

and William Shenstone in the next century.[31] [Fig. 36] Nearly forty years later Switzer commended the third Earl of Carlisle for creating walks in an easy natural style through Wray Wood at Castle Howard, but the credit for thinking of woodland as garden in the first place must go to Carlisle's father-in-law, the Earl of Essex.

> No man [Evelyn wrote] has ben more industrious than this noble Lord in Planting about his seate, adorn'd with Walkes, Ponds, and other rural Elegancies; but the soile is stonie, churlish and uneven, nor is the Water neere enough to the house, though a very swift and cleare streame run within a flight-shot from it in the vally.[32]

Evelyn also complained that, although the land was 'exceedingly addicted to Wood,' the coldness of the situation meant that only black cherry trees would grow there. Nonetheless he noted the use of 'treble rows of Spanish fir-trees' at the bowling green and the use of the cherry trees to make 'very handsome avenues.'[33]

Presumably Cook, whom Evelyn considered to be a skillful artist, told Evelyn something about the trees growing there, many of which predated the making of the garden of wood walks. Certainly Evelyn's remark that some of the cherry trees grow to be '80 foote long' echoes Cook's reference to 'a Cherry-tree in *Cashiobury* Wood-walk, . . . 85 foot high,' an observation published the previous year in his *The Manner of Raising, Ordering and Improving Forest and Fruit-Trees*.[34]

A previously unnoticed document in the Hertfordshire Record Office, called 'The Timber of the Manor of Cashio,' [Fig. 39] in fact lists all of the trees growing in the wood walks in the 1670s and confirms that (in Marvell's words) 'everything does answer use.' At the end of the catalogue of oaks, ash and beech there is 'Chery Trees there growing 152.'[35] Even that catalogue, while giving the number and value of the trees, does not list all of them. In his book Cook refers to planting limes at Cassiobury that had been raised at Hadham, where Essex himself had pruned them. These at Essex's instruction were planted 'to make three Walks of Line-trees, from the New Garden [the parterre south of the house] to the New Bowling-green.'[36] [Figs. 37, 38] Presumably, like the willows that Cook also records planting there, they were either too young or not considered good enough timber trees to be recorded in the timber valuation.

Certainly in his book, Cook notes that although the lime is a 'fine Tree, for Walks, Avenues or Lawns,' many planters do not like it 'because it is not good Timber.' Cook, who was as eager as Evelyn to reconcile use and beauty, argued that lime wood was both useful for carving and good for burning and charcoal, and that its scent was 'counted healthfull' and its red shoots 'very pleasing to behold in the Winter season.' Citing a letter of Sir Thomas Browne to Evelyn, published in chapter 29 of *Sylva*, he notes Browne's description of the tree as 'Large *and* Stately.' 'A single Rowe, to bound a Lawn round, set two or three Rod asunder, would,' he wrote, 'be mighty obliging to the Noblest Sense.'[37] Evelyn himself, recording the advice given by the royal gardener, André Mollet, noted that although elms were best at a distance from gardens (he had admired elm walks in Madrid), 'the Lime best in them by Walkes with the Garden.'[38] Cook also refers to Essex's giving thirty lime trees to Sir William Temple, one of the most influential garden writers of the late seventeenth century. Temple's espousal of *sharawadgi*, a way of planting 'without any order or disposition of parts, that shall be commonly or easily

39. Anonymous list of the trees growing in the Wood Walks at Cassiobury. Hertforshire Record Office.

observ'd,'[39] was consonant with Cook's earlier sense that limes so planted 'would shew themselves more clearly than when set in double Rows to make Walks.'[40]

For all its supposed practicality, Cook's *The Manner of Raising Forest Trees* is as full of aesthetic observations as Evelyn's *Sylva*. His recommendations for planting hedges are a classic attempt at reconciliation: 'There are and may be made many sorts of Hedges of one particular sort of Wood alone, some for Ornament only, some for Ornament and Profit, and some for Ornament, Profit and a Fence.'[41] Even in his account of the hornbeam (*Carpinus betulus*), where 'to hedge in Ridings, Causewayes, or to make close Walks or Arbours, this Tree is much to be commended,' Cook feels that its ornamental use (as at Hampton Court) needs to be reconciled with its use for firewood.[42] In this he appears to go beyond Evelyn who was content to praise the beauty of a hornbeam palisade at Tournay for its own sake and to repeat the recommendations of the designer of Hampton Court, André Mollet, that cherry laurel or beech be used for this purpose solely for aesthetic effect.[43]

Evelyn, however, had already declared his commitment to the mixture of use and beauty. Two years before the first publication of *Sylva* he engaged in a correspondence with his father-in-law, Sir Richard Browne, on just this subject. Writing of woodland as 'a foyle to your Garden,' Browne imagined a forest where the thinning of the oaks planted for their use to shipping might 'give us some resemblance of a Quincunx,' and where 'here or there an artificial or freshly raysd Arbor would be instead of the [regular] order.' Might not these 'Moderne acquisite [exquisite] Tempe's,' he wrote, be more naturally and easily 'inserted in a stately forrest, than Mounds pertierres [parterres] etc. by art devised in a Garden?'

In his reply, Evelyn answered his father-in-law's citation of *Georgics* II with a further quotation from it and went beyond him to explain what he had earlier meant by the inclusion of 'Terminus Arbors' in woodland plantations:

> As they that build houses and ships bestowe beauty and ornament on the fronts: soc if our Dutch gardeners and other, (I may one day say husbandmen), were by Forrest lawes, I meane decrees of such as undertake it, bound and regulated in their mounds, Gardens and fittest places, to plant and adorne their plantations, The Forrest might soone be made the glory, wealth, and beauty of England; their groves, thickets purifye the ayre of provinces, and sweeten the navigable streames.[44]

Some of this Evelyn was to take up later in *Sylva*, not least in the increasingly elaborated fourth book, 'Dendrologia'. That Cassiobury was to exemplify such recommendations within a decade indicates how welcome Evelyn's comments on the garden must have been to both Capel and Cook.

Cook frequently defers to *Sylva*, especially for examples of trees of a prodigious size, but for all his desire for experimentation he has none of Evelyn's deference to the recommendations of the *Georgics* about grafting. The controversy about grafting one species on another that the *Georgics* prompted in the last quarter of the seventeenth and the first quarter of the eighteenth centuries enters his pages only to be dismissed, even when it is propounded by Bacon and Evelyn.[45] His scientific curiosity, however, was as alert as theirs and his concern for the causes of things as lively as Virgil recommended. Writing of mutations in flowers, he observes: 'If you be a Lover of Plants, or a Servant of Nature, be diligent, and whensoever you see your Mistress step out of Door, then do you wait upon her to her Journey's end, for 'tis on the Diligent she bestows her Favours.'

Like other gardeners after him, Cook fancied himself a poet. He concludes many of his entries on particular trees with poems that, for all their doggerel rhymes, express arboreal sentiments that greater poets, such as Cowley whom he quotes, also expressed. The lime 'will to After-ages show / What Noble Essex did on us bestow,' and the oak, preserver of Charles II's life, instructs us in a lesson dear to Capel hearts: 'that we / Might thence Learn Lessons of true Loyalty.' Cook's best poetic effort is one written for Essex's brother, Henry, a poem in which he espouses a theme dear to neo-Pelagian fashion, that even fallen man preserves 'the green shoots of Him [Adam] th'Original Tree' which by the 'innocent old Trade' of gardening will bring profit to the country and honour to the king.[46]

Evelyn's praise for Cook, however, was not as a poet but as a gardener 'who is as to the Mechanic part not ignorant in Mathematics.'[47] Whereas the first two-thirds of his book are devoted to silviculture, the last third is given over almost entirely to what would now be called design: making walks, avenues, and figures.[48] [Figs. 40, 41] From it indeed emerges just how much Cassiobury

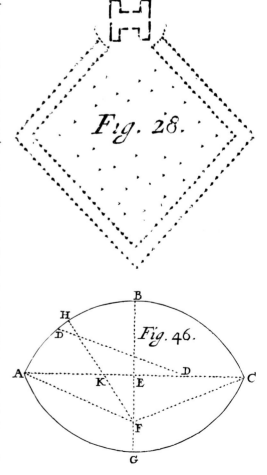

40 and 41. Designs Nos. 28 and 46 from Moses Cook, *The Manner of Raising, Ordering, and Improving Forest and Fruit Trees* (1679).

Fig. 28.

Fig. 46.

was Cook's creation. The last of his accompanying plans shows how the parterre was made and includes mounts planted with trees in a manner still employed sixty years later by Lord Petre at Thorndon. Another illustrates how to make an oval such as is shown as a termination of the three western walks in the Kip engraving. And the basic plan of the western side of the wood walks is illustrated in his figure 28 (figure 40 here), a figure that shows the house in the same place as in the Cassiobury plan.[49] Chapter 38 sets out not simply how walks, circles, and 'goosefeet' are to be made but Cook's own experience of doing so at Cassiobury. His description of the creation of the bowling green circle even lists the number of Spanish fir trees in each of the surrounding circles.

Cook was employed by the Capels long before the move to Cassiobury. Manuscript accounts of 1664 show him acting as a sort of steward,[50] and he was plainly involved in early stages of planting at Cassiobury even before the house was complete. By 1681, however, he had left to become one of the founding partners of the famous Brompton Park nursery. The Brompton nursery, gained its fame from the combination of nursery trade with essentially French landscape design. Indeed, London, who had been in France, was probably Evelyn's co-translator of La Quintinie's *The Compleat Gard'ner* (1693).[51] Moreover, Wise's plan for Melbourne in Derbyshire 'to suit with Versailles' is evidence of the continuing influence of the revolution in design in which Cook was instrumental. That he died in 1713 possessed of five properties in Essex and Hertfordshire is indicative of his success as both a plantsman and a designer.[52]

Evelyn did not agree with Cook in everything. He continued, like Sir Thomas Browne and Charles Cotton, to prefer trees planted in a quincunx arrangement, whereas Cook prefered them to be planted in a triangular pattern. Nonetheless, in the 1679 edition of *Sylva*, Evelyn praises Cook as 'that industrious Planter Mr. *Cooke*, from whose ingenuity and experience (as well as out of gratitude for his frequent mentioning of me in his elaborate, and useful work) I acknowledge to have benefited my self, and this *Edition*.'[53]

What both men shared was the belief that 'Almighty God hath Imprinted in the Hearts of most wise men such a Love to Plants in part, as their Father *Adam* had in his state of Innocency.'[54] Evelyn's friend Cowley went so far as to claim that the Tree of Life had been a 'Cedar till the Flood.' (*Thuyas* were still called '*Arbor-Vitae*' in the seventeenth century.) In the post-diluvian world it was a 'thorny shrub' but became, said Cowley, an evergreen again in a mind that was temperate and innocent.[55] Like Matthew Hale, whose *The Primitive Origination of Mankind . . . According to the Light of Nature* (1677) Evelyn owned, they believed that the Fall 'did neither alter the essential Constituents of Mankind, nor wholly raze out the Engravings of those common Notions, Sentiments and rational Instincts that were in them.' Indeed, Evelyn marked both this passage and another in which Hale said that men were called to husbandry 'to preserve the *Species* of divers Vegetables, to improve them and others.'[56]

In a similar passage in Browne's *The Garden of Cyrus*, Evelyn marked a reference to the vegetable creation as 'the first ornamentall Scene of nature.' He also noted Browne's praise of the 'Botanicall bravery' of the Persians and his famous observation about Eden, that 'Gardens were before Gardiners, and but some hours after the earth.'[57]

'The Excellency of Husbandry,' wrote Leonard Meager, in another work in Evelyn's library, 'appeareth partly by its Antiquity, as we esteem Things to be the more Admirable, the more Ancient, and the nearer they come to God, . . .

So that God was the Original and Pattern of all Husbandry, and the First Contriver of the Great Design, to bring that odd Mass, and Chaos of Confusion, unto so vast an Improvement.' Meager even outlined a sort of patriarchal succession in which Solomon was 'the Second Husbandman, or Improver of the World.' Like his earlier work, *The English Gardener* (1670), *The Mystery of Husbandry* (1697) was also a practical work on the improving of arable, pasture, and woodland. But 'improvement,' as for Cook and Evelyn, included an aesthetic pleasure that went hand in hand with profit. Woods are profitable, but 'they also yield pleasant and delightful prospects to the Eye, [and] serve as cool shades to retreat in the summer.' And Meager echoes Cook in praising the hornbeam which, when 'set in Walks or Avenues, produces a pleasant shade.'[58]

Underlying this affirmation of practical husbandry united with divine purpose was the physico-theological belief in (to use Evelyn's words) 'the admirable forme and usefulness of the parte of the Universe, particularly the Earth.'[59] Again and again in his marginal notations, Evelyn aligned himself with this belief in the manifest design of God in creation as opposed to Thomas Burnet's belief that the world before the Fall had a perfection no longer available or comprehensible to us. From Leeuwenhook's account of the circulation of the blood to John Woodward's assertion that even hurricanes 'are yet not without a very necessary and excellent *Use*,' Evelyn's marginal notes indicate an endorsement of conventional physico-theology.[60] Chiefly, as in the work of the pioneer botanist, John Ray, this provided a theological and philosophical framework for the study of plants. In his manuscript notes for *Sylva*, Evelyn writes: 'Mr Ray's Catalogue is most excellent greatly directive to accompany a generall hist of plants; and 'tis best as he finds, to distribute them into their severall families according to their differences (a method of exceeding use for the memory).'[61]

In an account of Ray's *The Wisdom of God Manifested in the Works of Creation* (1691) Evelyn has marked the reviewer's comment: 'Of Plants, he thinks, there are not fewer in the World than 18000.'[62] The enormous expansion in the repertoire of available plants in the last decade of the seventeenth century led to a frequently repeated complaint that botany was being confounded by botanists who, in Plukenet's words 'multiply *species* and confound *Botany*.'[63] Evelyn's marginal notations show him sympathetic to this complaint, but they reveal even more his voracious interest in new species, chiefly trees. Throughout his library any reference to the introduction or propagation of a new species is marked or annotated.[64] Frequently these annotations refer either to an etymological or classical reference as well, for Evelyn was concerned about the continuing presence in botany and husbandry of the wisdom of antiquity. He notes with approval the observation of Robert Plot, professor of chemistry and keeper of the Ashmolean Museum at Oxford, that '*Agriculture* was ever of high esteem, having exercised the pens of learned Men' in the time of Columella. Plot's frequent quotation from what he calls '*Georgical* writers,' moreover, underlines the essentially georgic cast of much of the writing that Evelyn admired.[65]

Works such as these provide analogies and sources for Evelyn's own thoughts about the spiritual use of trees in the treatise that was to become Book IV of *Sylva*. None, however, is a more obvious source than René Rapin's *Hortorum Libri IV*, a work published the year after the first edition of *Sylva* and subsequently translated by Evelyn's son. In a passage 'De Nemoribus' Evelyn marks a discussion of the usefulness of trees in protecting houses from wind. What interests him in this passage, however, is the testimony of the ancients to the beauty and pleasure of woodland. In this passage, annotated by Evelyn, Rapin invokes Cicero, Tacitus, and Virgil in praise of woodland as the height of rural ornament, offering a pleasure above even poetry or city life.[66]

Closest to Evelyn in sentiment, however, was Abraham Cowley, whose essay 'The Garden' was dedicated to him. Thomas Sprat, the secretary of the Royal Society who wrote the prefatory 'Life' to Cowley's *Works* (1668), struck a note that was particularly sympathetic to the Virgilian and royalist cast of Evelyn's mind: 'The two last [books] speak of Trees, in the way of *Virgils Georgics*. Of these the sixth Book is wholly Dedicated to the Honour of his Country. For making the *British* Oak to preside in the Assembly of the Forest Trees, upon that Occasion he enlarges on the History of our late Troubles.'[67] The fourth of Cowley's essays, 'Of Agriculture,' is one in which the georgic strain is very apparent, a strain that Robert Plot was to take up twenty years later: '*Citys* have flourish't well enough either without *Physitians* or *Lawyers*; but that they cannot subsist without good *Husbandmen* is plain and evident.'[68] Deploring the deleterious political effects of trade, Cowley observed that no husbandman was responsible for 'the twenty years ruine of his Country' in the Civil War. 'To be a Husbandman,' he wrote, citing the second book of the *Georgics*, 'is but a Retreat from the world, as it is mans; into the World, as it is Gods.'[69]

Cowley's association of Virgilian precept with Christian morality was not new, but it translated into the English landscape the agricultural (and thereby horticultural and silvicultural) implications of that union. If the simple country-man, like Virgil's Evander, is to be the backbone of his country, he must be trained to be so in an agricultural college in which such subjects as aration, pasturage, rural economy, and the management of gardens, orchards, and woods are taught. As headmaster, Cowley recommends none other than Samuel Hartlib, the educational reformer and friend of Milton who, only thirteen years earlier, had recommended that schoolboys be made to plant trees in their minority so that they might be able to harvest mature timber when they were older.[70] For Cowley, such colleges would extend the exegesis of Virgil's text into the practice of agriculture. The professors of his college were not to read the *Georgics* only 'but to instruct their Pupils in the whole Method and course of this study.' In this 'translation' what Cowley was propounding was similar to what Sir Thomas Browne had recommended in *Pseudodoxia Epidemica*, that 'those Geoponicall rules and precepts of Agriculture which are delivered by divers Authours, are not to be generally received; but respectively understood unto climes whereto they are determined.'

In the same year as Cowley's *Works*, John Worlidge published his *Systema Agriculturae*, a work that not only quoted Evelyn and Hartlib but celebrated Virgil's account of 'the pleasures and profits' of the country life and of agriculture in particular. Worlidge refers to *Sylva* as a work that recommends the planting of trees 'both for Timber, Fruits, and other necessary uses.'[71] In that he refers to the first edition, he can cite no reference in Evelyn to the aesthetic qualities of woodland, but he himself, both in the introduction and in the chapter 'Of Woods', celebrates the 'incredible delight and pleasure to all' afforded by trees 'arrayed with the most verdant Leaves, and adorned with the most excellent and curious Blossomes.'[72] Indeed, although Worlidge's historical account of the gardens of the ancients sounds like Browne, his praise of unadorned nature anticipates Shaftesbury. His celebration of the rustic life cites 'the Heathens of old,' but his language looks forward to Addison and Switzer. 'It is for no other reason that *Gardens, Orchards, Partirres, Avenues*, etc. are in

46

such request in Cities and Towns, but that they represent unto us Epitomized, the Form and Idea of the more ample and spacious pleasant *Fields, Groves,* and other *Rustick* objects of pleasure.'[73]

Throughout the chapter 'Of Woods', Worlidge stresses the particular beauties of the trees under discussion; indeed he devotes two pages to the cultivation of flowering shrubs that have no profitable use. In suggesting that timber trees be planted 'in Hedge-rows, Avenues, or any other way disposed or ordered about your Houses, Lands, Commons, etc.,' he in effect describes what the Earl of Essex was about to do at Cassiobury. In describing 'a Plump or Grove of Trees' planted near a country house in the north of England, he looks forward to that supposedly Kentian invention, the clump. In so doing and in celebrating the country as the place to find 'the most Secret and Mystical things that nature affords,' he both elaborates on Evelyn's earlier work and suggests the way in which Evelyn's *Dendrologia* will develop.

Worlidge was not alone in celebrating the philosophical pleasures to be cultivated in rural life. In his influential poem, 'St. James's Park,' published in 1661 (a decade before the first appearance of *Dendrologia*), Edmund Waller concluded with a picture of the newly restored Charles II holding his court, as Evelyn also describes him, amidst a 'living Gallery of aged *Trees.*' Evelyn himself had written of the 'solemness of the Grove' and the 'spacious Walks' at St. James's in his *A Character of England* (1656).[74] And several years later he made a note of the 'stately Elme Trees' that composed this gallery (the Mall) and of the size of the Mall itself, a note that he made in conjunction with observations about the size of the 'Paillemailles' at the Tuileries, Versailles, and St. Germain.[75] The conventions to which Waller's poem appeals—the sacredness of groves in antiquity and their suitability for philosophical and statesmanly retirement—were, as we have seen, the commonplaces of seventeenth-century writers. Waller's poem, however, sets them forth in unambiguous English terms:

> In such green Palaces the first Kings reign'd,
> Slept in their shades, and Angels entertain'd:
> With such old Counsellors they did advise,
> And by frequenting sacred Groves grew wise;
> Free from th'impediments of light and noise
> Man thus retir'd his nobler thoughts imploys:
> Here CHARLES contrives the ordering of his States,
> Here he resolves his Neighb'ring Princes Fates;
> What Nation shall have Peace, where War be made
> Determin'd is in this oraculous shade.[76]

At about the same time the poet Thomas Traherne copied into one of his notebooks an essay on groves from a work published by Thomas Jackson in 1624, an essay which argues for their spiritual use:

> If thou light on a Grove thicke set with trees of such unusuall antiquitie and height, as that they take away the sight of heaven by their branches over spreading one another: the height of the wood, and solitariness of the place, and the uncouthness of the close and continued shade in the open Ayre, soe joyntly represent a kinde of heaven on earth, and exhibit a profe unto thee of som divine power present.[77]

Jackson goes on in this work to renew the Horatian contrast between the city and the country life, to the customary advantage of the latter:

the frequency of sermons seems most necessary in cities and great Townes, that their Inhabitants, who (as one wittily observeth) be for the most part but the workes of men, may dayly heare God speaking unto them. Whereas such as are conversant in the fields and woods, continually contemplat the workes of God.[78]

Similar observations could also be found in John Aubrey's *The Remaines of Gentilisme and Judaisme* (c. 1668) or in Browne's *Garden of Cyrus* (1658) where the example of the 'retirement' of the Emperor Charles V was one to which Evelyn returned in his notes for *Elysium Britannicum*.[79]

The significance of Evelyn's *Dendrologia* was not so much its originality as its popularity. Attached as it was to a work of practical silviculture, it disseminated Shaftesburian ideas of nature to a rising middle class attracted to the Whig ideals of liberty that Addison describes in his account of the land of Liberty in *The Tatler*, number 161 (20 April 1710). French and Italian gardens provided the precedents for the mixture of garden and forest, but English essayists increasingly sought philosophical and aesthetic justifications for this practice, primarily in the writings of classic authors.

Stephen Switzer's criticisms of the defects of French gardening are, like Addison's, political and aesthetic. As John Dixon Hunt has pointed out, Switzer argues that a harmony 'between politics, agriculture and the poetic imagination'[80] is to be the genius of English gardens based on classical precedents. In the creation of these 'extensive' gardens, shrewd practicality in estate management was to be combined with both the planting of groves and the 'calling in' of existing woods into landscape plans by threading them (as at Castle Howard) with winding paths. Although the economic and aesthetic motives for tree-planting were various and took forms as widely different as the forest garden at Painshill and the more architectural design of nearby Claremont, Evelyn's work offered a precedent for thinking of silviculture as more than a merely remunerative or patriotic exercise. It provided the moral and aesthetic justification for what was to become a basic element of English landscape design.

Evelyn in fact cites Waller's already famous poem on St. James's Park in his fourth book, declaring that Waller 'shew'd himself as well a *Prophet as a Poet*'[81] in his celebration of the trees of that park. Much of what Evelyn has to say in defense and celebration of groves and woods sounds not only like Waller (and his predecessors) but a score of eighteenth-century apologists who were to come in his wake. Like Jackson, he is not unaware of the abuses of religion in groves and trees: 'by what degrees it degenerated into dangerous Superstitions: For the *Devil* was always *God's Ape*, and did so ply his *Groves*.'[82] The abuse, though, is no argument against the use, and he cites not only the historical garden precedents associated with Plato, Democritus, Thucydides, Cicero, Quintilian, Pliny, and Tacitus, but literary examples in Juvenal, Virgil, Horace, and Petrarch.

Aeneas's Elysium, he points out, is of '*Groves* . . . [and] *Ever-greens, the Dwellings of the Blest*,' and therefore, he concludes, 'Wise and Great Persons had always these sweet Opportunities of Recess, their *Domos Silvae* . . . not much unlike the *Lodges* in divers of our Noblemens *Parks* and *Forest-Walks*.'[83] In fact Evelyn here echoes his own earlier correspondence with his father-in-law, Sir Richard Browne, about the creation in England of just such Virgilian landscapes, Elysiums that he also identifies with the *Georgics*. Browne first explains how 'Moderne acquisite [exquisite] Tempe's' might be 'inserted in a stately forrest':

I prefer those arbors in which all trees are assisted to the compleatest perfection of growth, fruite, beauty, wherein full spreading branches on all sides keepe the Sun and windes at utmost distance, and then best when the sides yielde full shade and shelter, the middle has noe other Canopy than the Temple of Terminus, the fayre heavens.

Evelyn in reply recommends planting 'hedge roes and thickets in . . . affected wildness or plainesse,' and claims that 'these wild gardens will deserve the prayse, annexed to the name of Virgill.' They are, moreover, to be used 'to plant and adorne . . . plantations' i.e. woods. 'The result of all this [he says] is to limb what I meant by Terminus Arbors.'[84] In *Dendrologia*, moreover, like many an early eighteenth-century gardener, he domesticates the classical muses to the English landscape while echoing Juvenal in scorning the vices of the town: 'Here then is the true *Parnassus, Castalia*, and the *Muses*, and at every call in a *Grove* of Venerable *Oaks*, methinks I hear the Answer of an hundred old *Druids*, and the *Bards* of our Inspired Ancestors.'[85] In a letter from his ancestral home, Wotton, to Pepys in 1692, he writes: 'Here is wood and water, meadows and mountains, the Dryads and Hamadryads.'[86]

The religious associations of groves and woods, these 'nemorous Solitudes' as he calls them, are as important to Evelyn as their merely meditative and philosophical nature. '*Paradise* itself,' he says, 'was but a kind of *Nemorous Temple*, or Sacred *Grove*, Planted by *God* himself.'[87] Christ, Elijah, and St. John the Baptist all used woody wildernesses as spiritual retreats, and in the grove at Mambree the angels appeared to Abraham. 'And perhaps,' he continues, as if setting out a catalogue for an eighteenth-century garden, 'the *Air* of such retired Places may be assistant and influential, for the inciting of Penitential Expressions and Affections; especially where one may have the additional assistance of solitary *Grotts*, murmuring *Streams*, and desolate *Prospects*.'[88] It was just this vocabulary of natural effects that the Earl of Shaftesbury was to invoke only eight years later in one of the most influential treatises for the eighteenth-century landscape garden, 'The Moralists'.

4

THINGS OF A NATURAL KIND: SHAFTESBURY AND THE CONCEPT OF NATURE

Central to any discussion of nature in the early eighteenth century is the famous passage in 'The Moralists' by Anthony Ashley Cooper, Third Earl of Shaftesbury:

> I shall no longer resist the Passion growing in me for Things of a *natural* kind: where neither *Art* nor the *Conceit* or *Caprice* of Man has spoil'd their *genuine Order*, by breaking in upon that *primitive State*. Even the rude *Rocks*, the mossy *Caverns*, the irregular unwrought *Grotto's*, and broken *Falls* of Waters, with all the horrid Graces of the *Wilderness* itself, as representing NATURE more, will be the more engaging, and appear with a Magnificence beyond the formal Mockery of Princely Gardens.[1]

Until relatively recently Shaftesbury's position there was taken as an unqualified endorsement of the 'natural garden' that reached its apogee later in the century. This conventional assessment was first seriously challenged in 1984 in an article by David Leatherbarrow, setting out the apparent discrepancy between Shaftesbury's supposed endorsement of nature and his stated views elsewhere about the ideal forms of nature. Leatherbarrow's case seemed further to be confirmed by Shaftesbury's own practice in his garden at Wimborne St. Giles in Dorset where (a previously undiscovered document revealed) he had employed an essentially formal plan, a plan also depicted in the background of his portrait in the engraved frontispiece to 'The Moralists.'[2]

Neither the evidence of the garden nor the portrait, however, is so straightforward as Leatherbarrow claimed. In the first place, Shaftesbury's use of globe and pyramid yews does not, as Leatherbarrow asserts, necessarily constitute an allegiance to artificial shapes. To Shaftesbury, both forms would have represented the perfection of nature and the simplicity of antiquity.[3] In his garden, moreover, he saw them as part of the design to allow the eye to travel outward and not, as he says 'to stopp the Prospect from the House and Terrass.' In his note on this point, moreover, he recommends that 'Globe-Hollys' be used in just this way: 'a few to take of Eye but not so many or so high as to hide ye Prospect of ye Hills and rising ground behind,' a theme to which he returns several times.

Both sorts of yews (the conventional stock-in-trade of gardeners from Pliny's time to the present) were commonly used in the late seventeenth century, but largely for symmetrical or architectural effect.[4] Shaftesbury is exceptional in wanting them employed in his garden for overall effects of colour and shape. The globe yews, for example, 'will do better between the

42. The Yew Hedge in the Forecourt of Cirencester Park, Glos. Country Life Photo.

Sycomores on the South side of the Bowling Green' where the gardeners are to take 'away the double rows of little pyramids' because 'the Globe Figure of the Yew does better than the Pyramid, when between or under ye droppings of ye larger Summer Greens.' Equally the pyramid yews are to go more appropriately with the 'Scotch Firs'. Shaftesbury's specific objection is to the parading of these trees in the conventional way where 'no contrast [is] observed either of Figure or Species.' This is an important point, for it was not trimmed shrubbery in itself to which Pope and Addison and Switzer were to object, but the tortured falsity of contrived topiary shapes. Nor did they object to high yew hedges, such as Lord Bathurst used to enclose the forecourt at Cirencester [Fig. 42] and Lord Burlington at Chiswick. Indeed, the frontispiece to Switzer's *Ichnographia Rustica* shows a parterre walled in by a clipped hedge as tall as the house. Even Milton's Eden, after all, required pruning.

43 and 44. Dawley Park and Orchard Portman from Leonard Knyff and John Kip, *Nouveau Theatre de la Grande Bretagne* (1708).

Secondly, the gardens near the house, as described and depicted, were three plain parterres, surrounded by relatively simple shrubbery and trees that led the eye out into the surrounding landscape. One need only look at the contemporary gardens depicted in Knyff and Kip's *Britannia Illustrata* to see how much simpler Lord Shaftesbury's garden was. Those great estates commonly employed figured parterres surrounded by walls or palings, as indeed is the case with the three gardens to which Leatherbarrow compares Wimborne St. Giles: Dawley Park, Orchard Portman, [Figs. 43, 44] and Eaton Hall. The parterres at Wimborne St. Giles had the unfigured simplicity that Batty Langley was to recommend twenty years later. Nor did Shaftesbury's house dominate its landscape with radial avenues as Wollaton, Ragley, or Badminton [Fig. 29] did. The absence of hedges, walls, or palings, moreover, allowed the calling in of the country that was to be one of the central principles of Pope's garden aesthetic.[5]

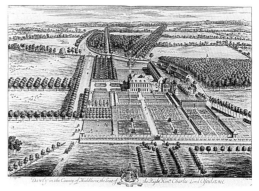

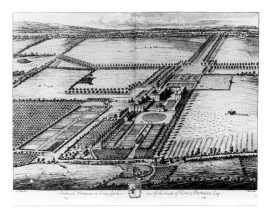

Like Pope, Shaftesbury also would have seen no discrepancy between nature and a grotto in his garden. By the end of the seventeenth century elaborate Italianate and emblematic grottos, such as the one at Wilton, had ceased to be fashionable. They were replaced instead by grottos filled with natural curiosities: shells, gems, and stones of all sorts. Even such a distinguished botanist as John Ellis was not above creating such a grotto, for which the Reverend William Borlase sent him spars, pyrites and corals in 1752.[6]

In its very plainness, Shaftesbury's garden invited a greater attention to 'the horrid graces of the wilderness' that lay beyond it. Indeed, it did so in a way that was more revolutionary or novel than even the practice of Stephen Switzer a decade later. Although Switzer was far more thoroughly committed to the natural implications of rural or extensive gardening, his imaginary 'Manor of Paston', for example, employs considerably more architectural or formal elements than Shaftesbury's garden, and his treatment of parterres discusses even the sculpting of yew into statues.

On the subject of discrepancies, for that matter, we would need to ask what 'use' it was that 'sanctified the expense' of making Pope's garden: the touchstone that Pope used for right gardening in his 'Epistle to Burlington'. And how was it that only four years after promoting the idea of *sharawadgi* or asymmetrical and irregular beauty in his *Upon the Gardens of Epicurus*, Sir William Temple created at Moor Park a garden (figure 14) that was almost entirely symmetrical and regular? In such company Shaftesbury, though a disbeliever in systems, was a model of rational consistency.

Even at Lord Bathurst's first estate, Riskins (figure 8), an early *ferme ornée* that Switzer included in the second edition of his *Ichnographia Rustica*, Pope was moved by its walled enclosure to suggest that a mount would have provided a vista into the landscape. Although there was a mount with a pavilion at Wimborne St. Giles, it was not necessary to use it to see into the landscape. The eye travelled out the garden's carefully designed linear perspectives to the 'rude rocks' of the distant hilly landscape. And the native hedge maples that formed the garden's outer boundary, though trimmed, served to effect just the transition from the architecture of the house to the larger garden of the landscape that Switzer was to recommend throughout *Ichnographia Rustica*.

That Shaftesbury was obviously not proleptically espousing the landscape designs of Kent or Brown does not mean that he was not sincere in his rejection of 'the formal mockery of princely gardens.' His rejection of what that phrase implies is not necessarily a rejection of formality. If it is an anachronism, in relation to Shaftesbury, to use the word 'nature' to mean what Horace Walpole meant by it in 1770, it is as great an anachronism to use the word 'formal' to mean merely 'symmetrical' or to leave the phrase 'formal mockery' unexamined in its context. Given Shaftesbury's concern with inherent form, it seems likely that the phrase means 'the mockery of form' by the imposition of what is not inherent in or appropriate to the genius of the thing. Certainly one does not have to be a philosopher to know that a garden without some form is an impossibility. Of what garden would Shaftesbury's *dictum*, ''Tis *Mind* alone which forms,'[7] not be true? Even Pope's garden, for all his insistence on variety, had 'formal unity'.

Shaftesbury's phrase 'formal mockery' rejects what Switzer was to call the 'Clipt Plants, Flowers, and other trifling Decorations fit only for little Town-gardens, and not for the expansive Tracts of the Country.'[8] That these were still the staple of virtually all the country gardens shown in *Britannia Illustrata* makes Shaftesbury's position one year later the more remarkable. And yet he was espousing principles and tastes that were to be echoed in a very few years by both Pope and Addison, principles and tastes that were founded on an appeal to nature. This nature, moreover, was closer to the nature of the Cambridge Platonists and John Ray's physico-theology than to Descartes or Bishop Burnet. And it is in the language of this kind of Platonism that

Shaftesbury's rural sage, Theocles, declares: 'whatever in Nature is beautiful or charming, is only the faint Shadow of that *First Beauty*.'[9]

Indeed, by the time that Shaftesbury wrote that, Ray's physico-theology had already united botany and theology. Ray, whose *Methodus Plantarum* was the standard botanic taxonomy in this period, published in 1691 *The Wisdom of God Manifested in the Works of Creation*, a work that went far to reconcile all aspects of nature to divine purpose and that was republished ten times before 1750.[10]

Whatever the circumstances of the famous outburst by the neophyte, Philocles, about 'Things of a *natural* kind,' it is little more than a less forceful repetition of what Theocles has already uttered in the previous dialogue. Theocles' remarks plainly identify 'the artificial Labyrinths and feign'd Wildernesses of the Palace,' with a world of false 'Monsters' where 'Nations now profane one another, war fiercer, and in Religion's Cause forget Humanity: whilst savage *Zeal*, with meek and pious Semblance, works dreadful Massacre; and for Heaven's sake (horrid Pretence!) makes desolate the earth.'

In opposition to that, the rural sage flies from the '*Desarts*' of civilisation to 'live alone with Nature . . . view her in her inmost Recesses, and contemplate her with more delight in these original Wilds.'[11] What he subsequently teaches Philocles is that beauty, far from being necessarily inherent only in geometric shapes, may be found in 'the wild *Field*, [and] these *Flowers* which grow around us.' By a process of dialogue Philocles comes to see the implications of his 'vulgar' prejudices, prejudices in which he 'cou'd never relish *the Shades, the Rustick*, or *the Dissonancys* . . . of such *Master-pieces* in NATURE.'[12] What is embraced is not a mindless revel in wildness but a reflective understanding of it. Even in the phrase 'horrid Graces of the Wilderness,' 'horrid' is a word inviting reflection as, in Pope's 'Eloisa to Abelard' (1717), the line 'Ye grots and caverns shagg'd with horrid thorn' suggests the interplay of reflection and sensation.

Each reflective person, Shaftesbury believed, could see two persons in the mirror of his mind: '*One* of them, like the Commanding Genius, the Leader and Chief . . . ; the *other* like that rude undisciplin'd and head-strong Creature, whom we our-selves in our natural Capacity, most exactly resembled.' To Shaftesbury the greatness of poets, and the reason they were judged wise men in antiquity, was that 'they were such well practis'd *Dialogists*, and accustom'd to this improving Method, before ever Philosophy had adopted it.'[13]

That such reflections should arise in a rural scene was a convention both of English poetry of the seventeenth century and of the *Georgics* that gave rise to it. Both Stephen Switzer and his patron, Charles Boyle, affirmed nature as a tamer of the passions. Out of the *Georgics* (II, lines 475–90 in particular) also came the desire for profounder insights into the working of nature. Shaftesbury's use of scientific terminology is one aspect of this; the linking of botanical research with georgic husbandry is another. An anonymous writer in the *London Magazine* in 1738 noted that rural nature 'reads continual Lectures, not only in speculative, but practical philosophy.'[14]

Much of this derives from the second *Georgic* where, as Richard Feingold has observed, Virgil used a very different landscape from that of the *Eclogues*, a landscape 'which could be used to express and interpret political as well as poetical experience.'[15] There the countryman with his caves and living lake dwells happily near the habitation of wild beasts (*Speluncae, vivique lacus . . . non absunt . . . ac lustra ferarum*), far from the lofty palace adorned with tortoise shell (*Si non ingentem foribus domus alta superbis . . . Nec varias inhiant testudine postes*) and safe from the very world of arms and fraud (*procul discordibus armis . . . nescia fallere vita*) of which Theocles complains in his 'Rhapsody'. Theocles, indeed, goes on to praise natural philosophy in Virgilian language: 'Happy he who can know the causes of things' (*Felix qui potuit rerum cognoscere causas*). That such scientific knowledge had already been identified, more than a century earlier, not with a past golden age but with a future enlightenment, is indicative of the potency for liberal enlightenment of the georgic tradition that Shaftesbury inherited.[16]

The knowledge of the causes of things, moreover, included the knowledge of botany with which in the early eighteenth century gardening was increasingly identified. In his sermon on *The Antiquity, Innocence, and Pleasure of Gardening* delivered in 1732 to 'a Meeting of Gardeners and Florists', William Harper praised 'the distinguish'd Elegance of the Age, that it has so far advanc'd *Hortensial Improvements*, and rais'd the *Botanic System* to so elevated a Pitch.' The '*Philosophical* Remarks,' as he calls them, lead him to remark: 'what a vast Room for Reflection does a small well-furnish'd Spot of Ground afford . . . ? If *Rome* and *Athens* had their *Pliny, Seneca,* and *Epicurus,* [he writes elsewhere in the sermon] we have had our more Renowned and Honourable *Bacon, Boyle, Evelyn,* etc. If *Rome* had her *Cicero, Virgil,* and *Horace*; we have had our equally Famous *Temple, Milton, Cowley,* and others.' Harper, who thought that 'among many other curious Improvements of the present Age, *Gardening* is now confessedly advanc'd to the highest Perfection,' saw botanical experiment as central to it. Even in a fallen world, he wrote:

> There might still be room for Man to exercise his Invention, and to please his Fancy by curious Experiments; by transplanting the Trees and Flowers; shaping them into such Forms, as were most agreeable to him; and by making, where he cou'd, such additional Decorations, as shou'd make Paradise it self still more Paradisiacal.[17]

Shaftesbury is also another instance of the georgic identification of agriculture and horticulture, a tradition that went back as least as far as the founding of the Georgical Committee of the Royal Society. This identification is clearly voiced by Evelyn: '*Gardining* is one of the noblest and most refined parts of *Agriculture.*'[18] The garden and the landscape into which it naturally leads are part of one redemptive enterprise. Shaftesbury corresponded with the agricultural writer, Edward Lisle, whose *Observations in Husbandry* include an account of a conversation with him about manuring. But Lisle places his work in a larger frame than a merely agricultural one, insisting in his preface on the connection between husbandry and the 'divine, moral, and philosophical conclusions' that come with such an occupation. Can anyone, he muses, 'propose a nobler entertainment for the mind of man than he would find in the inquiry he must make into all the powers and operations of nature wherein husbandry is concerned?' And he concludes:

> Add too, that scene of nature, which the country lays before us, has I know not what charms to calm a man's passions, and so to compose his mind, and fix his thoughts, that his soul seems to be got clear of the world; and the farther his education enables him to carry his inquiries, the higher are his reflections raised.[19]

These themes were also present in the writing of Evelyn's friend, Abraham Cowley, a Restoration poet whose work remained influential in the early eighteenth century, on Shaftesbury in particular.[20] Cowley's praise of the rural life in his essay 'Of Agriculture' makes the same identification of philosopher with husbandman and rebukes the world of 'civilised' man in the same georgic terms:

> We are here among the vast and noble Scenes of Nature; we are there among the pitiful shifts of Policy: We walk here in the light and open wayes of the Divine Bounty; we grope there in the dark and confused Labyrinths of Human Malice: Our Senses which are here feasted with the clear and genuine taste of their Objects, which are all Sophisticated there, and for the most part overwhelmed with their contraries. Here Pleasure looks (methinks) like a beautiful, constant, and modest Wife; it is there an impudent, fickle, and painted Harlot. Here is harmless and cheap Plenty, there guilty and expenseful Luxury.[21]

This georgic celebration of the natural world is also present in the double portrait of Shaftesbury and his philosophical brother, the Hon. Maurice Ashley, painted by John Closterman, c. 1701 [Fig. 46]. This self-consciously Augustan portrait invokes the classical sculpture of the heavenly twins, Castor and Pollux, that Closterman would have seen in the Odescalchi collection in Rome. But it also depicts a landscape in which Apollo, the god of wisdom, is associated both with a classical temple and with a natural landscape (a sacred grove) from which supernatural revelation arises. It seems very likely that the composition of this portrait was Shaftesbury's suggestion. He was certainly one of the earliest Englishmen to understand the principles of painting, and he communicated to Closterman his philosophical theories of portraiture. Both Shaftesbury and his brother 'were ardent neo-platonists, and Maurice probably points to the landscape to emphasise the neo-platonic commonplace that the beauty of nature is a visible reflection of the highest beauty, the mind of God.'[22]

Closterman also painted a portrait of Shaftesbury in the previous year, a portrait in which he stands dressed as a contemplative philosopher holding a book, possibly his own *Inquiry Concerning Virtue and Merit* (1699), by a column on which can be seen the works of both Plato and Xenophon, signifying the contemplative and the active life. In the background a man, usually identified as an attendant, enters in day dress, carrying a peer's robes as a reminder of the active life to which Shaftesbury is called as the head of the household and an active politician.

In that Shaftesbury's brother had translated Xenophon and that Xenophon represented the practical, moral, and political aspects of Socrates's teaching, whereas Plato represented the metaphysical and contemplative, it seems likely that the second man in the portrait is Shaftesbury's brother. Certainly he looks like the man in a pendant portrait by Closterman, a portrait where a groom in the background, who looks like Shaftesbury, fulfils a similarly emblematic function by restraining the horse of passion.[23]

This emblematic portraiture is significant because of Shaftesbury's use of the former portrait as the engraved frontispiece to his *Characteristics* (1711) [Fig. 45]. In this engraving by Simon Gribelin the attendant is replaced by a perspective that leads the eye from the library through the perfect order in Shaftesbury's garden outwards. In using the landscape as a quotation in this way, either Shaftesbury or Gribelin or both suggest the way in which, as in many seventeenth-century emblematic portraits, the landscape offers a moral commentary on the sitter. It provides an active field for its contemplative subject. But it also alerts us to the way that (from this period onwards) the

45. Simon Gribelin after Closterman, Frontispiece to *The Moralists* (1714). Thomas Fisher Library, University of Toronto.

The Right Honorable Anthony Ashley Cooper Earl of Shaftesbury, Baron Ashley of Winbourn St. Giles, & Lord Cooper of Pawlett.
J: Closterman Pinx.   Sim: Gribelin Sculp.

46. John Closterman, 'Anthony Ashley, 3rd Earl of Shaftesbury and the Hon. Maurice Ashley' National Portrait Gallery, London.

sitter gives meaning to the landscape in which he sits, translating into the setting his moral and literary values.[24]

My point is that, for Shaftesbury (as the perspective of his garden suggests) the 'woods beyond the garden' were a part of the variety of garden experience itself and in the same sort of dialogue with it as the *boschetti* of Renaissance Italian gardens. 'What would pastorals (for instance),' he writes, 'prove to one who had no relish of the real *paysage*? the *rus*, animals, and rural objects.' It is this very georgic point that he goes on to expound in his unfinished *Second*

Characters, a passage abbreviated by Leatherbarrow at just the point where, once again, Shaftesbury underlines the importance of natural wildness:

> Remember the several orders (as of old with Mr Clostr [Closterman] in Richmond Park and St. Giles's woods) into which it is endeavoured to reduce the natural views: the last and most sacred, like the Alpine kind, where the vast wood and caverns with the hollows and deep valleys worn by the cataracts in the very rock itself, pines, firs, and trunks of other aged trees. This attempted by Salvator Rosa, but without the just speculation. Witness the stickiness [i.e. stick-like-ness] of his noble trees (which he otherwise finely described), and his mangling them like artificial trunks and amputations made by man and with instruments—contrary to the idea of those sacred recesses, where solitude and deep retreat, and the absence of gainful, lucratible and busy mortals, make the sublime, pathetic and enchanting, raises the sweet melancholy, the revery, meditation. 'Where no hand but that of time. No steel, no scythe but that of Saturn's.' Secret suggestion of the world's ruin and decay; its birth and first formation, 'where neither art nor the conceit or caprice of man has spoiled their genuine order.'

Throughout this passage there are footnote references to the earlier 'Rhapsody' passage quoted at the beginning of this chapter. The later passage, from an essay 'Of the Scene, Camps, Perspective, Ornament,' is, says Shaftesbury, 'a repetition of what writ before in Rhapsody to which no occasion to refer here purposely.'[25] Indeed, the specific line he refers to is exactly the one in which Philocles espouses 'Things of a *natural* kind.' And this rhapsody is linked by his note to Theocles's moving depiction of mankind among the giddy precipices of ruinous mountain scenery, lost among the 'lofty Pines, the Firs, and noble Cedars' that present to him the 'various Forms of *Deity* . . . more manifest in these sacred Silvan Scenes; such as of old gave rise to Temples and favour'd the Religion of the antient World.'[26] That these sentiments are virtually a translation of a passage from the elder Pliny's *Natural History* (Book XII, chapter 1), cited by Rapin in his *De Cultura Hortensis*, only underlines the connection between horticulture and philosophy in celebrating a new kind of nature.[27]

This is a connection pursued even further by Shaftesbury's philosophical follower, Francis Hutcheson, in his *Inquiry into the Original of our Ideas of Beauty*, a work published in 1725, just as the first rural landscapes were beginning to be created. The Horatian and Georgic *topos* of retreat that runs throughout Shaftesbury's *Characteristicks* is once again prominent. Hutcheson notes even the desire of the *nouveaux riches*, when once 'they are got above the *World*, or extricated from the Hurrys of *Avarice* and *Ambition*,' to retire to nature and the 'Pursuits of *Beauty* and *Order* in their *Houses*, [and] *Gardens*.' This pursuit of Beauty, like that of Shaftesbury and Lord Burlington, he identifies with the poet and the man of taste. It is what sets them above the mere empiricism of the scientist, enabling them to see beauty in any 'Composition of Objects, which give not unpleasant simple Ideas.' 'A *rude Heap* of Stones,' he says, echoing Shakespeare, 'is in no way offensive to one who shall be displeas'd with *Irregularity* in *Architecture*, where *Beauty* was expected.'

It is this recognition too that allows for 'different Kinds of *Uniformity*, so there is room enough for that Diversity of Fancys observable in *Architecture*, *Gardening*, and such like Arts in different *Nations*.' 'Diversity of Fancys in the

Sense of Beauty' are based in Hutcheson's belief in the association of ideas for which he was an early apologist. And he gives as an example of association the identification of trees with various states of mind: 'The *Beauty* of *Trees*, their *cool Shades*, and their *Aptness* to conceal from Observation, have made *Groves* and *Woods* the usual Retreat to those who love *Solitude*, especially the *Religious*, the *Pensive*, the *Melancholy*, and the *Amorous*.'[28]

When Stephen Switzer came to write about planting extensive woodlands only ten years later, his complaint about the 'Set Wildernesses and Groves, so much us'd of late amongst us'[29] was that they were too artificial. To these he contrasted coppices and woods, but included such woods as Wray Wood at Castle Howard, where serpentine rides through a natural woodland had been created even before Shaftesbury wrote 'The Moralists.'[30] For Switzer, whose account of the history of English gardening ends with the extensive estates of his own time, the 'Religious and Rural Thoughts [that] highly possess and illustrate the Minds of the greatest Nobility'[31] arise from a celebration of a redeemed nature. Even the excrescences of nature, he argues, are not blemishes, since even from the hills the springs arise 'that refresh the Valleys, the Beauty of which adds such a Magnificence to our Gardens.'[32]

This is exactly the position adumbrated by Shaftesbury in 'The Moralists,' where his argument is from nature as design. 'Seeming blemishes' are reconciled in a definition of nature where '*Good* . . . is predominant; and every corruptible and mortal Nature by its Mortality and Corruption yields only to some better.'[33]

By the early 1730s Pope could write of the good man who 'takes no private road, / But looks thro' Nature up to Nature's God'[34] safe in the confidence that 'natural theology' was widely acceptable. That it was so is due in no small measure to the horticultural and botanical consequences of this new theology and the general recognition that the 'mighty maze' of creation was, in Pope's phrase, 'not without a plan.' What, in fact, Pope seems first to have written (in line 6 of the *Essay on Man*) is 'A mighty maze of walks without a plan.' Like Shaftesbury's use of the word 'formal', this revison demands that we re-examine the meaning of the word 'plan' as we have the meaning of Shaftesbury's word 'formal'. Pope's revision suggests that, whereas the sense of 'plan' as 'a scheme of action' or 'way of proceeding' was acceptable to him, its sense as 'a drawing, sketch or diagram' or even 'a scheme of arrangement' was not.

The last is the sense with which the *Oxford English Dictionary* identifies Pope's line from the *Essay on Man*, but Pope's revision of the line indicates the poet's increasing dissatisfaction with gardens laid out with elaborate symmetry based on diagrams. This is the very thing that he had earlier mocked in the 'Epistle to Burlington': 'Grove nods at grove, each Alley has a brother / And half the platform just reflects the other' (ll7–18). His 'mighty maze of walks without a plan,' however, suggests the sort of garden that, like the Earl of Burlington's additions to Chiswick, Pope thought of himself as planting.

Pope's friendship with Lord Bolingbroke, the man to whom he addressed the first of his *Satires*, offers a glimpse of the way another aspect of the *Georgics*, the political import, translated itself into England. The Augustan conviction that England had assumed the political mantle of ancient Rome was one shared by men of both political parties, but especially those in opposition to the government. If the true Virgilian golden age were to be created in England it would have to come from an alliance of true native liberty, ancient *virtus*, and an espousal of the values of the land. For this the text was, once again, the famous passage from the end of Book II of the *Georgics*, the passage idealising the life of the country and contrasting it to the corruption of city and court that Virgil had taken from Varro. Happy is he, says Virgil, who knows the gods of the countryside, far from the iron laws of the courts, the frantic forum, miserly avarice, or the thunder of the political platform (ll. 494–508).

Bolingbroke, who thought of himself as a rural philosopher and heir to Thucydides, more than once courted treason for his espousal of this sort of patriotism. Even in exile in France, he was the focus both of Augustan opposition to ministerial tyranny and of georgic idealism. After his return from exile in 1725, he bought Dawley Park and proceeded to dis-park it, turning it into an early *ferme ornée*, a combination of garden and model working farm. In the hall of the house he celebrated its agrarian idealism with the Horatian inscription, *Beatus satis ruris honoribus*. In 1732 Pope, using the myth of Jove instructing men in the arts from Book I of the *Georgics*, wrote of Dawley Farm that it 'Taught Patriot's Policy; taught Poet's Sense.' Bolingbroke in Pope's poem becomes a sort of English Jove who makes the ancient fiction true in the language of the Psalms:

> See! Emblem of himself, his *Villa* stand!
> Politely finish'd, regularly Grand . . .
> Here the proud Trophies, and the Spoils of War
> Yield to the Scythe, the Harrow and the Car;
> To whate'er Implement the Rustick wields,
> Whate'er manures the Garden, or the Fields.[35]

Bolingbroke, in Pope's celebration, has combined Hellenic and Hebraic, the restored villa of the ancients and the prophecy of Isaiah.

Although Bolingbroke had no time for the Platonism that inspired Shaftesbury, Pope had no difficulty reconciling Bolingbroke's espousal of the great chain of being with the Platonists' sense of God's manifestation in the physical universe. Both are present in the *Essay on Man*. What Bolingbroke provided was a political focus for disquiet about urban capitalism and its social consequences. 'There could not be a truer maxim in our government than this,' Swift wrote to Pope in 1721, 'that the possessors of the soil are the best judges what is for the advantage of the kingdom.'[36] This Augustan and Virgilian nostalgia for the land became increasingly focussed in opposition to Walpole and identification with Henry Frederick, the Prince of Wales. Bolingbroke's *On the Spirit of Patriotism* (1736), written during his second exile in France, is a plea to the noble and landed classes to recapture society from Walpole. It owes its arguments in part to *An Essay Upon the Origin and Nature of Government*, by Swift's one-time employer and patron, Sir William Temple.

What is obvious in all this is the connection between political disaffection and Virgilian myths of land, whether horticultural or agricultural. The word 'patriot', whether applied to opposition Whig or Tory, was associated with *pater* and 'patriarchal', as Augustus for Virgil had been *pater patriae*. It was also a signal that, so far as gardening was concerned, some sort of emblematic reading was called for. Gardens were texts into which ancient texts could be translated and from which the visitor was in turn expected to translate a contemporary exegesis.

For Pope's friend, George Lyttelton, opposition to Walpole took the form not only of literary attack in his *Persian Letters* (1735) but of encouraging the landscape poet, James Thomson, to write the drama *Edward and Eleonora* (1739), a 'patriotic allegory' in praise of the Prince of Wales to whom Lyttleton was secretary. Lord Lyttelton was to create his own garden at Hagley, but throughout this part of the century the garden most reflective of the landscape of opposition was that created by his uncle, Lord Cobham, at Stowe. Cobham, an opposition Whig, was altogether more moderate in his politics, but the temples that he erected in his garden told moral and political messages, not least the Temple of Modern Virtue, where the deliberately ruined fabric contained a headless statue of Walpole. In the Temple of British Worthies that stood across the Styx from it in the Elysian Fields, the bust of King Alfred [Fig. 47] was the same signifier of liberty as was his tower at Stourhead [Fig. 24]. In this company even Cobham's dog, Signor Fido, was more worthy of inclusion than Walpole or his ministers.

Even Dr. Johnson, who later denounced this sort of patriotism as 'the last refuge of a scoundrel,' defended the patriot dramatist Brooke against the government censors in 1739. Bolingbroke's *Idea of a Patriot King* (1738), coming as it did at the end of the first great phase of garden-making in the eighteenth century, repeated and elaborated the distinction between a country party and those who supported a single minister, a distinction that he had earlier made in his *Dissertation upon Parties* in 1733. This was also the message of Pope's 'Epistle to Burlington', published only two years earlier: the georgic theme of moral husbandry as opposed to the vulgar extravagance of time-serving politicians and new-made men. Pope's praise of the gardens of Cirencester and Chiswick—'Who plants like BATHURST, or who builds like BOYLE'—is, after all, Virgilian and Horatian in tone. It is praise of honest men out of power.

By 1738 Pope had despaired of georgic 'patriotism' having any effect upon the venal affairs of English politics. Even under the powers of theatre censorship recently given to the Lord Chamberlain, the patriot might have his futile say:

> A Patriot is a Fool in ev'ry age,
> Whom all Lord Chamberlains allow the Stage:
> These nothing hurts; they keep their Fashions still,
> And wear their strange old Virtue as they will.[37]

That the language of opposition, whether in poetry or gardens, was lost on the government periodical writers is evident in their rebuke to Lyttelton's *Persian Letters*. Let him, wrote *The Craftsman*, 'harmlessly amuse the *World* with *Tales* of his *Uncle*'s fine *Gardens*, and the wonderful Qualities of his *Italian Greyhound*.'[38] The argument about the original of 'Timon's villa' in Pope's 'Epistle to Burlington,' however, indicates that whether Pope intended it as a satire on Walpole's estate of Houghton or not, patriotism was identified with right stewardship and correct taste. That the government hacks on *The Craftsman* and *Fog's Journal* could read even the 'Epistle to Bathurst' as mere literature is indicative of how obscure the language of opposition politics, the language of Virgil's *ingentia rura*, was to the government philistines.

47. Bust of King Alfred, Temple of the British Worthies, Stowe.

KING ALFRED

THE MILDEST JUSTEST MOST BENEFICENT OF KINGS ;
WHO DROVE OUT THE DANES, SECURED THE SEAS PROTECTED LEARNING,
ESTABLISH'D JURIES, CRUSH'D CORRUPTION, GUARDED LIBERTY,
AND WAS THE FOUNDER OF THE ENGLISH CONSTITUTION.

5
RURAL AND EXTENSIVE LANDSCAPE: SWITZER AND *INGENTIA RURA*

In 1718, the year before Pope began to work on his garden at Twickenham and Lord Burlington on Chiswick, Stephen Switzer published his *Ichnographia Rustica*. Switzer, who described himself simply as 'Seedsman of Westminster-Hall,' had nonetheless worked under London and Wise, the most famous gardeners of the preceding generation, and published (in 1715) a work that was to form a large part of the first volume of *Ichnographia: The Nobleman, Gentleman, and Gardener's Recreation*.[1]

How far Switzer represented increasing hostility to what had been the prevailing mode in gardening is revealed in the *Proposals for Printing, by Subscription, A General System of Agriculture and Gardening* that he published in order to elicit subscriptions for the new work. His rejection of 'that Stiffness that is and has been very frequent in Garden-Designs'[2] is of a piece with what Pope derided five years earlier as 'the various Tonsure of Greens into the most regular and formal Shapes.'[3] In the second decade of the eighteenth century, this stiffness was usually identified with the legacy of Dutch gardening. French gardens, in contradistinction, were looked upon as *la grand manier*. Not until three decades later, in the 'Proemial Essay' to the second edition of *Ichnographia*, did Switzer recognise that the essentially French manner of London and Wise at Blenheim (on which he himself had worked) was also too regular, and cite Pope's 'grove nods at grove' in reproof to it.[4]

It is nonetheless an instructive paradox that the frontispiece to Switzer's *Ichnographia* shows not the 'rural and extensive' garden for which he was to become famous but the parterre of a great house walled in by clipped hedges. These are as tall as the house and filled with just the artificial topiary and regular nicety that Switzer decried as 'the stiff *Dutch* Way,' the sort of thing exemplified by Heemsteede in Holland [Fig. 48]. When in the second volume of *Ichnographia* he feels obliged to deal with parterres, it is with an embarrassed recognition that these are contrary to the 'simple, plain, and unaffected Method I have propos'd to myself.'[5]

Switzer's paradox no doubt arises from his wanting to espouse the extensive manner of French gardens and having, in the process, to take the smooth parterre with the rough irregularities of the open vista. His *credo* is spelled out clearly in the preface to volume I:

> By *Ingentia Rura* (apply'd to Gard'ning) we may understand that Extensive Way of Gard'ning that I have already hinted at, and shall more fully handle; this the French call *La Grand Manier*, and is oppos'd to those crimping, diminutive, and wretched Performances we every-where meet with, so bad,

48. J. de Moucheron, *Plusieurs Belles, et Plaisante Vues et la cour de Heemstede, dans le Province d'Utrecht* (1702).

and withal so expensive, that other Parts of a Gentleman's Care is often, by unavoidable Necessity, left undone; the Top of these Designs being in Clipt Plants, Flowers, and other trifling Decorations (which I shall speak more of by and by) fit only for little Town-Gardens, and not for the expansive tracts of the Country.[6]

Referring to gardens like the one at Pierrepont House in Nottinghamshire [Fig. 49], Switzer proceeds not only to oust 'Interlacings of Box-work' in favour of 'the plain but nobler Embellishments of Grass, Gravel, and the like,' but to seek to confine flowers to town gardens. The corollary of this is that country gardens are to rely for their effects on georgic elements: 'Woods, Coppices, Groves, and the busie and laborious Employs of Agriculture, with which *Gardening* is unavoidably as well as pleasantly mix'd.'[7]

This insistence on the interrelation between rural gardening and agriculture is rooted in Virgil's *Georgics*, a work that mediately and immediately was beginning to have a profound effect on the creation of the English landscape garden. Like the ancients to whom he appeals for authority, Switzer sees agriculture as a science 'with which Gard'ning is inextricably wove.'[8] By 1779 it was a cliché for the editors of the *Farmer's Magazine* to observe: 'What has been said with regard to the Farmer will in general hold good to the Gardener, who may be called a Farmer on a smaller scale.'[9]

Throughout *Ichnographia*, the theme of use and profit that Switzer shares with Pope's 'Epistle to Burlington' continues to emerge.[10] Like Pope, whose *Essay on Criticism* he deliberately misquotes in order to make it relevant to gardens, he also believes that following nature involves following the ancients. This, however, does not prevent him from observing that the ancients did not understand design so well as the moderns. It was Louis XIV, in Switzer's view, who brought gardening 'to the most magnificent Height and Splendour imaginable.' It is for the English to bring gardening to a perfection undreamt of even by the French.[11]

Switzer seems unsure about whether this sort of gardening is already practised in England; he contradicts himself on this in the preface. This may be a result of his awareness that the great tree-lined avenues of such estates as Badminton, for all their French *grand manier*, do not correspond to what he has in mind as 'rural gardening': 'the unbounded Felicities of distant Prospect, and the expansive Volumes of Nature herself, . . . not Wall'd round or Immured' but reliant upon beauties 'lightly spread over great and extensive Parks and Forests.' Here the 'Gardens for the Politer and Greater Genius's of Britain' will triumph over 'the 'so-much-boasted Gardens of *France*' just as Marlborough has over the forces of Louis XIV.[12]

This '*Forest*, or in a more easie Stile, *Rural* Gard'ning' depends both upon the interplay of art and nature that a later writer noticed at Dyrham 'where Nature and Art, vie with each other to forme this little Paradice.'[13] It also required an interplay of symmetry and variety that he calls *simplex munditiis*. 'When we come to assist Nature,' he says, echoing Shaftesbury, 'we are indispensably oblig'd to follow it.'[14] Indeed Switzer came to espouse variety not only in 'a Rude Coppice or amidst the Irregular turnings of a wild Corn Field,' but

49. Anon., 'Pierrepont House, Nottinghamshire' (c. 1708–13). Yale Center for British Art, Paul Mellon Collection.

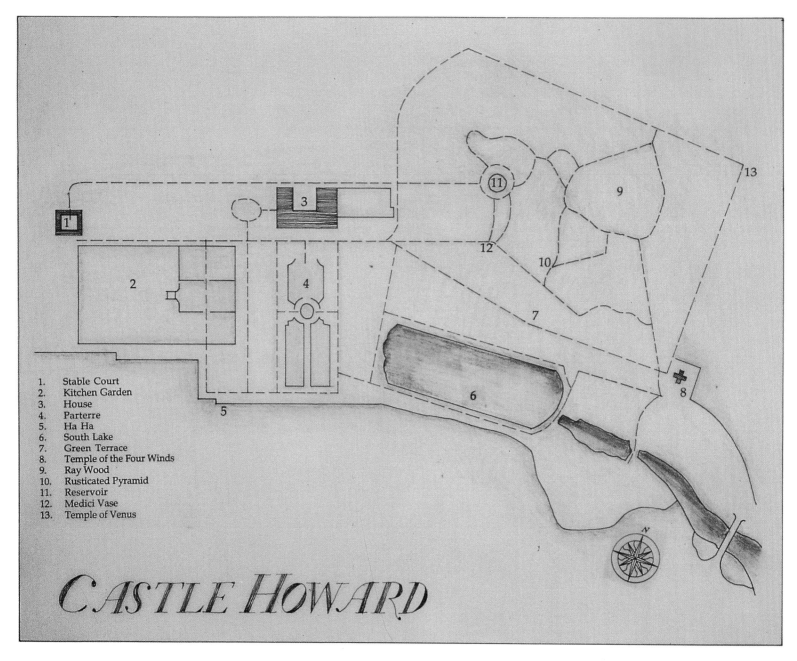

1. Stable Court
2. Kitchen Garden
3. House
4. Parterre
5. Ha Ha
6. South Lake
7. Green Terrace
8. Temple of the Four Winds
9. Ray Wood
10. Rusticated Pyramid
11. Reservoir
12. Medici Vase
13. Temple of Venus

CASTLE HOWARD

50. Todd Longstaffe-Gowan, Reconstruction Plan of Castle Howard (1727).

in the invocation of '*huge Forests mishapen Rocks and Precipices.*'[15] And his recommendation that, at the end of a court near the house, one plant 'large Hedges of *Dutch* Elm, or any other Hedge,' rather than build a wall is also consonant with Shaftesbury's earlier practice.[16]

Neither are plantations of woods to be made in which 'grove nods at grove' in exact facsimile, nor are straight rides to be imposed upon the woodland. This last was what George London had originally proposed for Wray Wood (or Ray Wood) at Castle Howard [Figs. 50, 51]: a scheme of star-rides contradicted by the Earl of Carlisle, Charles Howard, who was the son-in-law of Arthur Capel, the creator of Cassiobury. Like Addison, Vanbrugh, and the Duke of Richmond, all pioneers in different ways of the landscape revolution, Howard was also a member of the Kit-Kat Club. At Castle Howard, says Switzer, Carlisle achieved

the highest pitch that Natural and Polite Gard'ning can possibly ever arrive to: 'Tis There that Nature is truly imitated, if not excell'd, and from which the Ingenious may draw the best of their Schemes in Natural and Rural Gardening: 'Tis there that she is by a kind of fortuitous Conduct pursued through all her most intricate Mazes, and taught even to exceed her own self in the *Natura-Linear*, and much more Natural and Promiscuous Disposition of all her Beauties.[17]

Thomas Gent's elegy on Charles Howard, published in 1738, makes clear not only that the third Earl thought of himself as having escaped the treacherous life of the court described at the end of the second *Georgic*, but that Wray Wood exemplified that escape. Whatever the conventional range of emblematic statues,

> What Wisdom but my LORD's, could these display,
> My LORD, who all Things knew, was certain These
> Must give fair Lustre to his shady Trees.

Here the imaginative traveller, 'as tho' he enter'd into *Greece*, or *Rome*,' was encouraged to wander

> Where fair *Meander* Walks so sweetly lead
> To new-come Joys, in every Turn we tread!
> *Ray-Wood*, the Park, and Wilderness of Greens;
> With Downs, and Lawns, display the lovely'st Scenes![18]

51. Green Terrace and Temple of The Four Winds, Castle Howard.

In 1744 Philip Yorke wrote: 'What most pleased us in them [the gardens] was a wood of 60 [acres], cut out into walks of different levels and interspersed with trees of a venerable age.' By 1740, however, when Simon Yorke was improving the walks through the woods at Erddig in North Wales, what Switzer recommended had become a convention.[19]

Switzer's history of this sort of forest garden traces it back through Lord Rochester's New Park[20] and Sir William Temple's 'sharawadgi' (the 'natural' principle of 'Chinese gardens') to the forest garden at Cassiobury and John Evelyn's pioneering work on forestry, *Sylva*. Switzer traced to Evelyn's two translations from the French (*The French Gardiner* and *The Compleat Gard'ner*) the fact that 'Gard'ning can speak proper English.'[21] And it is to Evelyn's chapter, 'The Sacredness and Use of Groves,' that he traces the spiritual justification for tree-planting that is one of his major themes.[22]

The history of gardening in England that comprises most of Switzer's first chapter has a teleology that sees increasing openness as its defining characteristic. In recommending this he was preceded most immediately by Addison's famous essay in praise of the 'agreeable mixture of Garden and Forest' to be found in France and Italy, as opposed to the mere 'Neatness and Elegancy' of the gardens of England.

> But why may not a whole Estate be thrown into a kind of Garden by frequent Plantations, that may turn as much to the Profit, as the Pleasure of the Owner? A Marsh overgrown with Willows, or a Mountain shaded with Oaks, are not only more beautiful, but more beneficial, than when they lie bare and unadorned. Fields of Corn make a pleasant Prospect, and if the Walks were a little taken care of that lie between them, if the natural Embroidery of the Meadows were helpt and improved by some small Additions of Art, and the several Rows of Hedges set off by Trees and Flowers, that the Soil was capable of receiving, a Man might make a pretty Landskip of his own Possessions.[23]

By 1752 all this had become received wisdom. The amateur botanist, Peter Collinson, riding through the 'Rising Groves and Clustring Thickets' of his friend Lord Petre's twenty-year-old plantations could observe that the 'delightful Confusion of Objects so blended by Nature is the Great Plan and original from whence wee are to Coppy, and the nearer Wee approach to Her, Wee shall be sure always to please.'[24]

Addison's concern to link profit with pleasure is of a piece with his earlier (Whig) celebration of Liberty as a goddess inhabiting such a landscape, where Plenty and Commerce were also inhabitants. But he shared even with Shaftesbury and Bolingbroke, who were of a different political persuasion, a dislike for 'the little Labyrinths of the most finished Parterre' and indeed himself commended 'Woods . . . cut into shady Walks, twisted into Bowers' of the sort Carlisle had created at Castle Howard.[25] Although he was prepared to acknowledge the makers of parterres as the epigrammatists and sonneteers of gardening and to celebrate London and Wise as the heroic poets, his own taste was for what he called 'the *Pindarick* Manner,' a sort of ordered disorder which included 'the beautiful Wildness of Nature, without affecting the nicer Elegancies of Art.'[26]

Central to this development was the 'Planting and Raising of all sorts of Trees,'[27] an enterprise so much in the hands of his first master, George London, that Switzer gives him credit for this arboreal revolution. But that revolution, as we have seen, was well in train long before London, and there were many horticultural and botanical patriots in its van. For Addison, as for Evelyn, tree-planting was a patriotic duty. And if, for Switzer, William III was 'as great a *Gard'ner* as he was a *Soldier*,' it is equally true (as he cites Addison to say of gardening) that 'there have been Heroes in this Art, as well as in others,'[28] and Switzer's history consists in part of a catalogue of these heroes.

In spite of Switzer's dismissal of town gardens, he himself had a garden in Vauxhall. Perhaps, like Pope, he accepted Virgil's admonition to praise an extensive garden but cultivate a small one. Certainly some of his heroes were concerned more with horticultural botany than with extensive gardening. One such, the Duchess of Beaufort, although mistress of Badminton, confined her horticulture largely to botanical importation and experimentation, primarily with flowers. Although she was a sister of the Earl of Essex, there is nothing to connect the woodland plantations of Cassiobury with the extensive wooded rides created by the Duke of Beaufort at Badminton.

Similarly, Dr. Henry Compton, Bishop of London (in whose garden had been trained George London, Switzer's former employer) was celebrated for 'the Importation, Raising, and Increase of Exoticks' but not for garden design. Important as these early amateur botanists were to the development of gardening (as we shall see in the next chapter), their contribution was less significant to the creation of 'extensive gardening' than that of Lord Essex and Moses Cook, whose Cassiobury Switzer praised as 'a truly-delightful Place' where he was 'ravish'd with its Natural Beauty.'[29]

Though not so widely read as Addison's essays, Timothy Nourse's *Campania Foelix* (1700) was an important stage in the formulation of these new ideals of extensive gardening. Nourse is one of the predecessors cited by Switzer, and like him he celebrates the variety of new plants now available to the gardener: 'Curiosities of Plants, Fruit-Trees, Flowers, and other Rarities of the Gardens, brought over from Foreign Countries.' But what he shares most with Switzer is an admiration for the natural beauties of the countryside and a Horatian belief that use and beauty may be combined 'in matters relating to Husbandry and Planting, which would be of equal Pleasure with the Entertainments of a Garden.'[30]

Nourse's observation that 'a Seat which has nothing but the wide Plain for its object, affords but little pleasure to the Eye,' is also an affirmation of the importance of variety and a rebuke to the dullness of many French gardens. In this he was reiterating what had been observed as early as 1665 by John Rea:[31] an essentially Italianate and classical position that Switzer was also to adopt. Like Switzer, Nourse remained interested in the conventional Italian repertoire of garden effects (fountains, statues, etc.) in the pleasure garden near the house. His sense that the wilderness should be 'Natural-Artificial,' i.e. deceive the visitor 'into a belief of a real Wilderness or Thicket' is also Italian. In his cautious calling in of the country, however, he moves into a more distinctly English theatre, one where tree-planted walks in the landscape reflect Evelyn's earlier practice and recommendation.

Nourse's ideal of the country house is, moreover, a georgic one such as Switzer was also to espouse. His country house is to be somewhere between the mere toil of a farm-house and the mere *otium* of a villa or country retreat. It is to stand 'in the midst of a large Park . . . [which is] at the least a Mile and a half over every way.' This park he imagines planted between the entrance to the estate and the house, preferably with beech, and cut through with an avenue that contracts as it approaches the house. Moreover it is to have gravel walks sixteen feet wide cut through the woods parallel to this avenue.

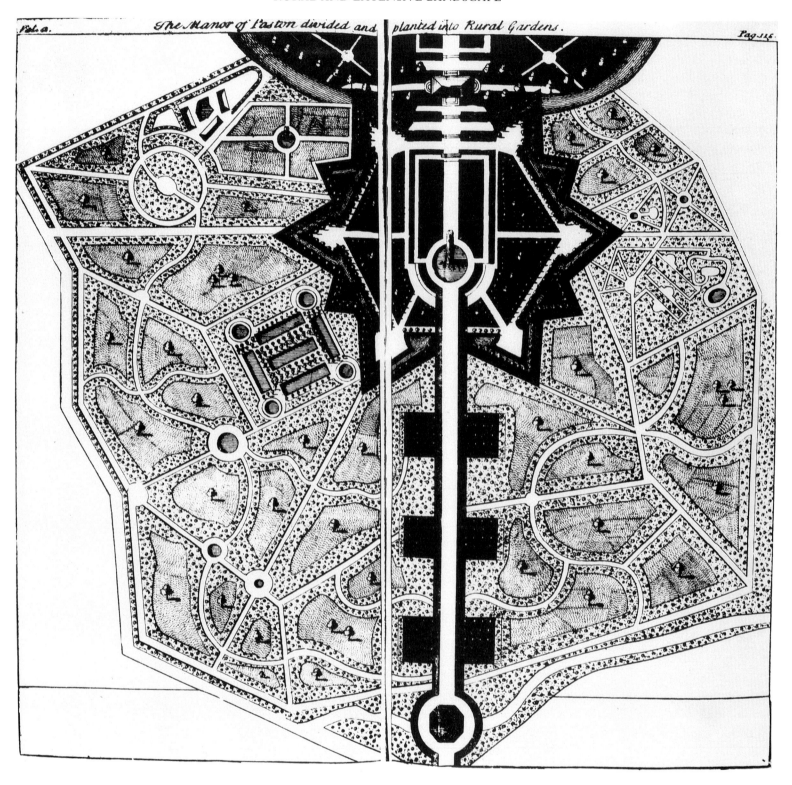

The Manor of Paston divided and planted into Rural Gardens.

52. 'The Manor of Paston' from Stephen Switzer, *Ichnographia Rustica* (1718). Trinity College Library, Toronto.

Although this is not so innovatory as the Earl of Carlisle's Wray Wood at Castle Howard, it is nonetheless an important endorsement of the sort of woodland garden that Switzer himself was to create at Grimsthorpe. Nourse's concern that the tops of the trees in this park rise no higher than the second floor also indicates his concern for both the overall effect and the details of tree plantation. Indeed, Nourses's stipulation that 'at length the Prospect may terminate on Mountains, Woods, or such Views as the Scituation may well admit of,' not only invokes the calling in of the country that the Earl of Shaftesbury was beginning to practice but looks back to the ideal landscape of Milton's 'L'Allegro' where the house 'Bosom'd high in tufted Trees' is the centre of an ideal landscape.

Another of Switzer's 'heroes' was the Countess of Lindsey, mistress of Grimsthorpe in Lincolnshire, for which Switzer designed woodland walks of the kind suggested by Nourse.

> This Lady was reputed to be a continual Attendant and Supervisor of her Works, without any regard to the rigid Inclemency of the Winter-season; and not only so, but also in the Measuring and Laying out the Distances of her Rows of Trees, she was actually employed with Rule, Line etc.[32]

Ichnographia Rustica is, in fact, dedicated to James Bertie, Marquess of Lindsay, the Countess's husband, to whom Dryden also dedicated the translation of one of Virgil's *Eclogues*. The first edition of *Ichnographia* in 1718 included an idealised plan of Grimsthorpe under the title 'The Manor of Paston divided and planted into Rural Gardens' [Fig. 52]. It showed the combination of fortification walls, serpentine paths, and extensive tree plantations that illustrate Switzer's indebtedness to Vanbrugh and Bridgeman on the one hand and his breakthrough into extensive gardening on the other. Although William Stukeley's drawing of the garden in 1736 shows the former rather than the latter [Fig. 53], Switzer's recommendation had, by the 1730s, been widely put into practice.

Contemporary with Grimsthorpe was the manor of Riskins or Richings (figure 8), an early *ferme ornée* created by Lord Bathurst on the Thames in Buckinghamshire. Pope was later to observe that it lacked variety and needed mounts to take the view, but Lady Hertford, who purchased it from Bathurst in 1739, described it , in Pope's phrase, as an '*extravagante bergerie . . .* nearer to my idea of a scene in Arcadia than I ever saw.'[33] And Switzer himself was to publish it three years later in the second edition of *Ichnographia* as the ideal of a *ferme ornée*.

Lady Hertford was married to Algernon Percy, Earl of Hertford and Duke of Somerset, to whom Switzer dedicated his influential book on water-works, *Hydrostaticks*, in 1729.[34] She was born Frances Thynne, a daughter of the

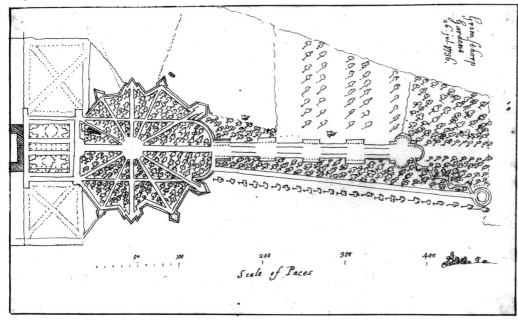

53. William Stukeley, 'Grimsthorp Gardens 26 Jul. 1736,' Bodleian Library Ms. TOP. gen. d.14. Bodleian Library, Oxford.

Pinus Americana quinis ex uno folliculo setis
longis tenuibus triquetris ad unum angulum
per totam longitudinem minutissimis crenis asperatis.

Lord Weymouths Pine.

Pinus Sylvestris folis oraviris
glaucis conis parvis albentibus.

The Scotch Firr vulgo

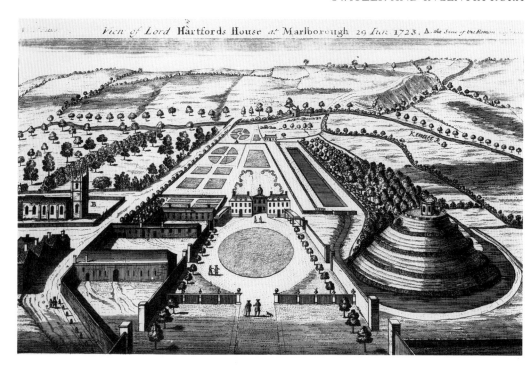

55. William Stukeley, 'View of Lord Hertfords House at Marlborough' (1723).

Thomas Thynne for whose gardens at Longleat all the partners in the Brompton Park nursery (the firm of London and Wise) were engaged as advisors and suppliers. Thomas Thynne, moreover, as Viscount Weymouth, gave his name to the white pine, an American import that was instrumental in creating the extensive landscape gardens that Switzer recommended.[35] [Fig. 54]

Riskins was not the only rural retirement for which the Duchess increasingly longed. At Marlborough in Wiltshire, she had another garden where the adjacent hayfields were part of the garden's effects [Fig. 55]. In this garden she widened the cascades, where she also laid out a little wilderness of flowering shrubs. She also had ruins constructed in the grounds and a grotto built beneath the mount. In 1731 she wrote a poem celebrating the garden's 'terraces and grove,' and a letter of 1741 to Lady Pomfret refers to a new terrace that 'perfumes the air.' There, after breakfast, she and her family walked among the lindens and willows, tending the roses and coming indoors only to have a work called 'the *Gardener's Toil*' read to them.[36] During her time at Marlborough, Stephen Duck wrote a poem in praise of the garden's 'beauteous Grot' furnished with 'rustic Moss' and 'shining Pearl, or purple Shell.' And it was at Marlborough that James Thomson composed his poem 'Spring', the second part of his long work *The Seasons* praising nature's negligence in Virgilian terms and celebrating the interchange of art and the imagination with an uncorrupted external world.[37] [Fig. 56]

Unfortunately there is nothing to connect Marlborough and Lady Hertford with the fruit garden that Switzer designed 'for a Lady of extraordinary Merit in *Wiltshire* on the Road to the *Bath*.'[38] Nonetheless, his third plan in *The Practical Fruit-Gardener* (1724) illustrates a mixture of grotto, cascade, fountain, and basin in conjunction with fruit trees and plantations that would certainly have been congenial to her taste [Fig. 57]. Switzer's concern to mix 'the *Utile* with the *Dulci*' is in contradistinction to what had been the practice at Blenheim. His practice, he wrote:

is and has been all along my Method when I could, to enclose these Fruit-Gardens within the larger Quarters of Wood, etc. whereby the Garden lies

56. Tardieu after William Kent, Title-page for Thomson's *Spring* (1742). Thomas Fisher Library, University of Toronto.

more commodiously to come to, and adds to the extent and Beauty of your Garden at once, and if well dispos'd, is one of the greatest Ornaments of a Design.[39] [Fig. 58]

It is a mark of how far silviculture had advanced both practically and theoretically in the 1720s that Switzer's essays in *The Practical Husbandman* (1733) are so much more knowledgable about trees than the 1718 edition of *Ichnographia*. In the latter his repertoire of trees (oak, ash, beech, chestnut, hornbeam, Scotch pine, silver spruce, elm, lime, and poplar) is no greater than what Evelyn had recommended over half a century earlier. It shows no recognition of botanic advances: that, for example, the Duchess of Beaufort's garden included African evergreen oak (*Cliffortia illicifolia*), or the American import, ironwood (*Sideroxylon*), let alone a number of new exotic shrubs. By 1733, however, he was insisting that 'any one that would strive to bring the

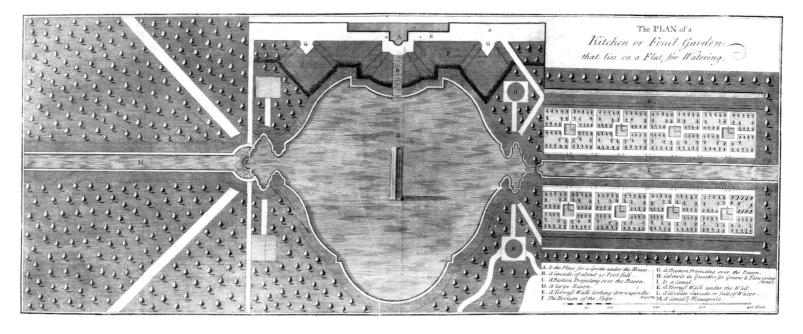

57. 'The Plan of a Kitchen or Fruit Garden' from Switzer, *The Practical Fruit Gardener* (1724). Trustees of the British Library.

raising and planting of Forest Trees to their utmost Perfection . . . ought not to be content with treating barely on those Plants which grow at Home.'[40]

Switzer's list, in *The Practical Husbandman*, of those who 'at all leisure Times apply themselves to Husbandry and Planting,' includes a number of important names in the advancement of silviculture: the Duke of Richmond, the Earl of Islay (later Duke of Argyll), Lord Bathurst, and William Benson, Wren's successor who created Wilbury. But his subscribers' list reveals even more about the advances that gardening had made in this period. Not only does it include Lord Burlington's gardener at Londesborough, Thomas Knowlton, a

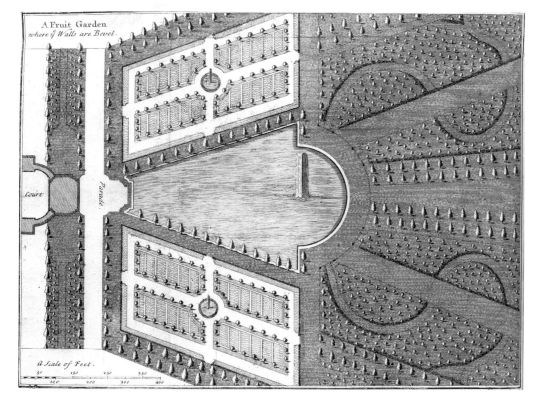

58. 'A Fruit Garden Where the Walls are Bevel' from Switzer, *The Practical Fruit Gardener* (1724). Trustees of the British Library.

man who was both a horticulturist and a designer, but Peter Aram, another Yorkshire gardener at Newby Hall, who was himself an author of a gardening book and celebrated the landscape designs of William Fisher at Studley Royal in a poem about that estate. The gardener to Sir Henry Goodrick, himself an experimental arboriculturist, is included, as is William Love, the head gardener at Stowe. So too is the gardener at Castle Howard and the gardener to Lord Lyttelton at Hagley, another estate associated with the poet, James Thomson, and largely dependent on trees for its effects.

A correspondence in the same year between Switzer and Henry Ellison, the owner of Gateshead Park in County Durham, is revealing about Switzer's relations with nurserymen. In ousting the former steward, Thomas Woolley, Switzer claimed to have refused to enter into the sort of exclusive agreement with a supplier that he believed his predecessor to have made with Henry Woodman, a Chiswick nurseryman. Woodman gives a different picture of Switzer, however, in a letter of 15 December 1731:

> I am not att all surpris'd that Mr Switzer has bin with you and in all yr. Neighbourhood seeing he has nothing else to recommend him (having not a foot of Nursery ground and wt. he sells must take of others) but his elaborate draughts and designs [.] and as every man is to be commended for his diligince and Industry I would not be thought to say any thing illnatur'd of him but confess 'tis a practice I was always asham'd of to thrust my selfe in or indevor to surplant any person that has bin us'd to serve a Gentleman . . . as to Flowering Shrubbs I have as great Variety as any of the trade and will sell 'em as cheap and perhaps as Mr. Switzer can bye 'em him selfe.[41]

It is not surprising that Lord Orrery, Switzer's patron, was a subscriber to *The Practical Husbandman*, but it is revealing that Henry Hoare, the Earl of Peterborough, and the Earl of Shaftesbury, all of them important creators of gardens in their own right, were as well. Hoare, who was the grandson of William Benson, was to create Stourhead in the 1740s, using chiefly wood and water to create its effects.

In 1733 Lord Peterborough was already an accomplished gardener at Parson's Green near London and one of the original co-operators with the Earl of Pembroke, Lord Islay, and Lord Bathurst in the making of Mrs. Howard's estate at Marble Hill. He had only just purchased his estate, Bevis Mount, in Southampton and begun to landscape it in a way that led Pope to invoke Cicero in praising him as a farmer and sage. That Pope, like Switzer, regarded this as an equal heroism is revealed in 'The First Satire of the Second Book of Horace.' There Peterborough the soldier 'whose Lightning pierc'd th'*Iberian* Lines, / Now forms my Quincunx,' i.e. the plan of the orchard in Pope's garden at Twickenham. Peterborough was, moreover, praised for his 'wilderness' of trees at Parson's Green, where a grove of cypresses and a fine tulip tree were distinguishing features, and Pope cited the pines of Virgil's *Eclogues* in its praise.[42]

The Practical Husbandman is not unlike much garden writing of the nineteenth and twentieth centuries in being a cross between a periodical and a book. In the last of the essays in volume I, Switzer steals a march on Robert Castell's *Villas of the Ancients Illustrated*, published five years earlier, and concludes this 'Dissertation on the Antient and Modern Villa's [sic]' by insisting on the importance of trees:

> To conclude this Part, the raising or planting of Wood in Hills rather than

Vales, adds greatly to the Beauty of any Place, when beheld from afar, which is visible in several Groves, Clumps or Compartments of Wood, many of them but small, which one sees at a Distance . . . it being certain, that one Tree on a Hill adds more Beauty to a Seat, and looks better than six, I had almost said ten, in a Bottom.[43]

Switzer is there writing contemporary with Kent's creation of the groves at Esher and a decade before Walpole was to deplore Kent's use of clumps at Euston in Suffolk. What he indicates is the intimate connection between the Palladian ideals of Lord Burlington and their arboreal translation into the English landscape. And that this was not merely a horticultural or even random aesthetic exercise is evident in a later essay in *The Practical Husbandman*: 'Of the Etymology, contemplative, and sacred Uses of Woods.' Here he steals a march on Book IV (*Dendrologia*) of the 1706 edition of Evelyn's *Sylva*, a section of which he seemed unaware in the 1718 edition of *Ichnographia*. There, in Evelyn's terms, he writes of 'these divine and pious Advantages, added to the Pleasure that all wise and virtuous Men naturally take in raising and planting of Woods, Walks, and Forests, with their own hands.'[44]

In Switzer's praise of silviculture, 'pleasure' is never divorced from 'advantage'; pleasure is as much in agricultural as in aesthetic improvement. The desire to have timber, he wrote in *Ichnographia* 'is, or indeed ought to be, the chief Aim of every Planter . . . had there been as great a number of Oak and Beech Trees rais'd in our *London* Nurseries, as there have been *Greens* [topiary shrubs], Posterity would have reap'd more Benefit by it than by them.' For this reason, although he subsequently became interested in extending the repertoire of trees for plantations, he never abjured his early view that, as at Cassiobury, 'the Method of Sowing and Raising Wood is certainly much cheaper than planting Exotics, etc. the Way that has been followed in all our Modern Wildernesses.'

To these 'Set Wildernesses and Groves, so much us'd of late amongst us,' he contrasts coppices and woods and in the process redefines the very word 'garden' itself in a way that was not to be recognised by dictionaries for more than a century. Even Dr. Johnson in 1755 still defines a garden as an enclosed space. Switzer's garden is its antithesis:

> these kinds of Rural Gardens shall be laid open to the extensive Avenues all round, in an open and unaffected manner, (not Wall'd round or Immured, as has been the Practice) when those large Sums of Money that have been buried within the narrow Limits of a high Wall, upon the trifling and diminutive Beauties of Greens and Flowers, shall be lightly spread over great and extensive Parks and Forests: I say, such seem to be Gardens for the Politer and Greater Genius's of Britain, especially if to it be added Water the Spirit and most enchanting Beauty of Nature, and when Parks shall be turn'd into Gardens.[45]

Within a few years of the first publication of *Ichnographia* Switzer was enjoying the patronage of Charles Boyle, fourth Earl of Orrery, to whom he dedicated his *Practical Fruit Gardener* in 1724. When in 1731 Orrery died, his son, John Boyle, assumed the title and began immediately to work on the family's Somerset estate, Marston Bigot, a project in which Switzer had been involved. This design, which appears in the fourth volume of Campbell's *Vitruvius Britannicus* (1739) [Fig. 59], shows fountains of the kind for which Switzer, the author of *Hydrostaticks* (1729), was celebrated: the sort of machinery, in fact, that was attractive to Boyle's father, the fourth Earl, from

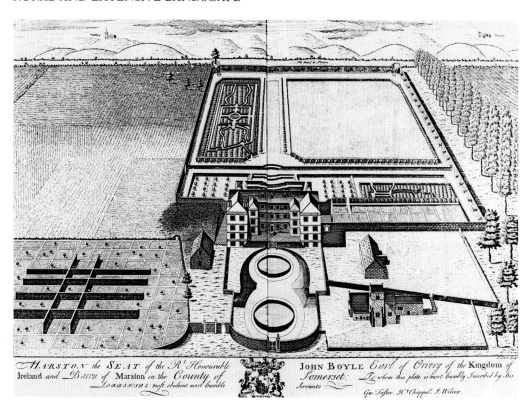

59. Richard Parr, 'View of Marston' (c. 1715) from Colin Campbell, *Vitruvius Britannicus* (1739). Thomas Fisher Library, University of Toronto.

whose library Switzer claimed to have gleaned much of his information. But the garden contained more walls and regular features than Switzer recommended, and it was only under John Boyle's direction that it began to extend into the landscape south and east of the house (figure 17) and to take on the appearance of what was espoused in *Ichnographia*: 'continued quite thro' the Woods and Parks . . . and no Appearance where the Bounds of the Garden is.'[46]

Boyle's own sense of the estate had been in gestation for some time. Writing to his friend William Cecil as early as 1726, Boyle described the grounds in georgic terms:

> The Gardens lie above the House and command a Prospect of a very rich Vale, surrounded by an Ampitheatre of Hills, too beautifull and too well wooded to tire the Eye with looking at: A thousand little Cottages are interspersed in the Woods and Fields;
> —*procul Villarum Culmina fulmant.*[47]

Years before John Boyle came into possession of the estate, he wrote of it as 'the Place I love best in the World.' And his vocabulary of retirement is that of the Augustan ideal: 'I am pleased with the Grandure of Palaces, yet I chuse humble Marston for my Dwelling.'[48] Indeed, when shortly after assuming the title, Boyle was faced with having to go to Ireland to settle the massive arrears of his estates there, he wrote to his friend Salkeld:

> I am sufficiently enamoured of Marston and the Muses to prefer that Place and their Company to the most considerable Advantages that can accrue to me by Law [i.e. in Ireland].
> > In the sweet Silence of the sacred Grove,
> > > Wrapt up in Ease, in Poetry and Love,
> > No Slave to Courts, but fixt in Honour's Rules
> > I chuse to leave the World to Knaves and Fools.[49]

Boyle's happiness in love was short-lived. His first wife died in 1732, but by 1733 he was writing to his friend, the dramatist Thomas Southerne, about the major work being undertaken at Marston:

> We are hard at work both within and without doors, but in the Gardens are outdoing Hannibal, and working thro' rocks more obdurate than the Alps . . . Near an Upper Fountain is to stand a Seat, and at each end two little Closets where you and Phillis may whisper your Loves, and where I may count my beads and say my Mattins. I am scratching out upon Paper ten thousand Designs for other parts, and my Plans commonly come all to the same Fate—they are flung into the Fire and forgott.[50]

In this work, the older Switzer was certainly consulted. Three years before the expanded publication of *Ichnographia* and six before his death in 1745, he was with Boyle at Marston and he seems to have been there again in 1741.[51] Boyle's taste for classical allusion and mottoes (a taste he also indulged later at Caledon) is Virgilian in inspiration and anticipates Shenstone's work at The Leasowes.

It is also of a piece with the Jacobite neoclassicism of his friend William King, the principal of St. Mary Hall, Oxford. Possessed of Irish estates and a friend of Swift, King had published in 1736 his best-known work, a satire called *The Toast* with a frontispiece by Bourgignon (Gravelot), the artist who also worked for Lord Petre. King's friendship was, for Boyle, just the sort that Pliny had celebrated in his letters, and the gardens at Marston were a recreation of the gardens in those letters, letters that Boyle was editing at this time.

> I have endeavoured, my dear Dr [he wrote to King in 1742], still to adorn the Fons Regius as Mr. Aulde [the parson at Marston] quibbingly [*sic*] calls the Spring dedicated to your name: I have placed, under an old Oak that is near it, a bench: the back of which is of stone, and upon it the following Motto is engraven.
>
>
>
> Ecce SCAMNIUM!
>
> Otia dat pigris, praebat solatia fessis
> Et senitus somnum, et mensam messioribus aptam,
> Praebat dura nimis sed grata cubila nymphis
>
> Orrery posuit 1742
>
>
>
> I have crowned the dedication Stone with Laurel, and Bays. Lady Orrery has planted roses, woodbines, and jessamin. I have hedged in a bit of Land by way of Garden, and have enclosed the stone work with a rail so that neither four footed nor two footed beasts can molest you. Oaks, Yews. Firs and flowring Shrubs, grace your Temple which if not the Temple of Liberty is at least the Temple of Evergreens. Thus your name and your poetry are sacred to us, your person shall be so whenever you descend, like some benificent deity from Heaven.[52]

'Extensive parks and forests,' though they were to be the principal feature of the garden that Boyle created at Caledon in Ireland in the late 1740s, were not possible at Marston. Boyle's early concern with the trees at Marston, however, was for more than the merely practical reason of protecting the house from southerly gales. A great deal of his correspondence with his wife in the mid-1740s has to do with tree-planting. Although some of these trees were planted near the house and were part of a replanting of the terraces, many of them were for plantations further out. 'I think to remove the great Trees, to form the front row of the new Grove, towards the South,' Lady Orrery wrote to her husband in January 1744. But her heart was set against cutting down or even trimming these trees, trees that she 'read' in political terms that would have made sense to the Capels at Cassiobury three-quarters of a century earlier. Doubtless the threatened invasion of the Pretender, which she mentions in a letter less than a month later, was in her mind when she wrote:

> As to the Trees, I cannot cut them down, it is like taking away a dozen of your best heads and honestest hearts from amidst your House of Lords: young ones may come up, but in the mean time both the Nation and Marston are exposed to terrible storms and want all the Shelter we can give it. Lord Cartert, will perhaps tell us he will lend us a Schreen [sic] of guilt Leather: but I am for hardy Elm, or sturdy English Oak.[53]

Throughout this period, when the invasion of the Pretender was daily anticipated, Switzer's successor, James Scott, was at work in the gardens. A builder as well as a garden designer, he was nicknamed 'the Great Surveyor' by the family,[54] and he seems to have alternated his labours there with work for the Duke of Norfolk, probably in the gardens designed by Lord Petre at Worksop. Under his regime the existing grounds at Marston were improved, the grotto (which still exists) created, the spring enhanced with a dedication to Boyle's friend King, a statue erected to Apollo, a monument to one of Boyle's dogs, and another to one of his horses.[55]

In fact it was left to Margaret Hamilton, Lady Orrery, to plan and oversee the major replanting of the trees at Marston in the winter and spring of 1744. Throughout this period her husband was in London, largely with his cousin Lord Burlington or with Pope, whose dog Bounce, bitten by a mad dog, was to have his death at Marston commemorated by one of Pope's last poems. Lady Orrery's fascinating correspondence with her husband throughout this period reveals both her horticultural vision and her managerial talents. It is she who, from January to March in that year, organised the replanting of the trees in the garden and the rebuilding of the terraces, though the latter proved impossible to alter and even the ha-ha was unsuccessful in keeping out thieves from the garden: 'I think to remove the great Trees, to form the front row of the new Grove, towards the South, it will be less expence no carriage and make a fine appearance but not one of them shall stir till your orders arrive.'[56]

Her letters refer to arbutus seeds (possibly to be used, as at Lord Petre's Thorndon, for an edging) and to including mulberries and cedars, oaks and ash with the existing elms in the grove. They also show her knowledgable about the trees she was using, more indeed than her husband who seems not to have been much of a plantsman:[57] 'There are 20 Mulberry trees coming down hither, and four Cedars, the part of the Garden you mentioned for their reception will not be large enough, as Mulberrys are a very beautifull Tree, they should be planted in some conspicuous Place. they love a moderat Shade, and Water, tho' I have seen them flourish extreamly exposed to the Sun.'[58]

A decade later Richard Pococke recorded the appearance of Marston. No longer the largely enclosed garden with fountains and cascades that Switzer had created for the fourth Earl, it had become a 'landscape of antiquity,' the sort of *ferme ornée*, indeed, that Switzer recommended in *Ichnographia*, full of literary and personal associations.

> The Earl is improving the place in very elegant taste. There is a Lawn with a Statue of Minerva at the end of it; then to the right another lawn with a plantation of Wood adorned with Busts and an open temple with an altar in

it and ancient statues. To the left of the first lawn is a winding walk to the Cottage built near the place where a person [a deprived Royalist clergyman] lived (in the times of confusion after K. Charles the first) . . . At the other end of the garden in a corner is a little Hermitage near finished for my Lords youngest Son, there is a deep way cut down to it with wood on each side, a Seat or two in it, one is made in the hollow of a tree, it leads to a little irregular Court with a fence of horses heads and bones . . . Two or three fields below the house is a cold bath [see figure 17, number 6], as in an enclosure of an ancient Cemitery, with several old inscriptions made for it and at the end is a small room very elegantly furnished, this I take to be Lady Orrery's place of retirement.[59]

All of this was consistent with Boyle's observations on Tusculum and Laurentinum in his edition of Pliny's letters, finally completed in 1751. Pliny's garden room (*diaeta*), which Boyle noted was confirmed by contemporary accounts of houses in the Near East, he compared also to 'edifices detached from the palaces of ULYSSES,' the sort of place to which Penelope, like Lady Orrery, might withdraw. It was, he wrote, 'the *horti diaeta*, rather than the *villa Laurentina* that engaged his heart': a preference for gardens over architecture that Bacon also had cherished.[60] Similarly, he wrote of baths: 'persons of distinction had private baths at their country seats,' and that Pliny's were 'rather convenient than pompous.'[61]

In 1746 Lady Orrery went with her husband to her own estate, Caledon, in Ireland, where they largely remained for the rest of the Earl's life. There Boyle's taste for 'extensive gardening' could be more thoroughly indulged, and a grove of Diana by a ford in the river seems to have been the earliest example of this.[62]

> I am jogging on in Mottos [he wrote to his friend Watkins in January 1747]. The Statue of Diana stands at the entrance of a wood, which by the turn of the river is formed into a Peninsula. Fields again on every side, the motto is:
>
> > En lucas et ara Dianae
> > Et properantis aquae per amoenos ambitus agros.[63]

Within a year he had built a 'bonehouse' which still exists, a hermitage, and a wood of 'natural winding walks' of just the sort Switzer had commended in *Ichnographia:* 'a faint Essay, and Copy of the sublime Thoughts of ancient and modern Poets on this Subject.'[64] That he thought of his life in literary terms is revealed in a letter to Pococke in 1748: 'Thomson's *Castle of Indolence* came to me last post. I have not read it yet. Such a poem will certainly be very proper to my hermitage, which is now in such beauty that I am impatient to see you there.' Two years earlier he was promising to install the bust of King (who was also a poet) there.[65] A year earlier he was inquiring of Thomas Birch, his source of English news, whether the work of another garden designer and classicist, Joseph Spence (presumably his *Polymetis*) had yet been published.[66]

Mrs. Delany, whose own garden at Delville Boyle thought would be revered 'much as the present Age honours *Praeneste*,'[67] described it in 1748:

> an *hermitage* which is about an acre of ground—an island, planted with all the variety of trees, shrubs, and flowers that will grow in this country, abundance of little winding walks, differently embellished with little seats and banks; in the midst is placed an hermit's cell, made of the roots of trees, the floor is paved with pebbles, . . . *Four little gardens surround his house*—an orchard, a flower garden, a physick garden, and a kitchen garden, with a

kitchen to boil a teakettle or so: I never saw so pretty *a whim* so *thoroughly well* executed.[68]

'Ours is Paradise in its first formation,' Boyle wrote to another friend. 'And methinks I am *the man whom the Lord God put into the Garden of Eden, to dress it, and keep it.*'[69] There his 'most noble grove' was 'like the awfulness of a Cathedral.' By 1748 Boyle could write to his friend Mead: 'I am planting millions of trees, making roads, forming avenues, doing great works, and am a kind of Sovereign among my tenants.'[70] He wrote in similar language to his friend Thomas Birch, observing that 'my Gardiner orders me to lay aside my pen and ink: and I must obey him, as he is the chief negotiator of my present important affairs.'[71]

Boyle continued to nourish the georgic myth of himself both as farmer preoccupied with potatoes and as landscape improver, a myth that was potent in his earliest descriptions of Marston. It was in part a myth that he had inherited from his ancestors, who were notorious improvers in planting in Ireland. Indeed, his great-grandfather, the first Earl of Orrery, was so 'sympathetic to schemes for the useful application of scientific and technological discoveries [that] . . . he had offered to assist the English horticultural reformer, John Beale,'[72] who was a friend of Samuel Hartlib and a correspondent of the fledgling Royal Society. What had been a mixture of pleasure with religious duty for his ancestors, however, had become for Boyle's father a more simply practical matter, a practicality reflected in Switzer's dedication to him of *The Practical Fruit Gardener* (1724).

John Boyle, however, espoused a more generalised ideological and neo-classical association of *utile* and *dulci*, one that Switzer had also championed in the third book of *Ichnographia*.[73] A century after his great-grandfather offered to assist Beale, he could write in these terms both of the hamadryads at Marston and the agricultural arcadia of Caledon: 'Lady Orrery and I enjoy the bowers we have planted: our roses bloom: our trees flourish: our cascades play; our meadows smile.'[74]

6

EVERGREENS AND AMERICAN PLANTS: THE EARL OF ISLAY AT WHITTON AND THE DUKE OF RICHMOND AT GOODWOOD

The revolution in landscape design that occurred in the first half of the eighteenth century depended for its execution primarily on the planting of trees and shrubs. Between 1701 and 1750, sixty-one new trees and ninety-one shrubs were introduced into England,[1] and between 1731 and 1768 the number of plants cultivated in England doubled. Writing in 1722, Richard Bradley noted that evergreen oak, not widely cultivated until six years previously, had now 'many Millions of them . . . been raised here from Acorns.' And he expressed the hope that 'in a few Years our Woods and Groves would be adorn'd with many rich and useful Trees, which at present, through the Fear we have of venturing such Curiosities abroad, are hardly esteemed worthy our Notice, or at least neglected as useless things in our Climate.'[2]

What Capability Brown came to be celebrated for—the disposition of trees in naturalistic settings—was not his invention. By the time that Brown came on to the scene (after 1750) not only had the designer William Kent led the way in the use of trees, but gardeners and botanists had vastly increased the stock of materials available. It is not an overstatement of the case to claim that the remaking of the English landscape in this period would not have been possible without this vastly increased repertoire of trees and shrubs.

Before mid-century, the major increase in tree and shrub importation occurred in the 1720s and '30s and coincided with the work of the pioneers of garden design: Bridgeman and Kent. Writing a hundred years later, J. C. Loudon ascribed this revolution not just to landscape theorists and designers, however, but to gardeners like Brown who had benefitted from the new discoveries in botany:

> Towards the middle of the century, the change introduced in the taste for laying out grounds, by Pope, Addison, and Kent; and the circumstance that Brown, who had been a practical gardener, was extensively employed in remodelling country residences according to this new taste, must have greatly contributed to increase the number of species employed in plantations.[3]

In fact Brown was more conservative in his use of new species than his predecessors. In his history of the importation and use of trees in the early eighteenth century, Loudon lists a number of landscapes and their owners that had benefited from using these new tree species: the Duke of Argyll at Whitton, the Duke of Richmond at Goodwood, Lord Peterborough at Peterborough House near London, Lord Petre at Thorndon Hall, Arthur

Capel, Earl of Essex at Cassiobury, Henry Herbert, Earl of Pembroke at Wilton, Spencer Compton, Earl of Wilmington, the Marquess of Lansdowne at Bowood, Sir Harry Goodrick at Ribston in Yorkshire, Charles Hamilton at Painshill, and Philip Southcote at Wooburn Farm.

> Subsequently to the year 1730 [Loudon writes], foreign trees and shrubs appear to have been planted in various country seats, and more especially in those laid out in the modern [i.e. landscape] style. Among the earliest of these are included Stowe, and part of the scenery at Blenheim. At the former are some fine old cypresses, cedars, and acacias, planted in Brown's time; and in the latter were till lately [1838] the oldest deciduous cypresses and Lombardy poplars in England.[4]

Loudon also mentions Brown's reworking of the Bridgeman/Kent landscape at Claremont for Lord Clive, a design that included 'a great many exotic trees, particularly cedars of large dimensions [and] large ilices, cork trees, tulip trees, red cedars, a large hemlock spruce, and many other fine specimens of foreign trees.'[5] But Brown's work there and elsewhere would not have been possible without the work of his predecessors both in botanical importation and experimentation and in planting out.

60. Todd Longstaffe-Gowan, Reconstruction Plan of Painshill Park (1738).

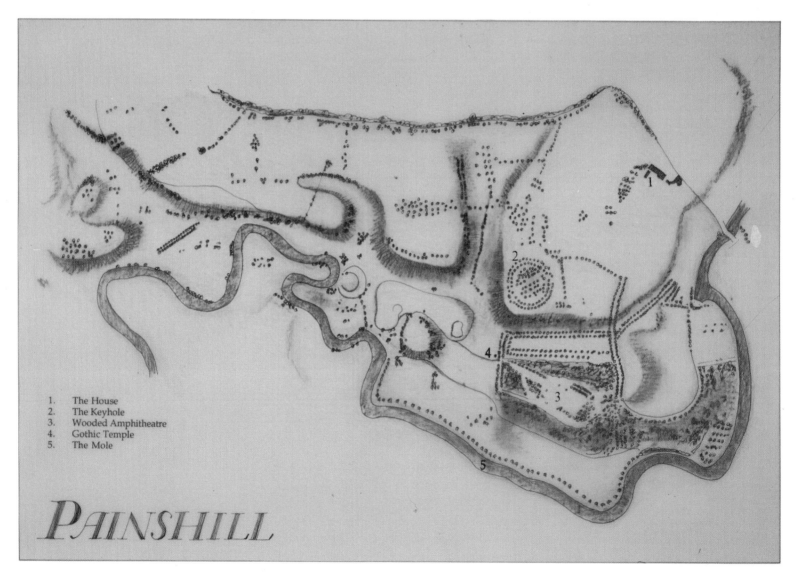

1. The House
2. The Keyhole
3. Wooded Amphitheatre
4. Gothic Temple
5. The Mole

PAINSHILL

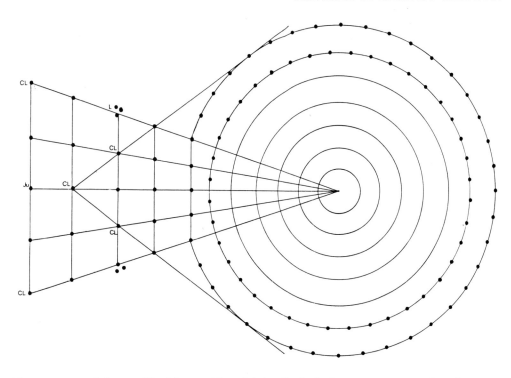

61. John Phibbs, Reconstruction of 'The Keyhole', Painshill.

About one of these, Sir Harry Goodrick, little is known except that he was an experimental botanist and planter. His plantations seem never to have been very extensive, and one of the rare glimpses we have of his work is in a letter to the amateur botanist, Peter Collinson, in 1726, in which he laments that the previous cold winter has destroyed many of his exotic trees, among them an arbutus and what was probably a viburnum from Carolina. But, he observes: 'the lebanon Cedars value not the cold, nor my young oaks of different kinds, which you sent me, viz 6 or 7 acorns (I think) from Pensilvania, nor the Tulip trees [*Liriodendron*], The Oaks I now value more than ever . . . I fancy the trees from that part of the world agree best with our climate . . . Variety of Oaks and other tall trees is what I most covet.'[6] Goodrick concludes, indicating that, whatever his achievements at Ribston (and the creation of the famous Ribston Pippin apple was one), his intention was to 'call in the landscape' with plantations of trees larger than those normally used near the house.

Loudon's history continues with an account of one of Brown's immediate predecessors in planting, Charles Hamilton. In the 1740s Hamilton, whose gardener, Peter Thoburn, later became a nurseryman in his own right in London, introduced a wide range of new trees both at his own estate, Painshill, and at Bowood. Painshill, as the finest 'forest or savage garden' (in Horace Walpole's phrase) was especially dependent on a variety of trees. [Fig. 60] Loudon lists 'silver cedars, pinasters, and other pines, American oaks, cork trees, and ilices, a tupelo tree (*Nyssa*), tulip trees, acacias, deciduous cypresses, Lombardy and other poplars'[7] as remaining there one hundred years later.

Perhaps Painshill's most outstanding arboreal feature was a plantation kown as 'The Keyhole' [Fig. 61]. Consisting of seven concentric circles of trees and with its principal axis aligned on Hamilton's house, its largest outer circle had a diameter of 378 feet. The four innermost circles were of beech, the fifth of Scots pine and beech mixed, and the outer two of Scots pine; but the outermost extended itself through a plantation of evergreen exotics, of which some cedars, larch, and juniper still survive. For all its 'formality', the complexity of the design and the mixture of tree types were enough to make it

62. The Gothic Temple, Painshill.

appear more like one of 'many clumps of forest trees'[8] and to be congruent with the old field structure that Hamilton inherited. Nonetheless, it served to frame views from the Gothic Temple [Fig. 62] and to distinguish other parts of the landscape. This tension between the regular and the irregular was already a feature of many landscape gardens. Nor were the trees used in 'The Keyhole' uncommon by 1740. Indeed, in spite of Horace Walpole's claims for Hamilton's originality in the 'forest or savage garden,' he was in fact the heir and beneficiary of considerable innovation in planting in the previous decade as well as of the recommendations in the writings of such men as Switzer and Langley.

Painshill's forest garden was distinguished chiefly in its use of conifers, especially pines, one of which, the Weymouth or white pine (*Pinus strobus*, see figure 54), had not been extensively cultivated in England before 1705 when the owner of Longleat, Lord Weymouth, had planted out large numbers of the tree.[9] [Fig. 54] Even as late as 1739 Peter Collinson could write of it as 'scarce and rare with us.'[10] Hamilton was able to plant conifers on such a large scale because he too had been preceded in the pioneering work of experimentation by men like the Duke of Argyll and others of Peter Collinson's circle. In the early 1720s, while he was still Earl of Islay, Archibald Campbell acquired Whitton in Middlesex and began by at least 1724 to plant it with exotic trees. The greenhouse (by James Gibbs) was built before the house itself.

Argyll's interest in horticulture was of a piece with his interest in husbandry and provides another instance of the georgic strain in British landscape gardening. By the 1740s the rage for 'improvement', whether agricultural or horticultural, had also taken hold in Scotland. Robert Maxwell's preface to the *Select Translations*, published by a Society of Improvers in Agriculture in 1743, cites Virgil's *Georgics*, Pliny, Varro, and Columella, just as Switzer had done thirty years earlier. And Maxwell introduces the same argument for hybridizing and introducing exotics—that native species are poor things—that Philip Miller had used in the *Catalogus Plantarum* more than a decade before. Indeed, he is able to cite not only the practice of the president of the society in making extensive public gardens 'where there was once a Morass' but the practice of the Earl of Islay in introducing 'the American and Balm of Gilead Firs, the Larix, and many other useful Plants.'[11] Maxwell's adjective, 'useful', echoes Pope's ''tis Use alone that sanctifies Expence' and indicates once again the strong moral and classical strain that runs through the apologetics for rural and extensive gardening in the early eighteenth century.

From the catalogue of Argyll's trees made later by his gardener at Whitton, Daniel Crofts, in 1765, we have some idea of the enormous range of species. In what was a relatively small estate (about fifty-five acres [Fig. 63] cut out of the unproductive ground of Hounslow Heath), Argyll began by planting cedars and went on to introduce such a range of exotic trees that Horace Walpole claimed that 'the introduction of foreign trees and plants . . . we owe principally to Archibald, Duke of Argyle.'[12] These included nearly 300 shrubs and deciduous trees, as well as about fifty different conifers.[13]

It is difficult to determine how many of these trees found their way from the nine acres of nursery to the rather larger pleasure ground that was laid out nearer to the house, but many of them must have. Contemporary engravings [Fig. 64] show the house surrounded by a wide mixture of deciduous and coniferous trees, and the long canal leading from the house to a Gothic Tower at one end of the grounds was lined by mature conifers in just the way that Batty Langley was to recommend in his *New Principles of Gardening* (1728).[14] The adjoining large, wooded plantation with its irregular winding paths— referred to as 'wilderness work' by Sir John Clerk who visited in 1727[15]—was obviously designed to make the most of the tree species planted there.

When Joseph Spence visited the garden, probably in 1760,[16] he gave an account of the appearance and size of the various trees. Nearest to the house were a number of enclosures 'for the more curious Trees; in little strait walks: running in and out; like borders.' Here, though Spence noted that there were probably a number of rarer curiosities that were not mentioned by the gardener guide, there was a 'Siberian Stone-Pine,' a 'Swamp Pine,' and a 'Portugal Laurel, clear'd up for about 7 f in the stem, with a beautiful shady head that wou'd look, most charmingly, alone on a Knole, with a seat around it'—an idea that Spence had proposed earlier for the countryside near his own garden in Surrey.

Spence did not approve of the Duke's old-fashioned taste in the layout of the 'Grove-Work with the old Serpentine Walks, and Openings generally for a single Tree,' but he was impressed with the specimens that he saw there: 'a Red Virginia Cedar [*Juniperus virginiana*], above 30 f high' as well as a scarlet oak and 'American Bird-Cherry Trees' of the same height. He also commented on 'the largest Larch I [ever] observ'd... supposd 55 f high,' which had come from Sir Godfrey Kneller's nearby garden. 'Swedish Maple' ('that kind of Tree, much esteem'd by his Grace') and 'Sr Charles Wager's Maple... commonly call'd the Scarlet-flowerd Maple' were also there with an unidentified German nut tree, some Weymouth pines ('near 50 f high') and some 'Pretty (open) Cypress.'

Where Spence is most interesting is in his account of the larger effects of tree-massing. The Gothic Tower, for example, seems to have been Miltonically 'bosomed high in tufted trees,' cedars of Lebanon in fact, and these in turn continued the effect of younger cedars of Lebanon that flanked the canal leading to the tower. But Spence was clearly most fascinated with what he calls

63. Todd Longstaffe-Gowan, Reconstruction Plan of of Whitton after Daniel Crofts (1765).

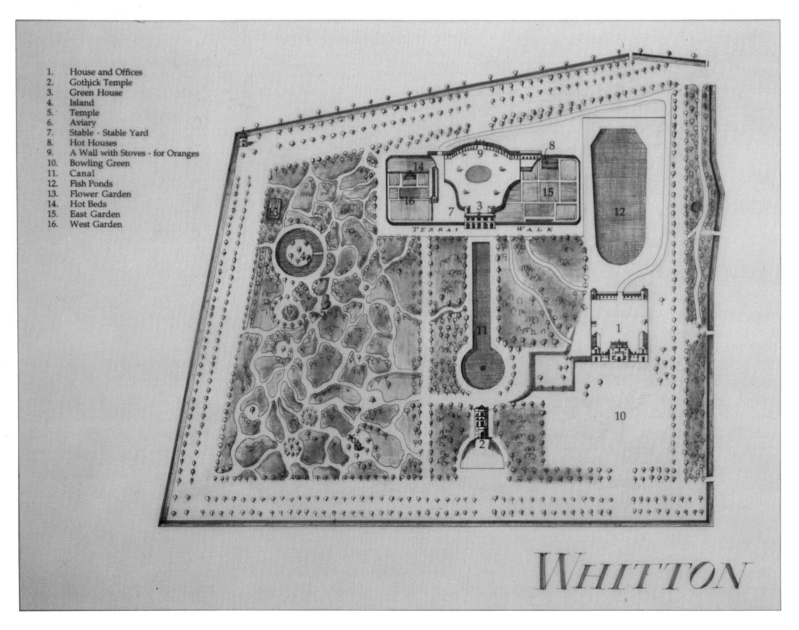

1. House and Offices
2. Gothick Temple
3. Green House
4. Island
5. Temple
6. Aviary
7. Stable - Stable Yard
8. Hot Houses
9. A Wall with Stoves - for Oranges
10. Bowling Green
11. Canal
12. Fish Ponds
13. Flower Garden
14. Hot Beds
15. East Garden
16. West Garden

WHITTON

A View of the House and part of the Garden of His Grace the Duke of Argyl at Whitton. —— London Printed for Rob.t Sayer Map & Printseller in Fleet Street.

Veüe de la Maison et d'une partie du Jardin de Mons.r le Duc d'Argyll a Whitton, a 4 lieues l'oüest de Londre.

64. View of Whitton (c. 1760).

'almost a Grovette [a small grove] of Weymouth Pines [*Pinus strobus*], on the farther side of the entrance.' The gardener's account of a visitor who 'spoke of his having seen Weymouth Pines, in America, of 150 f high' leads Spence to the reflection: 'what a pity it is, some Gentleman don't plant a grove of them here; which would draw up one another and bring them, perhaps, to a much greater higth [*sic*] than ever they have attain'd to here.'

As Spence depicts him, Argyll was thus not simply a botanical planter, but a gardener interested in adapting newly discovered trees and shrubs to what cannot have been a very promising landscape. Richard Pococke described it in 1750 as 'a plantation mostly of Evergreens and American plants' in which 'the whole is laid out much in the wilderness way, with a broad walk of grass all round.'[17]

Argyll in other words created a pleasure garden no less interesting than many others laid out in the same period. Although Spence later complained of its being old-fashioned, its combination of 'wilderness' plantation with a formal canal, for example, was consonant with the Italianate taste that Kent and Burlington espoused in the early 1720s and that could be found, for example, at nearby Twickenham Park or at Chiswick. It was certainly far in advance of the clipped regularity that Miller still used to illustrate a garden in his frontispiece to the *Gardeners Dictionary* (1724) or the *Catalogus Plantarum* (1730). Indeed, Argyll's advantage over Kent, as Walpole pointed out, was that

Kent, who did not know exotics, 'was therefore restricted in the effects he could achieve.'[18]

In 1732 Argyll took into his employ James Lee, a Scot who was later, in partnership with Lewis Kennedy at Hammersmith, to become one of the most famous nurserymen of the century. Indeed it was Argyll who promoted this partnership, having throughout Lee's employment continued his education and given him free use of his library. Lee's early biographer, Robert John Thornton, says of him that he 'studied Botany at a time when few persons in England had any knowledge of the science.'

It seems likely that Lee met Linnaeus when he was in England; certainly he corresponded with him and sent him specimens. Indeed it was through Lee's *Introduction to Botany* that many later eighteenth-century gardeners were introduced to Linnaeus's system. Among his later friends Lee counted Stephen Hales, the author of *Vegetable Staticks*, John Martyn, the second Professor of Botany at Cambridge, and Alexander Hunter, the York doctor who was to republish Evelyn's *Sylva* in 1776. Lee's nursery, says Thornton, 'was always open to the curious; nor was he ever backward in communicating knowledge.' Indeed, Thornton goes so far as to claim that the Hammersmith nursery, as a repository of new and rare plants, was second only to Kew, the botanic garden to which the trees from Whitton made such a large contribution after Argyll's death.[19]

But Argyll's garden was not merely a nursery of exotics; it was a pleasure ground as well. His Gothic Tower [Fig. 65] there succeeded an earlier temple with wooden columns and a grotto below. Built on a vaulted basement behind a tunnelled mound, the tower created the optical illusion of being built on the mound itself. This illusionism, and the framing of a perspective of the garden along the canal to the house, is similar to the optical tricks that Pope enjoyed in his grotto at nearby Twickenham. There boats passing on the river were framed by the grotto's entrance as a kind of diorama in a 'Perspective Glass'

65. Gothic Tower at Whitton (c. 1760).

Tour Gothique à Whitton au Duc d'Argyl.

and the grotto itself, in which there was a sort of camera obscura, led into surprise vistas of the garden.[20]

Argyll can hardly have been unaware of what Pope was doing in his garden at just this time. Pope was a frequent guest at Whitton and addressed several poems to him. Argyll, moreover, was one of the trustees appointed by George II to oversee the settlement made on his mistress, Henrietta Howard, and this included establishing her at Marble Hill, where Lord Bathurst and Pope were busy designing the grounds. His Gothic Tower, moreover, far from being a ruin as has sometimes been suggested, invoked the conventional Whig reference to Gothic liberty that can also be found later in Lord Cobham's similarly triangular Gothic Temple at Stowe or Henry Colt Hoare's 'Alfred's Tower' at Stourhead.[21]

That Argyll was familiar with the literature of botany is not in doubt. The 1768 catalogue of his library shows that it included many botanical and horticultural works in both Latin and English.[22] Among the former were two seventeenth-century continental editions of René Rapin's Latin poem, *Of Gardens*, as well as the botanical works of Commelin, Boerhaave, Gesner, Dillenius, Browall, Martyn, and John Ray. There were also many garden catalogues, including those of the French royal gardens at Blois and the botanic gardens in Montpellier and Paris; the *medical garden at Haarlem*; and the botanic gardens at Leiden, Amsterdam, and Göttingen; as well as the Physic Garden at Chelsea, and the nearby garden of William Beaumont, the French garden designer who created the famous topiary gardens at Levens Hall in Cumbria and England's earliest ha-ha.

Argyll owned John Clayton's *Flora Virginica*, published in Leiden in 1742, as well as William Hughes's *The American physitian; or, a treatise of the roots, plants, trees, shrubs, herbs &c, growing in the English plantations in America* (London, 1672), and many other horticultural and botanical works in English. These included a two-volume edition of Miller's *Dictionary*, John Worlidge's *Systema Agriculturae* (1681), Patrick Blair's *Botanick Essays* (1720), and John Wilson's *Synopsis of English Plants* (Newcastle, 1744).

One is not surprised to find included John Evelyn's translation of La Quintinie's *The Compleat Gard'ner* (1693), but it is interesting that Argyll owned the fourth (1706) edition of Evelyn's *Sylva*. For it was only in that edition (the last one before Evelyn's death) that the author included *Dendrologia*, his long essay on the aesthetic and philosophical reasons for tree plantations. There is a curious echo and invocation of that work in Pehr Kalm's account of his visit to Whitton on 4 May 1748. The Duke of Argyll, he noted, was a lover of science, 'but in particular of *Botanique,* and the branch of that science which is called *Dendrologie.*'[23] Kalm's use of Evelyn's word, 'dendrology', suggests that Argyll's attachment to the cultivation of trees was more than merely botanic, that it placed him in a sort of arboreal succession to the great gardens of the classical past invoked by Evelyn in his essay. The spirit of Evelyn's work still very much presided over this period. In an essay, 'Of the Etymology, contemplative, civil, and sacred Uses of Woods,' (1733) Stephen Switzer gives a sort of digest of Evelyn's *Dendrologia* and describes the 'divine and pious Advantages, added to the Pleasure that all wise and virtuous Men naturally take in raising and planting of Woods, Walks, and Forests, with their own hands.'[24]

Argyll was the uncle of Lord Bute, the effective creator of the botanic gardens at Kew, and many of the specimens in his collection passed there after his death in 1761. But his botanical interests were of a piece with aesthetic and even philosophical ones. Through his friendship with the amateur botanist, Peter Collinson, he was part of a circle of estate owners who were also interested in arboreal innovation: Charles Hamilton, Charles Lennox, the second Duke of Richmond, and Lord Petre of Writtle. From their labours in the 1720s and thirties one can see 'ornamental plantings on these estates as part of a movement giving new life, shape, and colour to the previously mainly native appearance of trees in landscape gardens.'[25]

Collinson interested himself in a number of estates, including the Earl of Jersey's (Middleton Park, Oxfordshire), the Duke of Newcastle's (Claremont, Surrey), and his brother's The Grove (at Esher in Surrey). A letter of 15 November 1737 about the laying out of Middleton initiated the Earl of Jersey's correspondence with Collinson, a correspondence that included a discussion of nurserymen and gardeners over the next two decades. Collinson's obvious interest in the design as well as the materials of *ingentia rura* is reflected in Jersey's gratitude for his 'great pains in instructing me to lay out to advantage and to beautify my little Spot of ground.' Collinson's inquiries about Jersey's progress with his plans prompted a lengthy reply:

> we have pulled down our Walls before the house and by so doing laid ourselves open to the Country, the Open Grove is freed from the Underwood and almost grubbed up, the Wall also that went round it is taken down to breast high by which means from any part of the grove we have a View all over the Country; the Kitchin garden I have greatly encreased in Size, and has been walled round some time though not yet planted, the chief reason, is the Nature of our Soile that woud not admit of the Borders being so soon prepared as in other Counties . . . We have deliberated much about the Visto's and Avenue's in Our Wood, and taken Several Sights to Agreeable Terminations, but find that carrying them quite throrough [*sic*] to the great Walk woud make such Slaughter with the Wood that my heart fails, and I am realy such a Cit. as to have a great Value for trees, this grand affair I have therefore deferred till I have better Opinions.[26]

These 'better opinions,'[27] he decided, should be those of Switzer, but in telling Collinson so he had occasion to twit him about the latter's preference for Bridgeman and Kent. This is probably a joking reference to Collinson's spending time at Claremont, where he sometimes dined with the Duke of Newcastle [Fig. 66]. In a letter of 1754 he wrote: 'Perhaps I ought not to say it but Mr. Pelham always showed Mee a particular Respect and indeed the Duke of Newcastle when I have been at Claremount has taken more notice of Mee at Sundry Times then I could expect.'[28]

This notice, it seems, went so far as soliciting Collinson's views about how the French were to be dealt with in North America. It may well have been Collinson's connections with such Pennsylvania Quakers as the botanist, John Bartram, that provided him with information about America. In writing to Newcastle, however, Collinson abandoned all traces of Quaker pacifism. Henry Fox (later Baron Holland), writing to Collinson about getting seeds from America recommended that Niagara 'be a place of Arms in *the extensive View you mention.*' It may also have been Collinson's desire to extend the botanical exploration of North America that led him to be so forceful in his belief in westward expansion. 'Those that remain Masters of the Ohio Country, will be undoubtedly Masters of all the Colonies,' he wrote to the Duke of Newcastle in 1754.[29]

Both Bridgeman and Kent contributed to the design of Newcastle's gardens

66. The Amphitheatre and Lake, Claremont.

at Claremont, which were described by Henrietta Pye as 'beautifully variegated,' and (in Bridgeman's 'theatre' there) 'planted as thick as possible with shrubs.'[30] Mr. Pelham, Newcastle's brother Henry, was the owner of The Grove at nearby Esher, where Kent was said to have been 'Kentissime'; in Pope's phrase, '*Kent* and Nature vye for PELHAM'S Love.' Celebrated for its 'improved taste,' its 'seats, ruins, temples and mausoleums . . . [were] picturesquely dispersed throughout the ample extent of the paradisiacal scenes of the GROVE.'[31] [Fig. 67] The rivalry of Kent and nature illustrates the co-

67. Thomas Medland after Melieux. Esher Place, Surrey (1792).

operation of design and propagation that Collinson's dearest friend, Lord Petre, had best exemplified, but in which the Pelhams plainly continued to be interested. The Duke's nephew and heir, Lord Lincoln, is referred to in a letter from the Duke of Richmond to Collinson in 1747 as 'quite mad after planting.' [Fig. 68] Indeed, one of the signs of Lord Lincoln's devotion to gardening was his continued patronage of his former mentor, the classical scholar, garden historian, and designer, Joseph Spence. Within a year of the Duke's letter, Spence began to create an extensive and rural garden in the landscape surrounding the vicarage at Byfleet in Surrey, of which Lord Lincoln was the owner and patron.

In that letter of 1747, Richmond suggests that some of the American pines (possibly *Pinus palustris*) that he had requested from Petre's Thorndon might be sent to Lincoln's estate (Oatlands in Surrey). 'You and I,' he continues to Collinson, 'must go, and see what he is about, and dine with him, and I agree with you that so good a taste ought to be encouraged.'[32] Some picture of what that taste achieved is given by Richard Pococke only three years later. Lincoln had transformed the symmetrical garden laid out by his father, a garden that had included a cruciform canal and a version of the Claremont ampitheatre, as well as an avenue giving a vista to Claremont itself some four miles away. [Fig. 69] The visitor to Oatlands in 1750, however, arrived at 'several acres of ground . . . laid out in fine lawns and planted with clumps of trees in a very beautiful manner.' Thence he was taken by 'a winding walk to the left through shrubberies, and so down the hills to a Nursery, laid out like an elegant Parterre.' Nearby, adjacent to lawns on which sheep grazed, there was an enclosure with exotic plants 'with boards plac'd over them on which their names are cut.' The banks of the 'Broad Water' had been enhanced by 'planting them in an irregular manner with withy [willow] and other trees.' Plainly the botanic spirit had been caught, and yet it was also associated with husbandry

68. Arthur Devis, 'Henry Fiennes Clinton, 9th Earl of Lincoln, with his Wife Catherine, and Son George' (c. 1751). Private Collection.

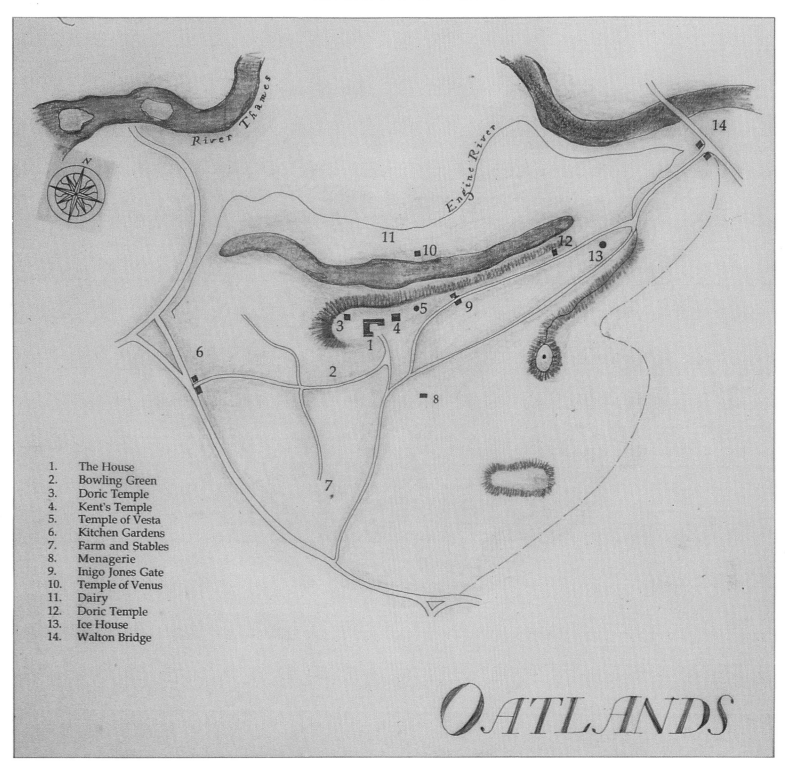

1. The House
2. Bowling Green
3. Doric Temple
4. Kent's Temple
5. Temple of Vesta
6. Kitchen Gardens
7. Farm and Stables
8. Menagerie
9. Inigo Jones Gate
10. Temple of Venus
11. Dairy
12. Doric Temple
13. Ice House
14. Walton Bridge

69. Todd Longstaffe-Gowan, Reconstruction Plan of Oatlands (c. 1750).

and Palladian design. In the midst, as an obvious testimony to Palladian values, Lincoln had restored in 1735 a gate originally erected at the nearby palace of Oatlands by Inigo Jones, the native hero of English Palladianism.[33]

A decade later Collinson himself was able to write to Lincoln commending 'the fine Effect of the plantations, as the Scene varies—Art and Nature [he went on] in this Paradice, conspire to Raise my Spirits and give a glow that I can't express.'[34] [Fig. 70] Perhaps another sign of the progress of Lincoln's horticultural tutelage is a letter addressed to him by Joseph Spence only four

70. Richard Farringdon, View of Oatlands (c. 1780).

years later. In it, Spence describes the many features of Stourhead's Virgilian landscape as if to an initiate in garden mysteries.[35]

Collinson, who provided cedars of Lebanon for Lord Lincoln, also provided seeds for the third Duke of Bedford, a keen advocate of reformed husbandry, whose tree plantations were among the best in the country. Writing to Bedford in 1734, Collinson offered his 'experience in plantations and gardens.' One form this took was Bedford's becoming a subscriber, even before Lord Petre, to Collinson's scheme of seed and plant importation from America.[36] By 1759 Collinson was able to take a proprietary interest in what had been achieved at Woburn, having been instrumental in getting Bedford some of Lord Petre's nursery trees. Offering the Duke some 'Sibiria White Firr Seed and Russia Larix,' he took occasion to give a little history of the creation of the Woburn landscape:

> It gives Mee real pleasure to hear of its prosperity—because with your Graces Leave I think my Self in some small Degree Interested In It—By procuring that Variety of North American, Pines, Firrs, and Cedars etc of which it is composed. For Mr Miller knowing I had Correspondence Abroad in our Colonies, Desired Mee to send for a Collection of Seeds from thence

for Yr Grace. Accordingly I brought over in the years 1742, 1743, and 1744. Each year, a Large Chest of Seeds of Trees and Shrubs etc from Pensilvania. From these I have hear'd, Sprang up the principal Materials for raiseing this Noble plantation, which I am informed Excells all others in this Kingdome.[37]

Collinson was on even friendlier terms with the second Duke of Richmond, another gardener who was interested both in design and botany. Richmond, moreover, had a family connection with Collinson's close friends, the Petres. In a letter of 1742 he referred to his 'uncle Southcote,' presumably Sir Edward, Lord Petre's former guardian.[38] A glimpse of the intensity of this interest is in a letter from Richmond to Collinson in 1742, a letter in which Richmond fears that if he does not get his order for trees in soon enough to the nurserymen 'the Dukes of Norfolk [Worksop], and Bedford [Woburn] will sweep them all away.'[39]

Richmond increased his estate (Goodwood in Sussex) from 200 acres to 11,000, thereby acquiring 'a rich and beautiful Landskip, bounded by the sea for 30 Miles in Sight.'[40] This estate is also another good example of the connection between 'rural gardening' and the Palladian revival where, as Rudolf Wittkower

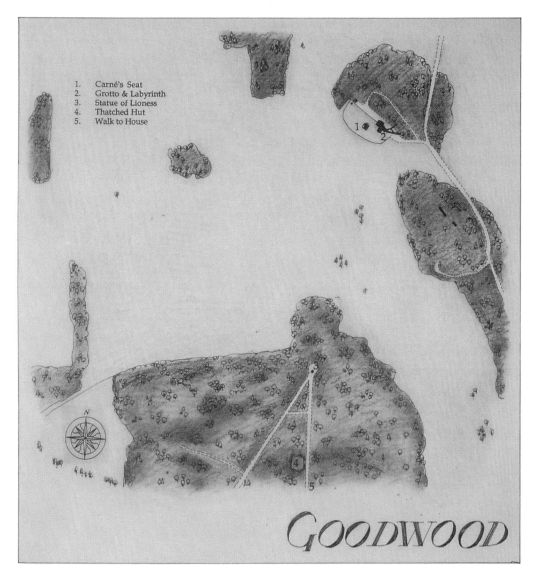

71. Todd Longstaffe-Gowan, Reconstruction Plan of Part of the Grounds at Goodwood (c. 1750).

1. Carné's Seat
2. Grotto & Labyrinth
3. Statue of Lioness
4. Thatched Hut
5. Walk to House

GOODWOOD

observed, 'classical houses were given "romantic" landscape-garden settings.'[41] In 1725 Colen Campbell included several plans for Goodwood in his *Vitruvius Britannicus*, the *locus classicus* of early eighteenth-century Palladianism. His plans for the house (interestingly similar to Roger Morris's plans for the Duke of Argyll's Whitton Park) were never realised, although a large plan for the estate seems partly to have been put into effect. Another large estate plan of 1731 also shows very similar gardens. Near the house both plans show dense wildernesses, one with a mount, threaded with serpentine paths; further out, a perimeter planting of loosely belted trees separates the estate from the surrounding downs. [Fig. 71] Because Campbell himself writes of 'the great Improvements Mr. Carné [Richmond's landscape gardener] has made in this delightful Place [which] will be lasting Monuments of his Art and Industry,'[42] it is not entirely clear what Campbell's contribution was. It seems that Carné's was primarily planting, as Campbell says that 'Carné's Oaks shall never be forgot.' Certainly the Duke, who believed in extensive plantations, esteemed Carné highly, as he built a Palladian temple in the grounds in 1743 and called it 'Carné's Seat'.

Either Roger Morris or the Earl of Burlington was the likely architect for the building, another effective example of the relation between Palladian values and landscape.[43] The dome of the roof in the porch contained the Duke's birth constellation and there was a banqueting room in the basement. There was also a nearby grotto, extensively decorated by the Duchess with shellwork later in the decade, in which a circular mirror was placed (as in Pope's grotto) to 'call in the country,' in this case to reflect the top of the steeple of Chichester Cathedral. And nearby there was an underground labyrinth.

Richmond, like Lord Petre and the Duke of Argyll, also kept an extensive menagerie of wild animals, another aspect of the re-creation of a paradisal landscape, in this case by zoological means. By the early 1740s, though, he abandoned his zoological garden for a botanic one.[44] 'Within these few years,' wrote a traveller in 1742, 'he has dispos'd of allmost all his beasts,' though not, it seems, without creating a different kind of emblematic statuary from the usual classical sort. The visitor gives an account of Richmond's celebration of what might be called zoological heroism: 'One of his Lyonnes's he has buried in his garden at the end of one of the walks, and has erected a monument of Portland stone over her.'

Apart from the view, this visitor found little to commend in what the Duke had done: 'The gardens, consist of a little wood taken out of the Park, in which are 2 or 3 pleasant vista's. In the middle of the wood is a thatched hut where the Duke dines sometimes in summer . . . The Park is but a barren spot of ground, and very indifferently planted.'[45]

Within a few years all that appears to have changed, but even in the 1730s the work had been begun. Although there is little in the estate accounts about the gardens, there is enough evidence from the Duke's correspondence to suggest that his extensive interest both in botany and in 'planting out' had started well before 1742. A letter to his steward, Labbé, on 2 December 1730 shows him already concerned with his plantations:

> tell the gardiner he must be sure to lay a great quantity of dung to the roots of all the trees of all sorts that are newly planted, in order to keep the frost from them. he must also throw a great deal of fresh dry straw upon the young *Algaroba* plants that are just come up; pease straw would be the best of any, for it is the dryest and will keep out the frost best. read this part of the letter to the gardiner that there may be no mistakes.[46]

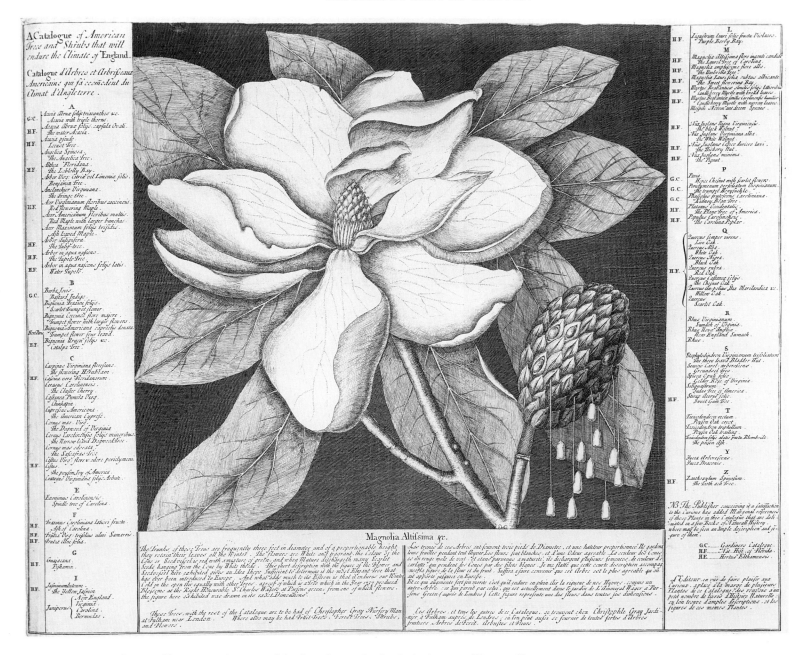

Magnolia Altissima &c.

72. Christopher Gray. *Magnolia Altissima* from *A Catalogue of American Trees and Shrubs that will endure the Climate of England*. 1737. Oak Spring Garden Library, Upperville.

By 1730 Richmond's nurseries would also have included the seedling off-spring of the 'Tubb of Acorns of the Ever Green Oak' that had been offered by a Robert Hayes living in Minorca to Carné in 1729. Goodwood continued to be sent seeds from Minorca. A letter of 1750 apologises to the Duke for sending seeds among which there were no rarities and mentions that they were meant to be divided with Hamilton, presumably Charles Hamilton of Painshill.[47] Rarities, however, came from Lord Petre. A letter from him on 23 March 1740 refers to sending Richmond 'two plants of the small *Magnolia* [*Magnolia grandiflora* or *virginiana*] . . . having as yet rais'd but very few plants of that kind.' In that the first recorded introduction of *Magnolia grandiflora* [Fig. 72] was in about 1730, Richmond was plainly honoured to be included among what Petre in the same letter referred to as 'my brother Gardeners.'[48]

An undated letter from Collinson to Richmond in the late 1740s shows that Lord Petre was not alone in thinking of himself as part of a society of 'brother Gardeners.' 'Yesterday,' Collinson writes, 'I kept the Fast at a Feast at Ld

Lincolns with yr Bottle Friend Lord Harcourt—Wee toasted you and all Lovers of planting These Worthy Good Men who have the cause of propagation att Heart.'[49]

Indeed, in the disposal of the trees from Lord Petre's nurseries after his death, Collinson turned to the Dukes of Argyll and Richmond as the obvious heirs to the contents of those nurseries. With these trees, Richmond's plantations got under way in earnest, plantations that were to be extended, with Collinson's help, by the third Duke in the 1760s.[50] In a letter to accompany some of the trees, Collinson wrote:

> When I was last at Thorndon I had these Specimens Gather'd to show my noble Friends the *Dukes* of Richmond & Argyle [that] by them they may form some tolerable Idea what they have, and what they want, No 1—I take to be the best [.] you raised several in the American Wood—and yett wether owing to *Thorndon Soil* has a different appearance from yrs—The Jersey Pine [*Pinus virginiana*] you have one or Two the Others you Want—Now my Good Lord Lett Mee Know What Number you will Have of Each Sort for I now can Secure them for you against a proper Season *to Remove* [.] for all the Plants in the Nurserys att Thorndon is likely to be bought by one person—so the like opportunity will not perhaps be again—and these you know are not to be mett with in any Nursery.[51]

In 1747, the date of this letter, the Jersey pine was still a relative rarity, having been introduced only in 1739. Where the Duke of Richmond's 'American Wood' is indicative of his being as committed to experimental plantations as Lord Petre, his collecting of new species is further evidence of the importance of botanical rarities to the making of *ingentia rura*.[52] Indeed, in a letter to Collinson in 1741, thanking him for seeds of trees which he already had, Richmond nonetheless went out of his way to assure him: 'I am extreamly obliged to you and assure you these things are not thrown away upon me, for no man liveing loves propagation (in an honest way) more than I do.'[53]

Throughout the period immediately after Lord Petre's death in 1742 the Duke was in correspondence with Collinson about what was needed at Goodwood. On 5 December he wrote to Collinson, thanking Lady Petre for an offer of some birds for his menagerie but expressing a greater interest to have 'some of the Curious plants from Thorndon, now those I stand most in need of,' he continues,

> are in the first place a particular fine plant of the Chinese Thuya [*Thuja orientalis*] about five foot high that would just match that one which I have already in my ever-green grove; and if there are any more of the same sort I should be very glad to have them, as also of my Lord Isla's swamp pine [*Pinus elliottii*], and some more of that small firr, with leaves like the Common Yew. These are the most desirable things that I can thinke of at present, butt as you know my collection, you also know what I wante better than myself.[54]

This letter reveals several interesting things: first, that as well as an 'American wood' (possibly planted later) Richmond had an 'ever-green grove'; second, that this latter grove already contained obvious rarities; and third, that he thought of his trees, as Lord Petre did, as a botanic collection.

Richmond was himself closely involved with the creation of his plantations. In his letters he writes frequently as if he were directly involved in the work. In the same letter of 5 December 1742 he writes to Collinson that he will have his 'hands full' with planting once the weather improves

for I shall have nine acres to plant this season, seven upon the top of a very bleak hill above my parke, and an addition of two acres to the Arbor Vite [*Thuja occidentalis*] grove. the Cerrus oake [*Quercus cerris*] I have gott is the true genuine one from Nottingham; I have one plant of it about six inches high and about sixteen good and fresh, though butt small, acorns which I have planted, some in the open ground and some in a tub.[55]

The seven acres of plantation 'upon the top of a very bleak hill' were probably adjacent to Carné's Seat, which the Duke, in the same letter, mentions as being about to be constructed. That a plantation well beyond Campbell's estate design and so far from the house should have been part of his plans is indicative of how much of the landscape Richmond intended to 'call in.' That he was doing it with a tree as rare as cerris oak (only introduced in 1735) is evidence of the great part that botanical experimentation and propagation played in the creation of his landscape.

At the end of December he wrote again to Collinson about trees from Thorndon, explaining more fully the nature of this new plantation. This was to be a mount that went beyond what Lord Petre had been able to create in the flat landscape of Essex by using the 'bleak hill' to create 'a mount Lebanon':

I want some small cedars of Lebanon, that is from six inches to three foot high, butt I had rather not have them higher than three foot, and about 100: of the common Thuya or arbor-vites [*Thuja occidentalis*] of any size providing they do not exceed four foot . . . I dont so much as mention the number of Cedars of Lebanon, because the more I could have the better, for I propose makeing a mount Lebanon, upon a very high hill, which to be planted close as they ought to be to draw one another up, I fear would take up to two hundred plants or more. and I have not above thirty by me.[56]

In 1739 Collinson wrote that tulip trees and 'Virginia Oaks' were planted,[57] but it is not clear which sort of oak 'Virginia Oaks' were. Possibly they were the tree identified as *Quercus marilandica* in the Whitton catalogue. Tulip trees (*Liriodendron*) were not rarities by this time; Richmond wrote that he could get them from Gray the nurseryman. Nonetheless he wrote that would be 'very glad of about 40, or 50' from Thorndon if he could get them. Although he insisted on paying for these trees, he recognised that he would have to take the rarities offered to him 'for love or mony, for . . . they are not to be gott any where else.'[58]

At about the same time hickory (probably either *Carya amara* or *C. porcina*), both introduced in the early seventeenth century, were also planted.[59] Cork oak (*Quercus suber*) had also been planted before this time, but neither it nor evergreen oak (*Quercus ilex*) was particularly new or rare. Nor was the American red oak (*Quercus coccinea*) to which Collinson was probably referring when he mentioned 'the large Echinated Cup Acorns' with which he hoped to supply the Duke, most likely for his experimental nurseries.[60] In the same letter, however, Collinson refers to Lord Pembroke's 'Carrus Oke' (*Quercus cerris*), which was still a rarity.

Throughout the 1740s Richmond's correspondence with Collinson shows him continually extending his plantations. In December 1742 he writes about wanting 'to make a mirtle hedge of about 180 foot in length,' and by February he is instructing Collinson that he wants 'forty or fifty of the broad leaved myrtles [*Myrtus communis*] . . . I would have those of a foot high for 9 *pence*.'[61] By 1746 he is able to tell Collinson, his chief supplier: 'All my plantations in general flourish prodigiously, and particularly the Weymouth Pine that have made vast shoots, and I have not lost one of them. and our verdure here is beyond what I ever saw any where. and Carné's seat as well as the whole parke and gardens, are in the highest beauty.'[62] Throughout this period, too, Richmond's correspondence continues to show him interested in propagating botanic novelties, though not at the expense of restricting the scale of his plantations: 'You see by my list that I have sent for the 400 Duch Junipers, butt I want to know in what they differ from the English Juniper, tho if they do not differ I should be glad to have them, for I want to make a great plantation of Junipers, for which reason I wish you could gett me a good quantity of the seed of it.'[63]

In all this, Collinson remained Richmond's chief supplier, either as agent for the trees from Thorndon or in providing trees from his own nurseries. From Richmond's correspondence with him, often about problems of carriage, we get a glimpse of the rarities the Duke was accumulating. In November 1747 he writes to Collinson to tell him about having received 'from Portugal two sorts of seeds of Cistus, not known I beleive [*sic*] here, and four new sorts of Genistas,' and enclosing 'the flower of one call'd *Piorno* in Portugueeze.'[64] In the following March he writes to assure Collinson that all the trees sent by him have arrived safely except the one that he valued most, a single example of 'the black American Larix' (*Larix pendula*) a rarity that had been introduced only in 1739. And he goes on to complain about the cost of other rarities, while acknowledging that he must have them: 'The small magnolias [*Magnolia grandiflora*] are confounded dear, . . . The white cedar [*Chamaecyparis thyoides*] is also excessively dear; 'tho I shant grudge that, if 'tis a good plant, as there is but one of them.'

Richmond also remained in touch with the Duke of Argyll, whose letter of 26 April 1748 shows that both men continued to extend the arboreal repertoire of the landscape garden:

> The Larix Your Grace mentioned is one I raised from Seed I had from Archangel [in Russia], which I bid my Gardener send with the plants I call the Russia Balm of Gilead [*Abies sibirica*]; this Larix I had forgot; but doubting whether Your Grace had any of them I thought to send it; I find these Russia Larix's seem to dislike hot Weather, and are plainly a different kind from that of Germany. I observe these Russian Balm of Gileads have a pale green bud instead of the purplish red bud of the New England kind, I have none larger than these I have sent your Grace, so I dont yet know what other differences they [*sic*] may be.[65]

Both of these trees were also rarities. *Abies sibirica* is said not to have been introduced into Britain until the nineteenth century. Russian larch does not appear in the catalogue of the trees at Whitton and as a result is difficult to identify with any modern larch.

After 1748 the correspondence stops, but what we have is enough to suggest how the landscape at Goodwood was transformed from relatively barren grassland to an arboreal arcadia, along the lines suggested in Campbell's 1725 plan. That the creation of this landscape was intimately connected with the Duke's botanical interests is reflected in a letter of 28 November 1750 from Collinson to the recently bereaved Duchess. In it he seems as much distressed by the possible sale of the Duke's nurseries as by the Duke's death itself.[66]

A letter from Collinson to the Duke (27 August 1744) asks that Philip Miller be given a root of 'Climbing Euonymas of which you have plenty.'[67] A climbing euonymus (*Celastrus scandens*, introduced by Collinson in 1736) can only have been used in the gardens near the house, gardens for which there exist detailed instructions for floral planting among the Goodwood papers.[68] But plainly the Duke's planting interests extended far more widely. That he was interested in both and the inevitable transition and treaty between the two suggests the significance of his friendship with the Prince of Wales, then creating interesting new gardens of this kind both at Carlton House and Kew. Indeed, the Badeslade and Rocque engraving of Kew is dedicated to the Duke of Richmond.

Richmond's plantations, continued by his son, the third Duke, were not without their vicissitudes. Collinson records that 40,000 seedling Scotch pines were killed by 'Cock-Chafers' (a beetle sometimes called a May-bug) in 1759. But forty magnolias counted there by Collinson in the same year were in even more flourishing condition when he visited again with the Duke of Argyll in 1765. In 1762 he wrote to H. J. Fox (later Lord Holland): 'I am agreeably surprised with the Wonderfull progress and growth of so many Exotic Trees, that I remember in their Infant State, that now requires a Skillful Hand to control their Exuberance, and prevent their stifling their underling Neighbours.' He went on to account for his time there: pruning, looking at nurseries 'and Informing great Designs, for Planting and Improving, the Environs.' What seemed to have pleased him most was the redemption of an otherwise barren soil to husbandry and beauty. It was, he wrote, 'a glorious Scene to see these Barren Moorlans [*sic*] Shaded with Verdant Woods. this extensive Plantation you know is Begun, the true Richmond Spirit will carry it one [*sic*], not only to give Himself pleasure, but Profitt to his Posterity.'[69]

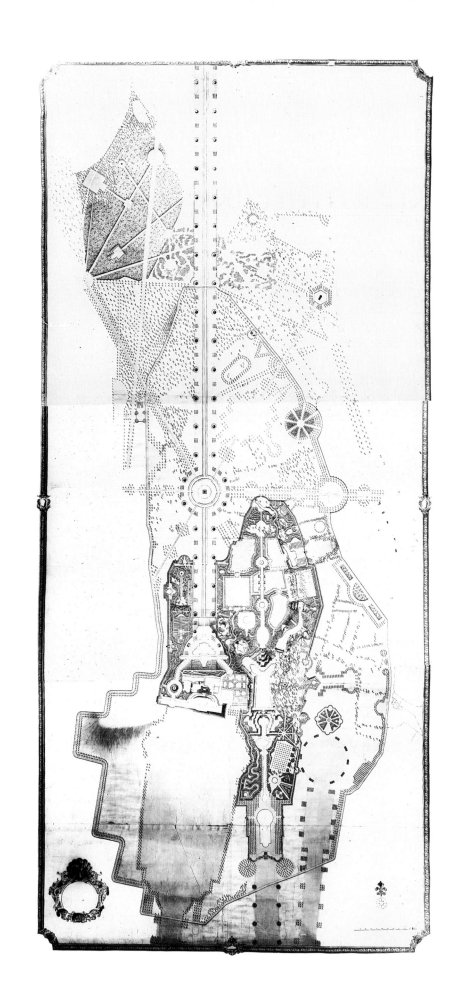

73. Robert James, Baron Petre,
Finished Plan of Thorndon Park,
Essex (c. 1740). Essex County Record
Office.

7

PAINTING WITH LIVING PENCILS:
LORD PETRE

Robert James, eighth Baron Petre of Writtle, came to gardening later than the Duke of Argyll but made up for it in the scale of his enterprise (over 1,000 acres as compared to Argyll's fifty-five).[1] At his estate, Thorndon Hall in Essex, [Fig. 73] Petre not only had a vast nursery (in fact a series of nurseries) but a large park. The amateur botanist, Peter Collinson, who himself introduced fifty-two species into Britain, described Petre in 1733 working continually at two great plans of his garden and park. These plans were the basis for the plan that survives, a finished version done by the French 'surveyor' Bourgignon d'Anville, who was later to become more famous as the engraver Gravelot.[2]

Nor were Petre's gardening projects confined to his own estate.[3] In 1738 he drew up a plan (once again rendered in a finished form by Bourgignon) for Worksop in Nottinghamshire, the seat of the Duke of Norfolk, a kinsman and fellow Catholic. [Fig. 74] There, for an estate even bigger than his own (1,700 acres), he created a design for a landscape garden of 370 acres that included a very much enlarged copy of Kent's Temple of British Worthies at Stowe (1735) and a copy of Lord Herbert's Palladian Bridge at Wilton (1737), which he used to link two islands in a proposed lake of 130 acres. [Fig. 75]

Petre also understood the theatrical use of receding spaces of different shapes to entice the viewer out into the landscape, a technique characteristic of William Kent's landscapes. Indeed, in his 'clumping' of trees for this purpose, Petre anticipated not only Brown's later designs but Kent's practice at Euston in the 1740s.[4] In the plans for both Thorndon and Worksop one can see the peripheral disposition of trees in the manner called for by Stephen Switzer in his essay 'A Dissertation on the Antient and Modern Villa's':

> To conclude this Part, the raising or planting of Wood in Hills rather than Vales, adds greatly to the Beauty of any Place, when beheld from afar, which is visible in several Groves, Clumps or Compartiments of Wood, many of them but small, which one sees at a Distance . . . it being certain, that one Tree on a Hill adds more Beauty to a Seat, and looks better than six, I had almost said ten, in a Bottom.[5]

Not surprisingly, Switzer's *The Nobleman, Gentleman and Gardener's Recreation* (1715) was in Lord Petre's library, along with such other classics of the new style as Batty Langley's *New Principles of Gardening* (1728), many copies of the three editions of *The Gardeners Dictionary* published before Lord Petre's death, and Richard Bradley's *A Philosophical Treatise of Husbandry* (1721).[6] By 1728, Langley could propose a graduated scheme for planting shrubs similar to

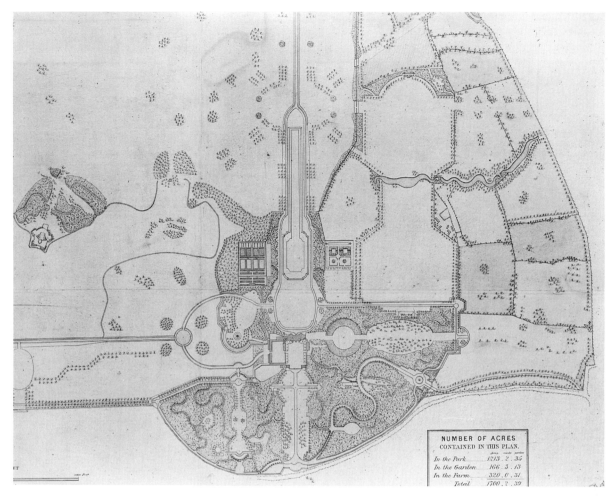

NUMBER OF ACRES
CONTAINED IN THIS PLAN.

	acres. roods. perches.
In the Park	1213 . 2 . 35
In the Garden	166 . 3 . 43
In the Farm	320 . 0 . 31
Total	1700 . 2 . 39

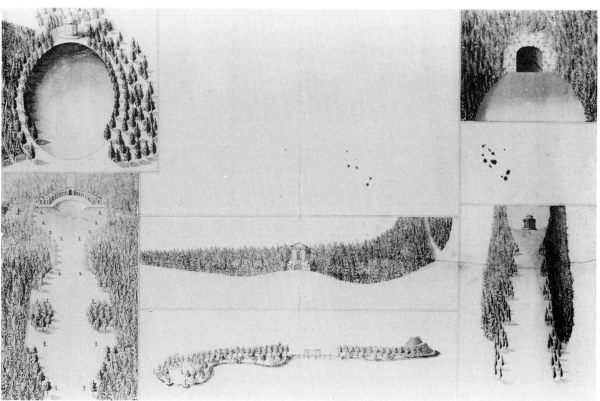

the disposition of trees and shrubs that Lord Petre was to use in the forecourt at Worksop. Referring scathingly to Bradley's claim to have invented such a method of planting flowers, he wrote that graduated planting was as well known 'as that seven Days make one Week, or twenty four Hours, a natural Day.'[7] But Petre was to go further in this than Langley or Miller suggested.

What Petre's plan for Worksop, like that for Thorndon, demonstrates is that 'calling in of the country' that Pope requested in the 'Epistle to Burlington' (1733) and for which Switzer's ideas of 'rural gardening' led the way. On the plan of Thorndon there are plainly arable fields to be seen in the midst of the design. We are a long way not only from the 'Modern [French] Designs [where] we see all at once, and lose, the Pleasure of Expectation,'[8] but even from the attempts by Batty Langley to break out of the constricting regularities of that and the Dutch style only a decade earlier in his *New Principles*. Even the work of Kent at Stowe, Claremont, or Carlton House was on nothing like this scale.

Nearly two decades before Hogarth's *Analysis of Beauty* defined it as a serpentine line within a geometrical form, Petre was putting into practice that very English contribution to variety at Worksop. His planting plans, more-over, show him committed to another aspect of variety in his use of many different sorts of trees and shrubs, a commitment by which Pope's friend, Joseph Spence, distinguished him from Kent.[9]

One need only compare his planting at Worksop with Lord Bathurst's two decades earlier at Cirencester to see how Petre's sense of colour and shape altered the scope of the design. The ground-plan of both estates would suggest that the planting near the house was very similar. Both houses had what amounted to a large circular forecourt surrounded by trees that, in Christopher Hussey's phrase, translated 'into vegetation such Baroque forecourts as that originally confronting Burlington House.'[10] But plans are not, in themselves, any more trustworthy evidence of what was there than plot summaries are representative of the novels they purport to encapsulate. Whereas the three-quarter circle at Cirencester was a monumental yew hedge twenty-five feet high, the ellipse at Worksop was an ampitheatre made of many trees of different colours, shapes and sizes. [Fig. 76]

Around the great oval lawn to the south of the house, Petre planned a belt of fourteen different evergreens some thirty feet deep, from Scotch pines (used as nurse trees) at the back to a box hedge at the front. This belt included spruce fir (*Picea abies*), silver fir (*Abies alba*), pinaster (*Pinus pinaster*), striped holly (*Ilex aquifolium* 'Ferox Argentea'), red cedar (*Juniperus virginiana*), laurel (*Prunus laurocerasus*), laurustinus (*Viburnum tinus*), yew (*Taxus baccata*), Swedish juniper (*Juniperus communis* 'Suecica'), arbutus (*A. unedo*), alaternus (*Rhamnus alaternus*), phillyrea (probably *P. latifolia*), and box (*Buxus sempervirens*). [Fig. 77] Petre seems here to have put elaborately into practice hints suggested by Miller in the 1731 and 1739 editions of *The Gardeners Dictionary*, both of which were in his library. Miller's concept of an evergreen wilderness containing varying lights and shades of green is reflected in Petre's practice, where 'the species are always disposed to contrast with the one behind.'[11] His choice of trees and shrubs here was more conservative than what he was employing in his own landscape garden at the same time, probably because Worksop did not have available the numbers of exotic trees that were readily to hand from the nurseries and 'stoves' at Thorndon. Firs, yews, alaternus, and phillyrea, for example, had been used in 1684 by Sir Robert Southwell in the creation of his garden at Kingweston in Somerset. At Thorndon, on the other hand, Philip

74 (facing above). Robert James, Baron Petre, Plan of Worksop, Notts. (1738) Country Life Photo.

75 (facing below). Robert James, Baron Petre, Architectural Elements for the Landscape at Worksop (1738). Essex County Record Office.

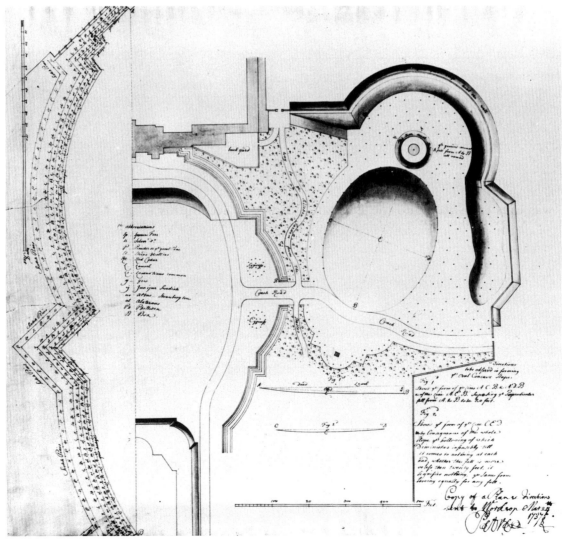

Miller's 1736 catalogue of the garden lists ten species of pine, six junipers, four laurels, and four laurustinus.

At both houses, however, Petre would have been concerned with the relation between house and landscape and the 'translation' between the two that also concerned Switzer. Like Switzer, he also looked to the Augustan sources of the new ideas of landscape. Not only did he sponsor John Martyn's edition of the *Georgics*, known as the *Flora Virgiliana*, but he supported the local classical scholar, Thomas Cooke, in his work. Cooke's 'Epistle the Third', dedicated to the Earl of Pembroke, praises him in conventionally georgic terms, terms that might even more forcefully be applied to Lord Petre:

> Hail to those Shades where now my Genius roves,
> Zealous to wait you thro the silent Groves
> I wait you there with philosophic Eyes,
> In your more boasted Titles, good and wise,
> Searching thro Nature all her perfect Laws,
> And tracing from th'Effect the secret Cause.[12]

Petre was also typically Augustan in his interest in Palladian architecture. Not only was his library well stocked with such English classics as Colen Campbell's *Vitruvius Britannicus* (1739), James Gibbs's *Book of Architecture* (1728), and Isaac Ware's editions of Inigo Jones's work, but he also had Ware's *Palladio in English* (1738) and the Italian edition of Palladio done by Giacomo Leoni in 1721. Leoni was, in fact, commissioned by Petre to design a Palladian house for him, a project never completed in Petre's lifetime.

What would have been most striking in his Palladian 'translation' of the architecture of the house at Worksop into the landscape, would have been the columnar form of the 'Red Cedar' (in fact, a Virginia juniper). Sometimes called the eastern red cedar, it was introduced in the late seventeenth century. Although it was recommended by Stephen Switzer in *The Practical Husbandman* (1733), it was only beginning to be widely used in the 1720s. Its pre-Linnean label, suggesting as it did the tree's similarity to the cypress (*foliis inferioribus juniperiis superioribus Sabinam vel Cypressum referentibus*), is a nice instance of garden 'translation'. The cypress, a tree associated with the classical Roman and Italian villa, was thus translated into the English landscape to accompany another translation, the Palladian villa, and was itself translated into another tree altogether, the American red cedar.

In its use of evergreen groves and in the species employed, Petre's planting at Worksop could be described as 'similar horticulturally to the planting of evergreen groves as described by Dezallier d'Argenville' in *La Théorie et la pratique du jardinage* (1709), another book in Petre's library.[13] Indeed both Thomas Fairchild (in *The City Gardener*, 1722) and Batty Langley (in *New Principles of Gardening*, 1728) described schemes of graduated planting of shrubs and trees according to height. Worksop, however, provides the first evidence of such recommendations being put into practice.

At this time Philip Southcote, who created the first acknowledged *ferme ornée*, Wooburn Farm, and was the son of Petre's guardian, compared Petre's work at Worksop to that of the well-known nurseryman, Christopher Gray of Fulham (1694–1763):[14] 'He was as much a nursery-man as Gray, and understood the colours of every tree, and always considered how he placed them by one another.'[15] In a letter written to Southcote in 1752, Collinson similarly praised as 'painting with Living pencils . . . the Mixture of Trees and their various Shades of Green' at Thorndon.[16]

76 (facing above). Forecourt of Worksop in the 1760s, from P. Russell, *England Displayed* (1769). Thomas Fisher Library, University of Toronto.

77 (facing below). Robert James, Baron Petre, Finished plan of Oval Forcourt with Plan of Hedge Planting, Worksop, 1738. Essex County Record Office.

78. Robert James, Baron Petre, Plan of Clumps for Worksop, (c. 1738). Essex County Record Office.

Another and rougher plan for Worksop, probably for hillside clumps south and east of the house, also exists. [Fig. 78] It is the only working drawing in Petre's hand that survives; except for some numbers put on the plan by Bourgignon, the writing is entirely in Petre's hand. Whereas the planting of the forecourt of the house has a detailed symmetry, the planting of the hillside clumps is free and in drifts in a way that seems quite modern. Petre's large finished plan of the estate shows the same blocks of regular and rectangular planting near the main vista that he also used in the landscape at Thorndon and Notley and at Gisburn[17] in Yorkshire. At Worksop and Thorndon, however, there were also irregular swirled and elevated clumps in which the planting itself was also swirled in drifts.

In the largest of these a roughly S-shaped clump has a central ridge of English oak and beech with 'Chesnuts intermixt all over ye Piece' and pine, Scotch pine, poplar, larch, and whitebeam (*Sorbus aria*) scattered throughout. A node of Scotch pine, pine, silver fir, larch, and pinaster sits about one-third of the way down this central plantation, and on the edges variously are plantations of Scotch pine and pinasters; beech, cherry, larch, and poplar; box backed by yew and laurel; a mixture of Scotch pine, pine, and spruce fir (*Picea alba* or *P. mariana*); evergreen oak with larch; and single smaller plantations of Scotch pine or pinaster.

108

Most of the edge plantations are numbered and Petre's notes on them are indicative of the meticulous care with which these arboreal landscape effects were created. Of the evergreen oak with larch, for example, he writes: 'Theas Clumps Must be from 20 to 50 feet diameter and irregularly dispers'd over the whole piece att from 80 to 150 feet apart.' That the effect of the larger clumps was intended to be as dramatic as Capability Brown's famous arboreal 'punctuation' is also evident in Petre's direction for the plantation of Scotch pine, pine, and spruce fir that occurs next to the previous group of evergreen oak and larch. 'This Long Clump of Sp[ruce] Fir Silver Fir. etc etc,' he writes, 'is intended to be plac'd upon that Knowl that was just above the Gate that was first sett in the new fence so that if t[h]ose not fall out right by the Plan it must be sett right and the piece of Box and of Yews and Holly must be plac'd just under it whear it is nearest to the out Line and the hill is most upright.'

Nothing is left to chance in these planting plans. It seems a wonder that Petre had any time to get on with his own estate; yet throughout this period he was still planting out thousands of trees at Thorndon from his nurseries. One of the other clumps on the Worksop plan is lettered to correspond to marginal plantations on a clump, and for each there are meticulous directions. 'Theas Clumps must consist of 5 or 6 trees each, and be plas'd att from 30 to 80 feet apart,' he writes of a group of yews and pinasters. And of another of box and spruce fir he sets down: 'it must also be observ'd that where *Some Yews towards this Line* are orderd it is intended that thay should be mix'd very full with the Box from 15 to 30 feet deep next the Line.'[18]

Instrumental in the planting of Worksop was Petre's friend Collinson, [Fig. 79] who in 1762 wrote an account of its inception and its present appearance:

> At the Request of Lord Petre of Thorndon Hall Essex I procured Stone Pine Tree Kernels for himself and for the Duke of Norfolk to Sow at Worsop [*sic*] in Notinghamshire From Leghorn Anno 1740 and a Hodshead of Italian Oaks—These Two Pines and Oakes are vastly grown and make a Noble Effect on the Hills planted with them In the Parke at Worsop—now anno 1762 . . . Anno 1741 I procur'd a Great Quantity of Silver Firr Cones for Lord Petre from Nuremberg for they Grow on all the Hills round that Citty . . . Bought great Quantity of Chesnutt for the D. Norfolk to be Sown at Worsop: 1741—now fine Trees 1762.[19]

That Petre's designs for Worksop were never completely executed, however, is scarcely surprising. In 1743–44, £1287 13s 1d. was spent on the grounds, and Philip Yorke then expressed the belief that the improvements were 'so vast and expensive that it is scarce possible they can ever be completed.'[20] Only six years later, however, Richard Pococke described the appearance and continuing implementation of Petre's plans and the reasons of husbandry that lay behind them:

> All the plantations are made on Lord Petre's Plan, who had the greatest genious for these improvements. and there are 1700 acres under improvements: the ground is very fine ['finely situated' cancelled] there being a low ground which winds round the higher Hills that open in one part: and on each side of it, are several little hills, divided by dales, which are planted with Clumps of trees, mostly Evergreens, and among them the Larch, which is very beautiful when they leave the boughes to grow from the bottom. On the top of the farthest hills to the west there is to be a Temple; and about the middle of the designed water, a bridge in the manner and style of Ld Pembrokes—and at the North East end of the water is to be a

79. Peter Collinson, from James Fothergill, *Works* (1781). Thomas Fisher Library, University of Toronto.

Grotesque building under a hill with a grotto, all which is drawn out according to Ld Petre's design—and they are ploughing up the Park by degrees in order to bring in the ground;—for the large Parks in this country seem for the most part originally to be large Commons enclosed, being a sandy poor soil, which naturally produces little but fern.[21]

At Thorndon Petre could plant and design as he liked, though the 'genius of the place' would have suggested extensive tree plantations, partly because, as at Worksop, the soil was very barren and would support little else, and partly because of the wooded appearance of the surrounding landscape. In 1735 John Loveday of Caversham said that 'this part of Essex [was] perhaps as wood-land a Countrey as any in England.'[22] Peter Collinson gives an extensive description of the wooded appearance of the estate only five years later, in 1740:

At Thorndon in Essex near Brentwood Lord Petre in the year 1740 Finished the Esplanade on the Top of the Park and then Planted the Two Mounts which He raised att a great Expence—the Mount near the new Church is Raised over the Ground about 91 feet high The Tops of the Mounts are planted with a Cedar of Lebanon about 6 or 7 feet High and Twenty years old from Seed there is four Smaller Ones on Each Side the Great One that are about Two Feet high and Tenn years old—The Larix's about them are 3 feet High and Tenn years old The Mounts are mostly planted with Red Virginia Cedars 3 yrs old being Raised from Seed from Pennsilvania with other Evergreens of His Raising The Four Clumps of Larix on Each Side the Road next the park gates was then about 7 or 8 foot High and Tenn years old.

Twenty years later, in 1760, he was able to add that the effect of these, mixed with Virginian red cedars, now 'made an amazing fine appearance.'[23]

All the other Plantations below the Esplanade was planted this year 1740 in April and May being mostly of Trees of his Lordships Raising from Seed . . . Some Sweet Chestnuts He planted when a Boye are being Removed from the Seed Nursery In Tenn Years Time arrived to 20 foot high and Two foot Next the Ground, this is a great Encouragement for all to plant.[24]

In 1762 Collinson also wrote a testimonial to one aspect of Petre's pioneering work in landscape design in his copy of Miller's *Dictionary*: 'Lord Petre, who was the ornament and delight of the age he lived in, removed, in the spring of 1734, twenty-four full-grown elms about 60 ft. high, and 2 ft. in diameter: all grew finely, and now (1764) are not known from the old trees they were planted to match.'[25] Loudon (who quotes this passage) goes on to observe that in 1738 Petre 'planted an avenue of elms 15 or 20 years old, cedars 20 years old, and larches 11 years old.'

This invention in landscape design has traditionally been credited to Capability Brown: his moving the trees of Bridgeman's regular design at Stowe to create a more irregular vista to the lake. It is further evidence of how Brown's work depended not just on the botanists and designers who preceded him but upon the co-operation between the two that was worked out in the early part of the century.[26]

In his large and uncollected correspondence, chiefly with other botanists, Collinson offers other testimonials to Petre's abilities. One of these correspondents was the American Quaker, John Bartram, whom Collinson employed to gather seeds and living specimens. [Fig. 80] When Collinson refers to 'a Gent that has a Villa planted on Every Side with Exoticks, collected

A List of Seeds of Forest Trees & Flowering Shrubs Gather'd in Pensilvania, the Jerseys & New York By John & William Bartram & sent over these years to their Correspondents, being the largest Collection that has ever before been Imported into this Kingdom Anno 1755

1 Benjamin or allspice Tree
2 Magnolia
3 Red Cedar
4 White Cedar or Cypress
5 Broad Leaved Evonymus
6 Cephalanthus, Button Wood
7 Judas Tree
8 Sugar Mapple
9 & 10 Myrtle
11 Dogwood
12 Holley
13 Evergreen Rhamnus
14 Jersey Tea plant
15 Nissa or Tupelo Tree
16 Dwarf Sumach
17 Hemlock, Silver Spruce firr
18 Sarsafrass
19 Three Leafed or Frankincense pine
20 Tulip Tree
21 Two Leafed Tough Pine
22 North American aria
23 Swamp Service
24 Viburnam with black...
25 poplar Leafed Birch
26 Female Cornus
27 Beach Sumach
28 Arrow Wood
29 Evergreen privet or Ilex Amis
30 acacia or Locust Tree
31 Horn Beam
32 Hop Horn Beam

33 Two Leafed Pine
34 White Ash
35 Balm Gilead Firr
36 deper Rhododendron or Mountain Laurel
37 Greater Ditto
38 Dwarf Pine
39 Beach Nutts
40 Toxicodendron
41 Hamamelis or Witch Hazel
42 Mountain Spruce Firr
43 White Walnutts
44 Celtis or Nettle Tree
45 Arbor Vitae
46 aralia spinosa angelica Tree
47 Scruby White Oke
48 Tough Twigg'd Viburnam
49 azalea or Honeysuckle
50 Mountain Red Oke
51 Great Shagbark Hickery or Hatter Nutts
52 Scarlet Oke
53 Willow Leafed Oke
54 Broad Willow Leafed Oke
55 Great Fern...
56 White Oke
57 Dwarf Red Oke
58 Prinos or Red Winterberry
59 Clethra, Sweet Spire
60 Mountain Red Oke
61 Three Leafed Mountain Pine
62 anona or papaw apple
63 Black Mulberry
64 Great Cranberries

65 Beach Cherry
66 Spanish Swamp Oke
67 Bastard Ditto
68 Climbing Evonymus
69 Swamp Chesnutt Oke
70 Mountain Ditto
71 Swamp Broadleafed Ditto
72 Sweet Gum Tree
73 Honey Locust Tree
74 Sumach
75 Black Walnutts
76 Evergreen Evonymus
77 Dwarf Cluster Cherry
78 Early Harth Service
79 Sweet Service
80 Andromeda
81 Lime Tree
82 Alder Tree
83 Staphylodendron
84 Deciduous Cypress
85 Platanus plane Tree
86 Ash Leafed Mapple
87 Red & White Pine... boom
88 Persimon Fruit
89 Upland Roses
90 Mountain Laurel is Thyme Leaves

91 Broadleaf'd Andromeda
92 Narrow Leafed Thorn
93 Great Cluster berry
94 Dwarf Round Leafed Cherry
95 Menispermum
96 Swamp Spruce Firr
97 5 Leafed Canada Pine
98 Dwarf Chesnutt Oke
99 Tall azalea
100 Toxicodendron

On the latter side of Oct.r 1764 — Old Tom the Favourite Cat of a Gentleman on the Excise after 3 Days illness Died aged 18 year & half a Rare Instance of the Longevity of this animal, Seldom attaining to 11:12 or 13 years in the usual length

80. Peter Collinson, 'A List of Seeds of Forest Trees & Flowering Shrubs Gather'd in Pensilvania.' Linnean Society, London.

by a person sent by me into america,' the 'Gent' is probably Lord Petre and the 'person' Bartram.[27] Indeed, Loudon credits Collinson with having introduced into England 'the greater number of species' of trees in the early part of the eighteenth century.[28]

In *The Practical Husbandman and Planter* (1733), it was one of Stephen Switzer's criticisms of Moses Cook that he 'confined himself only to Indeginous [sic] plants.' Whereas, Switzer continues,

> if there is any one that would strive to bring the raising and planting of Forest Trees to their utmost Perfection, he ought not to be content with treating barely on those Plants which grow at Home, but ought by all means to endeavour at such an Introduction of foreign Trees and Plants from Climates of equal Temperature, or (if possible) from Climates which are colder than ours is.[29]

Collinson himself pays frequent tribute to the work of Lord Petre in this naturalising of imported specimens. And just such a point had been made three years earlier in the *Catalogus Plantarum*, published 'By a Society of Gardeners' and probably written by the Chelsea gardener, Philip Miller:

> *As for such Persons who make little Account of the introducing* Exotick Trees *and* Plants *among us, it will be sufficient to desire them to look back and see what we originally had of our own spontaneous Growth, and in how poor a Condition we had still been, had not our Forefathers introduced those many noble Trees for Shade, and those many excellent Fruits for gratifying our Palates, and those numerous Varieties of beautiful and odoriferous Flowers to delight the Senses, which we now enjoy in such Plenty, few of which being the original Product of our own Island.*[30]

Although both Evelyn's *Sylva* and Cook's *The Manner of Raising Forest Trees* were in his library, Petre had moved far beyond what either man had been able to achieve botanically. In a letter to Bartram on 1 September 1741 Collinson writes:

> The trees and shrubs raised from thy first seeds, are grown to great maturity. Last year Lord PETRE planted out about ten thousand Americans [i.e. trees and shrubs], which, being at the same time mixed with about twenty thousand Europeans, and some Asians, make a very beautiful appearance;— great art and skill being shown in consulting every one's particular growth, and the well blending the variety of greens. Dark green being a great foil to lighter ones, and bluish green to yellow ones, and those trees that have their bark and back of their leaves of white, or silver, make a beautiful contrast with the others.
>
> The whole is planted in thickets and clumps, and with these mixtures are perfectly picturesque, and have a delightful effect. This will just give thee a faint idea of the method Lord PETRE plants in, which has not been so happily executed by any: and, indeed, they want the materials, whilst his lordship has them in plenty.[31]

In a letter to Philip Southcote a decade later, Collinson wrote specifically of the trees with which these effects were achieved.

> The Effect must be Charming to see the Dark Green Elm with the Lighter Shades of the Lime and Beach—or the yellowish Green planes with the Silver Leafed Abele the Chesnut the oak and ash and the poplar the Acacia and Horse Chesnutt *cum multis aliis*, when Fann'd by a Gentle Breese then how Beautifully the Contrast, how delightfully the light and shades fall in to Diversifie the Sylvan Scene.[32]

Miller's catalogue of nearly 700 species of plants growing in Petre's garden and nurseries in 1736 is evidence of the extent of these materials. Only occasionally, however, as in Collinson's descriptions of the planting of the avenues and mounts, do we get a glimpse of how these plants were disposed. What is evident in Miller's list, though, is the large place of new American species, from trees as understated as the American larch or the deciduous cypress to ones as startling as the 'Silk Cotton tree with a thick Marsh Mallow leaf and an oblong pod' (*Ceiba*).

What is noteworthy about Collinson's account of Lord Petre's planting is that his observations combine design with botany. He writes not simply as a taxonomist but as a practising gardener concerned with aesthetic effects—here, effects on a very large scale but dependent upon the minutiae of foliage arrangement. That Petre himself was concerned with both tree husbandry and aesthetic effect is evident even in his library. On the one hand were many such books of husbandry as Langley's *A Sure Method of Improving Estates By the Planting of Forest Trees* (1728) and on the other 'A Bundle of three large, two midling, and three small designs of American Trees etc., done in Colours.'

Petre's achievements at Thorndon would have been impossible, Collinson notes, without access to the materials readily to hand in his extensive nursery: 'His nursery being fully stocked with flowering shrubs, of all sorts that can be procured,—with these, he borders the outskirts of all his plantations: and he continues, annually, raising from seed, and layering, budding, grafting—that twenty thousand trees are hardly to be missed out of his nurseries.'

There is, unfortunately, no evidence of how Petre 'bordered the outskirts of his plantations' at Thorndon, but there is evidence of what he had available: four kinds of alaternus, three of holly (including one from Carolina), a golden cassinia described as being like a phillyrea that comes from Carolina but is called 'The Cashiobery bush' (*Viburnum cassinoides*), four kinds of laurel and of privet, and twenty-two kinds of roses. Peter Collinson, moreover, gives some hints about Lord Petre's planting at Thorndon in a 1752 letter to Petre's relation, Philip Southcote. Having talked about the importance of colour effects in the planting of trees and shrubs, what he calls 'painting in planting to show the Contrast of Light and Shade,' Collinson continues:

> These Observations lead the Late Noble Lord Petre at Thorndon in Essex to Coppy Beautifull Nature in his beautiful plantations on Each Side, enrich[ed] with the Trees of America from the Lodge in the Great Avenue up to the Esplanade at the Head of the Park. These was his first Essays or I may call them but Lines of the Grand picture Had he Lived, the Vast Variety of Materials that he had collected together would have shown with what a Masterly and Skillful hand He would have given the finishing Strokes, to his Extensive plans.
>
> This compound objects has the Like Good Effect on the Ever Grees [*sic*], the Pines and Firrs, the Yew and the Variegated Holley and Phileree etc. etc. how beautifull the Scene when Sufferd to Grow unconfined in Groves and Thickets.[33]

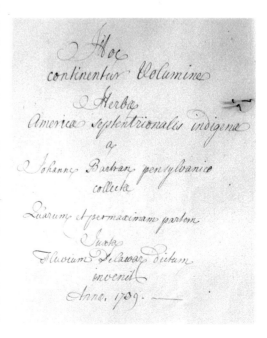

81. Title-page from Vol. 5 of Lord Petre's *Hortus Siccus*. Sutro Library, San Francisco.

To Collinson, as presumably to his friend Petre, there was no divorce between botany and the imagination. The landscape and the greenhouse were part of one continuum in his account of Petre's plantations of trees and the pineapples (of which Petre had four kinds) served at his table: 'When I walk amongst them [the plantations], one cannot well help thinking he is in North American thickets, there are such quantities. But, to be at his table, one would think South America was really there,—to see a servant come in every day, with a dozen Pine Apples—as much as he can carry.'[34]

Lord Petre's botanic importations from America are recorded in a *Hortus Siccus* or herbarium of plant specimens that extends to sixteen volumes and more than 1,500 pages.[35] [Fig. 81] Compiled at Thorndon around 1740, it reveals not only the enormous quantity of new botanic material but the great confusion in botanical nomenclature under which the science still laboured at that time. Petre's *Hortus Siccus* is composed of material from at least three sources.

Eleven of the volumes contain Caribbean plants gathered by the ship's surgeon, William Houstoun, whose plant-collecting Lord Petre underwrote in 1731–33. Two other volumes, of English plants and mosses, represent the collecting labours of Sir John Hill, an apothecary and enthusiastic botanist who appears in the correspondence of Collinson and the Duke of Richmond and against whom John Boyle wrote a mocking pamphlet. Hill also seems to have annotated and identified specimens in the other volumes. But, so far as Lord Petre's reshaping of his landscape at Thorndon is concerned, by far the most interesting parts of the work are the American contributions of John Bartram.

Miller's catalogue of the plants in the grounds was made in 1736, and Collinson's note on the flyleaf indicates that Petre's 'vast Plantations [were] greatly increased before his Death' in 1742. It is therefore impossible now to determine how many of the trees and plants included in the *Hortus Siccus* were actually cultivated at Thorndon. That collection nonetheless indicates the huge range of plant and tree materials suddenly available to Peter Collinson's circle of subscribers as a result of the collecting labours of John Bartram.

Representing Bartram's trips that extended as far north as Albany in New York State and as far south as Virginia, the plants in this herbarium indicate that, for example, Petre might have made use of a wide range of shrubs. These include many still uncommon viburnums, *Rhus* (probably sumach), bittersweet, holly, and elder. Although none of these plants was unknown in England at the time, the Whitton catalogue indicates that many new species were being brought in from America and that, in some cases, the Duke of Argyll did not have examples that were in Lord Petre's collection. Seventeen

82. *Pseudo acacia americana* from Vol. 6 of Lord Petre's *Hortus Siuccus*. Sutro Library, San Francisco.

83 (below right). *Acer Pensylvanica* with John Bartram's annotation, from Vol. 12 of Lord Petre's *Hortus Siccus*. Sutro Library, San Francisco.

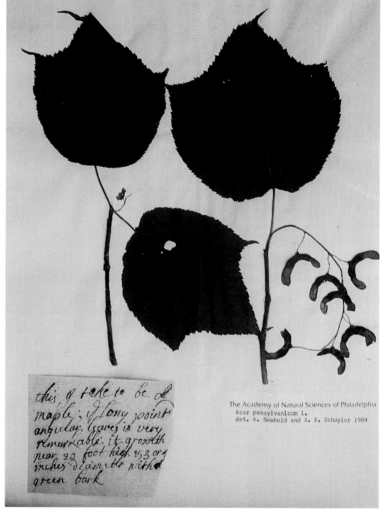

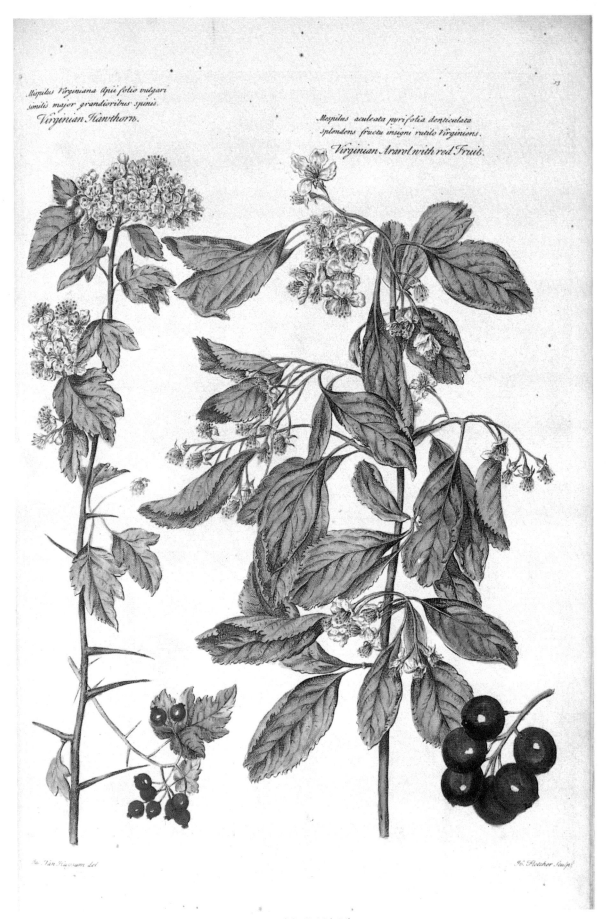

Mespilus Virginiana Apii folio vulgari
similis major grandioribus spinis.
Virginian Hawthorn.

Mespilus aculeata pyrifolia denticulata
splendens fructu insigni rutilo Virginiens.
Virginian Ararol with red Fruit.

84. Hawthorn from *Catalogus Plantarum* (1730). Trustees of the British Library.

85. 'Our black or saw gum' identified in John Bartram's hand from Vol. 12 of Lord Petre's *Hortus Siccus*. Sutro Library, San Francisco.

86. 'Our mountain hasel' identified in John Bartram's hand from Vol. 12 of Lord Petre's *Hortus Siccus*. Sutro Library, San Francisco.

sorts of acacia are also included (possibly encompassing both *Robinia* and *Gleditschia*)[36] [Fig. 82] as are six willows (Argyll had only three) and at least nine different maples. One of them, probably striped maple (*Acer pensylvanicum*) [Fig. 83], was plainly in his possession well before its recorded introduction in 1755, although it does not appear in Miller's list. 'This I take to be a maple,' writes Bartram; 'the long pointed angular leaves is very remarkable: it groweth near 20 foot high and 3 or 4 inches diameter with a green bark.'[37]

Doubtless the hawthorns (*Crataegus*) included several from Virginia identified in the Whitton list, though it is indicative of the problem in tracing them that at least three of them, the 'Great thorn'd Virginia Haw with red fruit,' [Fig. 84] the 'Carolina Hawthorn with large yellow fruit' and the 'American Hawthorn with a Narrow Almond leaf,' appear in Miller's list under a completely different genus, *Mespilus* (medlar). All of these descriptions raise the question whether Petre, like Joseph Spence later, thought of fruit-bearing trees in terms of their aesthetic effect. Certainly the bright fruit of the American hawthorns would have been a distinctive aspect of fall colour, a subject that also interested Sir John Hill. Miller's cataloguing also suggests that 'the double blossom peach' and 'The sweet scented Crab of Virginia' were just

The Academy of Natural Sciences of Philadelphia
Prunus maritima Marsh.
det. A. Newbold and A. E. Schuyler 1984

as important for their flowers as for their fruit.

Like Argyll, Petre appears to have had the American chestnut (*Castanea dentata*) long before its recorded introduction to England (1783).[38] The 'Black Gumm' [Fig. 85] referred to is probably a tupelo (*Nyssa sylvatica*) also recorded at Whitton in 1736, and his 'Mountain Hasel' is probably *Corylus cornuta* [Fig. 86] that is not recorded at Whitton until after Argyll's death. Argyll appears not to have had the *Toxicodendron* (poison sumach) or the sand cherry or 'Beech plum' (*Prunus maritima*) [Fig. 87] that appear in Petre's catalogue, though both men had the American Judas tree (*Cercis canadensis*) by the 1730s. Also known as redbud, its characteristic early dark-pink flowers would have made it attractive to a man as concerned with colour in planting as Petre was.

Within a decade, Bartram was to become one of the first naturalists to use Linnaeus's system of classification, but in 1739 he was unsure of the names of many of these specimens. So too was Lord Petre. His library contained most of the classic names of botanic literature: Bauhin, Commelin, Dillenius, Gronovius, Stephen Hales, Lobel, Malpighi, John Martyn, Mattioli, Plukenet, Plumier, Ray, Sloane, and Tournefort. There too was Linnaeus's *Hortus Cliffortianus* (1737) and at least seven others of Linnaeus's works tied up in

87. 'The beech plum or Chery' identified in John Bartram's hand from Vol. 12 of Lord Petre's *Hortus Siccus*. Sutro Library, San Francisco.

88. 'Lignum campechianum quoddam' from Vol. 8 of Lord Petre's *Hortus Siccus*. Sutro Library, San Francisco.

loose sheets in a bundle. But Linnean nomenclature was still not established, and the confusion of names, even to a man with (in Collinson's phrase) 'a great Ardour for every Branch of Botanic Science,' is reflected in the confusion of his *Hortus Siccus* and Miller's catalogue of his garden. Even with all the resources of this extensive botanical library, Petre was unable to identify *Lignum campechianum quoddam* which, he explains, the English call 'Logwood'.[39] [Fig. 88]

All of this puts into context his achievement at Thorndon where 10,000 American trees were planted by 1740, only five years after he began to subscribe to Collinson's scheme. It also explains the depth of Collinson's bereavement when Petre died in 1742. Collinson's grief at Lord Petre's premature death from smallpox was intense. 'I have lost my friend—my brother,'[40] he wrote to Bartram in 1742, and in 1744 he was still referring to Petre's death as 'the greatest loss that botany or gardening ever felt in this island.'[41] It is worth noting that he celebrated Petre not simply as a botanist but for the wide-ranging endowments of his mind:

> Few or none could excel him, in the knowledge of the liberal arts and sciences. He was a great mechanic, as well as a great mathematician; ready at figures and calculations—and elegant in his tastes.[42]

> His skill in all the liberal arts, particularly architecture, statuary, planning and designing, planting and embellishing his large parks and gardens, exceeds my talents to set forth.[43]

And elsewhere Collinson said that Petre had 'a fine Tast for Architecture and Drew and Designed well himself—a great Ardour for every Branch of Botanic Science—whoever sees his vast Plantations and his Catalogue will not doubt it—which was greatly increased before his death.'[44]

In 1740, eight years after the garden was begun, Lord Petre wrote to the Duke of Richmond that he was 'extremely taken up in finishing a large plantation which will contain about seven thousand trees.'[45] And Collinson noted in his copy of Evelyn's *Sylva*[46] a list of the 'Trees planted at the Upper End of the Park' at Thorndon. Of the fifty-three types listed, nearly 5,000 trees had been planted, and these constituted only about one quarter of the total plantation. A number of these had been introduced since the beginning of the century, some of them (such as the striped sycamore, probably *Acer pseudoplatanus* 'Variegata') by Petre himself through the agency of Bartram and Collinson.

Others, such as the Carolina oak (of which Petre had planted 230) and the weeping willow (161) had been introduced only a few years before he began work at Thorndon. The last had previously been planted by Pope in his garden at Twickenham, though it seems that Pope was not the first person to introduce the tree into England. Its first listing is in Robert Furber's catalogue of 1727, although Langley (in 1728) refers to its having been cultivated by Pope's landlords, the Vernons, at Twickenham Park. The red cedars (*Juniperus virginiana*) that Petre later used at Worksop are also recorded as having been used at Thorndon, where 562 were noted by Collinson as growing 'on upper Mount', 604 'on Lower Mount' and nineteen 'in clumps.' Although, like the 112 'Balm Gilead Firrs' also recorded there (the 'New England balm of Gilead' [*Abies balsamea*] catalogued at Whitton), they were introduced in the later part of the seventeenth century, their use seems not to have been common. Petre began to use them shortly after their first appearance in Furber's 1727 catalogue: the red cedars for columnar height, and the 'Balm Gilead Firrs' for a dense tree of medium height.

He also used larches extensively, possibly for the various effects of light against dark (noted by Collinson above) that are especially evident in this deciduous conifer. It was Collinson, in fact, who procured one species of larch (*Larix pendula*) for Lord Petre, and he gives an account both of this and the tree's introduction into England by Sir Theodore Janssen in 1712 in his marginal notes in *Sylva*:

> I went with Lord Petre to see them [he writes of the larches at Janssen's estate in Wimbledon] he was so charmed with them, that he procured Seed from Sr Theodore and Raised Vast Quantities and planted at the Head of the Park—in about 20 years. Some are a foot Diameter, his Example gave this fine Tree a Reputation and then Nursery Men began to Raise them—since they are seen in all plantations.[47]

In this mixed coniferous planting Petre satisfied, whether consciously or not, the thirteenth of Langley's Rules in *New Principles of Gardening* (1728): 'That the Slopes of Mounts, etc. be laid with a moderate Reclination, and planted with all Sorts of Ever-Greens in a promiscuous Manner, so as to grow all in a Thicket; which has a prodigious fine Effect.'[48]

Perhaps more importantly, Petre here began to move beyond the traditional use of the Mount as a place for vistas in a flat landscape: the sort of thing recommended by Pope to Lord Bathurst for his *ferme ornée*, Riskins, in Buckinghamshire. Here the mount became something not to be looked *from* but *at*; the density of its planting would have prevented any very satisfactory views. No longer a curiosity in a garden of various elements, it became itself a picturesque element in an overall composition. Throughout Thorndon, moreover, the planting itself invoked the landscape of antiquity: those 'Groves of Pines, Firrs, Cypress, Plane Trees, Beech, or such like' that Richard Bradley believed characterised the gardens of the ancients in contrast to the 'Knots or Flourishes' of modern gardens.[49]

Acacia Americana Abruæ foliis triacanthos. —
sive ad axillas foliorum spina triplici donata.

Three Thorn'd Acacia or Locust Tree.

H. Fletcher Sculp.

8

THE PRACTICAL PART OF GARDENING: BOTANISTS, GARDENERS, AND DESIGNERS

In 1730, just as Lord Petre was about to begin his horticultural career at Thorndon, a society of London gardeners published *Catalogus Plantarum ... A Catalogue of Trees and Shrubs*[1] that was intended to be the first of a series intended to include catalogues of other plants and flowers as well [Fig. 89] One of the members of this society was the gardener of the Chelsea Physic Garden, Philip Miller, who is also thought to be the most likely author of the preface to the *Catalogue*. Although the *Catalogus* was intended to address 'the practical Part of Gardening,' its dedication to the Earl of Pembroke indicates that its audience was larger than the owners of town and nursery gardens. What indeed is interesting in the list of pioneers and leaders of horticultural advancement is that it includes not only nurserymen and botanists but such makers of landscapes as the Earl of Islay (Whitton), Lord Wilmington (Wilbury), and the Earl of Pembroke (Wilton).

The ninth Earl of Pembroke's 'naturalistic' redesigning of his landscape has been adequately accounted for,[2] but what is sometimes overlooked is the importance of trees in accomplishing this landscape revolution. Miller might well be addressing many modern studies in garden history when he complains of books written about large pleasure gardens that 'many of them have been written by Persons of slender Skill in the Knowledge of particular Plants.'[3] His dedication to the Earl of Pembroke, moreover, makes plain the importance of botanical experimentation to the creation of new landscapes when he praises 'those noble Gardens at *Wilton*, where are a greater Number of the Trees here [in the *Catalogus*] treated of, and in a more flourishing Condition, than can be found in any one Garden in this Kingdom besides.'[4]

Were the *Catalogus* addressed only to botanical and horticultural experimentation or even the town garden, it would confine its observations to the kitchen garden and greenhouse with only an occasional aside on the pleasure garden. But much of the work addresses the suitability of trees and shrubs for 'wildernesses', i.e. the sort of wooded plantations for which the Earl of Pembroke is praised. And its concern for what is both practicable and practical in English landscape gardens is related to the problems of extensive planting. The advantage of knowing the various species of the genus *Quercus* (oak), for example, is so that 'we may continue a Plantation thro Soils of various Qualities, with trees of the same Genus.'[5] Where ground in such a plantation becomes marshy, the Carolina water-oak can be substituted for the English and the whole retain a unity of effect.

North American trees are indicative of the problem that vexed botanists and

89. Acacia from *Catalogus Plantarum* (1730). Trustees of the British Library.

121

gardeners increasingly by the beginning of the eighteenth century: the inadequacy of current taxonomic vocabulary to accommodate these '*new Kinds annually introduced into the* English *Gardens.*'[6] The *Catalogus* was published in the very year in which Linnaeus began to write his *Bibliotheca botanica*, the first essay in the work that was to emerge in 1753 as *Species Plantarum*, the foundation of modern botanical nomenclature. What the *Catalogus* reveals is the confusion of botanical names at the time, a confusion, says Miller, that means that '*Gentlemen very often send to Nursery Men for the same Kind of* Fruit, Plant, etc. *which they already have growing in their Gardens.*'[7] It was the apprehension that, with the introduction of many new plant types from other parts of the world, '*there was Reason to fear that the Confusion would still be greater,*'[8] that led the Society of Gardeners to publish the *Catalogus*.

The *Catalogus* was by no means the first evidence of the significance of botany to the makers of the new landscapes. Miller's claim that 'within the Space of fifty Years, the practical Part of Gardening began to rouze out of the long Lethargy it had lain in,'[9] was true both of botany and gardening, as his list of predecessors and contemporaries indicates. Mary Capel, sister of the Earl of Essex, who created Cassiobury, and wife of the first Duke of Beaufort, who created Badminton, was herself an eminent botanical pioneer both in her garden in Chelsea and at her great estate in Gloucestershire. Although she knew no Latin, she corresponded with the principal botanists and horticulturists of her time and employed one of those botanists, William Sherard, as a tutor for her grandson.

It is hard to say what effect her botanical introductions had on the great 'French' landscape of radiating avenues that her husband created at Badminton before 1700. Her obvious taste for exotic aromatic shrubs would have affected only the gardens near the house and many of her introductions, such as ironwood (*Sideroxylon*) and African evergreen oak (*Cliffortia illicifolia*), were not hardy in the British climate.[10]

Her contemporary, Henry Compton, Bishop of London (1675–1713), is a more telling case of this sort of influence. Peter Collinson described him at this time as 'a great lover of rare plants, as well such as came from the West Indies as from North America, and had the greatest collection then in England.'[11] In his botanically pioneering garden several future landscape gardeners worked, and of his influence on one of the partners in the London and Wise firm Switzer wrote: 'He was a great Encourager of Mr. *London*, . . . and probably very much assisted him in his great Designs.'[12]

Such botanical encouragement to owners and designers was not uncommon. In 1721 Richard Bradley, the future first Professor of Botany at Cambridge, published a translation and considerable revision of G. A. Agricola's *A Philosophical Treatise of Husbandry and Gardening*. Like the *Catalogus*, Bradley's translation was dedicated to the Earl of Pembroke, and its intentions were similarly to show 'the great Advantages that may be drawn from all the above described Methods, as well for the Improvement as the Encrease of *Plants*, whether in *Gardens, Plantations* about *Country-Seats*, or *Woods*.'[13] Bradley also writes of the enormous increase in trees and shrubs available to gardeners, and 'fine Exotick *Plants*, especially their number daily increasing, as it does at the Country-Seats of all Persons of Quality.'[14] His concern, expressed in the words of the French translator of Agricola, is that gardeners 'being only guided by Experience, are seldom led to make any Reflection upon the Principles of their Art.' Agricola, by contrast, 'joins Reason with Experience.'[15] This, Bradley says elsewhere, is what is required if gardeners are to be 'rank'd with great

Philosophers, and deserve Honour, rather than what the generality of Gardeners commonly meet with from the Publick.'[16] By insisting on the importance of reason to gardening experience, Agricola and Bradley also imply the converse: the importance of botanical experience to the theoretical conceptualising of garden design. More than a decade before Philip Southcote was to create his famous *ferme ornée* at Wooburn Farm and nearly a decade after Addison first suggested such a project, Bradley offers practical advice on how to effect such a combination of use and beauty. He advises his readers 'to multiply common FRUIT-TREES *to an almost infinite Degree; and to plant 'em in* GARDENS, FIELDS *and* WOODS.'[17]

Although Bradley published a *Dictionarium Botanicum* in 1728, it has almost nothing to say about trees and shrubs. His *Dictionary of Plants*, published in 1747, does, however, make a surprising number of comments about the utility of trees and shrubs in landscape gardening. By 1747 the 'arboreal revolution' was largely complete and Bradley was able to dedicate his book to 'the Improvement of Gardening and Plantations, which redounds so much to the Pleasure and Advantage of a Nation.'[18] Bradley's *Dictionary* in fact reflects his own practice and advice for the previous two decades. Certainly the *Dictionary*, in offering aesthetic advice, goes far beyond what its title suggests. Bradley's description of the beech, for example, offers advice which was originally contemporary with Lord Bathurst's extensive beech plantations at Cirencester in the 1720s and provides a justification for it that is a long way from merely practical silviculture: 'towards the End of Summer, a little before the Fall of the Leaf, a Wood of these Trees affords one of the finest prospects in Nature, giving us a View of the most agreeable Mixture of Colours I ever saw.'[19]

By the 1730s it was possible for Stephen Switzer to include even more 'philosophical' considerations for beech plantations in his *Practical Husbandman*. The beech, he wrote, is 'a Tree of that Elegancy and fine Verdure in Summer, and of so spreading a Nature, that under this Tree it might well enough be supposed (though Authors have given the Honour of it to another) that *Alexander* rested that Army with which he had almost over-run all the World.' Referring to Virgil's first *Eclogue*, Switzer says that it was under the beech, 'that *Virgil*, that Prince of Poets (in the Person of *Meliboeus*) introduces one of the best Poems that was ever wrote.'[20]

If Switzer exemplifies the close connection between design and husbandry in this period, Bradley also offers another instance of the close connection between botany and the putting of design into practice. He instances the sycamore as an unjustly despised tree and one that another eminent botanist, 'the ingenious Mr. *Peter Collinson*,' has discovered is 'the best Fence against violent Sea-Winds, where no other tree can thrive.'[21] This is confirmed by a 'particular Instance of the great Service, Benefit and Beauty of this . . . Tree . . . at *Morgam*, a Seat of Lord *Mansel*'s, near the Sea'[22] and followed by a recommendation the sycamore be more widely used in the Isle of Wight. One of Bradley's early patrons was Richard Balle, to whom Bradley dedicated his *Gentleman and Gardeners Kalendar* (1718). Balle's family possessed Mamhead in Devon, an estate celebrated for its plantation of forest trees. Indeed Balle's father, Sir Peter, is among the 'patriots of horticulture' that Loudon was to celebrate a century later.[23]

Writing of Bradley at the end of the century, Richard Pulteney remarked that it was Bradley's distinction 'to excite a more philosophical view' of both gardening and husbandry 'and diffuse a general and popular knowledge of them through the kingdom.'[24] One detects the tone of disapproval, however, in Pulteney's characterisation of Bradley as 'a popular writer on Gardening and Agriculture,'[25] a characterisation that reflects his dislike (in the same chapter) of the dubious means by which Bradley got the chair of botany at Cambridge.

Bradley's successor, John Martyn, was altogether more reputable and scholarly. Although he would have known some botany from his training as a physician, he made himself an accomplished botanist. He was also a classicist of some accomplishment and edited both the *Georgics* and the *Pastorals* of Virgil.[26] Martyn's particular affection for the *Georgics* was shared by Switzer and Pope and the first generation of 'rural gardeners', and he himself retired to a farm in Streatham in 1752. His edition, which includes both a translation and extensive botanical notes, is particularly impressive. The notes amounted, said his biographer, to a *Flora Virgiliana*, a botanical reconstruction of the Thessalian valley of Tempe from which Spence was to take the title of his uncompleted work on gardening and where a life of ease amid large farms had been the inspiration of Switzer's *ingentia rura*.[27]

If for Pope it was necessary to translate this Virgilian *ingentia rura* into English garden landscape, for Martyn it was necessary to reconcile ancient botany and modern practice. In the process he identified, for example, Virgil's cypress (*Georgics* II.443) as the Phoenician cedar (Linnaeus's *Juniperus phoenicea*) that had been introduced into England in 1683 and that, though cultivated by the Earl of Islay at Whitton, was still rare in the early eighteenth century.[28]

In writing this *Flora Virgiliana*, he not only affirmed the botanical work of such contemporary experimenters as Philip Miller and Sir Hans Sloane (both of whom subscribed to his edition)[29] but suggested what might be the materials of a poetic landscape. Even in his edition of the *Pastorals*, Martyn described the setting as 'a rural Scene, a sort of fine Landscape, painted by a masterly hand.'[30] If it is not surprising that John Dyer, the author of the famous landscape poem 'Grongar Hill' (1727), subscribed to Martyn's edition of the *Georgics*, then it is even less surprising that Lord Petre, the creator of such landscapes, was also a subscriber.[31]

What the botanical pioneers of the early eighteenth century ensured, as Pulteney observes, was that 'gardeners acquired botanical knowledge, and were excited to greater exertions in their art,'[32] an art that included garden-making as well as nursery horticulture. Of the four gardeners that Pulteney singles out for commendation—Thomas Fairchild, Thomas Knowlton, James Gordon, and Philip Miller—all were involved in garden-making in some way, and Knowlton and Gordon had worked for two of the greatest garden designers of the period, Lord Burlington and Lord Petre.

It is not clear upon what evidence David Neave claims that Thomas Knowlton was not enthusiastic about garden and landscape design.[33] Certainly Knowlton's antiquarian interests show that he was no mere botanist. In any case, the gardens and landscape at Londesborough had far more expended upon them, especially for trees, under his supervision than previously had been the case. Before 1739, to the west of the house, a 'wilderness' was made with serpentine paths that had strong similarities both to Pope's garden of twenty years earlier and to the gardens of Lord Burlington's relative, Sir Charles Hotham, nearby at South Dalton [Fig. 90].

The avenues in the park that Knowlton designed show the impact of botany on planting design. Two of these avenues were planted with Turkey oak (*Quercus cerris*) which had been introduced into England only in 1735. They would have been interesting to Knowlton (as they were to Lord Pembroke and the Duke of Richmond at the same time) not simply as botanical curiosities but

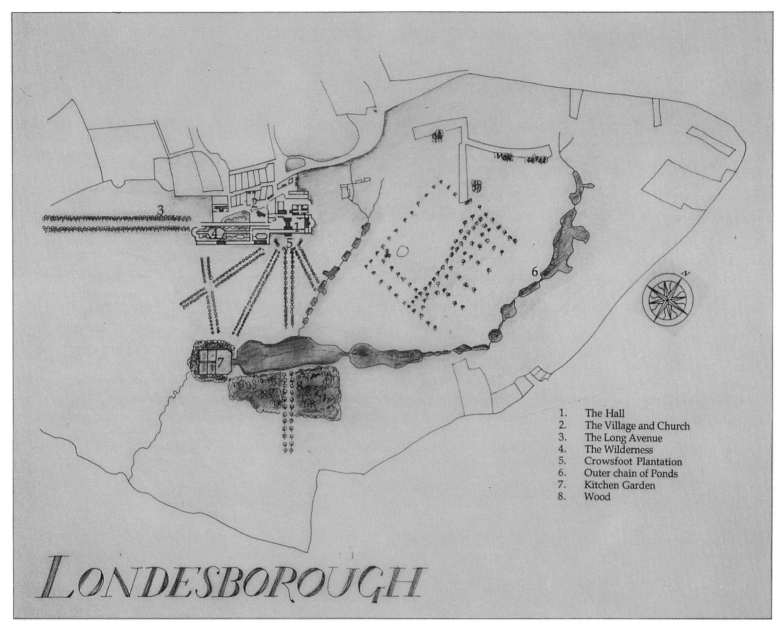

LONDESBOROUGH

1. The Hall
2. The Village and Church
3. The Long Avenue
4. The Wilderness
5. Crowsfoot Plantation
6. Outer chain of Ponds
7. Kitchen Garden
8. Wood

for the novelty of their pyramidal shape and the fact that they were fast-growing.[34]

Although the overall design of the park owes much to the *patte d'oie* plan associated with London and Wise, the park as a whole does not. What had originally been a canal, for example, Knowlton replaced with a nine-acre lake of a 'naturalised' irregular shape nearly thirty years before Brown was to do the same thing at Blenheim. That it was fed by a serpentine chain of lakes created to drain a marshy part of the park, moreover, fulfilled Pope's belief expressed in the 'Epistle to Burlington' written at the beginning of the decade: ''Tis Use alone that sanctifies Expence.'

Beyond the nine-acre lake, to the south, Knowlton made a wooded plantation, and he seems to have gone on planting clumps of trees both within the park and beyond it at exactly the time that Kent was making this one of the hallmarks of his landscape designs. That Knowlton was aware of Burlington's aesthetic principles in landscape and their implication for tree-planting in the park is revealed in a letter to John Ferret in 1751: 'By those little cuts thro' the

90. Todd Longstaffe-Gowan, Reconstruction Plan of Londesborough (c. 1730).

Thorns in the Ox Close it will have a Garden look, as having a little Art mix'd with Nature, so that the one beautifies the other.'[35]

What Knowlton is, in fact, describing is his development at Londesborough of an existing *ferme ornée* that one 'Mr. Wyld of Otley' praised at Londesborough as early as 1728, two years before Knowlton began his transformations:

> Next, from the Terras's exalted Height
> High tow'ring Trees attract my astonish'd Sight;
> Large Crops of Corn, rich Meads, and past'ring Groves,
> Where the fond Mother with her Lambkin roves:
> A youthful Wood on either hand appears,
> Whose Boughs with whistling Notes salute our Ears;
> Frequented with the airy feather'd Throng,
> Who praise their Dwelling in each tuneful Song.[36]

This earlier garden had been created by Knowlton's predecessors, Nathaniel Adams and Roger Looker, the latter a founder of the Brompton Park nursery. Knowlton brought to that georgic conception (the mixture of farm and pleasure ground) not only his own abilities in design but his familiarity with recent introductions of exotic species. In his practice the extension of the garden into the landscape seems almost the natural corollary of the extension of the scope of botany. His contemporary, John Martyn, had begun his career by amateur 'botanising' on St. George's Hill south of London and publishing the results, thereby bringing previously unnoticed native wild plants within the new taxonomy. Knowlton, on the other hand, with the introduction of Turkey oaks into the landscape at Londesborough, took botanical experimentation out of the 'stoves' (hot-houses) and offered a new 'vocabulary' of planting to the making of the English landscape.[37]

Throughout this period there is testimony to the increasing use of exotics in the writings of Bradley, Sir Hans Sloane, James Sherard and Peter Collinson. It was Collinson's distinction to encourage Lord Petre's botanical interests, interests which, like his own, extended to 'Natural History in all its parts, Planting, and Horticulture.'[38] Collinson's regret about the increasing specialisation of botany was that amateurs like Petre and himself would no longer have a place. As late as 1755 he wrote to Linnaeus complaining that 'we have great numbers of Nobility and Gentry that know plants very well, but yet do not make botanic science their peculiar study.' And yet these men, because of the alteration and addition of names in Linnaeus's *Species Plantarum*, would now be excluded from botany: 'Thus Botany, which was a pleasant study and attainable by most men, is now become, by alterations and new names, the study of a man's life, and none but real professors can pretend to attain it.'[39]

One such amateur was John Martyn's mentor, Dr. Patrick Blair, who wrote to Martyn in 1724 in a similarly cautionary tone about the way that discoveries in natural history had been made 'within these hundred years, . . . where the hints have been given by one, enlarged by the other, discovered by the third, and still greater improvments made by the fourth &c.' Martyn's predecessor, Richard Bradley, was just such a consolidator of earlier discoveries and his professorship at Cambridge an interesting example of the transition from amateur to professional botany.

Bradley's contemporary, Batty Langley, is usually thought of as a garden designer, thanks largely to the extensive use of plans in his *New Principles of Gardening* (1728). But in fact only three of the seven parts of this book deal with design; the four central sections are concerned with trees and shrubs. Langley's practice, chiefly at Twickenham Park, the estate of Pope's landlords, the Vernons, led him to be somewhat critical of Bradley's failure to experiment with his recommendations.[40] In *A Sure Method of Improving Estates* (1728), for instance, Langley used his experience at Thomas Vernon's estate to establish how Portugal (or Spanish) chestnuts ought to be planted. Because the limbs of one such tree there 'extend full fourscore Feet, . . . we may easily know, what Distances they should be planted for such rural Embellishments.'[41]

Bradley, who objected to the 'solemn stiffness' that characterised many gardens of his time, wrote of the horse chestnut that it had 'something in it so set and formal that I cannot admire it.'[42] But Langley, who was no admirer of what he called 'that *regular, stiff, and stuft up Manner*'[43] of the gardens that preceded him, nonetheless recommended the 'very fine Shade, and agreeable Figure'[44] of this tree. Taking his cue from Evelyn's praise of it, he recommended it for avenues, walks, and groves in a manner consonant with Lord Bathurst's contemporary practice in his 'Horse Guards Avenue' at Cirencester.

Langley's *A Sure Method* is very much in the shadow of Evelyn's *Sylva*, but the aesthetic spirit of Evelyn's fourth (1706) edition informs Langley's work as much as the forest-management practices of the first edition. Of the elm, he writes:

> But excluding all these many Advantages that arise from the Timber, its beautiful Verdure, and delightful Shade, is Encouragement sufficient for us to propagate it as much as possible . . . It makes as beautiful an Appearance as any Tree whatever, and more especially when Hedges, Groves, Walks, Avenues, etc. are planted therewith; for its Leaves are not only very beautiful in their Forms and Magnitudes, but of a pleasant Green, and one of the very last that falls in the Autumn.

And he goes on to give directions how to plant the elm 'to fill up the Quarters of a Wilderness' or 'in Groves, to cause an immediate Shade; so also in Espaliers, before a House, or on a Terrace Walk.'[45]

Langley, indeed, improves on Evelyn. Where the latter had expelled the variegated sycamore from gardens because it attracted flies and its leaves 'turn to *Mucilage*, . . . and spoil our Walks,' Langley sees that it may nonetheless have both an aesthetic and practical place 'in the middle of large Quarters' especially in 'dry hilly Lands, wherein few other Kinds of Forest Trees will live.'[46] And this, presumably, is exactly how Lord Petre came to use the 85 'Striped Sycamore' (probably the *Acer pensylvanica* discovered by John Bartram) that Peter Collinson records 'at the Upper End of the Park, [at Thorndon in Essex] in May 1740.'[47]

In the course of garden history, Langley is closer to the history of design than Bradley, although Bradley was also capable of writing about the making of such fashionable design features as cascades and conservatories for tropical fruit. But Langley is the more interesting precisely because he crosses the conventional borders. *A Sure Method* is inevitably more concerned with the practical side of silviculture than his *New Principles*, and yet even in the former he deals with hedges, for example, from both a practical and an aesthetic point of view. Writing of *Carpinus*, he says that 'there's none makes a more beautiful Hedge than the Hornbeam; provided that 'tis not planted too thick' and that limes (lindens) 'make very beautiful close Hedges,' even that (of chestnut hedges) 'there is none more beautiful, if they are skilfully order'd.' And yet he also notes that maple hedges prosper 'where nothing else will thrive.'[48] Not

91. Plan for a Summer House in a Grove from Richard Bradley, *A General Treatise Treatise of Husbandry and Gardening* (1726).

93 (facing left). Plan of James Johnston's Garden, Twickenham, from Batty Langley, *New Principles of Gardening* (1728). Trustees of the British Library.

94 (facing right). 'Design of a Rural Garden after the New Manner' from Batty Langley, *New Principles of ⌐dening* (1728). Trustees of the British Library.

surprisingly, these recommendations are more elaborate in his *New Principles*, where pyracantha, elm, Norway spruce, holm oak, and box are added to the list of trees suitable for making hedges.[49] These recommendations are rendered the more forceful by Langley's own experience of gardens in which they have been successful. Of hornbeam, for example, he writes with admiration of the 'many beautiful Hedges of this Plant' at the Earl of Stafford's house, Mount Lebanon, at Twickenham, at Secretary Johnston's house next door (where he had designed the garden plan), and at Twickenham Park, where he himself had 'embellished' the gardens with hedges of hornbeam.[50] And of holm oak he notes its commendable use as a hedge tree in neighbouring Ham House: 'In the Gardens of that beautiful grand Seat of the late Earl of *Dyzart* at *Ham*, near *Richmond* in *Surry*, are many fine Hedges of this Plant.'[51]

The importance of shade in a garden is a theme that both Bradley and Langley share—largely in opposition to the treeless parterres of their predecessors. Bradley has a long essay on the building of summer-houses on the edge of a wood 'where the Air can have due Liberty'[52] and where even water machines can be used to create a draft [Fig. 91]. And Langley's belief that 'without it [shade] *a Garden is nothing*' is in the context of his praise for '*proportionable Avenues* leading from the House' to '*Groves* and open *Wildernesses*.'[53] The planting of these groves, however, must not be 'regular, *like unto Orchards*' but in imitation of nature so 'that no three Trees together range in a strait Line; excepting now and then by Chance, to cause Variety.'[54]

Variety is central to Langley's aesthetic. It exemplifies English liberty as opposed to the 'strait' regularity of French gardens. He must have had to tread

128

warily in the recommendations he made for James Johnston (Secretary Johnston) at his estate, later known as Orleans House, in Twickenham. Johnston's house, built in 1710, had been designed by John James, who also dedicated his translation of Dezallier d'Argenville's *The Theory and Practice of Gardening* (1712) [Fig. 92] to Johnston. Certainly a sketch of 1711 shows a very regular garden[55] and it was within the confines of this regularity that Langley had to accommodate his 1728 proposal.

Johnston's garden, although it was not large, still exemplified the spirit of Switzer's *Ichnographia*. In any case, even so forceful a proponent of rural gardening as Switzer was prepared to allow an attention to minutiae in gardens within a few miles of London. Rocque's map of 1746 shows Johnston's garden to have been a good deal smaller than its near neighbour, Marble Hill, or even than Pope's garden. Langley's plan [Fig. 93] included the incorporation of both ha-has and a mount to add variety, but the major effects of the garden were to be achieved with trees: '*Wildernesses, Labyrinth, Groves, etc.*'[56] These were the instruments of what he called (echoing Switzer) the '*Grand and more Rural Manner.*'[57]

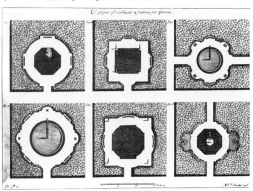

92. 'Designs of Cabinets and Salons for Groves' from A. J. Dézallier D'Argenville, *The Theory and Practice of Gardening* tr. John James (1712).

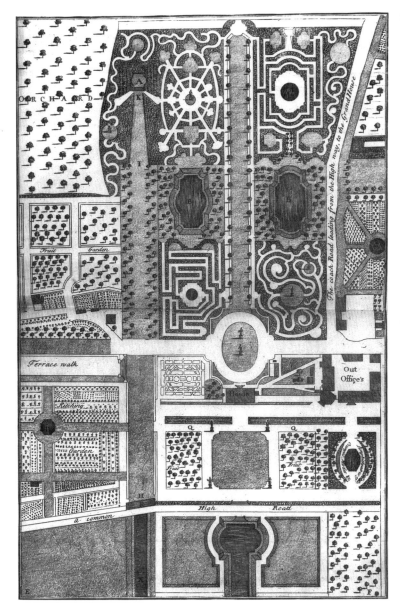

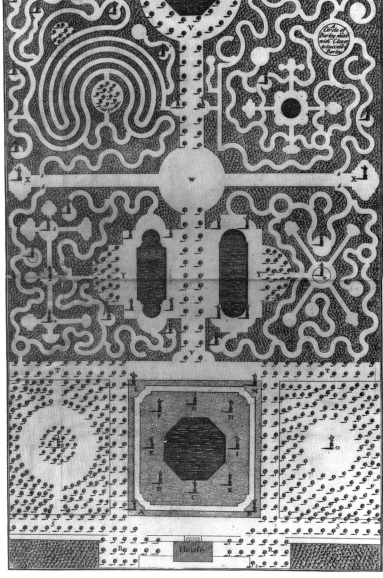

Langley also succeeded in 'calling in the country,' both across the Thames to the south and across the road to the north. The view of the major walk is carried over the canals next to the river 'and from thence over the *River Thames*, and there terminates in a pleasant Wood.' At the other end of the garden, 'there is a *Ha,Ha*, of Water, which is a Fence to the Garden from the Road, and admits of a *free View*, which Iron Gates or Grills cannot do.'[58]

We get a clearer picture of what this planting might have involved in Langley's not dissimilar 'Design of a *rural Garden*, after the new manner' [Fig. 94]. This garden appears to be no larger than Johnston's and yet it contains more than fifty different types of tree and shrub. Moreover, although Shenstone was later to deplore Langley's ignorance of the classics (he thought Minerva and Pallas different deities), Langley anticipated one of the chief features of the *ferme ornée*, the mixture of the useful and the beautiful: 'and indeed a beautiful Plantation should not only be adorned with entire Walks and Hedges of Trees of all Sorts, as well fruit as others; but intermix'd together in many parts, as if Nature had placed them with her own Hand. The *agreeable Mixture of Fruits in a Wilderness*, causes great Variety and Pleasure, as well as Profit.'[59] [Fig. 95]. Only the inclusion of fruit trees, he wrote a year later in *Pomona*, could make a garden '*truly Grand and Noble, as well as Proftable and Delightful.*'[60]

Even before Langley's proposals, Johnston had been celebrated by Defoe for his mixture of *utile* (a vineyard) with the *dulci* of art. In Defoe's account, the greenhouse was described as having 'a prospect every way into the most delicious garden,' and Johnston himself as 'a master of gardening.'[61] Richard Bradley also praised Johnston for 'many Improvements in Gardens' but especially 'that useful Discovery . . . of transplanting Trees with Safety in the hottest Summer-Months, which the World owes to Your solid Thought and extensive Knowledge in the Works of Nature.'[62] Johnston must have been called upon to employ this 'discovery' extensively if Langley's plans were put into effect.

Within what, in both the Johnston proposal and the 'rural Garden', remain very regular quarters of the garden, Langley's designs propose serpentine and irregular plantations. The range of trees and plants he employs, however, is fairly conventional. In it there are none of the exotics that the Earl of Islay was employing in nearby Whitton Park at this time. In the wilderness of his 'rural Garden', for example, of the fourteen trees he proposes to use only one, the weeping willow, was a novelty at the time. He refers to its having been 'brought from *Babylon*, and now in great Plenty and Perfection in England. Particularly, in the Gardens of the late *Thomas Vernon*, Esq; at his Seat in *Twickenham Park* in *Middlesex*.'[63]

For all his acquaintance with Pope's landlords, however, Langley's practice shows little of the radical change in design that Pope's garden itself demonstrates, even on Rocque's map. Like Bradley, though, he does propose a mixture of plantings that foreshadows what another of Pope's friends, Philip Southcote, was to put into practice in the following decade. In 1722 one of Bradley's correspondents, an 'R.S. of Surrey' recommended that a coppice be planted not 'according to any Plan or Figure; the Walks may be cut when it is grown up, and their Edges border'd with Cowslips, Primroses, Violets, and other wild Flowers to make it appear more Rural.'[64]

Something like what Addison also advocated—'Woods cut into shady Walks, twisted into Bowers'[65]—had already been created in Wray Wood at Castle Howard, where the French regular style of gardening represented by

95. 'Non-pariel [pareil] Apple' from Batty Langley, *Pomona* (1729). Oak Spring Garden Library, Upperville, Virginia.

London and Wise had had its first rebuke. Wray Wood, like the wood of Bradley's correspondent, was an extant plantation within which a labyrinth was cut out. Langley, echoing Switzer, went a small but important step beyond that in recommending that wildernesses be planted in this way in the first place, and that they introduce an industrious agricultural or georgic element as well. Referring to his plan of a 'rural garden' he writes:

> If we enter the Wilderness at bb,&c. we are led through their *pleasant Meanders*, with the agreeable Entertainments of *Flower Gardens, Fruit Gardens, Orangerys, Groves,* of *Forest Trees,* and *Ever-Greens, Open-plains, Kitchen Gardens Physick Gardens, Paddocks* of *Sheep, Deer, Cows,* etc. *Hop Grounds, Nurseries* of *Fruit* and *Forest Trees, Ever-Greens, &c. Vineyards, Inclosures* of *Corn, Grass, Clover,* etc. *Cones* of *Fruit Trees, Forest Trees, Ever-Greens, Flowering Shrubs, Basins, Fountains, Canals, Cascades, Grottos, Warrens* of *Hares* and *Rabbets, Aviaries, Manazaries, Bowling-Greens;* and those rural Objects, *Hay-Stacks* and *Wood Piles,* as in a Farmer's Yard in the Country. Which several Parts are disposed of in such a Manner, and Distance, as not to see, or know of the next approaching, when we have seen the first, so that we are continually entertain'd with *new unexpected Objects at every Step we take;* for the Entrances into those Parts being made intricate, we can *never know when we have seen the whole.* Which (if I mistake not) is the true End and Design of *laying out Gardens of Pleasure.*[66]

'By this Method of laying out Gardens,' Langley claims, 'those that are but small, will be made to appear *as very large ones,* and those that are spacious and large, *Grand* and *Noble.*' It is hard to believe, nonetheless, that a garden of a few acres, such as Johnston's, would not have seemed as overstuffed with such a catalogue as the earlier French gardens of which Langley complained. Much more persuasive is a recommendation, also made earlier by Bradley, to mix kinds of trees in a plantation 'as if Nature had placed them there with her own Hand. The *agreeable Mixture of Fruits in a Wilderness,* causes great Variety and Pleasure, as well as Profit.'[67] This in fact is what Evelyn had proposed seventy years earlier in his unpublished *Elysium Britannicum*: to treat such orchard trees 'as are proper for the decoration of a Garden of Pleasure, for avenues, Walkes, Groves, thicketts and other embellishments.'[68]

Like Langley's, Bradley's recommendations carry forward the theme of 'extensive or rural gardening' that was beginning to be put into practice in the 1720s and was to have its fullest manifestation in Philip Southcote's Wooburn Farm in the 1730s. Langley's Direction 9 sets down: 'That all the Trees of your shady Walks and Groves be planted with Sweet-Brier, White Jessemine [sic], and Honey-Suckles, environ'd at Bottom with a small Circle of Dwarf-Stock, Candy-Turf [sic], and Pinks.'[69] Although it was possible, in a garden as small as Secretary Johnston's, to put this into effect, Southcote's planting of the extensive hedgerows of his farm in this manner would have been more effective. And only there could the mixture of meadows and 'rural Enrichments' that Langley recommends in his Direction 19 have been put into effect.

Langley's treatment of tree plantations in *New Principles* also presumes a larger estate than most of the gardens in Twickenham afforded. Twickenham Park was an exception, and there Langley writes of having 'planted a Wilderness of *Oaks, Elms, Limes, Platanus* [Planes], etc.'[70] It is tempting to believe that the irregular plantation of trees, visible on Rocque's 1741 map north of the house and next to the canal, was Langley's 'wilderness'. Certainly it is far different from his plans for Secretary Johnston's garden and fulfills the pre-

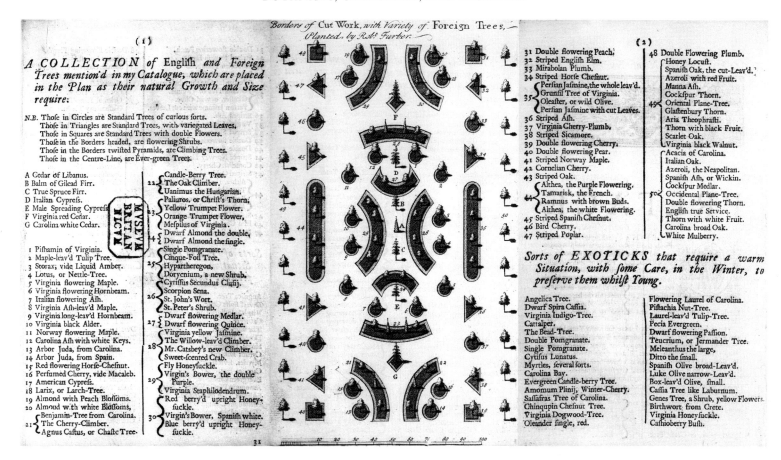

scription of his Direction 32: 'In the Planting of Groves, you must observe a regular Irregularity; not planting them according to the common Method like an Orchard, with their Trees in straight Lines ranging every Way, but in a rural Manner, as if they had received their Situation from Nature itself.'[71]

Plainly Langley's conception of nature was no less complex than Shaftesbury's or Pope's. His appeal to 'Reason, Art, and Nature' has to be read in the context of his 'Kentian' recommendation that painted ruins be included in the landscape. Presumably they were included within the debate among 'Reason, Art, and Nature,' whereas topiary—'those wretched Figures many Nursery-Men and Gardeners breed up their Hollies and other Ever-Greens in'[72]—could not be. His recommendations for planting 'follow Nature,' but a 'Nature methodiz'd' by a pleasing variety of disposition and plant types.

Although his wilderness at Twickenham Park did not employ them, his catalogue of recommended trees for wildernesses also includes 'Black Cherry and other Trees that produce Food for Birds, which will not a little add to the Pleasure thereof,' spruce ('promiscuously planted'), box ('very beautiful in the Quarters of a Wilderness'), and birch (presumably *Betula pendula*), which had only appeared in Furber's catalogue for the first time the year before.[73] [Fig. 96] And, as with his recommendations for hedges, he ties theory to practice, in recommending the tulip tree (*Liriodendron tulipifera*) for planting within a wilderness because Lord Peterborough, Pope's friend, had already successfully so used it in his garden at Parsons Green.[74]

It is not clear who planted the avenues at Twickenham Park that also appear for the first time on Rocque's 1741 map, but certainly Langley had recommendations for their plantation. Although he recommended elms for 'delightful Walks' as at Greenwich and could not imagine sacrificing their beauty for profit, he preferred beech or even black walnut to Dutch elms and lindens for avenues, and pine for '*large Avenues of boundless Views*'.[75]

What Langley exemplified was the concern of his generation of designers to accommodate the enormous increase in the numbers of available trees and shrubs to garden design. The full implication for gardens of this botanic explosion was not to be felt until the 1730s in Lord Petre's work at Thorndon, and yet Langley's book represents a wide horticultural audience already availing itself of an enlarged botanic repertoire in garden design.

The revolution in garden design that created the 'natural garden', however, was not carried forward by a few landowners or writers or even designers. It was 'translated' on the ground by a great many nurserymen and gardeners, a large number of whom are now known only from subscription lists and bills of account: men (and sometimes women) who adapted what were often only the vaguest of wishes or sketches to new and existing plant materials, especially trees and shrubs. Pope's John Serle, Lord Petre's James Gordon, the Duke of Argyll's James Lee: these are the men on whose backs and in whose minds the garden revolution was carried forward. And it is to them that we must now turn.

9

GARDENERS: FOREST TREES FOR USE AND ORNAMENT

At the beginning of Rudyard Kipling's Indian story, 'The Phantom Rickshaw,' the English narrator refers to 'the two or three hundred Civilians in his Province' and later to 'some fifteen hundred other people of the non-official caste' with whom he could expect to come in contact. The context of the story, however, makes it quite plain that these people are to be thought of only as English, not Indian. In his consciousness, the Indians are only the background, part of the scenery, nothing more. Something very similar has happened in the consciousness of many writers about garden history with respect to the gardeners themselves.

This book arose out of a lecture I gave several years ago on the relation between eighteenth-century English porcelain and the sources of its decoration in botany and landscape architecture. In the course of preparing that lecture I had occasion to use Philip Miller's *The Gardeners Dictionary* [Fig. 97]. Like many other eighteenth-century books, Miller's *Dictionary* was published by subscription, and the subscribers' list in the second volume provides an interesting insight into the audience for garden writing in the fourth decade of the century.[1] What caught my attention, however, was that the list contained not only the names of the famous theorists and practitioners of garden design in this interesting period—Pope, Burlington, Lord Petre, the Earl of Islay, Charles Hamilton—but that many of the other, now largely unknown, subscribers identified themselves as gardeners by profession. This raised the question: what did it mean to describe oneself as a gardener in the early eighteenth century? That question is itself related to genre theory in literary criticism, i.e. how does the name create the thing? When, for example, and why did Americans begin to think of themselves as Americans, and not simply as the English living abroad in a strange continent?

Whatever the answer to the gardener question, it is clear that at least *some* people thought of themselves as professional gardeners long before the nineteenth century, the period in which some writers have suggested the profession first appeared. As early as 1682, in *The Florists Vade-Mecum*, Samuel Gilbert advised '*those that understand not this Art in themselves in the hiring of a Gardiner [to] take Counsel of them that do, and give him assurance of his stay for five or six years.*'[2] This question is the more vexing in that many of the known garden designers of this period wrote of themselves not as gardeners but as nurserymen (London and Wise) or as seedsmen (Switzer). And one has fascinating glimpses of professional transition in this period as well.

Two interesting examples of this transition have been already been noted:

97. Frontispiece of Philip Miller. *The Gardeners Dictionary* (1743). Thomas Fisher Library, University of Toronto.

Blanche Henrey's *No Ordinary Gardener*, the history of Thomas Knowlton, Lord Burlington's gardener at his Yorkshire estate, Londesborough, and Peter Aram, who trained under London and Wise at the famous garden of Dr. Compton, the Bishop of London, before coming to Newby Hall. The publication of Aram's *A Practical Treatise of Flowers* in 1985 drew attention to another gardener who crossed the divide between 'mere' gardening and design. Writing of Aram's work at Newby indeed, Penelope Hobhouse used the phrase 'no mere gardener' when referring to Aram's 1716 drawing of a parterre garden of 'Pyramid Yews and round-headed Variegtaed Holly together with Flow'ry Decorations . . . intermixt.'[3] Aram's long poem about the nearby garden, Studley Royal, suggests not only his professional alliance with a circle of gardeners that included William Fisher (the Aislabies' gardener there) but with the 'philosophical' interests of his early contemporaries and mentors at London and Wise's Brompton nursery: Stephen Switzer, Charles Bridgeman, and even, indirectly, John Evelyn.

These two books suggest that there is a large area in garden history that has yet fully to be addressed: the history of the professional gardeners who made the gardens of the landscape revolution of the early eighteenth century. That subject in itself would constitute a book. Thirty years ago, before the influential work of H. F. Clark and his disciples, great estates such as Stowe were thought of primarily as the creations of their owners. We have since come to think of Stowe in relation to the work of its various designers: Vanbrugh, Bridgeman, Kent, and Brown. But what of the gardener (William Love) who oversaw and implemented these designs, and who in many cases had to choose the trees and shrubs and flowers that so give (or gave) the place its character? His name appears in the accounts at least by 1725 and he stayed until Capability Brown's advent in 1741. Not only did he lay out the Eleven-Acre Lake for Bridgeman but the Elysian Fields as well [Fig. 98]. Although the buildings in the latter were certainly by Kent, it seems likely that the overall design for the Elysian Fields (c. 1725) was by Bridgeman and that, 'since Kent did not appear on the scene until three or four years later,'[4] Love must have had a considerable

98. The Temple of Ancient Virtue in the Elysian Fields, Stowe.

role in its creation. If the question, 'How high was the grass in the Elysian Fields?'[5] is one that merits serious attention, it is clear that the man who made such a decision is one about whom we ought to know more.

Love certainly took his profession seriously, and like Knowlton and Aram was 'no mere gardener.' Not only did he subscribe to Switzer's *Practical Husbandman and Planter* (1733–34) but to Thomas Gent's *History of Rippon* (1733), a work in which such important contemporary gardens as Studley Royal and Newby Hall were described. And yet his important career at Stowe falls almost anonymously between the tenure of Edward Bissell (who may have come from the Brompton nursery) and Brown, nor does his name appear in Ray Desmond's extensive *Dictionary of British and Irish Botanists and Horticulturists* (1977).

The histories of such men and their careers are often lost in the obscurity of their situations, but there is enough evidence to suggest that some picture of the nature of their rising professionalism can be found. In the case of some, the papers of the families for which they worked preserve evidence of their contribution to the making of the landscape. The letters of the family at Rousham, including the account of the garden by the gardener, John MacClary, and some of the accounts relating to William Fisher at Studley Royal are cases in point.

But there is also a great deal to be discovered, about the profession generally and about some gardeners in particular, from both the wide range of periodicals in the eighteenth century and contemporary newspapers. Essays in the former and advertisements in the latter both give some picture of how gardeners were beginning to remove themselves from the station of mere household servants, who were often required to combine several jobs in one. This change in station was the result of two things: the need for gardeners to master the new botanical knowledge represented by Linnaeus, and the rage for 'place-making' (i.e. landscape designing) that came to the fore in the early eighteenth century and demanded a greater expertise in design.

In the development of garden history these two elements have often come to be treated independently. Those who come to garden history from horticulture, for example, often complain (with some justification) that garden historians pay little attention to the materials that composed the gardens being studied. One would look in vain in many recent books on garden history for any account of the trees and shrubs that were the essential elements of the landscapes under consideration. This is in large measure because designers such as Kent made only the most cursory reference to the type of tree or shrub required.

And yet the debate about the true nature of the picturesque, a debate conducted in the 1790s between Humphry Repton on the one hand and Uvedale Price and Richard Payne Knight on the other, was largely a debate about materials. Repton's objection to the aesthetic theories of Price and Knight was that they did not take into account the differences between painting and horticulture, differences that were essentially in the materials employed. Repton stood at the beginning of a movement that was to be called 'gardenesque', but he was no mere specimen planter, as some who followed him were. Indeed, the landscape changes visible in his famous 'Red Book' plans primarily involve the redisposition of trees and shrubs. In this, as he himself acknowledged, he followed in Brown's footseps, but he was also heir to Brown's predecessors. By establishing the equal importance of materials with design, these early eighteenth-century 'patriots of horticulture' (as Philip Miller called them) provided a botanical vocabulary of place-making that was at least as important as its syntax (design). And in many cases they provided the syntax as well.

In a recent interview, Roy Spring, the Clerk of Works of Salisbury Cathedral, deplored the modern tendency of architects to take sole credit for their buildings: 'I have a phobia about architects who stand back and say "I built this." . . . They didn't. They drew the pictures.' Credit for Salisbury, he believes, is due not to Canon Elias de Derham, the first architect, but to Nicholas of Ely, the master mason, and his staff of craftsmen.[6] What was true for medieval building was also true in the eighteenth century, and true for gardens as well. Plainly Lord Bathurst himself did not plant out the thousands of trees at Cirencester that he describes himself planting in his correspondence with Pope. Nor is it likely that Stephen Switzer, who worked as a designer for Bathurst, did so either.

Little is known about many of the gardeners who, in effect, created the great landscape gardens of the early eighteenth century. None of those who list themselves as gardeners in the subscription list to Switzer's *Practical Husbandman* (1733) is included in Desmond's *Dictionary*. And this list includes Thomas Harrison, the gardener to one of Miller's 'patriots of horticulture,' Sir Henry Goodrick at Great Ribston in Yorkshire, James Hoyland, the Earl of Carlisle's gardener at Castle Howard,[7] and William Hull, the gardener to Richard Edgcombe at Mt. Edgcumbe in Devon, a garden that Horace Walpole claimed as his favorite.

Another gardener who had an important role to play in the creation of landscape was John Field, gardener to the Duke of Bedford. Field, although he remained in the Duke of Bedford's employ, was also (like Moses Cook) a partner in the Brompton Park nursery and had, like London, been in the employ of Bishop Henry Compton. Although the redesigning of the gardens at Woburn in the 1670s was done by the surveyor, Philip Moore, Field created plantations there without Moore's direction and made use of Bedford's London gardener, Thomas Gilbank, to acquire plants from the garden of Lord Essex's brother, Sir Henry Capel, at Kew.[8]

Even Richard Bradley, who became the first professor of botany at Cambridge in 1724, worked earlier in his career on both the planting and the designing of the Duke of Chandos's legendary estate, Cannons.[9] Bradley, who acted as agent for the Earl of Essex's sister, the Duchess of Beaufort, in procuring plants in Amsterdam for her gardens at Chelsea and Badminton, was also (as we have seen) an extensive writer about improvement and garden history. Plainly he saw no division between garden design and gardening as horticulture. In his *Survey of the Ancient Husbandry* (1725), he praised Benjamin Townshend as both 'a Surveyor at Mr. *Whittmill*'s, [and] an ingenious Gardiner at *Hoxton*.'[10]

But Samuel Brewer (1670–1743), who was both a botanist and a gardener, ought also to have an honoured place among the patriot gardeners. He was a correspondent of Thomas Knowlton and a friend and near neighbour of another outstanding botanist gardener, Dr. Richard Richardson of North Bierly. Not only did he write an appendix to Dillenius's edition of Ray's *Synopsis* (after accompanying Dillenius on a botanical trip to Wales in 1726), he also ended his career in the early 1740s as head gardener to the Duke of Beaufort at Badminton.[11]

So too, the brothers Henry and James Scott, both nurserymen, remain more obscure than is their due. It seems likely that Henry was gardener to Lord Burlington, though he was also well established at Weybridge in Surrey as a

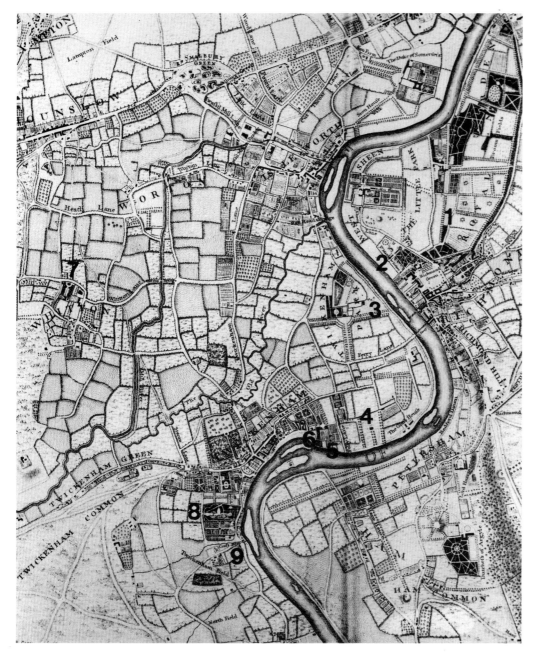

99. The Gardens of Twickenham and the Surrounding Area from John Rocque, *A Survey of London* (1741–45).
1. Kew Garden 2. Sir Matthew Decker's House 3. Twickenham Park (Vernon) 4. Marble Hill (Mrs. Howard) 5. Secretary Johnston's House 6. Earl of Strafford's House 7. Whitton Park (Earl of Islay) 8. Pope's House 9. Strawberry Hill (Horace Walpole).

nurseryman by the 1750s, advertising on a very Palladian trade-card that he 'performs any sort of Work in Gardens.'[12] He also appears in the subscribers' list to the second volume of Miller's *Gardeners Dictionary* (1739) as 'Gardener to the Right Hon. the Lord *Lovel*,' a list in which his brother James, a nurseryman of Turnham Green, is confusingly described as 'Gardener to the Right Hon. the Earl of Burlington.'

What role had men like the Scotts to play in the design of the gardens for which they were 'gardeners'? In Knowlton's case, the role was considerable. But what about John Teesdale, the gardener to Pope's friend Hugh Bethel? What was his role in 'translating' the 'natural taste in gardening,' and was he related to the two Robert Teesdales (father and son) who worked later at Castle Howard? Who was John Lee senior, the gardener to Mr. Secretary Johnston at Orleans House in Twickenham, and how was he involved in implementing Batty Langley's proposals for that garden? Plainly he was a man of some

GARDENERS

accomplishment, for Bradley dedicated the July issue (1722) of his *General Treatise on Husbandry* (1722–24) to him.[13]

Langley also commended the hedges in the garden of the Vernons, Pope's landlords, at nearby Twickenham Park, a garden in which the equally unknown Henry Timberlin was gardener. Langley describes Vernon as 'that late Encourager of Planting and Gardening,' but what role did his gardener play in designing the plantations of Portugal chestnuts (*Castanea sativa*) and black walnuts (*Juglans nigra*) that Langley praised there?[14] And what can be discovered about John Wyat, the Earl of Strafford's gardener at Twickenham, whom Langley also lauded?

> In the Gardens of the Right Honourable the Earl of Strafford, at Twickenham in Middlesex, are many beautiful Hedges of this Plant [hornbeam]; some of which are upwards of twenty Feet high, whose uncommon Beauty and Stature is in great Measure due to the extraordinary Skill and Management of that ingenious and well experienc'd Gardener, Mr. John Wyat, Gardener to that Honorable and truly Noble Lord.[15] [Fig. 99]

Langley, who was himself the son of a gardener, Daniel Langley of Twickenham, is also a valuable source of reference to the pioneering work of early nurserymen in providing the arboreal materials of the landscape garden. In *New Principles of Gardening* (1728) he refers to '*Peter Mason*, Nursery-Man at Isleworth' as having 'the only Nursery, that I know of, as has this Tree [the spruce fir, either *Picea glauca* or *P. mariana*, both first introduced about 1700], with all other Ever-Greens, Fruit and Forest-Trees, Flowering Shrubs, etc. in their best Perfection.'[16]

If, in '*Esher*'s peaceful grove,' as Pope wrote, '*Kent* and Nature [vied] for PELHAM's Love,' who was the real creator of the effects that so pleased the Prime Minister, Henry Pelham, there? In that garden, as Horace Walpole wrote, Kent may have been 'Kentissime', but it is hard to believe that a designer who made such insufficient reference to arboreal materials in his plans could have achieved those effects without the considerable assistance of the gardener there, John Greening.[17] Indeed, in 1760, one James Shiells who advertised himself as 'late Gardener to the Right Hon. Lady Katherine Pelham,' begged 'leave to acquaint the Nobility and Gentry, that he surveys, and plans Estates neatly and accurately; lays out Parks, Pleasure and Kitchen Gardens, in the most useful, elegant, and modern Taste; Makes artificial Rivers, or Pieces of Water, in the most natural and agreeable Manner.'[18]

Lady Katherine (or Catherine) Pelham was the wife of Henry Fiennes-Clinton, the Ninth Earl of Lincoln, who was the close friend and patron of Joseph Spence. And though Shiells may have worked at Oatlands, Lincoln's first estate, it seems more likely that he worked at Esher, which Lincoln inherited from his uncle, Henry Pelham. Shiells, then, provides an interesting instance of just what a gardener who worked in Kent's most famous garden might be expected to know and do. By 1766 Shiells had become the successor of Richard North, who had a small nursery in Lambeth. There, among other things, he had 'an ample stock of the *Carolina poplar*' which had been introduced in 1738, and he later supplied the Seaton Delaval estate in Northumberland with tree seeds.[19]

Another unknown subscriber to Miller's *Dictionary* was John Searing, who described himself as 'Gardener to his Grace the Duke of *Somerset*.' What role had he to play (along with Switzer) in the transformation of Lord Bathurst's Riskins into the 'extravagant bergerie' that it became under the reign of

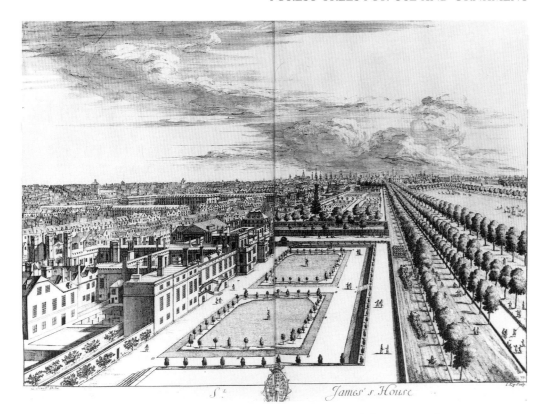

100. The Mall with Mr Rose's Garden in St. James's from Leonard Knyff and John Kip, *Nouveau Theatre de la Grande Bretagne* (1708).

Shenstone's friend, the Duchess of Somerset? And how much is owing to Searing in, Shenstone's georgic celebration of the Duchess's garden?

> In some fair villa's peaceful bound,
> To catch soft hints from Nature's tongue,
> And bid Arcadia bloom around.[20]

Like London and Wise, many of the nurserymen of the late seventeenth and early eighteenth centuries had considerable influence on the design of gardens.[21] Indeed, from the early eighteenth century onwards, the increasing wealth of plant materials made the services of a skilled nurseryman indispensable. At Blenheim, for example, London and Wise determined that the trees and shrubs used there would come almost entirely from the stock of their own Brompton Park nursery.

Their predecessor, John Rose (1619–77), the royal gardener at St. James's,[22] [Fig. 100] had similarly combined both design and the nursery trade. A correspondent of the famous gardener-writer, Sir Thomas Hanmer, Rose was also an accomplished florist and participated in the great craze for auriculas that began in the 1650s. But John Rea also celebrated him as a grower of evergreens, at Essex House in the Strand, [Fig. 101] in his *Flora* (1665). And Rose, who had been trained by Le Nôtre, subsequently (after 1661) laid out the garden in St. James's that was parallel to the new Mall.[23]

As has already been mentioned, many nurserymen began their careers in famous gardens. James Lee and Lewis Kennedy, former gardeners respectively to the Duke of Argyll at Whitton and Spencer Compton, Earl of Wilmington (another arboreal pioneer), were the founders of the most influential nursery of the period, the Vineyard in Hammersmith.[24] Many of these influential nurserymen were Scots, the two Scott brothers, Lee, Kennedy, and James Gordon among them.

Gordon began his career as gardener to Dr. James Sherard at Eltham, a

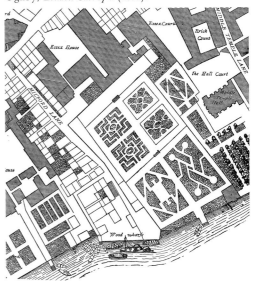

101. Essex House Garden in the Strand from John Ogilby, *London Survey'd* (1677).

garden famous for Dillenius's catalogue, published in 1732, just after Gordon replaced Thomas Knowlton who had gone to Londesborough. After Sherard's death in 1738 he became Lord Petre's gardener, and after Lord Petre's death in 1742 he became an important nurseryman in the East End of London and continued Petre's tradition of arboreal importation. In 1760 he gave notice in the *Daily Advertiser* that he had on show 'the Umbrella-Tree (*Magnolia tripetala*), from North America.' Although it had been introduced eight years earlier and noticed in Miller's *Dictionary*, Gordon notes that it has 'not yet been mentioned by any of the curious Writers on Plants to have blown in Europe before.'[25] It is a testimony to the high esteem in which he was held that John Ellis insisted on naming the rare 'Loblolly Bay' tree found in North America after him as *Gordonia lasianthus*.

Similarly, Christopher Gray, to whose colour sense Lord Petre's was compared, was a friend and supplier to Peter Collinson, Lord Petre's friend and one of the greatest English botanists of the century. His 1755 catalogue claimed that there was in his nursery 'a greater Variety of Trees, Shrubs, Plants and Flowers . . . than perhaps can be found in any other Garden for Sale, not only in England, but also in any part of *Europe*.'[26]

By the 1740s the mania for garden artifices of all kinds was in full spate. The town beau monde, who frequented 'Perrott's Artificial Garden in the Five Fields, Chelsea,' with its orchard of wax oranges, lemons, peaches, and nectarines, doubtless also supplied the custom for the many shell suppliers for 'Gentlemens Grottos' of the elaborate sort designed by Pope's correspondent Aaron Hill.[27]

There were, however, many serious nurserymen who influenced the creation of landscape gardens. At the simplest level, they supplied trees, as London and Wise had done. A notice in the *Daily Advertiser* for 30 October 1733 offers 'PLANTS of the True SCARLET OAK' (*Quercus borealis maxima*, first introduced in 1691) 'To be sold at John Pain, the Green Lettice near Brownlow-street end in Holborn, and at Mrs. Oran's Nursery Garden at Knightsbridge, and at George Handcock's, Gardener, the Adam and Eve in Islington, where they may be seen growing.' They were also to be found in the collection of Joseph Allerton, nurseryman of the Old Spring Gardens, Knightsbridge, who subscribed to Switzer's *Practical Husbandman* and wrote to him on 16 April 1733 to inform him that 'we have now great Quantities in our Plantations.'[28]

Unfortunately, nurserymen like this are frequently as unidentifiable as the vendors of trees and shrubs in the innumerable paintings of Covent Garden by Hogarth and his contemporaries. Some, however, had a higher profile. Drake's *Eboracum* (1736) credits John Telford (1689–1771), a nurseryman of York, with being 'one of the first that brought our northern gentry into the method of planting and raising all kinds of forest trees, for use and ornament.'[29] Indeed, Telford, who supplied Thomas Knowlton with trees at Londesborough, was the first of three generations of nurserymen; his son and grandson produced a *Catalogue of Forest Trees, Fruit-Trees . . . and flowering shrubs* in 1775.[30]

Thomas Fairchild (1667?–1729), the author of the influential work, *The City Gardiner* (1722), [Fig. 102] was both an experimental botanist and a contributor to the new zeal for gardening. Remembered for his work on the Guernsey lily (*Nerine sarniensis*) and the first successful raiser of a scientific hybrid (*Dianthus caryophyllus* x *barbatus*), he possessed in addition the largest collection of aloes and succulent plants in the country.[31] But he was also concerned with the place of his work within philosophy and theology. A neighbour and friend of Whitmill at Hoxton, he left a legacy there for a sermon to be preached annually

102. Title-page of Thomas Fairchild's *The City Gardiner* (1722), reproduced in Richard Bradley, *A General Treatise Treatise of Husbandry and Gardening* (1726).

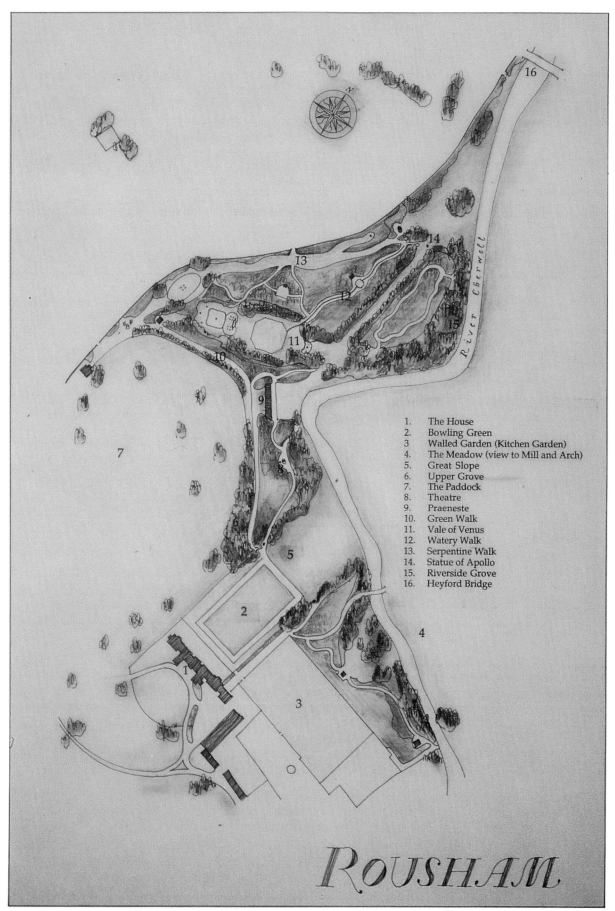

1. The House
2. Bowling Green
3. Walled Garden (Kitchen Garden)
4. The Meadow (view to Mill and Arch)
5. Great Slope
6. Upper Grove
7. The Paddock
8. Theatre
9. Praeneste
10. Green Walk
11. Vale of Venus
12. Watery Walk
13. Serpentine Walk
14. Statue of Apollo
15. Riverside Grove
16. Heyford Bridge

ROUSHAM

103. Todd Longstaffe-Gowan, Reconstruction Plan of Rousham after Bridgeman (c. 1750).

104. Venus Vale, Rousham.

105 Watery Walk, Rousham.

on the 'Wonderful works of God in the creation.'

Although Fairchild's considerable botanical experimentation was directed largely to town gardens, he was nonetheless highly commended by Richard Bradley both in his *Philosophical Account of the Works of Nature* (1721) and in his *General Treatise of Husbandry* (1726). Fairchild's collection of exotics from North America anticipated both Christopher Gray's *Catalogue of North American Trees* (1737) and Lord Petre's extensive plantations at Thorndon in the 1730s.[32]

Contemporary with Lord Petre's later work was the creation of the landscape garden at Rousham in Oxfordshire [Fig. 103]. It was designed by Kent and is the best-preserved of his gardens, but earlier designs by Bridgeman are not the only evidence that Kent relied upon the work of others. The estate correspondence reveals, as Kenneth Woodbridge noted, 'Kent's dependence on men such as White [the steward] and how decisions about detail were, in the end, taken by those on the spot.'[33] Even more telling are the references to the work of John MacClary (or Clary), the gardener, in White's correspondence with his employer, Lieutenant-General James Dormer. Writing of the parapet wall next to the river, White notes the General's approval of and determination to execute 'the gardener's new plan.'[34] Woodbridge observes that phrases such

as that, and White's subsequent reference to reading a plan 'with the gardener's advice,' 'suggest that it was ultimately John MacClary who bore the brunt of the work':[35] that it was MacClary, indeed, 'who had as much to do with making it [the garden] as Kent did.'[36]

Dormer was a friend of Lord Burlington, through whom he probably first met Kent and Pope. The sources of the garden's inspiration are thus difficult to discriminate. Pope certainly visited Rousham during the time of Kent's work there and Walpole may well have been right to attribute to him the 'model' of the garden 'at least in the opening and retiring shades of Venus's Vale.'[37] [Fig. 104] It is equally possible, however, that Kent may have been influenced at Rousham by his familiarity with Philip Southcote's contemporary *ferme ornée*, Wooburn Farm. Rousham, for all its georgic invocation of the landscape, is not a *ferme ornée*, but Southcote's prescriptions for the planting of perimeter walks and his deployment of shade are similar to what was done there. Southcote, for example, used trees, as Kent was to do, in the creation of prospect. 'There should be leading trees, or clumps of trees,' he wrote, 'to help the eye to any more distant clump, building, or view.'[38] He also had a great belief in the importance of shading. 'Even the least risings and falls in a Bank,' he said to Joseph Spence, 'make some variety of lights and shades.'[39] [Figs. 105, 106] 'We

106. Statue of Apollo (Antinous), Rousham.

107. River Walk and Heyford Bridge, Rousham.

should prevent the rays of the sun from falling too strongly on the eyes by a proper interposition of shades, which when above, helps the eye like a hat or umbrella (or on the sides, as one sees a picture much stronger when the sidelights are broken all round by a proper holding up of the hand).'[40]

The plantation of trees on either side of the Great Slope at Rousham certainly leads the eye out to the Temple of the Mill (a picturesque building beyond the estate proper) in the way that Southcote recommended. And the view from the south end of the serpentine walk on the northwestern perimeter of the garden originally included a view under trees and across the oval fishpond to the Eyecatcher (a mock-ruined arch, also outside the estate in the distance).[41] What is not clear is who was reponsible for the use of flowering shrubs in the walks at Rousham. MacClary describes the effect of this in his famous letter, 'The Way to View Rousham,' written in 1750, but the nature of the planting he describes was quite different from Southcote's:

> their you see the deferant sorts of Flowers, peeping through the deferant sorts of Evergreens, here you think the Laurel produces a Rose, the Holly a Syringa, the Yew a Lilac, and the sweet Honeysuckle is peeping out from under every Leafe, in short they are so mixt together, that youd think every Leafe of the Evergreens, produced one flower or a nother.[42]

Most of the plants used were the same as Southcote employed, nor were they any more uncommon than the trees that MacClary also lists: 'Oaks, Elms, Beachs, and Black Cherrys.' But Southcote did not mix evergreens and deciduous shrubs in the way MacClary describes, nor did he back his trees with a beech hedge as MacClary did. All of this suggests that, far from MacClary's getting beyond his station as steward/gardener and posing as an ersatz gentleman,[43] he was no more than describing what he himself had in large measure created.

White's letters show him, as one would expect, 'taking up the alders, beech and oak in the roundabout walk [the walk in Bridgeman's wilderness] and planting them in the wood,' or 'planting near the building in Aston Field [the Eyecatcher] two forest trees and five in Heyford field.'[44] [Fig. 107] Kent's initial specifications for planting at Rousham were remarkably inexplicit. On the plan of 1738 he listed no more than 'Forrist trees standing in grass,' 'Underwood' [undergrowth or dense shrubbery], and 'Evergreens standing in grass.' A letter from White in 1741 suggests that both Kent and General Dormer interested themselves in the choice of evergreens and 'flowering trees,'[45] but throughout White's correspondence Kent's absence from the garden was a frequent subject of anxiety and regret. Kent, moreover, was interested in immediate dramatic effects. 'His clumps were puny,' Horace Walpole wrote. 'He aimed at immediate effect, and planted not for futurity.'[46] The result must have been that many of the decisions about planting were made on the spot by MacClary.

But the gardener went far beyond that. He also made aesthetic decisions that were of great consequence. In December 1740, White described MacClary's alteration of the Great Slope to improve the primary prospect in the garden: [Fig. 108]

> to remove the two seats six foot nearer the house, and raise the ground about three foot where they are to be fix'd so that you are to go from the terrace upon a level to the seats from whence a better prospect will be had than heretofore. The head of the slope is then to break in twelve foot from the green walk and the slope thereby gain eighteen foot in depth. By this

method and by this only says Clary, the descent will be made perfectly easy and the slope look magnificent.[47]

This was a major design decision, made not by Kent but by MacClary, who, moreover, was able to play with the vocabulary of classical allusion, even in the theatrical mode that Kent had made his own. In his 1750 letter, he describes having constructed (daringly close to Kent's Vale of Venus), a comic 'mock-epic' worthy of Pope or Rowlandson:

> a pretty little Gothick Building, (which I designed for Proserpines Cave, and placed in it five Figures in Bass Relife, done by the best Hand in England, the two princeable figures, was pluto and proserpine, the other three, was proserpines Chaplain, Doctor, and her Apothecary, but my Master not likeing the Doctor, I chopt them all down.)[48]

Even the self-mockery of the desire for georgic sufficiency that John Dixon Hunt has noted in Pope's 'Second Satire of the Second Book of Horace Paraphrased' (1733/34)[49] enters MacClary's account of Rousham's beauties. A serpentine path leads, at last, 'to the Kitchin Garden Door, which when you enter in, it makes you forget all they Beautys you have seen befor, it look more like paradice then a Ketchen Gardn . . . Look to the Left and you see as pretty a set of pigg Stighs, as aney is in England.' [Fig. 109]

If Pope was 'content to piddle here [in Twickenham] / On Broccoli and mutton,' MacClary's mistress (he comically suggests) ought also to be content with the paradisal sufficiency of her estate. Pope's Horatian paraphrase contrasts such content with the false affluence of 'the Lord of thousands' in '*South-sea* days.' One such was John Aislabie, Chancellor of the Exchequer, who resigned and retired in disgrace in 1721 after the South Sea Bubble scandal. In spite of government prosecution, Aislabie retained both Waverley Villa in Surrey and Hall Barn in Buckinghamshire, though he subsequently renounced the latter (which he had inherited from his wife) in favour of his step-son, Henry Waller, a descendant of the poet, Edmund Waller, who had first laid out

108. Seat and Scheemaker's Statue at the Edge of the Prospect, Rousham.

109. Former Kitchen Garden, Rousham.

the grounds in the French style in 1651. At both houses, however, Aislabie showed his Palladian colours, colours previously evident in his subscription to Castell's *Villas of the Ancients*, in his support of William Benson as Wren's successor, and his championing of Colen Campbell. At Waverley, moreover, where the house overlooked the ruins of Waverley Abbey, there was early evidence of Aislabie's taste for ruins, a taste he himself was never able to gratify at Studley Royal but in which his son, William, succeeded by the purchase of Fountains Abbey.

By the time of his fall, however, Aislabie was already more interested in Studley Royal (an estate that his father had acquired by marrying the heiress) where he further developed ideas for the garden already used at Hall Barn.[50] His correspondence for 1717 shows that work was already proceeding there in the grounds before the building of the house.[51] Indeed, an undated letter (possibly of 1713) questions the steward's account that included charges for the gardener 'for going to Nottingham 1711' twice.

Aislabie's correspondence also indicates that the then steward, George Storzaker, was already having difficulties with William Fisher (who is only ever referred to as 'the gardiner'). As early as 20 August 1715 Aislabie wrote: 'tell the gardiner, if he will not work and do as he used to doe, I have no further occasion for his Service and will bring owne [an] other.'[52] Fisher seems nonetheless to have been given a largely free rein in making the landscape [Fig. 110]. Indeed, it seems that despite Aislabie's friendship with Vanbrugh, Hawksmoor, Campbell, Roger Morris, William Benson (of Wilburg), and Lord Burlington, Fisher may have been tutor to both father and son in the principles of landscaping.[53] Aislabie subscribed to Kent's edition of *The Designs of Inigo Jones* (1727) and indeed his son named one of the buildings at his later garden 'Kent's Seat' after him. But Kent did not begin to design landscapes until the early 1720s and cannot have been an influence on Aislabie's initial conception of his garden.[54]

Certainly Fisher was celebrated as a designer by a near neighbour and fellow gardener, Peter Aram, in the dedication to his poem, 'Studley Park,' published in Thomas Gent's *Antient and Modern History of the Loyal Town of Rippon* (York, 1733): '*Learn'd in Design, of quick inventive Thought, / That hast this PARK to such Perfection brought.*' Aram's poem, moreover, places Studley Royal within the context of such landscape poems as Denham's 'Cooper's Hill,' Waller's 'St. James's Park,' Pope's 'Windsor Forest,' and Garth's 'Claremont.' Although specific in citing Studley Royal's *topoi*, it compares the estate to lost Eden and the haunts of the muses. It concludes (as a tour of the gardens would) with Fountains Abbey and the taste for ruins, but it also includes a long passage celebrating the estate's georgic context:

> See Golden Ceres wave the rip'ning Grain
> And fertile Tellus crown the Tiller's Pains:
> Here in sweet Prospect scatter'd Groves arise,
> And there the peaceful Village meets our Eyes.[55]

Plainly, whatever the strong direction offered to Fisher by his employer, to another gardener, such as Aram, Fisher had a central place. Certainly in the early phase of the garden's building (before he was replaced as supervisor by the designer and builder, Robert Doe, in the late 1720s) Fisher had a strongly supervisory, if not creative, role in the making of the gardens, not only as planter but as overseer of the construction. Aram's poem celebrates him as '*Adept in all the GARDEN Mysteries, / Of Herbs and Flow'rs, in Legumes, and in Trees,*' but Aislabie's correspondence shows that not only was Fisher in regular direct contact with him but that he was organising the carriage of the stone from the moors to the garden.[56] He was, in fact, superintendent of the operations generally. Throughout this period Aislabie continued to try to expand his holdings at Studley Royal, but he seems also to have encountered opposition to his improvement of the estate, probably from locals who were used to hunting there. There was a fire (probably arson) at the house late in 1716, after which Storzaker was advised to have a man to help Fisher guard the house and to 'look to the park and work with the Gardiner etc.'[57]

For all that, Fisher, like Aram and Knowlton, was paid at very low rate. Where Moses Cook had been paid about £180 a year in 1680 at Cassiobury, Fisher was paid £26 a year.[58] By comparison, John Simpson, a stonemason hired to do work at the Cascade, [Figs. 111, 112] the earliest part of the garden, was in 1719 paid £37 11s 9d, and even Robert Marbery and his two sons were paid £71 11s 6d 'for breaking Stones' in February of 1720. These were the stones that, like the 'Timber to the Canall' for which Thomas Stephenson was paid £127 11s 8d in 1719 and Simpson £111 10s 1d in 1720 , were used to build the Canal that, with the Ponds and the Cascade, formed the initial phase of the garden between 1716 and 1720.[59]

As early as 7 March 1713 Aislabie was complaining that Peter Burnard's

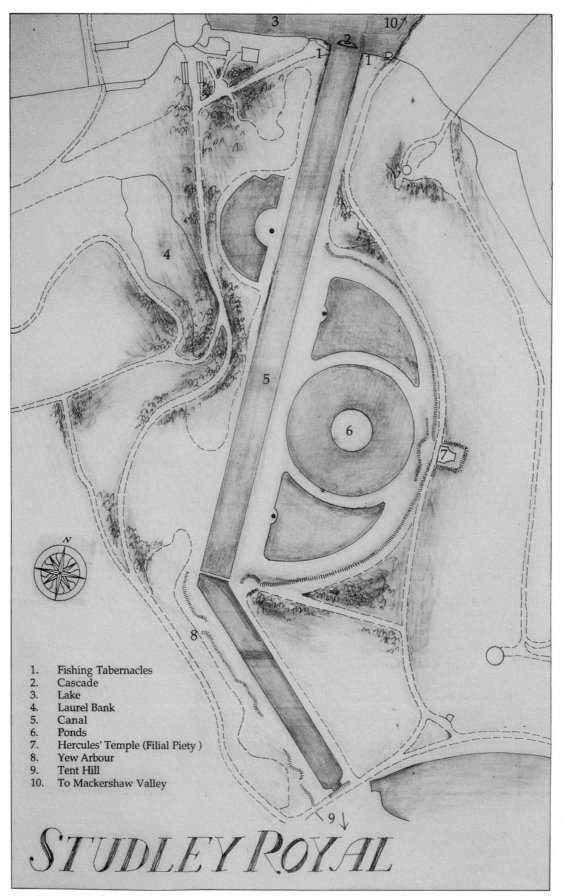

1. Fishing Tabernacles
2. Cascade
3. Lake
4. Laurel Bank
5. Canal
6. Ponds
7. Hercules' Temple (Filial Piety)
8. Yew Arbour
9. Tent Hill
10. To Mackershaw Valley

STUDLEY ROYAL

110. Todd Longstaffe-Gowan, Reconstruction Plan of Studley Royal (c. 1750).

111. Balthassar Nebot, 'The Cascade, Studley Royal' (c. 1730). Private collection, photo, The National Trust.

charge for 'the work that was done at the Wears' was exorbitant and by 31 January 1716, Aislabie was writing to his steward about making 'the pond heads in the warren.' On 19 January 1719 he wrote again: 'I gave the gardiner orders to make a pond in the Leas, and if it be possible to make it hold water or to bring any to it, and wou'd therefor have you give orders about it, and if it succeed, I will then alter the wall.'[60] Plainly Fisher was concerned as superintendent with more than the simple planting of the gardens above the Cascade. In March 1719 Aislabie wrote to Storzaker's son, John, the new steward, to 'give orders for the wood in the park to be fenc'd in, where the gardiner writes 'tis wanting.'[61]

Not surprisingly, though, Fisher's primary concern was with trees—their planting and preservation. The trees at Studley seem to have come from four sources: John Kirke's nursery in Brompton, London, near the nursery of London and Wise; the nursery of the Perfect family in Pontefract; John Telford's nursery in York; and what appears to be local coppicing.[62] The trees from Kirke must have been very expensive in carriage. Two bills for 1719 are for £22 2s 0d and £73 12s 0d respectively.[63] Generally the bills from Perfect were much lower and of course his nursery was much more convenient.

112. The Cascade, Studley Royal.

113 (below left). Statue of Neptune and Temple of Filial Piety (formerly Temple of Hercules), Studley Royal.

114 (below right). The Canal, Studley Royal.

Frequently Fisher went there to fetch trees and Perfect continued to supply trees to the estate in the 1730s.[64]

In the late 1720s Fisher was demoted from his position as superintendent and replaced by Robert Doe, but he remained as gardener. A letter to him from Aislabie on 11 February, 1728 reminds him that 'your first work must be planting which now the Season requires.' And Fisher replied on the 18th that 'we have made the Ground at the head of the great Dam fitt for planting' and that he has levelled and grassed the slope in Kelder walk.[65] Certainly there is abundant evidence that the planting went forward on a large scale under Fisher's direction. In October 1735 he was moving beech trees and a month later we read that 'the Carpenters have been Boxing the New Trees and them that was moved.' In February of the following year he is 'planting Walnutts, Chesnutts, etc. in Mackershawes [the deer park later developed as a wild picturesque valley] as your Honor order'd him.'[66]

Fortunately Hallot, Aislabie's agent at this period, sent him very careful letters, recording the doings of the estate on the right-hand side and the accounts on the left. His letter of 18 March 1736 shows Fisher still very much in command:

Went to Mr Blackets [Newby Hall] and brought 150 firrs They was that night and Wedensday [sic] Planting them by Wattle Hall Herculis's Temple and Thursday Staking Trees and felling Alders by the high fall—munday and to Day Planting firrs (out of Math. Beams Nursery) upon the hill by the

115. William Hallot, Letter of 18 March, 1736. West Yorkshire Archives.

153

low fall—The Cart has begun to lead the Wall from behind the New Stable to the Place orderd your Gardener.[67] [Fig. 115]

Plainly, demoted though he might have been, Fisher continued to exercise considerable sway. On 16 April Hallot wrote again in justification of his accounts:

> The Gardener says there is so much Cleaning in the Walks mowing and Tying of trees in the Cascade and the Nursarys that itt is Impossible to Do with a Less number of men to have things in order—he says by your Honor's Direction he begins next week to make some alteration in the Walk behind Hercules's Temple.[68] [Figs. 113, 114]

On 12 February 1737, he wrote once more to Aislabie: 'The men have been removeing some firrs (by Mr. Aislabies [presumably William's] order) from the left hand going to the lower to Plant in a sweep on the back side answerable to the bank side of Hercules's temple [later the Temple of Filial Piety].'

At the end of that year Hallot wrote again to say that 'the Gardener says he's had a Letter from York [presumably John Telford's nursery] that there is 300 Spruce firs the size your Honor mentioned but they bcg to know if your Honor would have them all.'[69] Presumably Aislabie did take the spruces, for a letter of 5 February 1738 confirming the arrival of a large shipment of elms from Perfect also states: 'The gardener says he shall be ready on Wednesday night for the Spruce firrs which I shall take care to send for to be here that night.' These spruces were then planted, like the earlier ones, 'above the first row by Hercules's temple.'[70]

What is not entirely clear is Fisher's role in determining this very important planting, planting that gives that whole section of the garden its character by softening the architectural quality of the design. On April 30 Hallot wrote: 'Everything that's been done before Mr. Aislabie came here was fully by the Gardeners Directions.' But quite when (William) Aislabie arrived to take

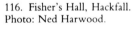

116. Fisher's Hall, Hackfall.
Photo: Ned Harwood.

charge is not stated. Throughout that March the gardener's men had been clearing walks in the wooded banks, preparing 'Borders for the hedges in the walks,' and removing oaks from the nursery to another walk. By 2 April they had finished planting hollies and tying trees at the Cascade and were beginning 'att the hill by the temple to clear it of wood and Stones.'[71] Fisher continued to modify and alter these plantings. On 8 April Hallot wrote that 'he's this week been cutting lower some of the Hedges in the Cascade,' and a year later he had moved the spruces from Hercules's temple along with the elms to the Rustic Bridge that was at the furthest end of the garden. There the plantings at the foot of Tent Hill were designed to conceal the termination and included eighty spruces and twenty-seven yews near the grotto.[72]

It would be mistaken to rate Fisher's place at Studley even so highly as MacClary's at Rousham. For all his directive and horticultural skill, he was not given so free a hand by John Aislabie as MacClary was by Kent and General Dormer. And yet his legacy seems to have been significant. Although he died in 1743, before William Aislabie began seriously to cultivate the wild romantic landscape of his nearby estate, Hackfall, his name was commemorated there in the octagon building called 'Fisher's Hall' [Fig. 116].

In his *Tour through the Northern Counties of England and the Borders of Scotland* (1802), Richard Warner thought that William Aislabie's intention at Hackfall was to induce the public to 'compare Hackfall with Studley' and to convince them 'of the superiority of the natural style of gardening [Hackfall] over the meretricious system, which in his days it was the fashion to adopt.'[73] If so, 'Fisher's Hall', rather than 'Kent's Seat' marked the *locus* of a new world of gardening, the world that Joseph Spence and many others were discovering at the same time, where 'the visitor was confronted with the sights and sounds of tumbling streams and foaming rapids, gazed upon bold rock faces and precipitous heights and contemplated one's human scale in the isolating presence of impenetrable woods and remindful ruins.'[74] If, as Edward Harwood believes, it was Fisher who directed William Aislabie on to this new path, then it is appropriate that he should have been commemorated in this building where 'the short physical distance from Kent's Seat to Fisher's Hall marked an intellectual leap from one generation's aesthetic ideals into the next.'[75]

10

NATURE'S STILL IMPROV'D BUT NEVER LOST: PHILIP SOUTHCOTE AND WOOBURN FARM

In 1734, only two years after his father's ward, Lord Petre, had begun to transform Thorndon, Philip Southcote bought Wooburn Farm near Chertsey in Surrey and began to alter it into the most famous *ferme ornée* of the early eighteenth century. [Fig. 117] Indeed, Southcote is generally credited with the invention of the *ferme ornée* although in fact the idea for such a georgic garden goes back at least to Addison's 1712 *Spectator* essay and even beyond to ideas first formulated by Evelyn in the 1650s. Even in the previous year, Switzer began to adumbrate the ideas of an 'Ornamental Farm' that came to fruition in the second edition of his *Ichnographia* in 1742.[1]

Writing what became one of the classic accounts of the *ferme ornée* in 1770, Thomas Whately (who was then a near neighbour to Wooburn) ascribed 'the vicious taste which long prevailed in gardens' to the divorce between profit and pleasure, farm and garden. For him the word 'improvement' ought to have included both agriculture and horticulture and improvement achieved 'by opening the garden to the country.' His phrase, 'to blend the useful with the agreeable,' betrays the Horatian origins of the *ferme ornée*, and to this he allies 'the ideas of pastoral poetry' in a way that William Shenstone was also to do in the 1740s at The Leasowes.[2]

In fact, although Whately begins his account with The Leasowes, he ends with Wooburn Farm, the place where he believed the idea of the *ferme ornée* had been most completely realised. His account is not uncritical. Indeed, he concludes with the point that he earlier raises: that the proper simplicity of a farm is often 'lost in such a profusion of ornament' as is suggested by 'beds of flowers . . . rather too profusely strewed.' In spite of Southcote's 'rifling' the flowers of the meadow for the garden and vice versa, the georgic '*simplex munditiis*' has, he believes, been lost sight of.[3]

It was for just this simplicity, however, that the anonymous author of *The Rise and Progress of the Present Taste in Planting* (probably Lady Irwin) had celebrated Wooburn only three years earlier. Comparing Southcote's estate to 'injur'd' nature at Studley Royal, he writes:

> Wooburn for me superior charms can boast
> Where Nature's still improv'd, but never lost;
> Here rob'd in soft simplicity she shines,
> And all the paint and pomp of Art resigns,
> Pleases alone by her intrinsic grace,
> And wears the native beauties of her face.[4]

117. Luke Sullivan, 'A View of Wooburn Farm in Surry' (1759). The Trustees of the British Museum.

Where Wooburn was most to be praised, Whateley believed, was in the georgic combination of farm and garden: the division of the farm into pasture and grain fields, the former divided into 'lawns' by the sandy walk that also surrounds the whole and is itself planted as a linear garden. [Fig. 118] 'With the beauties which enliven a garden, are every where intermixed many properties of a farm.' These include 'the bleating of the sheep' and 'the clucking of the poultry' as well as 'the corn-fields [which] are the subjects of every rural employment.'[5]

Although Wooburn had two pleasing views into borrowed landscape, Whately most admired the scenes through which the walk led, which were 'truly elegant, every where rich, and always agreeable.' His praise for the 'peculiar chearfulness [that] overspreads both the lawns'[6] echoes both Joseph Spence's response to Wooburn and his account of Pope's response. Southcote's uncle, the Abbé Thomas, was credited by Pope with saving his life, and Pope himself visited Wooburn and commended its beauties.

> When I told Mr. Southcote that the sight of his ground near his house was always apt to lead me into a pleasing smile and into a delicious sort of feeling at the heart, of which I had nothing when I was in his much nobler views along the brow of the hill, he said that Mr. Pope had often spoke of the very same effect of it on him.[7]

The early years of Southcote's life are something of a mystery. When he was in his early thirties, it seems likely that he was taken abroad by Lord Petre when he went to France in 1729–30. It also seems likely that Lord Petre, with whose family Southcote's was intermarried, continued to support him. Certainly Southcote, who believed that Lord Petre had gone beyond Pope and Kent in the practice of 'painting in gardening,' thought of himself as '*Lord Petre's* élève.'[8] It is also not unlikely that Southcote's repertoire of shrubs and flowers owed something to Petre's influence, though Southcote had neither the extensive botanical contacts nor the greenhouses to support planting of

157

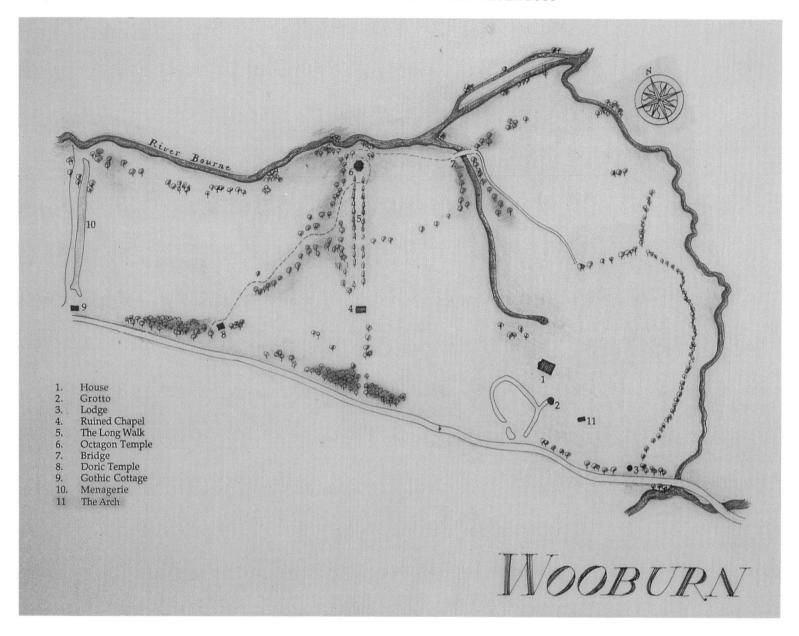

1. House
2. Grotto
3. Lodge
4. Ruined Chapel
5. The Long Walk
6. Octagon Temple
7. Bridge
8. Doric Temple
9. Gothic Cottage
10. Menagerie
11. The Arch

118. Todd Longstaffe-Gowan, Reconstruction Plan of Wooburn Farm (c. 1750).

Petre's kind.

For some time in the early 1730s Southcote appears to have been in the retinue of the Duke of Lorraine, both at Lunéville in France and in London, but in 1733 he married the Dowager Duchess of Cleveland, who settled £16,000 on him. In a letter to Stephen Fox in December 1731, Lord Hervey makes mocking reference to this intended match, describing Southcote as 'the Duke of Norfolk's disagreeable, cherry-cheeked captain' and 'a fool without either title or estate.'[9] In spite of Southcote's marrying the Duchess for her money, not everything in his financial arrangements went smoothly. In 1745 (a year before his wife's death) he and his wife were sued by other members of her family for a more equitable disbursement of her inheritance, a suit which considerably diminished her portion of that legacy.[10] Nonetheless a document of 1750 records the conveyancing of further land in Chertsey to Southcote, obviously an addition to Wooburn Farm that he was able to make with his wife's estate.[11]

Wooburn seems ultimately to have contained 125 acres[12] and to have included a temple designed by Lord Burlington.[13] [Fig. 119] What Southcote's education for such an enterprise might have included, in the absence of more complete records, can be only grounds for speculation. Certainly, through Pope at least, he would have known of Riskins, the Earl of Bathurst's *ferme ornée* in Buckinghamshire. He also knew Lord Petre's contemporary work at Thorndon and Worksop, and very likely was familiar with Worlies, the early *ferme ornée* established a century earlier by John Evelyn near Thorndon.

For that matter, it seems that he had something to do with the laying out of his father's grounds nearby at Witham in Essex. Horace Walpole, writing to George Montagu in 1749, mentions Witham as 'with Southcote's help . . . one of the most charming villas in England. There are sweet meadows falling down a hill, and rising again on t'other side of the prettiest little winding stream you ever saw.'[14] A survey of 1762 shows a triangular plantation containing a serpentine water and a lake behind the house. 'Bath Field' beyond it has a bath, 'Home Field' a statue, and at the end of the meadow is a cascade.[15] This combination of agricultural and aesthetic certainly looks like an early essay in what Wooburn Farm was more effectively to achieve.

There are not, unfortunately, anything like so many descriptions of Wooburn as of William Shenstone's The Leasowes. Thomas Whately's *Observations on Modern Gardening* (1770) gives the most extensive description of Wooburn, but it was published twelve years after Southcote's death. Perhaps more trustworthy as contemporary records are the observations made by Joseph Spence, Richard Pococke, and Horace Walpole. Spence's account of Wooburn and Southcote occur in his manuscript notes on gardens and gardening made in the early 1750s; Pococke's is in the travel notes made by him in 1757, and gives a good sense of the overall design:

> This is the first improvement in the Farm kind, and is esteem'd the most elegant, in England. It consists of walks to the left, first round two meadows on rather high ground and then round another on low ground, on the right side of them, through the further side of which a canal is made from the poultry house, which is in form of a temple, and extends towards the Thames. These walks are adorn'd not only with plantations of wood but

119. Samuel Ireland, 'Wooburn Farm' (c. 1770). Gothic Cottage and View of Burlington's Temple. The Trustees of the British Museum.

with spots and beds of flowering shrubs and other flowers to fill up angles, and other shrubs to diversifie the scene. From the end next the house and behind it is a piece of water form'd like a river, over which there is a bridge that leads to several small fields mostly of corn and some meadows with walks and plantations round them.[16]

Spence, who seems to have accepted Southcote's claim to have been 'the first that brought in the Garden-Farm; or Ferme Ornée,' notes too that Kent had been 'most struck at the Temple.' He also gives an account of Southcote's original conception that accords well with what Pococke observed: 'All my Design at first was to have a Garden on the middle high ground, and a Walk all round my Farm; for Convenience, as well as Pleasure. For from the Garden, I could see what was doing in the Grounds; and by the walk, could have a pleasing access to either of them where I might be wanted.'[17]

Spence, however, gleaned from Southcote not just the elements of a *ferme ornée* but the means whereby the landscape could be 'called in'. A letter from Lord Petre's widow to Peter Collinson on 4 June 1747 indicates that 'the Sweets and beautys of Wobourn' included as much of those further prospects that were 'without the bounds of Mr. Southcotes Dominions as within them.'[18] And by 1761 (three years after Southcote's death), Shenstone's friend and publisher, Richard Dodsley, noted how Wooburn 'joins to the Earl of Portmore just beyond it . . . [and] has a deal of variety and many prospects which are remarkably beautiful and picturesque.'[19] Even as late as 1795, in his second edition of *An Essay on Design in Gardening*, George Mason remembered Southcote for 'enlivening every path with casual pieces of perspective.'[20] Just such a consideration of perspective at Wooburn Farm was noted by Spence in about 1752:

> In Mr. Southcote's gardens, from the line that leads to the house, the foreground is the meadow; the mid-ground a winding stream with clumps and trees scattered about it; and the background is the rising of the hill and the line of trees to the ruined church. These are all of a moderate size, and well-proportioned.[21]

What Southcote taught Spence in the use of perspective had initially been practised by Pope in the placing of the obelisk to his mother's memory in his own garden in 1735. In that garden, however, Pope never had occasion or opportunity to use this device to 'call in the country'. The closest he came to such effects was the optical illusion of passing traffic on the Thames created by the grotto in the garden.

For Southcote, however, Pope's observation that 'all gardening is landscape-painting' deserved to be applied to a larger canvas than Pope addressed. 'Perspective, prospect, distancing, and attracting, comprehend all that part of painting in gardening,' he remarked to Spence in the early 1750s.[22] By this he meant also 'borrowed landscape' for which he used the word 'attracting,' or alternately 'foreshortening' or 'contracting': 'By attracting I intend to bring St. Anne's Hill at least one third *nearer to me* (by planting in the middle, so as to hide the ground behind). The trees I plant, when grown up, will fall in with the trees near that hill and make but one slope of foliage, and so unite that part to my own as to the eye.'[23] St. Anne's Hill was also one of the prospects from Spence's own garden. At the very time that he himself was foreshortening the view from *his* garden to St. Anne's Hill, he observed that Southcote had used 'prospect, looking *by* trees, but the line open at top (clear view)' from the

A.   *A.*   *A.*   *A.*

B.   *B.*   *B.*

Beech,   Bl: Poplar,   Hornbeam,   Abèle,   Alder,   Chesnut,   Nut-tree,   Crabtrees.

o Siringo,   o Sw: Willow,   o Laburnum,   o Lilac,   o Whitethorn,   o Honeysucle,   o Span: Broom.

o Rose,   o Laurel,   o Sw: Briar,   o Holly,   o Frutex,   o Com: Broom.

o Lillies,   o Holyhoaks,   o GoldenRod,   o Columbine,   o Starwort,   o Honesty,   o CrownImperial,   o Snaps,   o Piony,   o Primrose-tree,

o Stocks,   o Rose,   o Sw:Will,   o CantlBell,   o Wallflr,   o Catchfly,   o Carnations,   o Lavender,   o Scabions,   o Marjoram,   o Lavender Cotton,

o Crocus,   o Hypia,   o Snowdrops,   o Primroses,   o Jonquils,   o Snowdrops,   o Crocus &c

D.   *D.*   *D.*

E.   *E.*

F.   *F.*   *F.*

A. The Old Hedge-Row.   D. Sandwalk; 5f wide.
B. Plantation; 5f. wide.   E. Fence.
C. Border; 2f.½.   F. The Field, or Meadow.

120. Joseph Spence, 'The Order of Planting after Mr. Southcote's Manner.' Beinecke Library, Yale University.

temple 'in his own gardens, the view to the old church . . . and to the trees on St. Anne's Hill.'[24]

If Lord Petre's planting of his mounts was a prelude to this inclusion of prospect, Southcote's planting was more modest in its repertoire of trees. Among those included in the plantations that fronted his old hedgerows were beech, black and white poplar, alder, crabapple, chestnut, and other unnamed nut trees. He also used gum tree, hemlock, hickory, cypress, and various sorts of pine and acacia.[25] 'In all plantations made to cover the pale, or fence of your Boundary, [Southcote wrote] where there is room for it, it is remarkably fine and agreeable to see different plants rise one above another from the shrub to the tallest trees of various kinds.'[26] [Fig. 120] Fronting these trees, in a plantation no larger than five feet wide, were first large shrubs, such as lilac, laburnum, honeysuckle, Spanish broom, whitethorn, and philadelphus, and then smaller shrubs such as roses, laurel, sweet briar, spirea, holly, and common broom. This sort of planting, as we have seen, was being practised contemporaneously at Worksop by Lord Petre, though Southcote's was far denser. Like Petre's, however, Southcote's must have been intended to be thinned.

By 1735, none of these trees or shrubs was very extraordinary. Indeed, much of Southcote's plan and repertoire could have been suggested by Philip Miller's description of a 'Wilderness' in the 1731 edition of the *Gardeners Dictionary*.[27] Southcote was more innovative in his use of trees in the creation of prospect: 'There should be leading trees, or clumps of trees, to help the eye to any more distant clump, building, or view.'[28] Southcote also had as great a belief as Petre in the importance of shading. 'Even the least risings and falls in a Bank,' he said to Spence, 'make some variety of lights and shades,'[29] and he repeated, 'We should prevent the rays of the sun from falling too strongly on the eyes by a proper interposition of shades, which when above, helps the eye like a hat or umbrella (or on the sides, as one sees a picture much stronger when the sidelights are broken all round by a proper holding up of the hand).'[30]

Writing to Southcote in 1752, Peter Collinson made particular observations on how what he called 'painting with Living pencils' these effects might be best achieved using the dark and light green foliage of a number of trees to 'Diversifie the Sylvan Scene' (see p. 112). Although without Lord Petre's resources for botanical importation and experimentation, Southcote was nonetheless interested in scientific advances and understood the place of both Newtonian optics and planting in creating perspective effects. In his collection of 'Materials for Designing a Garden' he included an observation by his friend Dalrymple: 'The Gradations of Colors in the deciduous Trees, differs from that in the Evergreens: for in the former the gradation should be, Light-green, Deep Green, Yellow Green; whereas in the Evergreens, it shou'd be, Light Green, Yellow Green, Deep Green.'

Across the page from that Spence has noted: 'His way of trying them in Flower Pots; and in the Fields—Has also planted trees; (in circles, up a Mount).'[32] Elsewhere Spence's notes show Southcote aware of the importance of evergreens in enhancing sculptural effects and of black poplar as 'one of the best thickeners for the solids: because it is spiral, grows very fast, and may be cut away whenever better things grow up and spread.'[33] Southcote's deployment of flowers is outside the scope of this study. Suffice to say that at a time when (it has been wrongly thought) flowers were no longer important to gardens, his peripheral walks relied upon them and his mixture of bulbs with perennials was striking. He told Spence that he had 'prevailed on Kent to resume flowers in the natural way of gardening,' and that certainly is what he himself put into practice at Wooburn where, in William Mason's phrase 'The simple Farm eclips'd the Garden's pride' by encompassing it.[34]

Twenty years earlier, John Parnell, the great-nephew of the poet, Thomas Parnell, made a tour of England that included Wooburn. Like Mason he praised Southcote's combination of the agricultural with the horticultural, the *utile* with the *dulci*: 'I think Mr. Southcote's is more complete and more desirable than any improvement I know which carries their idea of beauty to such a length as to exclude the *utile* intirely.'[35]

Mason saw Southcote in the tradition of 'the English style of gardening' introduced by Kent. The notes written for his satirical 'Heroic Epistle to Sir William Chambers' by Horace Walpole, however, distinguish Kent's 'garden that connects itself with a park' and Southcote's *ferme ornée*. While noting the arcadian inspiration of Southcote's work, Walpole also voices some disquiet with the unreality and expense of the enterprise: 'The Profusion of flowers and the delicacy of *keeping* betray more wealthy expence than is consistent with the oeconomy of a Farmer, or the rusticity of labour. Wooburn farm . . . is the habitation of such Nymphs and Sheperds as are represented in landscapes [i.e. paintings] and novels, but do not exist in real life.'[36] Southcote nonetheless came to be celebrated, in contradistinction to Kent, as the champion of a rural ideal that had been praised by Horace and Pliny and the Virgil of the *Georgics*. As Miles Hadfield put it: 'Kent strove to create an Elysium: a classical paradise seen through the eyes of a Claude. Southcote's ambition was an Arcady: the ideal countryside.'[37]

When Joseph Warton, in *The Enthusiast* (1744) celebrated 'Shakespeare's warblings wild' over 'the lays of artful Addison,' he also exalted the taste of Southcote and his friend, Joseph Spence, over Kentian artifice.

Can Kent design like Nature? Mark where Thames'
Plenty and Pleasure pour through Lincoln's meads,
Can the great artist, though with taste supreme
Endow'd, one beauty to this Eden add?

'Lincoln's meads' at this time were not Lord Lincoln's later estate at Esher,[38] but Oatlands, the estate near both Southcote's Wooburn Farm and Spence's Byfleet, where Spence prided himself in having encouraged Lincoln 'into an Inclination for Planting and Gardening.'[39] Indeed, as we have seen, one of the principle views within Wooburn Farm was an invocation of just such a scene of the Thames as Warton describes.

Southcote's greatest legacy was not the *ferme ornée* itself but two of its instruments: the use of flowers and the peripheral belt of trees. By 1803, the *ferme ornée* had become in England almost as much of an artifice as Marie Antoinette's *hameau*, and Repton ridiculed it in his *Observations on the Theory and Practice of Landscape Gardening*. But Repton's extensive use of flowers owed something to Southcote's having 'prevailed on Kent to resume flowers in the natural way of gardening'[40] and to the 'rosary' that was one of Southcote's first creations there, with the help of Lord Petre. Spence may have thought the latter 'one of the first (and worst) things that was done there,'[41] but its legacy to the gardenesque movement is obvious.[42]

Southcote's other legacy was primarily to Capability Brown and his pupils: the peripheral belt that came to be simplified generally to a beech ride. In their hands, however, what had been a peripatetic experience of intimate and prospective effects became a ride or a carriage drive to underline the extent of ownership by concealing the bounds of the estate.

11
PROSPECTS AND THE NATURAL BEAUTIES OF PLACES: JOSEPH SPENCE

In the early 1750s, looking back over the previous two decades, Joseph Spence noted that Ephraim Chambers, in his *Cyclopedia* published in 1728, had heard nothing at that time of the 'new taste in gardening.' 'The very name of Gardens,' Spence wrote elsewhere, 'has shifted it's meaning among us, within these few years. It us'd to signify only Kitchin-Gardens, or at best Flower-Gardens; whereas its principal use now relates to the disposition of the Land, Water, Plantations and Views about our Villas in the Country.'[1]

Spence's own career offers an interesting example of the way in which this shift came about. Having achieved critical prominence in 1726 by his commentary on Pope's translation of the *Odyssey*, he became both Professor of Poetry at Oxford (and lectured on the *Aeneid* in the following year)[2] and subsequently Professor of Modern History. He also became a good friend of Pope, and Pope's extensive aesthetic influence on him is attested by the large number of anecdotes and observations, many of them on gardening, that are included in Spence's *Anecdotes*.

But Spence had the advantage of Pope in being able to travel to the continent, which he did three times between 1730 and 1741. Even on the earliest of these trips, when he went as the companion of the young Lord Middlesex, his letters are full of observations on the interplay between nature and art, garden and landscape, horticulture and agriculture. In Rome it was the 'mixture of city, country and gardens;' near Pisa, a countryside that was 'a little paradise of evergreens and perpetual shrubs of myrtle, all in flower;' and at Florence, the great estates of the Duke de Medici, with their mixture of *utile* and *dulci*: 'You go to it [Cascine] through a range of vast Scotch fir-trees: on your left hand is a long run of groves and pretty artificial islands full of arbours, and on the right lie the vineyards and cornfields interspersed, which is the manner all about Florence (as in Lombardy).'[3]

In his *Anecdotes*, moreover, Spence suggested that Southcote's 'idea of a Ferme Ornée' came similarly from 'Fields, going from Rome to Venice.'[4] This mixture of the useful and beautiful remained one of Spence's principles in the creation of a garden. In a famous letter to his friend, the Reverend Robert Wheeler, in 1751, he laid it down as the eleventh of his rules of landscaping, 'to mix useful things even in the ornamental parts, and something of ornament even in the useful parts.'[5]

Pope may have offered Spence painterly instructions on the art of planting, but Spence's practice shows far more evidence of horticultural knowledge than anything recorded of Pope. Indeed, although Pope gave Spence general advice

From mr Dalrymple.

The most obvious Dis-
-tinction for the colors of
Trees is the Light-Green,
as the Ash; the Yellow-
-Green, as the Lime: & the
Deep-Green, as the Black-
-Cherry.

The same Division runs
in the Evergreens. The Light
-Green, is the Weymouth-Pine;
the Yellow-Green, is the
American Spruce; & the
Deep-Green, is the Silver-Fir.

Each of these Divisions
contain a number of Sub-
divisions under it.

The Gradation of Colors
in the deciduous Trees, dif-
-fers from that in the Ever-
-greens: for in the former
the Gradation shou'd be, Light
-green, Deep Green, Yellow Green;
whereas in the Evergreens, it
should be, Light-Green, Yellow
Green, Deep Green.

mr Walker's List
of Trees &c, fro.
him & Dick; &c.
&c &c Dilg...

His way of trying them
in Flower-Pots; & in ye Fields.
Has also planted thus; (in circly
up a Mount.)

121. Joseph Spence, 'From Mr Dalrymple': On Colours in Tree-Planting. Beinecke Library. Yale University.

about perspective and the disposition of masses and colour, it was Southcote's planting plan for the walks at Wooburn that Spence transcribed in his notes. And if Southcote could describe himself as Lord Petre's pupil, Spence was, in a sense, the pupil of that pupil. What Lord Petre did with colour effects in clump and hedge planting at Worksop, Spence also planned in 1750 at Horwood, where he owned the living. There the plantation, which was a mixture of deciduous and coniferous trees, was arranged to show off their colours in the way that Southcote, citing Lord Petre, commended to him.[6] Spence in turn recommends 'placing trees of different greens and flowers of different colours by one another' in his 1751 letter to Wheeler, an idea that he may have got from Sir David Dalrymple (later Lord Hailes). [Fig. 121]. In boundary planta-tions, he also commends the gradation from lower shrubs to taller trees that Lord Petre had earlier used at Worksop.[7]

In a letter to his patron and former pupil, Lord Lincoln, Spence recorded the extent of Southcote's influence on him: 'I was the other morning, in great Happiness, for above three Hours, at Mr. Southcote's. He show'd me every thing, and let me into all his future Designs; and I think, I can see, that the Part which was the Flower-Garden, (and what he did the very first, of all his designs,) will be extreamly improv'd.'[8]

It was with Lord Lincoln that Spence spent the longest of his three trips abroad, between September 1739 and November 1741. Spence's correspondence from this trip says little about gardens. Although he records going to Pratolino in his notebook, he describes only Giovanni da Bologna's 'Apennino' there. Apart from his final letter to his mother, on 11 November 1741, about the Tuileries and the Luxembourg Gardens ('which would be charming if they were not so regular'), his only other interesting remarks are about the pretty walks in the countryside near Turin and the 'white villas and the little groves about them' that he admired near Rome.[9] He later wrote to Lord Lincoln, however, that one of his intentions had been 'an endeavour of leading you into an Inclination for Planting and Gardening, by pointing out Prospects, and the natural Beauties of places, as we pass'd.'[10]

Spence's own agenda for this trip (as for the two previous ones) was the pursuit of the culture of classical, and especially Virgilian, antiquity. He was particularly interested in the visual arts as they illustrated and confirmed ancient literature, and ultimately this study was to result in the publication of *Polymetis* (1747) and *Crito: or a Dialogue on Beauty* (1752).

'What further recommendation can a language want or have,' Leonard Welsted had written to Sir Robert Walpole in 1727, 'after it has once transfus'd into itself the soul of the Classical ages, where *Greece* and *Rome* reflourish in it and when the fountains of ancient and modern wit and science are laid open by the industry of its writers.'[11] Spence, however, was not simply on the side of the ancients in the controversy over ancients and moderns. Like many of his contemporaries, he saw Britain not only as the heir of antiquity but as superior to what the ancients had achieved in gardening:

> I have sometimes been apt to doubt, whether this taste of Gardning was ever receiv'd as a National Taste in any part of the World known to the Greeks and Romans; or ever practis'd since the fall of the Roman Empire, before it was introduced so lately among us . . . Knowledge and the Arts, of old, are suppos'd to have flourisht first among the Assyrians; and then, among the Egyptians: from Egypt they pass'd into Greece; and made their last settlement in Italy. I don't find, in any of the Nations just mention'd, any evident signs of the Art in Question: either from their Rules about Gardning in general, or in the particular Descriptions of their Gardens, with which I have hitherto met.[12]

This task had fallen to Britain, Spence believed, and had been exemplified in the gardens created in the previous thirty years. As an apostle of this 'new taste in gardening' Spence, like Sir William Temple before him, turned to Chinese ideas of natural irregularity. Unlike Temple, though, Spence knew whereof he wrote. He had looked at plates of the Chinese imperial gardens, first drawn in 1744 by T'ang Tai and Shen Yuan and engraved in Paris in 1749.[13] His translation of Jean-Denis Attiret's *A Particular Account of the Emperor of China's Garden* (1752),[14] moreover, was an affirmation of his belief not in the sort of chinoiserie espoused by Sir William Chambers but in the 'natural style.'[15] And it was these Chinese principles of extensive and open gardening that also informed his letter to Wheeler the previous year:

In the mixing of lights and shades, to let the former have the prevalence, or, in other words, to give the whole a joyous air rather than a melancholy one. In this again the Chinese seem very much to exceed our pleasure-ground makers. They have scarce any such thing as close or thick groves in any of their near views: they fling them all on some of the hills at a distance.[16]

In 1731, the year before Lord Petre began to remake his estate at Thorndon, Spence made his first experiment with garden design. In this garden he declared his allegiances by including statues of Virgil and Pope near the study and Homer and Milton by the greenhouse. This design, however, was for a small garden not unlike the town and suburban gardens that almost exclusively he was to design over the next two decades. I do not propose to give a complete account of Spence's gardening career.[17] What distinguishes it is neither these early small gardens nor his later participation in the taste for a combination of beauty, horror, and immensity in landscape. His genius was in his ability to break the bounds of the landscape garden of his time: to translate *ingentia rura* even further. Where Marvell had stepped from the enclosed garden into the landscape and seen (long before Kent) that all nature was a garden, Spence not only 'called in' distant views of the country but made that countryside part of his garden. Even at Kent's Rousham, where buildings outside the property led the eye into the landscape, the garden visitor was not invited to walk out into that landscape, let alone to use it in turn as a theatre from which to view the landscape through which he had passed. Wooburn Farm had two views of borrowed landscape, but neither could be called a 'bursting prospect.' Its circuit walk, like Shenstone's at The Leasowes, still kept the visitor within the bounds of its controlled referents. Even Pope's Twickenham had only one glimpse out of the garden: a kaleidoscopic vista through the grotto of the distant Thames. The mount in his garden offered a survey only of his own 'little kingdom'.

Spence's great admiration for Pope and his garden must, in some sense, have been a restraint on his own originality, for it was only in 1748 (four years after Pope's death) that he began to go beyond Pope's practice at Twickenham and to call in the country in a way that neither Pope nor Lord Petre had ever managed. In that year, thanks to the generosity of his patron, the Earl of Lincoln, Spence was offered a house in Byfleet in Surrey, near Lincoln's own estate, Oatlands. [Fig. 122] It was, as he wrote in Horatian terms to his friend Massingberd on 20 November 1748, 'absolutely separated from the Village; free from all disturbance, and calculated for ease and quiet.'[18]

The grounds of the house at Byfleet were not in themselves very extensive, but within a year Spence was already replacing the planting of the village land that led from his vicarage to the bridge. He had by then begun to incorporate walks and plantings in his neighbours' fields, and shortly thereafter he was to begin to incorporate the landscaping and 'calling in' of more distant hills. This 'more extensive and rural' landscaping was only possible because Lord Lincoln was also the leaseholder or owner of most of the surrounding land. Doubtless Spence's continental tours served to confirm the principle that he had also learned from Pope: that a garden should include distant picturesque views (although, in fact, Pope's garden included none).

Indeed, within a year of Pope's publishing his 'Epistle to Burlington', Spence wrote from Italy in praise of the sort of aesthetic that Pope also encouraged in the landscape garden: surprise, variety, and a concealment of the bounds. What pleased him in Rome, for example, was the apparent confusion of town with country.

A View of Oatlands in Surry the Seat of the Rt Honble the Earl of LINCOLN.   Vue d'Oatlands dans la Comté de Surry la Maison & Jardin Magnifique du Comte de LINCOLN.

Published according to Act of Parliament. March 1st 1759.   — Printed for I. Bowles in St Pauls Church Yard, John Bowles & Son in Cornhil, Robt Sayer in Fleet Street, Eliz. Bakewell & Hen. Parker in Cornhil, & I. Ryall in Cheapside.

122. Luke Sullivan, 'A View of Oatlands in Surry' (1759). The Trustees of the British Museum.

Several of the nobler palaces have gardens to them as large as if they were in the country . . . This mixture of city, country, and gardens, with the inequalities of the ground . . . gives several views of an uncommon sort, and more beautiful than are to be met with in most other cities. In many parts you have little groves of pine-trees rising above the houses, here you see a long Garden, with statues and fountains sloping down half the side of a hill . . . and there a dark wood running along the side of a Market-place.[19]

It was on this trip too that Spence seems first to have acquired a taste for the wilder sort of picturesque, anticipating Horace Walpole's famous response to the Alps seven years later: 'Precipices, mountains, torrents, wolves, rumblings, Salvator Rosa.'[20] He was not, however, able to satisfy fully his taste for such landscape until his appointment as a prebendary at Durham in 1754. His later designs for Bishop's Auckland there and for Raby show him incorporating truly wild landscape into garden design.

As early as March 1748, however, fully nine months before he moved to Byfleet, Spence began to consider how his garden might break out of the walled bounds that contained it. A plan of that date shows him considering how his orchard might be combined with a grove. Although he seems not to have given up the idea of retaining a regular orchard until August of that year, his early observation, that the 'Grove work [be] cornered with Hawthorn or some white blossomd Tree, that Blows as early as the peach, almond and cherry,' shows how he intended to mix the useful with the decorative.

Spence's sense of the dimension of this new grove continued to change throughout the spring, but his conviction that it should become part of the larger landscape became firmer: 'to fall in with the Quickset Hedge behither the great Lime Walk,' he suggests in a note of 21 May. By June he had planned a grove, largely of Scotch pine, with serpentine paths and a central opening of fifty by twenty-five feet, surrounded by almonds, cherries, larches, laburnums, 'French Ash,' acacia, double peach, pear, lilac, 'May bush,' and spruce. Beyond it was to be a piece of water.

What Spence was proposing here was not new either in theory or practice. As early as 1662, nearly ninety years earlier, John Evelyn had praised the mixture of wild and tame flowers in what he described as 'wild gardens... annexed to the name of Virgil... Full hedge roes and thickets in such affected wildness or plainesse will some times please better than costly art and expensive Works which are a Luxury fit to be reformd by lawes.'[21] But although something like this mixture was present in gardens by the 1730s, Evelyn himself had never put such precepts into practice. His own garden, Sayes Court, though it contained a mixture of various sorts of trees, did not venture into the landscape to break down the barrier between garden and countryside as Spence proceeded to do. Indeed, only Evelyn's correspondent, John Beale, seems to have glimpsed the principle that Spence came to espouse. Writing to Evelyn in 1662, Beale praised 'the Ecstasy of lofty Mountaines and broken cliffs, and craggy rocks which are the foyle and by a nice retreat give the Elysian delightes to the flowry bankes, paynted allyes, the August and Ancient Ornam[en]ts of Greenwich and Windsore.'[22]

By 12 July Spence had integrated his grove into his landscape in his 'First Plan for Continuation,' and by August he had incorporated a 'Raised Ground', introduced serpentining water, and had terminated the view with a 'willow Fence'. In all of this, as he writes in another plan of 1 August, [Fig. 123] his concern was 'to leave the Orchat-Trees, [of which he had already done a survey] according to their goodness and beauty; where they don't break in too much upon the Views' and to carry those views outwards.

In the centre of the plan of 8 August, though hidden by the grove, is a mound around which the serpentine water turns and on which is a building very like the Nightingale House, for which Spence did several designs. The grove itself, he wrote in September,

> should not be penetrable by the Eye, from the gravel-walk; (That the Whole may not seen at once, and that the Walk may be private.) It must be penetrable, at the Corner [furthest from the house] for the Alcove View [on the south-west side] of the Hills; and partly... not to cramp the view from the House Door, too much. This thinning to be more by Evergreens, than by close Planting.—Those not Hedge fashion, but in little clumps; or unequal sprinklings.[23]

Spence's increasing commitment to the view outwards is reflected in his theoretical writing about gardens, particularly in his unpublished work called *Tempe* or *Heads for Garden Letters*. In the appendix to that work he elaborates the connection between landscape painting and the making of landscape views, a connection which he credits to Pope in his *Anecdotes*. In so doing he cites that

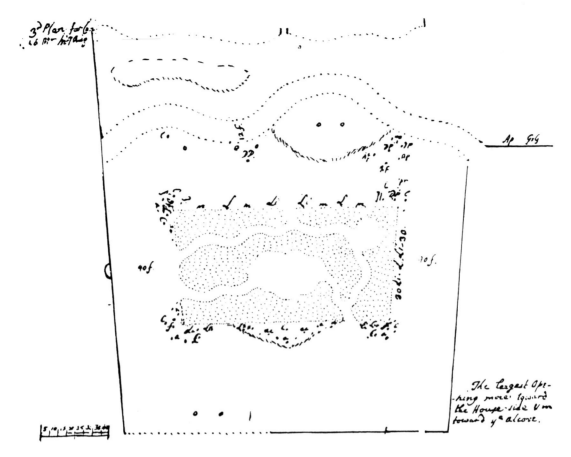

Front Trees of the Line-Walk, cramp the
water at first too much; ? to take them in
& allow a larger space between y² water &
the Walnut-trees: to make the best point of
view (each way,) within the Garden. } 'twill be so, as this is.

15 f of water, too much for y² swell
of y² ground.
Rising of 60 f, by 40; 3 f high in y²
midst: sloping from the Walnut trees.

To leave the Orchat-Trees, according
to their goodness, & beauty; where they
dont break in too much upon the Views.

To contrive as much as one can
to leave a line of them answering
the line of Oaks; at 20 f distance, at
the least.

To make the others as irregular
as possible; with cutting down, & planting.

To leave more on y² side to St George's
Hill, than on y² Hamshire-Hills-side.

If a Tree is good, & must be mov'd;
to transplant him, (if possible) into
the Garden.

To leave, or plant, so as to take
off the cornering of the Oak-Walk; with
little clumps of the Filbert Trees,
to be left; to irregularize the other fruit
trees: at unequal distances.

123. Joseph Spence, '3rd Plan for Continuation of the Garden, 1 Aug' (1748). Beinecke Library, Yale University.

other great influence on his garden theory and practice, Philip Southcote, his near neighbour at Wooburn Farm.

> In all the finest Lanscapes of the best Painters, there is what they call, The Foreground, the Middle-Ground, and the Lontananza, or Background. In laying out any large Pleasure Ground, these should be all very well consider'd; and, as far as may be, proportion'd to one another. If the Foreground be a large extended Lawn, the Middle shou'd have Groves or Woods of substance enough to answer it; and the Lontananza ought to be of a wide extent.—In Mr Southcote's Gardens, from the line that leads to the House, The Foreground is the Meadow; the Mid-ground, a winding Stream, with Clumps and Trees scatter'd about it; and the Back ground is the Rising of the Hill, and the Line of Trees to the Ruin'd Church: these are all of a moderate size, and well-proportion'd.[24]

By 1749 Spence's notes of 'Things to be done' took him similarly out from the gardens near the house to the grove and meadow. The dead trees in the former were to be made good with 'Scotch Firs, Silver Firs, Cluster Pines,' and 'Weymouth' Pines. The replacements, like the originals (which had been beeches and cherries) were from Lord Lincoln's at Oatlands. But Spence was also getting chestnuts from Chelsea and laurustinus from his neighbours.

Of the meadow he noted that he had already taken the 'Great Oak' there into his scheme and raised the ground as well as levelling it elsewhere 'for the Natural Arbor.' But there remained to hide the willow fence with lilacs, to plant seven or eight trees by the thick part of the hedge, 'to ballance the Diamond of Limes,' to remove more of the old fruit trees, and to fill out the farther planting by putting 'Scotch Firs and Evergreens' near the duck pond and even near the lime walk, along with almonds and double-blossom peach.

By this time Spence was already concerned with the views beyond the garden: the 'borrowed landscape'. His last memorandum is for 'Views' and includes 'View to General Cornwalls [his neighbour to the north-east] to be open'd, from the farther Mount. Trees in the Hedge-row before the best view, to be cut down.' In fact he notes to himself that he has already 'stript up' the latter, that is, removed its lower branches in the way recommended by Kent to improve vistas. In what seems to be an addendum to these instructions to himself, Spence has given a very detailed picture of the nature of these outer clump plantings on raised ground. '*Hilloc, by Field-Gate*: Firs to stand; and Forest-trees to be remov'd.—*Intervals, and Back*: Hiders to the right; and Forest Trees scatter'd to the left, and all behind; chiefly Beech, Wild Cherry, and Spanish Chesnut, in front.—Sycamores, by *elbow*—Abeles, Asp, Poplar, and Osier, about Bamlets Pond.' All of this practical advice to himself Spence complements with theory in the appendix to *Tempe*:

> Perspective, Prospect, Distancing, and Attracting, comprehend all that part of Painting in Gardening. Mr S[outhcote] (By Perspective he meant looking *under* trees to some further object; or by Prospect, looking *by* Trees, but the line open at the top. As for Instance, from the Burlington in his own Gardens, the View to the old Church is of the former kind, and to the Trees on St. Ann's Hill of the latter. Attracting he at first call'd Foreshortening.)

Spence goes on to cite Southcote's examples: what Pope did by 'narrowing the Plantation' in his garden to distance the obelisk at the end of it and what Southcote himself did to 'attract' St. Ann's Hill by staggering the plantation of trees, so that when mature they would 'fall in with the Trees near that hill; and

124 (this page and facing). Joseph Spence, List of Trees to be Planted, 23 Oct., 1749. Beinecke Library, Yale University.

make but one slope of Foliage: and so unite that part to [his] own, as to the eye.'[25]

This was a lesson that Spence learned well. Shortly after planning clumps in the middle landscape, he also began to concern himself with a scheme for planting in Parsonage Lane at Byfleet. The plan included alders, willows, horse chestnuts, oaks, and beeches—150 trees in all. At the end of the lane, he notes, is to be an 'Oval Grovette . . . on all the raisd ground. 20 Horse Chesnuts to South, and other forest Trees.' Throughout this plan, trees were to be used to enhance, reveal, and conceal. This 'first scheme' of 21 September 1750 was followed almost at once by a second of 31 October, in which the trees were spelled out in more detail. The 'grovette' is now to have 'about 20 Chesnuts and Limes' and to have a 'Seat, under one of the best Trees.' This last was a feature that Spence much favoured, one that he was to recommend for the Duke of Argyll's garden more than a decade later.[26]

By this time Spence had gone even farther in the appropriation of landscape. On 13 July 1750 he made the 'first Sketch' of St. George's Hill, the high barren heathland to the northeast of Byfleet which had been the site of a Roman or British camp[27] and which had also been the source of sand for his walks. There he set out to plant 'all the hither line of it . . . with clumps of firs, which in a few years will make it part of my garden: for the tops of the trees in my garden-grove unite (to the eye) with the trees in my hedgerows, and both of them will hereafter unite with the trees on the hill.'[28]

His plans were not uniformly successful in execution. In a note 'Trees, that have fail'd (Oct: 1750)' he lists alder, beech, birch, firs, horse chestnut, and oak, and records that ten of these were at St. George's Hill.[29] Nonetheless,

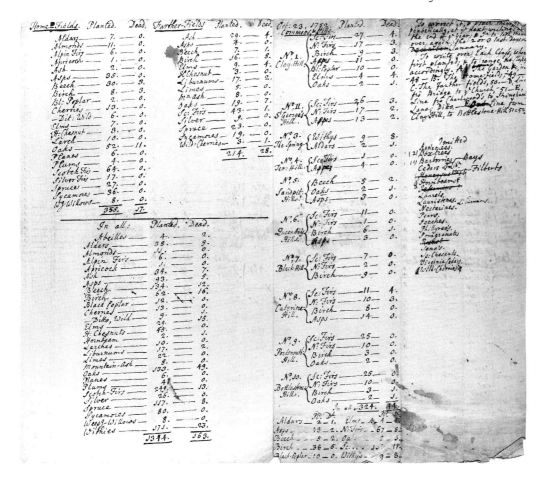

what he went on to create in the view to that hill was in imitation of what he had noted (in his 'Heads for Garden Letters') in the work of the Shaftesburian, Francis Hutcheson: an imitation of *belle nature* in its wildnesses. 'Thus we see that strict Regularity in laying out of Gardens in Parterres, Vista's, parallel Walks, is often neglected to obtain an Imitation of Nature even in some of its Wildnesses: and we are more pleasd with this Imitation, especially when the Scene is large and spacious, than with the most confident exactness of regular Work.'[30]

Spence's preliminary plan involved planting 'all Scotch Firs' but suggested that 'two or three Norway Firs' be tried as well, either there or on a neighbouring hill. On the site of this 'Plantation for the South Line, of St. George's Hill,' he began to elaborate what he labelled 'Abroad' in his 'Things to be done (by Spring 1751)': 'To plant the Camp-Line' (a reference to its having been the site of a Roman camp). In the same memorandum (which includes another reference to planting Parsonage Lane), he also notes plans for a 'Seat on St. Anns Hill' on a knole. In that St Ann's Hill lay, as we have seen, beyond Southcote's Wooburn Farm and five miles to the northwest of Byfleet, this was appropriation on a large scale indeed!

By the end of 1751 Spence's 'Things to be done' included relandscaping and planting trees in his neighbours' fields to improve views. In one of the fields belonging to Lord Lincoln, he made a note 'To find out a place for a Seat . . . to catch St. Ann's Hill,' and, while suggesting a seat in another neighbour's field, he went on to remind himself 'to clear away a little for the Visto, for the seat under the Oak.'

Spence's extension of his essentially flat site, in other words, included ways in which what was in effect a *ferme ornée*[31] could also invoke more striking views, such as he was to admire at Matlock in Derbyshire in the course of making these views. Writing to his friend Massingberd on 2 October 1752, he described the view of 'my great Favourite, Matlock:'

> The View from hence, as possibly you may remember, consists of three very different parts. In the midst, you see a very pleasing hill, all green and agreeably tufted with Trees; . . . To the left of this, you see a gentle turn of the Darwent, quite pleasing and undisturb'd; which joins in extremely well with a rising view of the Country, and all verdurous soft, and lively. And to the right of it, (or the side toward the great Torr,) is an Alpine View, of Rocky and Woody intersperst; very much like some pieces in Gaspar Poussin's Landscapes.[32]

Less than a month later, on 23 October, Spence's inventory shows him having appropriated ten 'Commons, and Hills' and having planted 324 trees. This is above and beyond the 355 trees planted in his home fields, 214 in his 'Farther Fields,' and 451 in Parsonage Lane [Fig. 124]. This was an astonishing amount of tree-planting for a man of Spence's means. It included 1344 specimens of twenty-eight different species of trees, of which about twelve per cent had not survived. What distinguishes his work is not the trees that he used; his list would largely have been available to a planter in the late seventeenth century. But his mixture of sweet-scented and flowering fruit trees with deciduous and coniferous trees *was* interesting, and his appropriation of the surrounding landscape for the purpose was quite astonishing, given that the land so appropriated was not his.

The planting of St. George's Hill (or 'the Point' as he called it), moreover, was not simply to provide a 'visto'. Spence devised an increasingly elaborate plan for the planting that transformed the site into a woody theatre from which to look out over the surrounding landscape, 'a woody theatre of statliest view,' such as Milton describes Eden as being in *Paradise Lost* IV. Between 7 and 11 November 1752 Spence worked through four increasingly elaborate plans for the Point that first included clumps of larch, poplar, and fir, interspersed with a mixture of all these, and then came to include birch and finally Scotch firs and pinasters. The third plan shows a transverse walk with a gravel oval at its centre twenty-four feet across. The fourth has elaborated that design to connect the circle through an open grove of black and white poplars to an amphitheatre at the south end that looks out over the surrounding countryside and includes seats under the poplars [Fig. 125]. For this plan Spence has specified beds of grass seed 'intermixt with the seed of Violets, Cowslips, Primroses, and Wild-Strawberries' next to the path.[33]

Spence's concern with the ascent to this natural eminence is reflected in his two versions of an ascending serpentine path to the site. Both have a bench part way up the slope, and the revision reflects his early note, scribbled on the back of a playing card: 'How to ease the Ascent to the Seat.' His sense of this landscape, then, was both prospective and peripatetic, static and kinetic. To Southcote's peripheral walk with its views into the *ferme ornée* Spence had added not only a distant prospect but one that included his own extended garden in an *ingentia rura*.

In 1758 Spence, on his journey to the north, went to The Leasowes, accompanied by Robert Dodsley, the publisher of Spence's translation of Attiret and the author himself of a poem in praise of The Leasowes, written in 1754.[34] It is not surprising that the two gardeners, Shenstone and Spence, liked

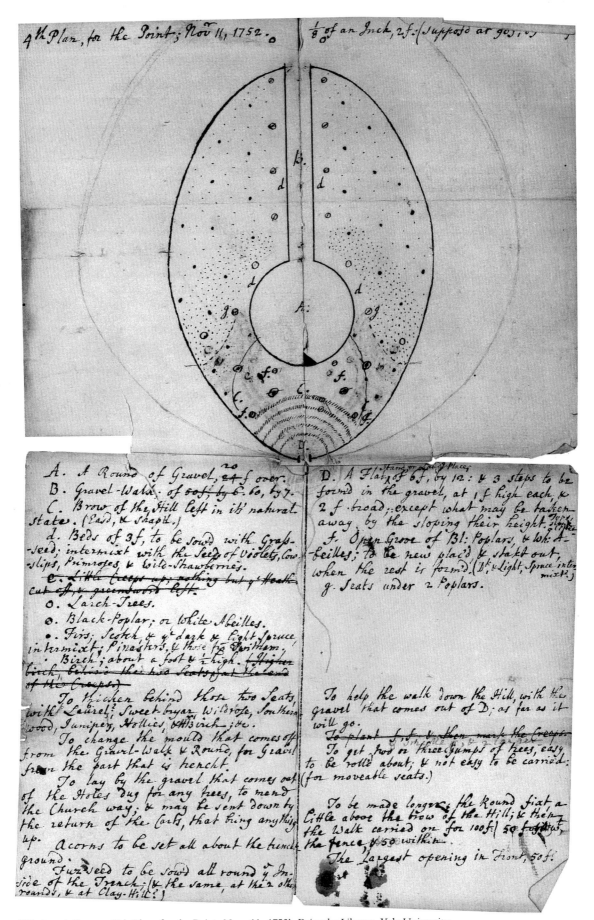

125. Joseph Spence, '4th Plan, for the Point; Nov. 11, 1752'. Beinecke Library, Yale University.

one another, or that Shenstone dedicated a seat to Spence's friendship.[35] Spence was not uncritical of Shenstone's work. Although he noted little about the extensive range of monuments and inscriptions in the garden, he thought some of the walks might be made less regular and more open. Predictably, what he found most praiseworthy were the views outwards into the borrowed landscape, and his notes suggest that these might be improved.[36]

By the time that Horace Walpole came to write his 'History of the Modern Taste in Gardening' in the 1770s, the pleasures of The Leasowes seemed insipid in comparison to the bursting prospect that Thomson celebrated and that Spence had begun to create at Byfleet in the 1740s. 'Prospect, animated prospect,' he wrote, 'is the theatre that will always be the most frequented,' and it was indeed just such prospects at Hagley (the nearby garden of Shenstone's friend, Lord Lyttelton) in 1753 that Walpole praised.[37] Such alpine prospects as Walpole had first praised in 1739 were to be of the essence in Spence's northern gardens of the 1760s as *ingentia rura* was further translated beyond garden-making to a new way of looking at landscape itself.

12

SMOOTHING OR BRUSHING THE ROBE OF NATURE: WILLIAM SHENSTONE AND THE LEASOWES

By the time that Philip Southcote bought Wooburn Farm, the poet and essayist William Shenstone had already become interested in the art of landscape design. After leaving Oxford in the 1720s, Shenstone spent several years in independent study of the classics with his friend, the poet Richard Graves, at Graves's home at Mickleton in Gloucestershire. Part of the inspiration to create a classical elysium on his own estate, The Leasowes in Shropshire, must have come from this experience, although plainly the idea of creating such a garden did not arrive all at once. Before 1745 Shenstone still had no overall consistent plan. In 1749, when Shenstone took the advice of his friends and demolished a summerhouse that he had built in 1742, he spoke of that earlier time as one when he 'had no Thoughts of laying out my environs.'[1]

Whether, as tradition has it, Shenstone's first landscaping was an avenue planted between Mickleton and Kiftsgate in Gloucestershire, it was certainly through the Graves family that he first heard of Southcote. Moreover, Graves himself was the principal heir of the owner of *Worlies* (or Warley Place) in Essex, an estate that had briefly belonged to John Evelyn before he began work on Sayes Court. At *Worlies*, Graves writes in his *Recollections of Shenstone*, the grounds had been remodelled 'from hints . . . borrowed from Mr. Southcote's, and other places.' Although the ground was flat and 'under the natural disadvantages of want of wood and water,' it had been improved 'by removing or concealing the fences, and shewing to advantage the few groups of trees' and had thus given the place 'a park-like appearance.'[2] These were the elements that Shenstone was to celebrate at The Leasowes in his poem 'The Landskip':

> How sweetly smil'd the Hill, the Vale
> And all the Landskip round!
> The river gliding down the Dale,
> The Hill with Beeches Crown'd![3]

Shenstone did not take up residence at The Leasowes until 1743, but even before that time he had cut an avenue through the wood and built a hermitage and a summerhouse. Graves wrongly credits him with being the first to observe that a landscape painter would make the best English gardener, but his sense that The Leasowes ought to be compared to Rosa or the Poussins is indicative of one of the garden's main inspirations. Another was Milton. Shenstone's manuscript notes on *Paradise Lost* survive and show how attracted to the landscape descriptions of that poem he was. Citing the fourth book as 'my Fav'rite', he goes on to quote lines 156–59 with their description

126. James Mason after Thomas Smith, 'A View in Virgil's Grove' (1748).

of the 'gentle gales,' 'odoriferous wings,' and 'balmy spoils' of Eden in order to observe: 'This is a pretty thought. The Idea we Conceive from this Description, must be of a very Beatifull [sic] Landscape.' Similarly, the description of Eve in Book IX, surrounded by roses that 'about her glowed,' leads him to a more general point about paradisal landscape: 'Milton, as it were by stealth and *aliud agens* [doing something else] Conveys to us Idea's of Beauties of Paradise another shining Instance together with many Inferior ones have occurrd in the former Books.'[4]

Graves also compares The Leasowes with the work of the poet James

127. D. Jenkins, 'A View of the Leasowes' c. 1770.

128. Virgil's Grove, The Leasowes.
Photo: Robert Williams.

Thomson, whose patron was Shenstone's near neighbour at Hagley, Lord Lyttelton.[5] Like Thomson, Shenstone was a Virgilian; the first part of his extensive plan for The Leasowes to be realised was 'Virgil's Grove' [Figs. 126, 128]. Indeed, even before that Shenstone wrote to Graves (in June 1742) about buying a 'model of the tomb of Virgil, an urn, and a scheme or two more of like nature.'[6] What made The Leasowes more than an itinerary of inscriptions, however, was Shenstone's concern with recreating antique landscape: *locus* as *lucus*, the genius of the place as the sacred grove of antiquity, translated into England as surely as the genius of ancient poetry and politics had been.[7] If he did not attempt the newly fashionable landscape of sublimity, it may have been in part because the topography of The Leasowes provided little opportunity for it (except by 'borrowed landscape') and partly because Virgil does not suggest it.

The combination of beauty with utility that Graves noticed in Shenstone's designing a worker's cottage as a Gothic ruin [Fig. 127] is also indicative of the influence of the second book of the *Georgics*. So too is Shenstone's later reply to Pitt, who had commented that at The Leasowes 'Nature had done every thing for him.' Shenstone cannot have been unaware that, in the words of a recent editor of the *Georgics*, man 'succeeds by transforming the natural order' in Virgil's poem.[8] His reply to Pitt was certainly in those terms: that 'he hoped he had done something for Nature too.'[9]

179

'How polish'd nature charms our Eyes' he wrote in a poem to his friend Mrs. Knight.[10] And in 1749 he wrote in a similar vein to his friend Lady Luxborough (Lord Bolingbroke's sister), whose estate, Barrels, he described as 'a perfect Arcadia': 'Taste in Gardens etc: has little more to do than *collect* the Beauties of Nature into a compass proper for it's own observation...The necessity of smoothing or brushing the Robe of Nature may proceed entirely from the same Cause.[11]

One of Shenstone's other friends was the widowed Duchess of Somerset, who had been born Frances Thynne, daughter of the 'inventor' of the Weymouth pine at Longleat. Later, as Countess of Hertford, she bought Riskins, Lord Bathurst's early *ferme ornée*, that had been celebrated by Switzer in the third volume of *Ichnographia Rustica*. Shenstone's poem 'Rural Elegance' was addressed to her memory and celebrates what he himself was to be celebrated for: the creation of a country retreat in georgic terms. Among its themes are a condemnation of the abuses of power, deploring drunkenness, a lament for litigation over land, and a treatment of the relation between use and pleasure, art and nature in the creation of landscape. All of these are themes central to Book II of the *Georgics*, and especially potent in the idealised description of country life at the end of that book.

If the distinction between William Kent's Rousham and Southcote's Wooburn Farm is between Elysian fields and Arcadia, this is a distinction that Shenstone further elaborated as his ideal in combining the agricultural with the aesthetic.[12] The Duchess of Somerset's achievement was, he writes,

> In some fair villa's peaceful bound,
> To catch soft hints from Nature's tongue,
> And bid Arcadia bloom around...
> No sounds inelegant and rude
> Her sacred solitudes profane
> Unless her candour not exclude
> The lowly shepherds votive strain
> Who tunes his reed amidst his rural cheer.[13]

Spence's friend, the rural poet James Woodhouse (1735–1820) celebrates The Leasowes in similarly georgic language in his praise of Shenstone's achievement. Here, he writes, in his poem 'Lessowes', is 'fair Agriculture's rich Economy,' and for it Shenstone deserves 'the Patriot's noble name.' If that honour is given to a botanical hybridizer,

> How much more He who plants the steril plain,
> With fruitful gardens, and rich fields of grain?
> And, still increasing genuine social joys,
> Makes pleasing domes, and happy hamlets, rise![14]
> [Fig. 129]

These are also the georgic terms that Shenstone himself uses to celebrate his *ferme ornée* in his poem 'Hope':

> My banks they are furnish'd with Bees,
> Where murmur invites us to sleep;
> My Grottos are shaded with Trees,
> And my hills are *white-over* with sheep.[15]

Shenstone's publisher and friend, Robert Dodsley, praised The Leasowes in the vocabulary of the *Georgics* when he first visited it in 1754. [Fig. 130] The

129. William Shenstone, A View of the Leasowes. Wellesley College Library.

language of his poem in its praise invokes the diction of the end of the second *Georgic*, the vocabulary of ideal rural landscape that had been so appealing to Shaftesbury too. And this his poetic persona finds confirmed by the 'powerful incantations, magic verse, / Inscrib'd on every tree.' A decade later, in his 'Description of the Leasowes,' he lists the specific texts, placed there by Shenstone, that gave rise to his earlier georgic response: the combination, for example, of the famous description of Tempe from *Georgics* II with a distant view 'diversified with a cottage, and a road that winds behind a farmhouse and a fine clump of trees.' That Shenstone's poem addressed to the Venus de Medici rebukes 'the vicious waste / Of pomp' and 'the sumptuous glare / Of gold' only confirms the tone of Virgil's poem.[16]

This side of Shenstone's achievement, the georgic side, needs to be stressed, if only because most of the traveller's accounts of The Leasowes mention only its 'ornaments and mottoes, and names of the groves.'[17] What attracted the anonymous author of *Four Topographical Letters* (written in 1755) was partly the quality of 'unaffected Nature' where everything was 'so elegantly rude, so rural and romantic' that the visitor might believe 'that the poetic Descriptions of *Arcadia* and *Fairyland* are not altogether Fictions.' More significantly, though, is his praise for Shenstone's combination of use and pleasure: 'He has laid out very pleasant Walks round his Fields, which are confined to the Hedge-side, without encroaching on the Pasture, and at proper Distances has placed Seats which command delightful Views over different Parts of the Country, each Prospect being terminated by some agreeable Object.'[18] This, it seems, was entirely the way in which Shenstone hoped The Leasowes might be 'read'. In the late 1750s (c. 1759), his friend Thomas Hull wrote: 'On the Whole, you are

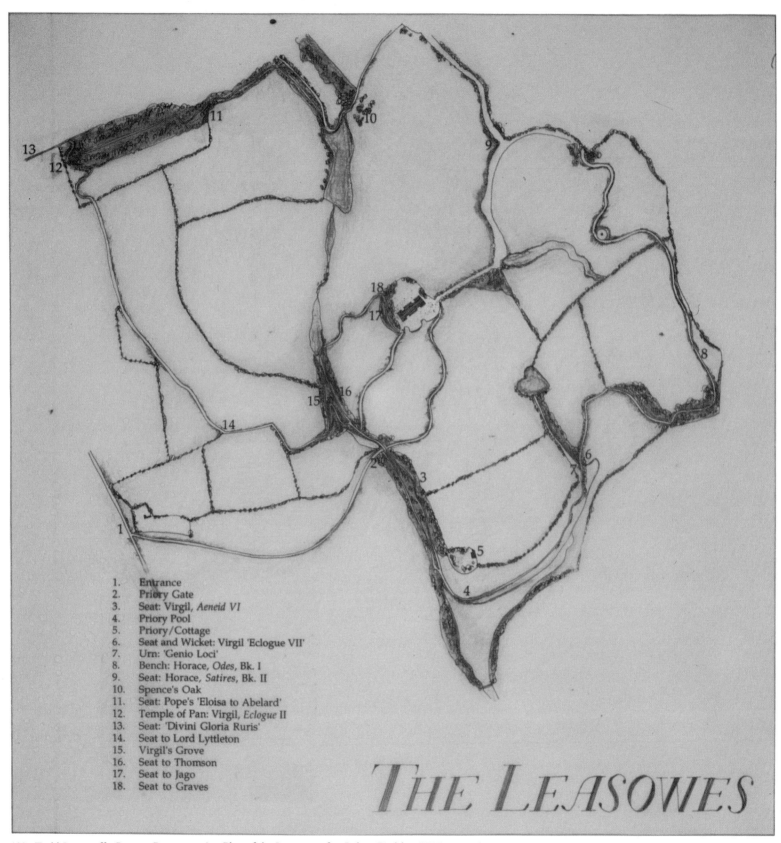

1. Entrance
2. Priory Gate
3. Seat: Virgil, *Aeneid VI*
4. Priory Pool
5. Priory/Cottage
6. Seat and Wicket: Virgil 'Eclogue VII'
7. Urn: 'Genio Loci'
8. Bench: Horace, *Odes*, Bk. I
9. Seat: Horace, *Satires*, Bk. II
10. Spence's Oak
11. Seat: Pope's 'Eloisa to Abelard'
12. Temple of Pan: Virgil, *Eclogue* II
13. Seat: 'Divini Gloria Ruris'
14. Seat to Lord Lyttleton
15. Virgil's Grove
16. Seat to Thomson
17. Seat to Jago
18. Seat to Graves

THE LEASOWES

130. Todd Longstaffe-Gowan, Reconstruction Plan of the Leasowes after Robert Dodsley (1764).

to look on this sweet Spot (according to it's glorious Master's own Description to *me*) merely, as a Farm.'[19]

There are, however, few references to farming in Shenstone's correspondence. He continued to refer to The Leasowes as 'my little farm' but his sense of what that meant is best conveyed in a letter to Graves in 1748: 'The French have what they call a *parque ornée*; I suppose, approaching about as near to a garden as the park at Hagley. I give my place the title of a *ferme ornée*; though, if I had money, I should hardly confine myself to such decorations as that name requires.'[20] Shenstone's sense of 'such decorations' was much like John Evelyn's: 'including cascades, temples, grottos, hermitages, greenhouses.'[21] By 1743 he could boast to his friend Richard Jago: 'I have an alcove, six elegies, a seat, two epitaphs (one upon myself), three ballads, four songs, and a serpentine river to shew you when you come.'[22] To the end he remained convinced that The Leasowes was a sort of arcadia, but pastoral as well as georgic: one with analogies to Poussin's, where such inscriptions as *Et in Arcadia Ego* on a memorial urn, rather than the shepherds themselves, would invoke the *topos*.[23]

Joseph Giles, celebrating The Leasowes in a poem to which Shenstone himself 'made some very considerable alterations and emendations' invoked just this pastoral topos:

> Behold what hills and pleasing vales!
> Where shepherds tell their rural tales,
> In artless strains of love:
> The flow'ry dingle, bushy dell,
> The mazy wood, without a spell
> Except the plaintive dove . . . [stanza 4]
>
> Here, woods and groves, and flow'ry fields,
> Have ev'ry blessing nature yields,
> While herds and flocks abound:
> Here sloping lawns so smooth and green,
> With many a bounteous, rural scene,
> Adorn the prospect round. [stanza 17][24]

No fewer than twelve of the eventual seats and monuments at The Leasowes employed quotations from Virgil. The first was a memorial seat to Thomson himself (with a quotation from *Eclogues* V) to be erected in Virgil's Grove. Dr. Johnson's famous objections to the artificiality of The Leasowes are in part answered by Richard Graves's defence of his friend in his *Recollections*,[25] but it is difficult not to find some preciosity in Shenstone's pasting up verses weekly 'upon a strip of Deal' which were then placed 'upon my skreens or Garden-seats, for the Amusement of my good friends the Vulgar.'[26]

What was obviously most important was the completion (in 1749) of the path around the whole estate. The most extensive account of this itinerary was given after Shenstone's death by Robert Dodsley in 1764. It provided a guide to all the monuments, seats, and points of vantage on the circuit of the grounds. It also drew attention to the importance of trees, both those planted by Shenstone and those 'improved' by him. Near the house Shenstone, like Southcote and Spence, showed himself knowledgable about the use of different shades of green (holly and laurel) for effects of 'distancing and approximating.' For the former he recommends 'a strait lined avenue that is widened in front, and planted there with ewe trees, then firs, then with trees more and more fady, till they end in the almond-willow, or silver osier.' In the 'forest ground'

Dodsley saw exemplified Shenstone's (and Pope's) principle of variety: 'wild green slopes peeping through dingle, or irregular groups of trees, a confused mixture of savage and cultivated ground, held up to the eye, and forming a landskip fit for the pencil of Salvator Rosa.'[27]

Dodsley's 'Description' was much imitated and repeated by subsequent accounts. What many of these accounts stressed, however, was not so much the monuments as the prospects that the garden provided. *The Modern Universal British Traveller* (1779), for example, gives a good sense of the mixture of classical inscription, grove, and borrowed landscape that characterised The Leasowes. It exemplified, indeed, what Shenstone wrote in his 'Unconnected Thoughts on Gardening' about the importance of variety in planting, 'that variety, which the natural country supplies every where; in a greater or lesser degree.'[28]

This walk satisfied at least two of Pope's criteria: variety and a confusion of the bounds by calling in the landscape. The most striking example of the latter was the view from an octagon seat in 'a clump of stately firs upon the summit' of a hill of the famous mount, the Wrekin, thirty miles away. This effect was of a piece with Shenstone's recommendations to Lady Luxborough. At Barrels, he said, she might have 'an opportunity of making some pretty open seat on a small mount at the very lower end of your Grove just by the Gate, which shou'd command (by lowering the Hedgerow) the Walk of Trees on the Hill the Temple and the country towards Henley etc.'[29] Shenstone made other views outward; he cut down a tree to incorporate a view of the ruin at Hagley and ensured another vista of the Earl of Stamford's grounds at Envil.

Shenstone's calling in of the country, however, remained a matter of opening views at appropriate places from The Leasowes into the surrounding landscape. It remained for an even more committed classicist, Joseph Spence, to extend the *ferme ornée* by appropriating and redesigning that *ingentia rura* to include the 'fine variety of savage prospects'[30] that Addison had admired at Fontainebleau half a century earlier.

13
NONE BUT REAL PROFESSORS: CONCLUSION

'Gardens,' said Sir Thomas Browne, 'were before Gardiners, and but some hours after the earth.' Like Joseph Spence's history of gardens, *Tempe*, Browne's *The Garden of Cyrus* suggests that there is little truly new in gardening, that invention is, in its old sense, only the rediscovery of what was already there. Even Addison, who has often been credited with first proposing the 'rural or extensive garden,' recognised its indebtedness to *Paradise Lost*. And Milton's paradisal garden is both an impossible re-creation of Eden and a recognition that the gardens of Italy might be a way of translating that lost landscape into the English imagination.[1] For all its rejection of the 'beds and curious knots' of many seventeenth-century gardens, however, Milton's garden of Eden was, as I have suggested, consonant with a growing awareness (from at least the early 1650s) that extensive landscape was part of the experience of the garden. Milton's 'woody theatre of various view' creates a treaty between landscape and horticulture that Marvell had already described in 'Upon Appleton House' and that he himself had celebrated thirty years earlier in 'L'Allegro' and 'Il Penseroso.'

For whatever reasons, and an increasing neoclassicism was one of them, the landscape of antiquity was already an appealing concept even in the late sixteenth century. It animates Sidney's *Arcadia* as it does Chapman's translations of Homer, and this landscape translates itself on to the stage of the Stuart court just as classical mythology had provided the vocabulary of Elizabethan monarchy. The 'King's Arcadia' was not an invention of Charles I. It was there in the first decade of the seventeenth century, in the neoclassicism of his brother, Prince Henry, whose portraits as an Augustan ruler are echoed by the restoration of a classical landscape in such court masques as *Prince Henry's Barriers* and *Oberon*.[2]

The collecting of antiquities by James I's favorite, the Duke of Buckingham, and by the Earl of Arundel, translated itself into the fashion for neoclassical architecture that Inigo Jones brought back in the form of Palladianism. The spirit of antiquity was thus re-created either directly, in the copying of antique fragments in contemporary buildings,[3] or indirectly, through Palladio's invocation of Vitruvius. This imbibed Palladianism was most startlingly represented by Jones's Banqueting House, the first stage of a neoclassical Whitehall Palace.[4]

What we associate with the eighteenth century in England was, as Lord Lincoln recognised in re-erecting one of Jones's gateways, the legacy of Jones and, more indirectly, the legacy of his patron Lord Arundel.[5] It was he who took Jones to Italy, and it was the great wealth of classical sculpture in his garden in the Strand that induced Francis Bacon to cry out, 'The Resurrection!' when he first saw it. The recreated arcadias (however fragile) of the Shakespearean romances indicate that the literary and imaginative act of translating classical landscape was not confined to the world of the court. If Elizabeth I as Diana could invoke an antique mythological world by performing in Sidney's *The Lady of May* at Kenilworth, so Oberon and Titania, for example, could inhabit the world of Peter Quince. Athens could be London and the landscape of Arcadia England, as surely as the Medici had believed Florence to be a generation earlier.

Dover's Cotswold Games, that attempt to revive the Olympics in Gloucestershire nearly three centuries before their revival, was another manifestation of the same impulse, an impulse that had already led Ben Jonson to perform the part of a Roman soldier when fighting with Leicester's army in the Low Countries.[6] Sejanus and Catiline, Caesar and Coriolanus were even more real to the Stuart audience than they were to the eighteenth-century Augustans, and the verbal and visual language of imperial triumphs, represented by Mantegna's *The Triumph of Caesar*, continued to animate even the statecraft of the Protectorate.[7] Spenser's invocation of the 'Brute' myth in *The Faerie Queene* could offer England the chance to see itself as 'Troynovant,' the Rome that ought to have been. Evelyn could believe that Britain was the elysium of the ancients, and Inigo Jones that Stonehenge was a Roman temple.

Why should not gardens also reflect this re-creation of the lost world of classical wisdom and glory? Plainly Lord Arundel's did so with the materials of antiquity. But the neoclassicism of modern artists also offered a way to re-create that antiquity in gardens, a re-creation that increasingly appropriated or invoked landscape. What otherwise are we to make of the gardens created for Prince Henry at Richmond, gardens that consisted of islands and bridges that connected the palace to the river, translating the architectural into the natural as Marvell was to do in 'Upon Appleton House?'[8]

To all of this, even to the sense of a landscape beyond the garden already apparent in William Lawson's *A New Orchard and Garden* (1618),[9] the great upsurge in garden- and place-making in the later seventeenth century was heir. The insistence on the primacy of groves and prospects over gardens of flowers, supported by Evelyn's friend, John Beale, looked back to Sir Henry Wotton's *Elements of Architecture* (1624), itself a formulation of principles already conveyed by Wotton to Constantin Huygens in the Netherlands a decade earlier.[10] If Traherne's defense of spiritualised groves in the 1670s was indebted to Thomas Jackson's earlier formulation of such concepts in 1624, so too the sense of a redeemed nature in which gardens had their place was the legacy of the 1630s; Pope was the heir of Hakewill.

Looking back from 1768, George Mason could recognise the liberation from rigid garden formalism already implicit in *Paradise Lost* and the *Arcadia*: 'MILTON, as well as SIDNEY, lived at a time when rural graces were but little understood; yet *his* model of EDEN remains unimpeachable.'[11]

Late seventeenth-century botany was also heir to the work of pioneers earlier in the century, both the Tradescants (father and son) and Jacob Bobart, the first Keeper of the Oxford Botanic Garden, among them. If the Tradescants began the extensive importation of foreign plants, especially from America, the botanic garden in Oxford imported the continental arrangement of plants according to genera and species. Henry Compton and the Duchess of Beaufort, to name but two of the late seventeenth-century patriots of botanical importation, followed in the footseps of the Tradescants. Tournefort Ray, Dillenius, and Linnaeus, pursued continental attempts at universal taxonomy in the context of the work already done at Oxford and Chelsea.

'Rural and extensive gardens' may in part have arisen out of a dissatisfaction both with the grandiose boredom of gardens on the French model or the 'crimping, diminutive, and wretched Performances'[12] of the Dutch, but they relied both upon long-standing native practice and upon the practical and theoretical advances of the new science of botany. What the Earl of Carlisle did at Wray Wood was not new; it was the reaction of long-established practice against recent francophile taste. What Switzer, Langley, and Bradley recommended, and what the Earl of Islay, Lord Petre, and the Duke of Richmond put into practice, was possible because a vastly expanded range of new trees and shrubs made it so. This was the case because there had arisen a large army of amateur botanists and nurserymen-gardeners who were interested not only in importation and propagation but in planting and design.

The landscape of antiquity animated the imagination of Elizabethans and Stuarts and translated itself into a world of pastoral that was both English and antique. By the late seventeenth century, however, it had become a cliché that in turn required a georgic text for its reanimation. What the *Georgics* offered was a renovating argument from use, an argument that carried with it an ability to yoke the divine glory of the countryside to the Tempe of Greek Arcadia, the extensive landscape of agriculture to a knowledge of the causes of things. If Blake's Milton could inhabit a landscape where the 'countenance divine' might 'walk upon England's pastures green,' so too the eighteenth-century makers of those pastures might imagine them a place fit for Virgil.

The *ferme ornée* was only the most overt yoking of agriculture with horticulture within a syntax of Virgilian reference. But its translation of the *Georgics* was part of a larger exercise that included Castell's literal translation of Pliny and John Boyle's translation of those texts into his landscapes. And in all these cases, trees and shrubs were the primary vocabulary of the translation.

In 1751 Capability Brown left Stowe. What he left behind as his contribution to the garden there was the Grecian Valley, a landscape whose primary palette was not temples but trees. But Brown's trees were not the theatrical 'ten of spades' clumps that had characterised Kent. They had become emblems in their own right, the punctuation of a silent speech that was the landscape itself. Two decades later he would be able to explain this in a famous conversation with Hannah More:

> He illustrates everything he says about gardening [she wrote] by some literary or grammatical allusion. He told me he compared his art to literary composition. 'Now *there*,' said he, pointing his finger, 'I make a comma, and there,' pointing to another spot, 'where a more decided turn is proper, I make a colon; at another part, where an interruption is desirable to break the view, a parenthesis; now a full stop, and then I begin another subject.'[13]

Brown may well have been speaking in a language that he knew Hannah More would understand and appreciate, but his remarks draw attention to the way in which the concept of nature continued to change its meaning. By the time Hannah More wrote down that conversation, the botanic and topographic face of England had changed almost beyond recognition. Gone almost without a trace were the parterres and allées of the gardens that Kip and Knyff had recorded. Gone too were the topiary excesses that Pope and Switzer had deplored. Gone in many cases also, thanks to the enclosures, were the old hedgerows with their native growth of hawthorn and elm and maple. In their place frequently was grazed parkland, punctuated by arboreal plantings designed to look more natural than nature itself: what Peter Collinson called 'Hints Borrowed from Nature . . . improved when executed by a Skillful Ingenious hand.'[14]

In the latter part of the century, however, the 'Skillful Ingenious Hand' was more likely to be that of a gardener-designer like Brown than that of an owner who was a politician or a botanist concerned to make his own statement. And the materials available were beyond the imagining even of Lord Petre or Philip Miller.

When Miller published the eighth edition of his *Gardeners Dictionary* in 1765, Joseph Banks and Daniel Solander had yet to come back from their voyage to the South Pacific and Australasia with Captain Cook. That southern Grand Tour (as Banks saw it) was to substitute botanical curiosities for plundered antiquities and to confirm the divorce between the sciences and the humanities that characterises the modern western world. Cook's botanists would return to an England prepared to catalogue their discoveries with the lexicon of a new taxonomy, a taxonomy that had profoundly altered ways of seeing, substituting description and analysis for the great chain of being. 'Landscape' now meant as much what was 'out there' as what was on the canvas, and that 'there,' whether topographical or botanical, was increasingly outside the vocabulary of traditional neoclassicism. 'Neo-classical theory had stressed the supreme importance of the unity of mood and expression in the highest forms of landscape art. Analytical and empirical observations, however, tended toward the disruption of such unity, forcing the artist to look at the world as a world of disparate things.'[15] These 'disparate things' were to be the repertoire of a new kind of garden, one where plants were curiosities to be admired closely rather than materials of an extensive landscape, as most of the North American imports had become. This, ultimately, was the legacy of Linnaeus: the world seen through the spectacles of classification.

What had begun in the mid-seventeenth century as the appropriation of landscape to the garden had ended by the mid-eighteenth century as the appropriation of the world to this new taxonomy. In the process the botanic world had been renamed ('translated' in Brian Friel's use of the word)[16] to suit a Eurocentric and increasingly (thanks to the expansion of the British Empire) Anglocentric model. Indeed, botany provided both a language (and a classicised language at that) of imperial expansion and a mythology of progress to sustain it.[17]

As 'garden' had come increasingly to mean not 'enclosed space' but 'landscape,' the landscape had also been transformed by exotic trees and shrubs imported primarily from America. As a result whole counties changed their appearance and what had at one time been foreign now seemed natural, (like conifers in Surrey). Moreover, as 'picturesque' ceased to be inspired by Claude Lorrain and came more and more to be a response to Gaspar Dughet and Salvator Rosa, coniferous trees became the vocabulary for translating the wild sublimity of mountainous scenery. What Joseph Spence had first admired in Italy and then at Matlock in Derbyshire was translated arboreally on to St. George's Hill in the relatively placid landscape of Surrey.

Edmund Burke's essay *Of the Sublime and Beautiful* (1757) codified an interest in the sublime that was increasingly at the expense of the more placidly beautiful. The taste for sublimity had been growing at least since the translation of Longinus's essay in the late seventeenth century. Burke, however, provided a vocabulary for responding to such created 'wild' landcapes as

Hagley, Hackfall, and Hawkstone that represented the acme of taste after 1750 for at least three decades.

Where Defoe had found Derbyshire merely dangerous and horrifying, Joseph Spence found it exhilarating and liberating. Indeed, the wilder the landscape, the less the corrupting hand of man that Shaftesbury deplored had been upon it. The cry of 'fair liberty' and the natural man had as their corollaries a landscape untrammelled by traditional rules and unmeasured by taxonomy. Niagara and the caves of Malabar offered an *extasis* that had no place for designed or planted effects.

This kind of wild sublimity, however, needed little botanising. Its landscape was one of terror and exaltation: Horace Walpole's 'Precipices, mountains, torrents, wolves, rumblings, Salvator Rosa.'[18] Like gothicism its grace was beyond the reach of art or at least beyond what had conventionally been thought of as the horticulturist's art.

Although William Shenstone continued to make his Virgilian *ferme ornée* well into the 1760s, the classical sources of horticultural reform and change became less consequential. The translation of antiquity had been so effective that a classical vocabulary (whether verbal or visual) was no longer necessary. Dryden's *Georgics* and Pope's *Odyssey* took their places alongside *Paradise Lost* as the canon of a domesticated classicism, teaching Homer and Virgil to speak good English.

Natural history, moreover, had outstripped the classical world and given a whole new meaning to *rerum naturae causas*. Dr. Hunter, the York doctor who republished Evelyn's *Sylva* in 1776 looked back to Evelyn as Evelyn and the early Augustans had looked back to Rome. A native *res publica* of learning had been established in which botany had achieved respectability in company with the classics.

If Collinson was right in lamenting to Linnaeus that the publication of the *Species Plantarum* in 1753 meant the end of botany as a gentleman's study, botany nonetheless became a much more popular pursuit among the middle and lower classes and with both sexes. This was especially the case among the newly urbanised, whether refugees from the agricultural revolution or not. For them the writings of Richard Bradley and Thomas Fairchild's *The City Gardener* gave direction, and of them Francis Coventry's portrait of Squire Mushroom in *The World* (1753) and Robert Lloyd's *The Cit's Country Box* (1757) made fun.

But botany now came down from on high, from the 'professors' as Collinson called them. Only the vocabulary might be expanded, and that solely by post-Linnaean license. Its grammar and syntax were established. What many of the natural historians involved in the founding of the Royal Society had feared was that the strongly mathematical and experimental cast of the society's work would mean that botany had no place. What had come to pass was that a highly mechanical model of the natural world had displaced the very men who were the pioneers of botany. 'I have had the pleasure of reading your *Species Plantarum*,' Collinson wrote to Linnaeus in 1754,

> a very useful and laborious work. But, my dear friend, we that admire you are much concerned that you should perplex the delightful science of Botany with changing names that have been well received, and adding new names quite unknown to us. Thus Botany, which was a pleasant study and attainable by most men, is now become by alterations and new names, the study of a man's life, and none but real professors can pretend to attain it.[19]

No wonder the poet John Clare, who owned the Linnaean *Introduction to Botany* published by the nurseryman James Lee, described it, in Milton's phrase for hell, a 'system of darkness visible.' Botany had become part of what Blake saw as the mechanising of the world: the 'dark Satanic mills' of Newton and Locke, where the 'mind-forg'd manacles' were fabricated and the 'ratio of the five senses' had replaced the imagination of the ancient world.

In the process, botany also became less democratic. The Society of Gardeners who published the *Catalogus Plantarum* in 1730 were prepared to recognise and include among their 'patriots of horticulture' men from the highest to the lowest station in society. And Evelyn, in 1660, declared to Sir Thomas Browne that he had written his *Elysium Britannicum* 'that persons of all conditions and faculties, which delight in Gardens, may therein find something for their advantage.'[20] By the 1760s John Ellis had to argue with Dr. Alexander Garden of Carolina (commemorated himself in the *Gardenia*) that the 'Loblolly Bay' be named after a nurseryman (Lord Petre's former gardener, James Gordon). What had been the centre of a co-operative and in most cases amateur enterprise, Chelsea Physic Garden, however, came to be replaced in influence by the royal foundation at Kew, itself in part plundered from the garden of another amateur, the Duke of Argyll.

In the process too, horticulture and agriculture came apart. The georgic impulse that inspired Stephen Switzer and the Duke of Argyll both to improve farming and to create an extensive or rural garden was no longer an animating force for either science. In a sense the *ferme ornée* had become a victim of its own success. The taste for planting that appeared natural had in turn created a taste for apparently untouched nature; Charles Hamilton's Painshill was praised for being 'savage', i.e. *sauvage* (wild).

By the end of the eighteenth century also, georgic had become almost as artificial as pastoral. Marie-Antoinette's ersatz agricultural *hameau* was as 'easy, vulgar and disgusting' to most sensibilities as the pastoral form that Dr. Johnson dismissed with that phrase. Humphry Repton asserted that there was an essential contradiction between farming and gardening and that, therefore, the joining of the two in a *ferme ornée* was a nonsense. Even George III's playing at farmer with his merino sheep at Richmond seemed a sign of mad Nero's fiddling while America burned. What had been a belief in the union of both kinds of improvement was now the appropriation of agriculture for the purposes of play.

However debased and corrupted, the neoclassical ideals of early eighteenth-century Augustanism sustained a living (and argued) mythology that extended back at least to the late sixteenth century. By the later eighteenth century, neoclassicism was as much a pastiche as the ersatz gothicism that angered the architect Pugin. Neither bespoke a social ideal. Both had become mere fashions in taste, a taste based on feeling divorced from moral sense.

Equally, the *ferme ornée* had become, in Whately's account, an 'ornamented farm.' No longer dependent on the georgic treaty between agriculture and horticulture, it had degenerated into a sort of farm museum, a collection of monuments and buildings meant to signify a nostalgia for a rural ideal made increasingly impossible by the enclosures and the gentrification of the rural hierarchy. The traditional rural virtues celebrated in Ben Jonson's 'To Penshurst,' however tied to particular economic, political, and social circumstances, remained a living ideal in Pope's praise of 'the Man of Ross' in the fourth *Moral Essay*, and may still be recognized in Fielding's Squire Allworthy. By the end of the eighteenth century, sentimental rural buildings were at the expense of such marginalised poor as the inhabitants of Goldsmith's 'Deserted Village,' and only Crabbe's 'The Village' could adequately reflect the decay into which that ideal had fallen.

In the process neoclassical ideals had become the stuff of interior decoration, and an intellected and deracinated Hellenism had produced the architecture of monumentality that was, to the ideals of seventeenth- and eighteenth-century Palladianism, as the chinoiserie fripperies of Sir William Chambers were to the Chinese origins of naturalism explained by Sir William Temple and Matteo Ripa.

Out of the divorce between thought and feeling, implicit in the gothic 'forgeries' of Chatterton and explicit in *Northanger Abbey*, the reconnection of emotion with recollection and imagination with the natural world remained the task of a new generation: the Romantics.

★   ★   ★   ★   ★

A recent French catalogue of the work of the 'land artist,' Andy Goldsworthy, refers to his constructions of leaves and stones and branches as *structures éphémèrales*. It is hard to imagine a better phrase for gardens themselves. Based upon aesthetic conventions that are continually changing, deferring to a horticultural vocabulary that is protean, and employing materials that are continually in metamorphosis, their nature as works of art defies the vocabulary and syntax of ordinary criticism.

Nowhere in the history of gardens in England was this truer than in the century between 1650 and 1750. And the fate of most of the gardens discussed in this book seems an appropriate manifestation of their nature as metaphors of change. Marston and Caledon have fallen into decay; Cassiobury, Thorndon, Oatlands, and The Leasowes have disappeared under golf courses; Whitton and Byfleet, like Evelyn's Sayes Court and Pope's garden at Twickenham, have been swallowed by the suburbs. Perhaps, for all that, they live the more potently in the mind: emblems of a dialectical treaty between man and the natural world that is as potent and necessary as when they were created.

APPENDIX:
THE MYSTERY OF 'SIEUR BOURGIGNION' AND THORNDON HALL

One of the more interesting landscape gardens of the first half of the eighteenth century was Thorndon Hall in Essex, created by the eighth Baron Petre in the decade after 1732. The surviving 1733 plan of the garden is attributed to a 'Sieur Bourginion,' a shadowy figure who appears in the Petre correspondence and in a roll of household servants after Lord Petre's death in 1742 as 'Mr. Burginioing Surveyor.'[1]

The various spellings of the 'surveyor's' name are not surprising in documents of this date, but they ought to alert us to the possibility that the French name in question is different from either spelling. Who then is the likely candidate among Frenchmen working in England at that time?

The name 'Bourgignion' does not appear in any French biographical dictionary, but the spelling 'Bourgignon' leads one to two brothers, both well-known. The first was the famous geographer, Jean-Baptiste Bourgignon d'Anville, who, however, seems never to have travelled outside France. The second was Hubert-François Bourgignon, better known as the engraver Gravelot.

As a young man Gravelot was a sort of scapegrace. His father sent him to Santo Domingo from which he returned to Paris ill, but not before (his brother tells us) he made a map of the island (that was subsequently engraved) so accurate that it might well have been done by the geographer brother.[2] In Paris Gravelot studied drawing with Restout and Boucher, but gave up painting to come to England in 1732 when he was 33.

Gravelot was well received in England by English painters and seems to have been one of the early movers towards the establishment of the Royal Academy. He took up jewelry design but he also began the engraving practice for which he was to become famous. Among his projects were an illustrated edition of the *Theatre of Shakespeare* and illustrations for Richardson's *Pamela* and Gay's *Fables*.

At this time, apart from doing caricatures of both Walpole and Burlington, he wrote a treatise on perspective and did several 'prospect' drawings, some with George Buck, and one at least (a 'View of London, from One Tree Hill, Greenwich') on his own. In the year of Gravelot's return to Paris (1745) Buck also published views of Worksop Manor in Nottinghamshire, an estate whose landscape was redesigned by Lord Petre for his kinsman, the Duke of Norfolk.

The estate plan of Thorndon is described as 'Design'd by the Sieur Bourginion,' but the word 'design'd' here is closer to the French *dessin* than to our modern sense of it. Similarly, in the early eighteenth century the word 'surveyor' also meant one who created topographical drawings or plans. Indeed, Gravelot engraved the maps for John Pine's edition of plates of the Armada tapestries that were then hanging in the House of Lords. In the list of subscribers to that edition is Lord Petre's name.

In his 'Eloge' of 1774[3] Gravelot's brother refers to his wide reading and his wide architectural knowledge from the study of architecture. But he also refers to Gravelot's polymathic flightiness: the ease with which he was distracted into other projects and areas of interest.

Gravelot remained in England until the outbreak of the war with France in 1745. He was in England, in other words, at just the time when Lord Petre was creating the park at Thorndon. From the preliminary drawings of that estate in the Petre papers, it seems likely that the design was Petre's own. Peter Collinson, Petre's close friend, wrote of him, for example, that he had 'a fine Taste for Architecture and Drew and Designed well himself.'[4]

It seems likely, however, that the final design was drawn up by Gravelot/Bourgignon. A similar working relationship between the two men can be found in the infinitely more extensive 1738 plans for Worksop, where Petre is described as the creator (*inv.*) but 'Bourguignon' as the designer (*delineavit*).[5]

If, as Sir George Clutton and Colin Mackay suggest in their article on Thorndon, the function of Petre's surveyor was no more than 'to make working drawings from his employer's designs,'[6] this is certainly a role that Gravelot could have played. That he seems subsequently to have played a similar role at Worksop may also explain his being on the roll of household servants at the time of Lord Petre's death. And is it not likely that an employer like Petre, who had travelled to France and retained Parisian connections,[7] would have employed him for this purpose?

NOTES

CHAPTER 1. THE PATRIOTS OF HORTICULTURE

[1] J. D. Hunt, *The Figure in the Landscape* (Baltimore: Johns Hopkins Press, 1976). Similarly, David Jacques's *Georgian Gardens: The Reign of Nature* (Portland, OR: Timber Press, 1984), by beginning its account in 1733, leaves out of account the botanic and horticultural foundations of the English landscape revolution in the late seventeenth and early eighteenth centuries.

[2] In the Georgian Group *Journal* (1990) Jane Clark ('For Kings and Senates Fit,' pp. 56–62) claims that Burlington was a Jacobite whose Masonic connections served as a cover for his activities and that Chiswick House was designed as a palace for the restored Stuart dynasty. See also her 'The Mysterious Mr. Buck,' *Apollo* 129 (1989), pp. 317–22.

[3] L. Welsted, *A Discourse to the Right Honourable Sir Robert Walpole . . . For Translating the Whole Works of Horace* (London, 1727), pp. 6–7. Harley was also a patron of the landscape architect, Charles Bridgeman, who, in company with Pope, visited him at Wimpole in 1724.

[4] David Jacques (*Georgian Gardens*, p. 22) points out that although Stephen Switzer's early clients were Whigs, he dedicated his *Practical Kitchen Gardener* (1727) to Lord Bathurst, 'a notable Tory.'

[5] *The Correspondence of Jonathan Swift*, ed. Harold Williams (Oxford: Clarendon Press, 1963), II p. 464.

[6] For the negative see Carole Fabricant, *Swift's Landscape* (Baltimore: Johns Hopkins Press, 1982), especially the chapter 'The Subversion of the Country House Ideal.' For the positive see Edward Malins and the Knight of Glin, *Lost Demsenes: Irish Landscape Gardening, 1660–1845* (London: Barrie & Jenkins, 1976), pp. 33–34.

[7] See Howard Erskine-Hill, *The Social Milieu of Alexander Pope* (New Haven: Yale University Press, 1978), p. 316.

[8] Letter of 28 January 1660, Christ Church, Oxford, Evelyn MS. 39a, Epistle 161.

[9] Swift, *Correspondence*, II p. 464. It might also be observed that John James's translation of Dezallier d'Argenville's *The Theory and Practice of Gardening* (London, 1712) was subscribed to equally by Edward Harley and Lord Bathurst on the one side and by Addison, John Aislabie, and Robert Walpole on the other.

[10] These two terms have been used respectively by J. C. D. Clark in *English Society 1688–1932* (Cambridge, 1985) and E. P. Thompson in *Whigs and Hunters* (London: Allen Lane, 1975). In a useful survey of the controversy about how to read the history of this period, Joanna Innes has written 'Jonathan Clark, Social History and England's "Ancien Regime",' *Past and Present* 115 (1987), p. 176.: 'If to a social history which gives more place to agency, a political history which pays more attention to structure could be coupled, then we would really have moved a significant step closer to being able to do away with some obstructive and unnecessary boundary lines traditionally drawn within historical enquiry.' See also 'Progressive Ideology and Conservative Ideology' and 'Historical Models for Conservative Narratives' in Michael McKeon, *The Origins of the English Novel 1600–1740* (London: Century Hutchinson, 1988), pp. 205–11, 226–37.

[11] This phrase was used by Petre's friend, Peter Collinson, to describe the planting of one of his friends, in a letter to Philip Southcote, 9 December 1752. Linnean Society, Collinson MSS. Large Book, p. 31.

[12] Dubois was not simply a gardener, however. He was a Fellow of the Royal Society and Treasurer of the East India Company.

[13] Preface to the *Iliad* (1715). *The Poems of Alexander Pope*, Twickenham edition (London: Methuen, 1967), VII p. 3.

[14] Society of Gardeners, *Catalogus Plantation* (London, 1730), sig. [b3].

[15] Ibid. sig. [b3].

[16] Joseph Spence, *Observations, Anecdotes and Characters of Men*, ed. J. M. Osborn (Oxford: Clarendon Press, 1966) I:606, p. 252. Pope was a friend of the painter John Wooton (1682–1764) and owned Wooton's *Classical Landscape with a Temple*, a painting that depicts the Claudean interchange of antique architecture and groves of trees that Pope himself praised in the landscapes of Cirencester, Esher, and Stowe.

[17] See my article, '"Wild Pastoral Encounter": John Evelyn and the Renegotiation of Pastoral in the Mid-17th Century,' to be published in *Writing and the Land in Renaissance England* ed. Michael Leslie & Timothy Raylor (Leicester: Leicester University Press, 1992).

[18] Virgil, *Georgics*, ed. Richard F. Thomas (Cambridge: Cambridge University Press, 1988), I p. 5.

[19] *The Rambler*, no. 134, 2 July 1751, in *The Works of Samuel Johnson* (New Haven: Yale University Press, 1969), IV p. 351.

[20] The obvious exceptions would be the three volumes Blanche Henrey's monumental *British Botanic and Horticultural Literature before 1800* (London: Oxford University Press, 1975) as well as her posthumous book *No Ordinary Gardener: Thomas Knowlton* (London: British Museum (Natural History), 1986) on Lord Burlington's gardener. Frank Lowenstein's edition of Peter Aram's *A Practical Treatise of Flowers* for the Leeds Philosophical and Literary Society (Leeds, 1985), John Harvey's considerable researches on nurseries and nurserymen and especially his article on the Earl of Islay's garden at Whitton (in *Garden History* 14 (1986), pp. 149–72), and George Clarke's two articles on the horticultural materials for the making of Stowe: 'Where Did All the Trees Come From?' *Journal of Garden History* 5 (1985), pp. 72–83 and 'How High Was the Grass in the Elysian Fields?' an unpublished paper delivered at the American Society for Eighteenth-Century Studies conference in Toronto in 1986.

[21] See D. D. C. Chambers, 'The Tomb in the Landscape: John Evelyn's Garden at Albury,' *Journal of Garden History*, I (1981), pp. 37–54.

[22] George Mason, *An Essay on Design in Gardening* (London, 1768), p. 32.

[23] John Ogilby's *Virgil*, first published in 1649 and then more sumptuously in 1654, certainly played a large role in the definition of pastoral and georgic in the mid-seventeenth century, but Ogilby was largely eclipsed by Dryden, who used the same plates in his edition.

[24] Annabel Patterson notes Francis Bacon's invocation of the same Virgilian text in service of

the new science in *The Advancement of Learning*. See her *Pastoral and Ideology: Virgil to Valéry* (Oxford: Clarendon Press, 1988), p. 135.

25 BL Add. MS. 15950, fo. 153. Cf. Evelyn's elaboration of much of this in the fourth chapter of his *Elysium Britannicum*.

26 Browne's work was probably indebted to *Hortorum Libri Triginta* (Lyons, 1560), a work on the history of gardens by Benedictus Curtius (Benoît du Court) which Evelyn was actively searching for in the 1650s.

27 Evelyn's source was Selden's *Historia Anglicus*, possibly chapters 9 and 10 of Selden's *The Reverse or Back-face of the English Janus* (London, 1682), which Evelyn owned. But Evelyn goes on to assert: 'Tis certain that Pope Clement the VI (about 300 years since) thought so.' BL Add. MS. 15950, fo. 153. He also notes (fo. 169) that 'Dr. Taylor would have me call it Paradysus, not Elysium, as a word usd by the Hellenist Jewes to signifie any place of spiritual and immaterial pleasure, yet excludes not the material and secular.'

CHAPTER 2. THE TRANSLATION OF ANTIQUITY

1 A. Patterson, *Pastoral and Ideology: Virgil to Valéry* (Oxford: Clarendon Press, 1988), p. 163.

2 Houghton Library, Harvard University, MS. Eng. 218.2 (1), fo. 13–14.

3 J. F. Félibien, *Les Plans et les descriptions de deux des plus belles maisons de campagne de Plinie le consul* (London, 1707), pp. 11, 8.

4 Robert Castell, *The Villas of the Ancients Illustrated* (London, 1728), pp. 89, 117.

5 Matteo Ripa, *Views of the Imperial Summer Residence at Jehol, Manchuria*, 1713. Two of the sets, one at the Bibliothèque Nationale in Paris and the other at the Canadian Centre for Architecture in Montreal, have further explanations of the significance or use of the respective sites. The elaboration here is drawn from the latter set (DR 1981:072:013).

6 *The Letters of Pliny*, ed. John Boyle (London: Paul Vaillant, 1751), I p. 351. In his gardening practice, Burlington may also have been influenced by the writings of John Evelyn, especially the *Sylva* and the *Elysium Britannicum*. The latter was largely unpublished, but much of it had become generally known in manuscript. Evelyn was a friend and correspondent of Burlington's grandfather, the first Earl of Burlington, who did not die until 1697.

7 *The Letters of Pliny*, I p. 161. Writing to her husband in 1744, Lady Orrery praised Burlington 'as the restorer of decayed and fallen Arts, as well as a fine Gentleman, and what is more valuable a truly worthy and honest Nobleman.' Houghton Library MS. Eng. 218.26, letter of 12 January 1744.

8 Sir William Temple, *Upon the Gardens of Epicurus, or Of Gardening in the Year 1685*, *Miscellanea* Part 2 (London, 1690), p. 132. A letter from Chufon in China of 22 November 1701 describes the agriculture of China as creating fields that 'somewhat resemble Gardens.' See *Philosophical Transactions of the Royal Society* 23 (1702), p. 1208.

9 Castell, *Villas of the Ancients*, p. 117.

10 Houghton MS. Eng. 218.2 (3), pp. 58, 355. Throughout the Orrery correspondence there is frequent reference to farming, both at Marston and Caledon.

11 John Boyle, *The First Ode . . . of Horace Imitated* (London, 1757), p. 13. Anthony Low notes how Boyle's friend Pope uses georgic for similar purposes of private withdrawal in his 'Ode on Solitude'. See *The Georgic Revolution* (Princeton: Princeton University Press, 1985), p. 274.

12 Virgil, *Georgica . . . P. Rami illustrata* (Paris, 1584), p. 204. A manuscript note in Latin in John Boyle's copy (in Trinity College, Cambridge) says that in this place the philosophical and rustic lives are joined together.

13 Houghton, MS. Eng. 218.2 (5), Letter to the Rev. Mr. F., 24 June 1747.

14 The Countess of Cork and Orrery [E. C. Boyle], *The Orrery Papers* (London: Duckworth, 1903), I p. 209.

15 Houghton, MS. Eng. 218.2 (3), p. 249.

16 Houghton, MS. Eng. 218.2 (1), fo. 22.

17 Houghton, MS. Eng. 218.2 (2), fo. 45. Letter to Salkeld.

18 *Orrery Papers*, II p. 56.

19 A letter to Baron Wainwright, 13 October 1739, in *The Orrery Papers*, I p. 268.

20 *The Letters of Pliny*, I p. 174. The theme of retirement had been much canvassed in the seventeenth century as well. See *Public and Private Life in the Seventeenth Century: The Mackenzie–Evelyn Debate*, ed. Brian Vickers (New York: Scholars Facsimiles and Reprints, 1986).

21 Houghton, Autograph File, Letter to John Duncombe, 19 June 1756.

22 Houghton, MS. Eng. 218.26, Letter of 6 February 1744.

23 *Letters of Pliny*, I p. 174.

24 *Orrery Papers*, II p. 115.

25 *Orrery Papers*, I p. 224.

26 It is equally likely to have been the ampitheatre and woodland grave-enclosure made by Johann Moritz von Nassau-Siegen at his garden in Cleves in 1663. See Hans Peter Hilger, 'Das Grab-monument des Fürsten Johann Moritz in Bergendael bei Kleve' in *Soweit Der Erdkreis Reicht: Johann Moritz von Nassau-Siegen 1604–1679* (Kleve: Städtisaches Museum Haus Koekkoek, 1979), pp. 205–212.

27 Virgil, *The Georgics*, III.10–11, translated into English verse by L. P. Wilkinson (Harmondsworth: Penguin, 1982), p. 99.

28 James Thomson, *Alfred: A Masque* (London, 1751), sig. [A]. Boyle's copy with his original prologue on the fly-leaf is in the library of Trinity College, Cambridge.

29 Anthony Low's account of the *Georgic* tradition in the seventeenth century also indicates the important role played by Milton (especially in *Paradise Regained*) in accomodating georgic ideals to English poetry. See *The Georgic Revolution*, chapter 7.

30 John Chalker, *The English Georgic* (Baltimore: Johns Hopkins Press, 1969), p. 88. I am generally indebted here to Chalker's account of Georgic poetry. With reference to what follows, see also Patricia A. Johnston, *Vergil's Agricultural Golden Age* (Leiden: E. J. Brill, 1980), Gary B. Miles, *Virgil's Georgics: A New Interpretation* (Berkeley: University of California Press, 1980), and the introduction to volume I of the edition of the *Georgics* by Richard F. Thomas (Cambridge: Cambridge University Press, 1988).

31 For a discussion of Virgil's indebtedness to Lucretius see Philip Hardie, *Virgil's Aeneid: Cosmos and Imperium* (Oxford: Clarendon Press, 1986).

32 David O. Ross has suggested that because Virgil's praise of the country life is a parade of familiar clichés, it should be read within the conventions of epideictic rhetoric as the inverse of praise (*laudatio*). In this account the phrase *si bona norint* indicates that farmers do *not* know their own good fortune and that therefore the passage is a kind of *vituperatio* or converse of the praise it seems. See his 'Laudation and the Lie' in *Virgil's Elements: Physics and Poetry in the Georgics* (Princeton: Princeton University Press, 1987), pp. 109–27.

This point is also made by Richard Thomas in his edition of the *Georgics*, where he suggests that the vocative *O* sets this golden age passage apart from the real world of the rest of the poem. I can detect no evidence that eighteenth-century readers were aware of this sort of irony in the Virgilian text unless it be that the mock-epic so favoured by many writers of Georgic conveys this dubiety of praise/dispraise.

33 It seems unlikely that Virgil, who was aware of proper botanical description, meant his claims for grafting to be taken seriously. 'Of the six grafts,' Richard Thomas notes, 'four are not possible, and the other two, in that they are not of the same genus, are at least unlikely' (*Georgics* I.161). They alert the reader to the tricks of epideictic rhetoric within which the poet is working and draw attention to the theme of man's transforming the natural world that is central to the book. If, however, only the most literal-minded dullard would mistake these suggestions for botany, there was nonetheless a protracted debate among English botanists of the Restoration and Augustan periods about grafting's possibilities. See David O. Ross, *Virgil's Elements*, p. 118.

34 *P. Virgilii Maronis Opera cum notis Thomas Farnabii* (London, 1677), pp. 64, 61.

35 John Worlidge, *Systema Agriculturae* (London, 1669), sigs. B2, [C3], and [C4v].

36 Castell, *Villas of the Ancients*, pp. 124–25.

37 William Harper, *The Antiquity, Innocence, and Pleasure of Gardening. In a sermon . . . at Malpas . . . Chester* (London, 1732).

38 William Benson, *Virgil's Husbandry, or An Essay on the Georgics: Being the Second Book . . . with notes Critical and Rustick* (London, 1724), pp. vi, xvi. Cf. John Boyle's observation, in his commentary on Pliny's description of his estate, Tusculum, that 'although in many parts splendid

and great, [it] seems inferior to our chief seats in *England*, which are scarce equalled, and, I believe, not out-done in any parts of the known world.' *The Letters of Pliny*, I p. 393.

39 Benson, *Virgil's Husbandry*, p. v. Annabel Patterson (*Pastoral and Ideology*, p. 187) has noted how Dryden's essentially Jacobite translation of the *Aeneid* was frustrated in its political intent by the Whiggish engravings provided by his publisher Tonson, engravings in which William III not Charles II was seen as the modern Aeneas.

40 Benson, *Virgil's Husbandry, . . . the Second Book*, p. xx.

41 Anthony Low (*The Georgic Revolution*, p. 123) notes that the shift from a martial ideal, as espoused in the *Aeneid*, to a 'georgic ideal that is proper to a newly centralized and peaceful nation-state' was consonant with a new view in Britain of 'what constitutes virtuous and public-spirited behaviour.'

42 Benson, *Virgil's Husbandry, . . . the Second Book*, p. xii. Annabel Patterson (*Pastoral and Ideology*, p. 153) notes a similar 'reading' of the Virgilian text in the translation of La Mothe le Vayer's *Of Liberty and Solitude* (1649). There the anonymous commentator sought to prevent the apparently republican sentiments of *Eclogue* I by praising the 'more equal & excelent form of Government' of Charles I.

43 James Ackerman observes that both Palladianism and the new landscape garden 'represented a rejection of the Continental Baroque, an avowal of simplicity and independence in contrast to grandeur and authority.' See *The Villa: Form and Ideology of Country Houses* (London: Thames and Hudson, 1990), p. 183. Among the subscribers to Campbell's work were Joseph Addison, John Aislabie (of Studley Royal), Lord Bolingbroke, Henry Hoare (of Stourhead), the architect/garden designer John James and his patron Sir William Johnston, the Duke of Newcastle (Esher), John Boyle and his father-in-law the Earl of Orkney, the Duke of Richmond (Goodwood), the Duke of Somerset (on whose gardens at Marlborough Switzer worked), Vanbrugh, and Viscount Weymouth (the propagator of the White Pine.)

44 Benson erected the monument to Milton in Westminster Abbey and gave William Dobson £1000 to translate *Paradise Lost* into Latin. He also encouraged Christopher Pett's translation of the *Aeneid*.

45 Christopher Hussey, 'Wilbury Park, Wiltshire,' *Country Life* (3 December 1959), p. 1018.

46 Ibid. Benson's gardener in this period was Lewis Kennedy, the subsequent partner with James Lee in the Vineyard Nursery in Fulham, probably the most important and influential nursery of the mid-century. See E. J. Willson, *West London Nursery Gardens* (London: Fulham and Hammersmith Historical Society, 1982), p. 35.

47 See Kenneth Woodbridge, *Landscape and Antiquity: Aspects of English Culture at Stourhead 1718–1838* (Oxford: Clarendon Press, 1970), pp. 33–37.

48 The text of the poem cited is that given in *Major Poets of the Earlier Seventeenth Century*, ed. Barbara Lewalski and Andrew Sabol (New York: Odyssey Press, 1973), pp. 1133–60.

49 For a more complete discussion of this to which I am indebted, see Keith Thomas, *Man and the Natural World* (London: Allen Lane, 1983), especially chapters V and VI.

50 Horace Walpole, 'On Modern Gardening' in *Anecdotes of Painting in England* (London, 1827), IV p. 264.

51 Cf. R. I. V. Hodge's sense of the poem as a journey that 'moves between Art and Nature, which thus become key terms in the dialectic of the poem,' in *Foreshortened Time: Andrew Marvell and Seventeenth-century Revolutions* (Cambridge: D. S. Brewer, l978), p. 141. Ann Bertoff suggests that the poem's dialectic is the result of the transformation of the life of nature by virtuous action: 'What is lost and what is gained, what is changed and what is created.' See *The Resolved Soul: A Study of Marvell's Major Poems* (Princeton: Princeton University Press, 1970), pp. l93–94.

52 BL Add. MS. 28726, fo. [154v]–155. Collinson's punctuation is so confusingly erratic that I have omitted some semi-colons and altered others to commas. Cf. the preface to the *Catalogus Plantarum* (1730) where one of the advantages claimed for its publication is that 'we shall be led to admire the great and bounteous Author of Nature, who has left scarce any Spot of Earth intirely unfurnished.'

53 The two poems cited by title are from *Poems, Centuries and Thanksgivings*, ed. A. Ridler (Oxford: O.U.P., 1966), pp. 35, 98–99. The others are from *Commentaries of Heaven*, BL MS. 63054, fo. l85, 71.

54 Milton, *Paradise Lost*, IV.141, *L'Allegro*, l. 58, *Il Penseroso*, l. 133.

55 Sir Thomas Browne, *The Garden of Cyrus* in *Works*, ed. Geoffrey Keynes (London: Faber, 1928) I p. 216.

CHAPTER 3. A GROVE OF VENERABLE OAKS

1 4 August 1690. *Diary and Correspondence of John Evelyn*, ed. William Bray (London: Routledge, [1906]), pp. 688–89, hereafter cited as *Correspondence*.

2 *Sylva* (London, 1664), sig. [A3v]. *Sylva* went through four editions between 1664 and 1706. In the last, which Geoffrey Keynes calls 'the handsomest as well as the most elaborate' (*John Evelyn, A Study in Bibliophily* (Cambridge: Cambridge University Press, 1968), the title was first spelled *Silva*. Curiously, Keynes notes neither the 1776 edition nor that the 1706 edition was the first to include *Dendrologia*.

3 Christopher Hussey, *English Gardens and Landscapes 1700–1750* (London: Country Life, 1967), p. 15.

4 Writing of Sir Baptist Hicks's incorporation of working mills in the garden layout of Campden House, Paul Everson notes Gervase Markham's recommendation (in 1614) that the mixture of orchard walks with fishponds combined pleasure with profit. See 'The Gardens of Campden House, Chipping Campden, Gloucestershire,' *Garden History* 17 (1989), pp. 119–20. See also Stephen Daniels, 'The political iconography of woodland in later Georgian England' in *The Iconography of Landscape*, ed. Denis Cosgrove and Stephen Daniels (Cambridge: Cambridge University Press, 1989), pp. 43–82.

5 Evelyn, *Correspondence*, p. 689.

6 Evelyn probably took his title from James Howell's *Dendrologia: Dodona's Grove or the Vocall Forrest*. First published in 1640 and included in Evelyn's library, it uses trees as a royalist allegory of the political troubles of the times. The key to the work explains that the King is an oak, the Nobility poplars, the Commons elms, and the two universities 'dainty *Groves of Laurels*.' Some of the material in *Dendrologia* is derived from Book II, chapter VII ('Of Groves') of the unpublished manuscript, *Elysium Britannicum* (Christ Church MS. 38).

7 Keith Thomas ascribes this to political motives: the Duke of Beaufort's desire to demonstrate 'that all local avenues of power converged upon him.' See *Man and the Natural World* (London: Allen Lane, 1983), p. 207.

8 *The Diary of John Evelyn*, ed. E.S. de Beer (Oxford: Clarendon Press, 1955), III p. 89. See also note 31 below.

9 Evelyn, *Diary*, III p. 591, IV pp. 116–17. Evelyn's correspondence reveals a large group of people who sought his advice about tree and hedge planting, advice as much about botany and propagation as about horticultural design.

10 Edmund Waller, *Poems, &c. Written upon several Occasions* (London, 1668), p. 183.

11 Evelyn MSS., Christ Church, Oxford, Ms. 38, fo. 186.

12 Hussey, *English Gardens* p. 155.

13 Ibid., p. 156.

14 In Walter Blith's *The English Improver Improved* (London, 1652), a book that Evelyn owned and annotated, the author refers to the lime as 'newly discovered' (p. 171).

15 *Correspondence*, pp. 659–61.

16 *The Miscellaneous Writings of John Evelyn, . . .* collected with occasional notes by William Upcott (London: Henry Colburn, 1825), p. 693. One of the pre-Linnaean names for *Pinus strobus* was *Pinus virginiana, conis longis*. A letter from Robert Ball to Evelyn on 30 January 1688 (*Correspondence*, p. 674,) says that Ball is sending acorns of the cork tree as well as 'two or three sorts of seeds of evergreens that grow about Leghorn.'

17 'Prefatory Letter' to John Smith, England's Improvement Reviv'd Evelyn's annotated copy, like the other annotated works referred to below, is now in the British Library.

18 *Philosophical Transactions* (1699), XXI pp. 437–38. Evelyn's early interest in the foundation of the Royal Society is evident in his marginal notation to the call for such a society in Samuel Hartlib's *Hartlib His Legacy* (1655), p. 205. His credulity about grafting (see note 45 below), however, suggests that he was as susceptible as

many of the members of the Royal Society to improbable stories about natural curiosities. See Michael McKeon, '"Natural History" as a Narrative Model' in *The Origins of the English Novel 1600–1740* (London: Century Hutchinson, 1988), pp. 58–73.

[19] Roy Strong, *The Renaissance Garden in England* (London: Thames and Hudson, 1979), p. 181.

[20] The drawing is in the Hertfordshire County Record Office. Roy Strong shows a view from beyond the exterior wall of the garden in *The Renaissance Garden in England*, plate 118.

[21] Hertfordshire Record Office, MSS. 224, 224a. As early as 1649, John Ogilby's royalist translation of Virgil (in *Eclogue* I) cites 'Sequestrations' as a consequence of civil war and thereby identifies royalism with a lost arcadia. See Annabel Patterson, *Pastoral and Ideology Virgil to Valéry* (Oxford: Clarendon Press, 1988), p. 171. Evelyn himself refers to the Commonwealth's destruction of woods 'to satisfie their impious (and hellish) avarice, which were the glory and oernament of this Nation.' *Elysium Britannicum*, Book II, chapter VII, fo. 109. I am indebted to John Ingram for permission to quote from his transcription.

[22] Evelyn, *Sylva* (London, 1664) sig. A3. René Rapin's *Hortorum Libri IV* (a book owned by Evelyn) also cites the elder Pliny (12:1) on the worship of oaks in the golden age, a worship shared by the Druids and revived in Restoration society by the institution of 'Oak-apple Day' in celebration of Charles II's escape at Boscobel from the Parliamentary forces after the Battle of Worcester.

[23] See BL Add. MS. 40627, fo. 42–52. This manuscript also shows Essex adding to the property from 1662 to 1681 by buying up parcels of land in Watford.

[24] Evelyn, *Diary*, IV pp. 199–200. As Lord Lieutenant of Ireland, Essex was also in correspondence with the first Earl of Orrery, and as a government minister he arranged to bring fruit trees from Copenhagen for Lord Arlington (BL MS. Stowe 200, fo. 168.)

[25] BL MS. Stowe 211, fo. 3. May describes the sculptor only as a stranger (i.e. a foreigner) but tells Essex: 'wee have seene things done by him in litle, and Modls of Clay.'

[26] Hertfordshire Record Office, MS. 10448. This manuscript also records a payment of £23 9s 4d to John Love 'for the Carriage of 33 loads and 63 feet of stones and 13 Tunnes and three hundred weight of iron' from London to Cassiobury.

[27] Henry Capel was also part of an extensive network of plantsmen. He exchanged plants with Evelyn, and orange trees that he had received from Spain through the offices of the Irish Catholic, Viscount Dungan, he passed on to Sir John Temple, brother of the author of 'Upon the Gardens of Epicurus,' for planting at his estate, Palmerston, in Ireland. The gardener there, Thomas Simpson, had also worked for Evelyn at Sayes Court. See T. C. Barnard, 'Gardening, diet and "improvement" in later 17th-century Ireland,' *Journal of Garden History* 10 (1990), pp. 80, 81.

[28] John Britton, citing John Aubrey's *Letters from the Bodleian Library* (1813) in *The History and Description of Cassiobury Park* (London, 1837), p. 16.

[29] It may, however, be argued that there is some English precedent for this. In the second edition of *A New Orchard and Garden* (1623) William Lawson indicates walks in woods beyond the garden proper. It also seems likely that the wilder wooded parts of many Dutch (or Dutch-influenced) gardens of the early seventeenth century were created under the influence of Sir Henry Wotton, who was tutor to Constantin Huygens in 1614–15 and whose *Elements of Architecture* (1624) was translated into Latin for a Dutch audience. Huygens's son was, like Evelyn, a member of the Royal Society and keenly interested in the forthcoming publication of *Sylva* as early as 1662.

[30] Switzer commends Cook in *The Nobleman, Gentleman, and Gardener's Recreation* (London, 1715), p. 46.

[31] Evelyn himself owned what may have been the earliest *ferme ornée*, Worley or Warley Place in Essex. Purchased from his wife's uncle, Sir William Pretyman, in 1649, it may well have included some of the experimentation with hedge-row planting about which he later corresponded with Browne. Certainly by the 1730s it had come to be regarded as a *ferme ornée*. See *Diary*, II p. 554, and note 44 below.

[32] *Diary*, IV p. 200.

[33] Ibid. In *The Manner of Raising, Ordering; and Improving Forest and Fruit Trees* (London, 1679), p. 140, Cook gives 1672 as the date when these firs were planted.

[34] Ibid., p. 67. The rest of Cook's title makes plain its relevance to Cassiobury: '*Also, How to Plant, Make and Keep Woods, Walks, Avenues, Lawns, Hedges etc.*' Cook is also credited with the authorship of *The Art of Making Cyder*, published with Evelyn's works. See S. Felton, *On portraits of English Authors on Gardening* (1830), p. 31.

[35] MS. 6542. This undated document, apparently a valuation of the timber from the whole estate for sale to the Earl of Elgin, is in the same sort of ledger book as those used for dated accounts of the 1670s. In the latter are recorded two payments to Cook for his work in the gardens: one of Christmas 1679 for £45 12s 2d for a quarter-years's wages (MS. 10448) and one 'from Dec. 25th 1679 to the 16th of September 1680' for £157 16s 3d (MS. 10449). Throughout this period there are a number of payments to James Ewre for looking after Lovesden Wood at Cassiobury (MS. 10449). The same manuscripts record several large payments to Arthur Wankford for 'worke done in the Park.' One of 1679 (MS. 10447) shows Wankford receiving £220 15s 5d, a sum almost as large as Cook's annual salary.

[36] Cook, *The Manner*, p. 21. Hertfordshire Record Office, MS. 10447 also records a payment to Thomas Scott 'for carrying a load of lyme trees to Cashiobury.' In the preface Essex is praised for having sown 'many thousands' of trees which Cook had raised.

[37] *The Manner*, sig. [av], pp. 70–71.

[38] Evelyn MSS, Christ Church Oxford, *Misc. Mss. Relating to Sylva Etc.*, fo. 152, 186.

[39] Sir William Temple, *Upon the Garden of Epicurus: or, Of Gardening, in the Year 1685, Miscellanea*, part II (1692), p. 132.

[40] Cook, *The Manner*, p. 71. Temple's estate, Moor Park in Surrey, was, however, quite small: about five acres, the size of Pope's later garden.

[41] Ibid., p. 95.

[42] Ibid., p. 74. Rapin also cites Cicero's praise of topiary in walks.

[43] Evelyn MSS., Christ Church Oxford, MS. 38, fo. 140, 208.

[44] Evelyn MSS., MS. 38, fo. 206, 208. Letters of [2] November 1662. See below, pp. 00–00.

[45] Cook, *The Manner*, sig. [a2v], pp. 2, 83. In his essay, 'The Garden,' Cowley wrote of grafting and imitating divine creation: 'It does, like Grace, the Fallen Tree restore / To its blest state of Paradise before' *Works* (1668), p. 119. Evelyn's deference to the *Georgics* is also reflected in his 'Plan of a Royal Garden: Describing, and Shewing the *Amplitude*, and *Extent* of that Part of *Georgicks*, which belongs to *Horticulture*' which is contained in his outline of *Elysium Britannicum* (1699). In the manuscript notes relating to *Sylva* Evelyn speculates 'whether the Peare (as some say) will graff on the Ash, Chesnutt, Medlare' or whether there is 'a way of graffing plums in walnut stock' as Pliny recommends. Evelyn MSS., Christ Church, Oxford, MS. 38, fo. 34, 36.

[46] Cook, *The Manner*, pp. 23, 49, 52.

[47] Evelyn *Diary*, IV p. 200.

[48] Evelyn's fascination with the parterre figures of French *broderie* is evident in his designs for them in BL Add. MS. 15950, fo. 173, 174. On the latter is written: 'See in the notes of Husbandry for the true draught of the Garden at Sayes Court.'

[49] Cook, *The Manner*, pp. 180, 177, 146.

[50] BL Add. MS. 40630, fo. 299–301.

[51] Evelyn's letter to his brother George suggests that even the first edition (1693), attributed solely to him, was not all his own work. *The Retir'd Gardener*, published by London and Wise in 1706, was a further translation of two works by François Gentil and Louis Liger. Evelyn commends the Brompton Park nursery in the 'Advertisement' to *The Compleat Gard'ner* and his *Diary* (V p. 176) records taking Richard Waller, the Secretary of the Royal Society, there on 24 April 1694.

[52] Cook's will of 24 September 1713 is Hertfordshire Record Office MS. D/Ex 285.Z1.

[53] Evelyn, *Sylva* (3rd ed., 1679) p. 59. Evelyn refers to Cook four times, most interestingly on design, pp. 239–40.

[54] Cook, *The Manner*, sig. [A4v].

[55] Cowley, 'The Garden,' in *Several Discourses by way of Essays, in Verse and Prose, Works* (London, 1668), p. 118. The previous year, in *Paradise Lost*, Milton had depicted a similar metamorphosis of the garden of Eden itself into a barren island after the Fall.

[56] M. Hale, *The Primitive Origination of Mankind* (London, 1677), pp. 355, 370.

57 Sir Thomas Browne, *The Garden of Cyrus* (London, 1658), pp. 90, 92. Evelyn also commments several times in the work on Browne's praise of the quincunx.

58 L. Meager, *The Mystery of Husbandry: or Arable, Pasture, and Wood-land Improved* (London, 1697), pp. 1–2, 108, 117.

59 Recorded on the verso of the last blank folio in Hale's *Primitive Origination*.

60 The former is on p. 144 of Evelyn's copy of Charles Leigh's *The Natural History of Lancashire* (1700). The latter is on p. 236 of Woodward's *Natural History of the Earth* (1702).

61 Evelyn MSS., Christ Church, Oxford. *Misc. Mss. Relating to Sylva Etc.*, fo. 95.

62 *Philosophical Transactions of the Royal Society*, 17 (1693), p. 611.

63 *Philosophical Transactions* (1700), p. 589. In reviewing a catalogue of Jamaican plants, Hans Sloane also complained that 'the Compilers of general Histories of Plants . . . have repeated one and the same Species, found in far distant Countries by various Observers, and differently described, once, twice, thrice' *Philosophical Transactions* (1696), p. 294.

64 Evelyn, for example, marked a passage in Plot's *The Natural History of Stafford-Shire* (1686) in which the author recommends planting acorns with furze (*Genista spinosa*) as a nurse shrub.

65 Robert Plot, *The Natural History of Stafford-shire* (Oxford, 1686), p. 339.

66 René Rapin, *Hortorum Libri IV. Cum Disputatione de Cultura Hortense* (Paris: E Typographia Regia, 1665), p. 187.

67 Cowley, *Works* sig. [c2v]. Michael Hunter cites Sir Robert Southwell spending his time out of office 'between Virgil's *Georgics* and Mr. Evelyn *On Trees*' in *Science and Society in Restoration England* (Cambridge: Cambridge University Press: 1981), p. 101.

68 Plot, *The Natural History of Stafford-shire*, p. 340.

69 Cowley 'Of Agriculture,' *Several Discourses*, *Works* (London, 1668), p. 98. In *The Georgic Revolution* (Princeton: Princeton University Press, 1985), p. 131, Anthony Low notes Cowley's indebtedness to Bacon's *Advancement of Learning*, and specifically to Bacon's potent phrase, 'these Georgics of the mind.'

70 Cowley, 'Of Agriculture,' pp. 101–02. Hartlib had transcribed and published Cressy Dymock's *An Essay for Advancement of Husbandry-learning. Or Propositions for Erecting a Colledge of Husbandry* in 1651. Evelyn, who was already interested in agricultural reform, records visiting him on 27 November 1655. See Low, *The Georgic Revolution*, pp. 143–45.

71 J. Worlidge, *Systema Agriculturae*, sig. D2.

72 Ibid., sig. D.

73 Ibid., sig. [Dv]. As Anthony Low notes, 'the darker side of Virgilian labor' is absent in Worlidge's georgic (*The Georgic Revolution*, p. 152). This, however, is consonant both with the gradual adaptation of pastoral *otium* to georgic ideals and with an increasingly utopian natural theology. What both Low and Annabel Patterson have remarked, the increasing accommodation of pastoral to georgic in the Restoration, in fact began in the 1650s with such royalist sympathisers as Evelyn and Edward Benlowes. See my article, '"Wild Pastorall Encounter:" John Evelyn and The Renegotiation of Pastoral in the mid-17th Century,' in *Culture and Cultivation in Early Modern England*, ed. Michael Leslie and Timothy Raylor (Leicester: Leicester University Press, 1992).

74 Evelyn, *A Character of England* (London, 1659), pp. 61–62. He was nonetheless disparaging of the park during the Commonwealth, comparing it unfavorably to the Tuileries.

75 BL Add. MS. 15950, fo. 146. In a letter of 29 September 1659, Browne says that, 'as soon as the weather and my leasure permitts you shall have the account of our Paille-mailes: which are here only three (viz) The Thuilleries, the Palais Royal, and the Arsenal, all which I will pace and take the distance by the Inglish foot.' BL Add. MS. 15857, fo. 149.

76 Edmund Waller, 'A Poem on St. James's Park As Lately improved by his Majesty' (London, 1661), pp. 6–7.

77 Traherne's copy is in Bodleian MS. Eng. poet. c. 42. Jackson's original is from *A Treatise Containing the Original of Unbelief, Misbelief, or Mispersuasions, Concerning the Attributes of the Deity* (London, 1624), Book V, chapter XX, p. 4, as republished in *The Works of Thomas Jackson* (Oxford: Oxford University Press, 1844), IV p. 178. Cf. this to Book II, chapter VII p. 107 ('Of Groves') in the manuscript of *Elysium Britannicum*: 'there is nothing strikes a more awfull (and solemne) reverence into us, then the gloomy umbrage of some majesticall groves . . . extreamly apt to compose the mind, and infuse into it a kind of natural Devotion, disposing to prayer, and profound meditation.'

78 Jackson, *Works*, p. 182.

79 BL Add. MS. 15950, fo. 153.

80 John Dixon Hunt, *Garden and Grove: The Italian Renaissance Garden in the English Imagination: 1600–1750* (Princeton: Princeton University Press, 1986), p. 187.

81 Evelyn, *Silva* (4th ed., London, 1706), p. 347.

82 *Silva*, p. 331.

83 *Silva*, p. 337. Writing to Evelyn as early as 1656, Jeremy Taylor referred to Sayes Court by the name of one of Pliny's villas, 'Tusculanum.' Letter of 16 April 1656 in *Correspondence*, p. 568. Forty years later, however, Evelyn thought ancient gardening 'certainly nothing approaching the elegancy of the present age. Letter to William Wotton, 28 October 1696 in *Correspondence*, p. 710.

84 Christ Church, Oxford, Evelyn MSS., MS. 38, fo. 206, 208. Letters of [2] November 1662.

85 *Silva*, p. 339.

86 *Letters and the Second Diary of Samuel Pepys*, ed. R. G. Howarth (London: Dent, 1932), p. 229.

87 *Silva*, p. 329.

88 Ibid., p. 330. Cf. Evelyn's catalogue in the 'Outline of the "Elysium Britannicum",' in *The Genius of the Place*, ed. J. D. Hunt and P. Willis (Cambridge: M.I.T. Press, 1988), pp. 67–69.

CHAPTER 4. THINGS OF A NATURAL KIND

1 Shaftesbury, 'The Moralists' in *Characteristicks of Men, Manners, Opinions, Times* (London, 1714), II pp. 393–94.

2 D. Leatherbarrow, 'Character, Geometry and Perspective: the Third Earl of Shaftesbury's Principles of Garden Design,' *Journal of Garden History* 4 (1984), pp. 332–58. Leatherbarrow's argument is accepted by John Dixon Hunt in *Garden and Grove* (Princeton: Princeton University Press, 1986), p. 182.

3 In Castell's later translation of the account of the garden at Tusculum, he describes how the shrubs 'in some Places . . . grow like Cones, and in other Globular.' See *The Villas of the Ancients Illustrated* (1728), p. 89.

4 The mixture of the two was a commonplace of the Anglo-Dutch garden, and is illustrated, for example, in an anonymous painting of Winchendon House (Bucks.) and another of Dynevor (Carmarthen), an anonymous drawing for a 'wilderness garden' at Badminton (Glos.), George London's drawing for a parterre at Blythe (Notts.), and William Williams's engraving of Trinity College, Oxford in *Oxonia Depicta*. See *The Anglo-Dutch Garden in the Age of William and Mary*, *Journal of Garden History* 8.2–3 (1988), nos. 87, 95a, 98b, 103, 108. That both pyramid and globe Yews continued to be commonplace in small estates in the early eighteenth century is illustrated in many of the plates in T. Badeslade's *Thirty Six Different Views of . . . Kent* (London, 1720).

5 Even at Shaftesbury's town house in Chelsea, the gardens not dedicated to kitchen gardening seem, in Kip's engraving of its neighbour, Beaufort House, to be very plain. As with Pope's other *dictum* ''tis Use alone that sanctifies Expence,' it seems that Shaftesbury, even in calling in the country, was more Popean than Pope, in his garden practice at Twickenham, was himself.

6 See Spencer Savage, *Calendar of the Ellis Manuscripts* in the library of the Linnean Society (London: Taylor and Francis, 1948), p. 8.

7 Shaftesbury, 'The Moralists', II p. 405.

8 Stephen Switzer, *Ichnographia Rustica* (2nd ed., London, 1742), I p. xviii.

9 Shaftesbury, 'The Moralists', II p. 395.

10 Like many of the early botanists, Ray was no narrow scientist. He showed a keen interest in antiquities, polity, government, legislation, and philology. Switzer describes him as 'our own pious and worthy Philosopher *Ray*', in the appendix to the third volume of the 1742 edition of *Ichnographia Rustica*, p. 31.

11 Shaftesbury, 'The Moralists', II p. 388.

12 Ibid., II pp. 424, 402.

13 Shaftesbury, 'Advice to an Author,' *Characteristicks*, I pp. 195–96.

14 Quoted in Marie-Sophie Røstvig, *The Happy Man* (Oxford: Basil Blackwell, 1958), II p. 103. This paragraph is largely indebted to Røstvig.

15 R. Feingold, *Nature and Society: Later*

Eighteenth-Century Uses of the Pastoral and Georgic (Hassocks, Sussex: Harvester Press, 1978), pp. 16–17.

16 Anthony Low cites a speech by Wisdom (Sophia) to this effect in Bruno's Lo Spaccio della Bestia Trionfante (1584). See The Georgic Revolution (Princeton: Princeton University Press, 1985), p. 137.

17 William Harper, The Antiquity, Innocence, and Pleasure of Gardening (London, 1732), pp. 14, 13, 9.

18 Elysium Britannicum, Christ Church, Oxford, Evelyn MS. 45, p. 41.

19 Edward Lisle, Observations in Husbandry (London, 1757), p. xi.

20 See Maynard Mack, The Garden and the City (Toronto: University of Toronto Press, l969), p. 80, n.4.

21 Abraham Cowley, Several Discourses by Way of Essay, Works (London, 1668), p. 100.

22 Malcolm Rogers, 'John and John Baptist Closterman: a Catalogue of their Works,' The Walpole Society 49 (1983), p. 259. In his essay, 'Shaftesbury as a Patron of Art,' Edgar Wind claims that Shaftesbury's published and unpublished writings show him to be a follower of Socrates but of the Socrates that Xenophon not Plato recorded. See Hume and the Heroic Portrait: Studies in 18th-century imagery (Oxford: Oxford University Press, 1986), pp. 64–68.

23 Ibid., plates 57, 58. Cf. the well-known engraving 'The Taming of the Passions' by Andrea Bocchi in Symbolicae Questiones (Bologna, 1574).

24 Wind also points out that Shaftesbury's A Notion of the Historical Draught or Tablature of the Judgment of Hercules is a 'philosopher's "Advice to a Painter"' and that he continued to give direction to engravers and artists who worked for him about emblematic subjects. See 'Shaftesbury as a Patron' in Hume and the Heroic Portrait, p. 66.

25 Shaftesbury, Second Characters or The Language of Forms, ed. Benjamin Rand (Cambridge: Cambridge University Press, 1914), p. 163.

26 Shaftesbury, 'The Moralists,' II pp. 390–91.

27 Arbores fuere numinum templa, priscoque ritu simplicia rura etiam nunc Deo praecellentem arborem dicant. René Rapin, Hortorum Libri IV Cum Disputatione de Cultura Hortensi (Paris, 1665), p. 188.

28 Francis Hutcheson, Inquiry into ... Beauty (London, 1725), pp. 89, 66, 33, 76.

29 Switzer , Ichnographia Rustica, I p. 272.

30 Leatherbarrow asserts (p. 334) that 'gardens designed with uncut trees and winding paths did not appear until the 1730s and '40s.' Such 'woodwalkes', as we have seen, were proposed early in the seventeenth century; the trees at Cassiobury (created in the 1670s) appear to have been left uncut; and the serpentine wooded paths at Sir William Temple's contemporary Moor Park are also to be seen in other gardens in Britannia Illustrata. Wray Wood is one instance of serpentine walks combined with uncut trees.

31 Switzer, Ichnographia, p. 85.

32 Ibid., p. 86.

33 Shaftesbury, 'The Moralists,' p. 216.

34 Pope, An Essay on Man, Epistle IV, ll. 331–32.

35 Pope, 'Dawley Farm,' ll. l9–20, 29–32, in Select Letters taken from Fogs Weekly Journal (London, 1732), reprinted in Alexander Pope, Minor Poems (London: Methuen, 1964), p. 452. Dawley Farm has been dealt with in Peter Martin's Pursuing Innocent Pleasures: The Gardening World of Alexander Pope (Hamden, Conn.: Archon Books, 1984). Bolingbroke's French estate, La Source, is the subject of an article by Kenneth Woodbridge in Garden History 4 (1976), pp. 50–64.

36 The Correspondence of Jonathan Swift, ed. Harold Williams (Oxford: Clarendon Press, 1963), II P. 372. Much of what follows is indebted to Isaac Kramnick, Bolingbroke and His Circle (Cambridge, Mass.: Harvard University Press, 1968) and to Bertrand Goldgar, Walpole and the Wits. The Relation of Politics to Literature 1722–1742 (Lincoln, Neb.: University of Nebraska Press, 1976).

37 One Thousand Seven Hundred and Thirty Eight. A Dialogue ... By Mr. Pope (London, 1738), ll. 39–42. Although not included in the Twickenham edition of Pope's poetry, the poem is credited to Pope by the Eighteenth-Century Short Title Catalogue.

38 The Crafts of the Craftsman: Or a Detection of the Designs of the Coalition (London, 1735), p. 13.

CHAPTER 5. RURAL AND EXTENSIVE LANDSCAPE

1 First published in 1718, it was revised and expanded in 1742. Switzer worked under London at Blenheim. Subsequently he worked at Grimsthorpe, Marlborough, Marston, Spy Park, Dyrham, Cirencester, Riskins, Nostell Priory, Leeswood Hall, and perhaps other gardens, including some in Scotland. John Harris has recently suggested that the garden of Stamp Brooksbank's 1728 house in Clapton (near London) was also by Switzer. 'A Tour of London's Gardens with John Rocque,' in London's Pride: The Glorious History of the Capital's Gardens, ed. Mireille Galinou (London: Anaya, 1990), p. 117.

What follows does not purport to be a thorough account of Switzer's work. A brief account is given in David Jacques's Georgian Gardens: the Reign of Nature (Portland, OR: Timber Press, 1984), pp. 18–23. Other articles dealing with aspects of his career include: W.S. Brogden, 'Stephen Switzer "La Grand Manier"' in Furor Hortensis, ed. Peter Willis (Edinburgh: Elysium Press, 1974), pp. 21–30, and 'The Ferme Ornée and Changing Attitudes to Agricultural Improvement,' Eighteenth-Century Life 8 (1983), pp. 39–43. Although recent work on Switzer has revealed his involvement with other gardens, Brogden's University of Edinburgh thesis on Switzer remains the most thorough account of his career. See also James Turner, 'Stephen Switzer and the Political Fallacy in Landscape

Gardening History,' Eighteenth-Century Studies 11 (1978), pp. 489–96; Anthony Mitchell, 'The Garden and Park at Dyrham' in The National Trust Yearbook 1977–78 (London: National Trust, 1978), pp. 83–108; Peter Willis, Charles Bridgeman and the English Landscape Garden (London: Zwemmer, 1977), pp. 22–25.

2 Switzer, Proposals for Printing, (London, [1718]), [p. 1]. On p. 2 Switzer cites Addison's famous Spectator essay no. 414 of 25 June 1712.

3 The Guardian, no. 173, 29 September 1713.

4 Switzer, Ichnographia Rustica (London, 1742), I p. 10.

5 Ibid., II p. 190.

6 Ibid., I p. xviii.

7 Ibid., I pp. xix, xl. In Proposals for Printing (p. 2) Switzer refers to Ichnographia Rustica as 'containing the Business of an Husbandman and Woodward, as well as Gardener.'

8 Ibid., I p. vi.

9 A General Dictionary of Husbandry, Planting, Gardening ... by the Editors of the Farmer's Magazine (Bath, 1779), I p. vii.

10 The desire to produce timber, Switzer writes, 'is, or indeed ought to be, the chief Aim of every Planter' (Ichnographia, I p. 328). 'I am never fond of any Tree that gives no hopes of future Profit as well as present Beauty' (II p. 244).

11 Ibid., I pp. 273–74.

12 Ibid., pp. xxxv–xxxvi, 273–74. Consonant with this 'patriotism' is Switzer's observation, when dealing with the origins of the ha-ha, that its military origins will be 'very pleasing to all the martial Genius's of our Country' (II p. 174). He notes also that the ha-ha was first used at Marlborough's seat, Blenheim.

13 Letter to Peter Collinson, Linnean Society, Collinson MSS., Small Notebook, p. 104.

14 Switzer, Ichnographia, I p. 327.

15 Ibid., III pp. 5, 7.

16 Ibid., III p. 74.

17 Ichnographia, I p. 87. For a fuller account of the creation of Wray Wood, see Charles Saumarez Smith, The Building of Castle Howard (London: Faber, 1990), pp. 124–130. Saumarez Smith identifies as the three distinguishing features of Wray Wood that it used existing mature trees, that its scale was adapted to a walking pace, and that it was asymmetrical. He traces the last to the influence of Sir William Temple's Moor Park, which Carlisle visited in 1697. Carlisle's rejection of London's plan is also a rejection of the French style espoused by John James's book, The Theory and Practice of Gardening (1712), to which he had subscribed.

18 Thomas Gent, Pater Patriae: being, An Elegiac Pastoral Dialogue (York, [1738]), pp. 12–13, 15.

19 'The Travel Journals of Philip Yorke,' Publications of the Bedfordshire Historical Record Society 47 (1968), p. 130. See also Merlin Waterson, The Servant's Hall: A Domestic History of Erddig (London: Routledge, 1980), p. 152.

20 Cf. Samuel Molyneux's account of New Park 'beautifully and wildly dispos'd into Slopes.' Letter of 14 February 1713 in J. D. Hunt and Peter Willis, eds., The Genius of the Place (Cambridge, Mass.: MIT Press, 1988), p. 149.

[21] Switzer, *Ichnographia*, I p. 59.

[22] Ibid., I p. 191. Switzer seems not to be using the latest edition of *Sylva*, the 1706 one, as he refers to a 'Chapter' in Evelyn's book, whereas by 1706 this had become a distinct Book.

[23] *The Spectator*, no. 414, 25 June 1712. Switzer echoes this in p. vi of the preface to volume III of *Ichnographia Rustica* (1742): 'an even decent Walk carry'd thro' a Corn Field or Pasture, thro' little natural Thickets and Hedge Rows, is as pleasing, as the most finish'd Partarre that some Moderns have been so fond of.'

[24] Linnean Society, Collinson MSS., Large Book, p. 29.

[25] *The Tatler*, no. 161, 18–20 April 1710; *The Spectator*, no. 414, 15 June 1712, and no. 37, 12 April 1711.

[26] *The Spectator*, no. 477, 6 September 1712.

[27] Switzer, *Ichnographia*, I p. 82.

[28] Ibid., I pp. 56, 279.

[29] Ibid., I p. 62.

[30] Timothy Nourse, *Campania Foelix*, (London, 1706), pp. 19–20.

[31] Nourse, *Campania Foelix*, p. 299; John Rea, *Flora* (London, 1665), pp. 1–3. See J. D. Hunt's discussion of this in *Garden and Grove* (Princeton: Princeton University Press, 1986), pp. 178–79.

[32] Switzer, *Ichnographia*, I p. 73.

[33] Helen S. Hughes, *The Gentle Hertford* (New York: Macmillan, 1940), p. 98.

[34] Percy was properly a member of the Seymour family, the Marquises of Hertford, who, like the Capels, had suffered severely in the royalist cause during the Civil War. To one of his ancestors, William Seymour, John Ogilby had dedicated his very royalist translation of Virgil in 1649.

[35] See David Burnett, *Longleat: The Story of an English Country House* (Wimborne, Dorset: Dovecote Press, 1988), pp. 76–78, 111, and David Green, *Gardener to Queen Anne* (London: Oxford University Press, 1956), pp. 9–12. Frances Thynne was also the granddaughter of Anne Finch, Countess of Winchelsea, a poet whose poem 'A Tree' (1713) reflected the new affection for woods.

[36] Hughes, *The Gentle Hertford*, p. 132. Probably this was Philip Miller's *The Gardeners Kalendar*, first published in 1732. Hazel Le Rougetel notes that 'under each month could be found directions for work to be done in the kitchen garden with notes on its produce, the pleasure or flower garden with plants then in flower, and the greenhouse and stove with their plants in bloom.' *The Chelsea Gardener: Philip Miller 1691–1771* (London: Natural History Museum Publications, 1990), p. 103.

[37] G. E. L. Cotton, *The Antiquities of Marlborough College* (Marlborough, Wilts., 1855), pp. 17–19.

[38] Switzer, *Ichnographia*, p. 308. The garden referred to is more likely Spy Park.

[39] Ibid., p. 300. See also William A Brogden, 'The *Ferme Ornée* and Changing Attitudes to Agricultural Improvement' in *British and American Gardens in the 18th Century*, ed. R. P. Maccubin and P. Martin (Charlottesville: University of Virginia Press, 1984), pp. 39–43

[40] Switzer, *Practical Husbandman* (April), (London,

1733), I p. liv.

[41] Quoted in John Harvey, *Early Nurserymen* (Chichester: Phillimore, 1974), p. 180.

[42] Peter Martin, *Pursuing Innocent Pleasures: The Gardening World of Alexander Pope* (Hamden, Conn.: Archon Books, 1984), pp. 187–88, 180.

[43] Switzer, *Practical Husbandman*, p. 22.

[44] Ibid., II.ii, pp. 68–69.

[45] Switzer, *Ichnographia*, I pp. 328, 343, 335, 273.

[46] Ibid., I p. 337.

[47] Orrery Papers, Houghton Library, Harvard University, MS. Eng. 218.2, vol. 1, fo. 22.

[48] Countess of Cork and Orrery [E. C. Boyle], *The Orrery Papers* (London: Duckworth, 1903), I pp. 66, 48.

[49] Ibid., I p. 113.

[50] Ibid., I p. 121.

[51] A letter to Dr. William King of 27 August 1739 says jokingly that '*Switzer* talk'd of planting Thistles and Crab-Trees' when King departed from Marston. Harvard, Houghton MS. 218.2 (3), p. 58. Lady Orrery writes from Ireland to Boyle at Marston, imagining him walking through 'the new Beautys of Marston' with 'the great Switzer.' Letter of 8 April 1741. Harvard, Houghton MS. 218.26.

[52] Letter of 15 November 1742. Harvard, Houghton MS. 218.2 (3), pp. 324–25. Switzer's 'Proemial Essay' (p. 12) to the 1742 edition of *Ichnographia*, however, rebukes 'the misplacing of Buildings, Statues, and other Ornaments, with which some of the best of our modern Designs have been crouded.'

[53] Houghton Library, MS. Eng. 218.26. Letter of 16 January 1744.

[54] Perhaps this is an ironic comment on his bills. Lady Hamilton refers to them as 'very large' in a letter of 9 February 1744. MS. 218.26.

[55] See Michael McGarvie, *The Book of Marston Bigot* (Buckingham: Barracuda Books, in association with Yeoman Foster Ltd., Frome, 1987). I am very much indebted to Mr. McGarvie for his elucidation of the Boyle correspondence and of the gardens at Marston and Caledon.

[56] Letter of 12 January 1744. MS. 218.26.

[57] Boyle nonetheless quarrelled with Dr. Johnson's definition of the laurel as 'barren'. Letter to Thomas Birch, 30 December 1747. BL Sloane MS. 4303, fo. 133.

[58] Letter of 18 February 1744. MS. 218.26.

[59] Richard Pococke, 'The Travels through England 1750, 1751 and later years,' BL Add. MS. 22999, fo. 62v–63. Boyle wrote to his friend, Dr. Barry, in 1752 about purchasing a farm adjacent to Marston that had once been a park: 'many of the trees stand and are very beautiful. Time may repark it.' Harvard, Houghton MS. 218.2 (7), p. 51.

[60] *The Letters of Pliny the Younger*, ed. John Boyle (London, Paul Vaillant, 1751), I, vi, p. 159.

[61] *Letters of Pliny*, pp. 171, 173.

[62] Lady Orrery refers to repairing flood damage there in a letter of 31 May 1746. *The Orrery Papers* (London: Duckworth, 1903), II p. 220.

[63] *Orrery Papers*, I p. 307. There was also a statue of Minerva near the river (Blackwater).

[64] Switzer, *Ichnographia*, III p. 107.

[65] Letter to King, 30 November 1746. Harvard, Houghton MS. 218.2 (5), p. 9.

[66] Letter of 29 February 1747. BL Sloane MS. 4303, fo. 120. Boyle's copy of the second edition of Spence's *Essay on Mr. Pope's Odyssey* (London, 1737) is now at Trinity College, Cambridge.

[67] Letter to Southerne, 23 December 1737, Houghton MS. 218.2 (7), 57.

[68] *The Autobiography and Correspondence of Mary Granville Mrs. Delany*, first series, (London, 1861), II pp. 492–93. Michael McGarvie also records the use of the hermitage for the birthday of Boyle's daughter in 1750 when 'the Trees and Hedge-Rows were beautifully illuminated.' 'John, Earl of Orrery, and the Caledon Demesne, Past and Present' in *Home is House and Garden*, ed. M. McGarvie (London: Ancient Monuments Society; Oxford: Garden History Society, 1984), p. 32.

[69] Letter to Lady Spelman, 16 May 1747. Harvard, Houghton MS. 218.2 (5), p. 39.

[70] Ibid., p. 204.

[71] BL Sloane MS. 4303, fo. 146.

[72] The gardener to the first Earl of Orrery's nephew, the Third Duke of Cork, also consulted John Worlidge about the gardens at Lismore, and a copy of the 1698 edition of Worlidge's *Systema Agriculturae* was in the library at Marston. T. C. Barnard, 'Gardening, diet and "improvement" in later 17th-century Ireland,' *Journal of Garden History* 10 (1990), pp. 78–79.

[73] Switzer (*Ichnographia*, III p. vi) echoes Addison in his belief that 'an even decent Walk carry'd thro' a Corn Field or Pasture, thro' little natural Thickets and Hedge Rows, is as pleasing, as the most finish'd Partarre [sic] that some Moderns have been so fond of.' It seems, though, that he was thinking of the Duke of Shrewsbury's estate at Heythrop 'with its winding walk, cold bath and miniature cascade' which he had seen while he was working at Blenheim in 1710. See Mavis Batey, 'Landscape Gardens in Oxfordshire' in *Of Oxfordshire Gardens*, ed. Stephen Butler, Sarah Ross, Alison Smith (Oxford: Oxford Polytechnic Press, 1982), p. 55.

[74] Houghton MS. 218.2.

CHAPTER 6. EVERGREENS AND AMERICAN PLANTS

[1] J. C. Loudon, *Arboretum et Frutecetum Britannicum; or, The Trees and Shrubs of Britain* (London, 1838), I pp. 80–81.

[2] Richard Bradley, *A General Treatise of Husbandry and Gardening*, August–September, 1722 (London, 1724), pp. 161, 159.

[3] Loudon, *Arboretum*, I p. 54.

[4] Ibid., I p. 70.

[5] Ibid., I p. 71. In fact, most of these were not recent introductions by the 1740s. In the 'Catalogue... drawn up of fine Exotick *Plants*' that Richard Bradley gives in his translation of G. A. Agricola's *Philosophical Treatise of Husbandry* (1721) most of the specimens listed are shrubs and hot-house varieties and virtually all

are seventeenth-century introductions. See p. 246.

6 Letter of 9 April 1726, Linnean Society, Collinson MSS., Small Book, fo. 138. Collinson records the Tulip Tree among 'the First Seeds I had given Mee' in a list of 'Seeds from America' [Maryland], 1723. Small Book fo. 32.

7 Ibid., Silver cedars, deciduous cypresses, and Lombardy poplars were probably later plantings. See also David Jacques, *Georgian Gardens: The Reign of Nature* (Portland, OR: Timber Press, 1984), p. 64.

8 Sir John Parnell, 'An Account of the many fine seats of nobles I have seen, with other observations, made during my residence in England in 1763' in James Sambrook, 'Painshill Park in the 1760's,' *Garden History*, VIII (1980), p. 95.

9 The Weymouth pine had, in fact, been discovered nearly a century earlier in Maine by a merchant called George Weymouth; see fig. 54. In introducing large plantations of it at Longleat at the beginning of the 18th century, Thomas Thynne, second Viscount Weymouth, 'ennobled' the tree. The 1768 edition of Miller's *Gardeners Dictionary* also notes the early use of the tree in groves by Sir Wyndham Knatchbull in Kent. Miller credits that plantation as the source of most trees raised in England, specifically those of the Duke of Argyll.

10 Richard Darlington, *Memorials of Peter Collinson* (London, 1849), p. 128. Even half a century later the pine was thought of as having been introduced 'within these forty years' and as having been propagated chiefly from Argyll's nursery at Whitton. *A General Dictionary of Husbandry, Planting, Gardening . . . by the Editors of the Farmer's Magazine* (Bath, 1779).

11 *Select Transactions of the Honourable The Society of Improvers in the Knowledge of Agriculture in Scotland* (Edinburgh, 1743), pp. viii, vi.

12 Horace Walpole, *Anecdotes of Painting in England* (London, 1827), IV pp. 266–67. Argyll probably got his first American specimens in the 1720s from the traveller botanist, Mark Catesby, but by the 1730s he was also participating in the scheme organised by Peter Collinson whereby John Bartram sent boxes of seeds and plants to be distributed among several noblemen who subscribed five guineas a box.

13 See *The Catalogue of the Collection of Trees and Shrubs formed by Lord Islay (later Duke of Argyll) at Whitton, Middlesex* made by Daniel Crofts, the gardener, in 1765 and reproduced with notes in Michael Symes, Alison Hodges, and John Harvey, 'The Plantings at Whitton,' *Garden History* 14 (1986), pp. 149–171.

14 Batty Langley, in *New Principles of Gardening* (1728), p. 149 wrote of Pines as 'most proper to be planted in *large Avenues of boundless Views*, to environ *Canals, Basons, Bowling Greens*, &c.'

15 Clerk of Penicuik Papers, Scottish Record Office, GD 18/21007, 9 April 1727, cited in P. Foster and D. H. Simpson, *Whitton Park and Whitton Place* (Twickenham: Borough of Twickenham Local History Society, 1979) Paper no. 41, p. 4.

16 The following account is in the Spence Papers (Box 9) in the Beinecke Library, Yale University. The date, 1760, seems likely because Spence mentions a Cedar of Lebanon planted '36 Years ago.' It was probably one of the early trees planted and the garden was begun in 1724.

17 'The Travels through England of Dr. Richard Pococke . . . 1750, 1751 and later years,' BL Add. MS. 23001, fo. 34.

18 Walpole, *Anecdotes of Painting in England*, I pp. 266–67.

19 James Lee, *An Introduction to the Science of Botany . . . from the Works of Linnaeus* (4th ed., London, 1810), pp. vi, x, xvi, xiv.

20 See John Dixon Hunt, *Garden and Grove* (Princeton: Princeton University Press, l986), p. 204.

21 Gothic, in other words, was not simply Palladianism made (in Walpole's phrase) 'to speak good English,' but a statement about Whig beliefs in the ancestry of liberty in England.

22 *Catalogus Librorum A.C.D.A.* [Archibald Campbell, Duke of Argyll] (Glasgow, 1758). I have corrected the titles where necessary.

23 *Kalm's Account of his Visit to England on his way to America in 1748*, trans. J. Lucas (London: Macmillan, 1892), p. 31.

24 This is from *The Practical Husbandman and Planter*, a work published in six monthly parts in 1733 and attributed to 'a Society of Husbandmen and Planters.' It was, however, largely edited, compiled, and written by Switzer. See II, part 2 (August), pp. 68–69.

25 Symes, Hodges, and Harvey, 'The Plantings at Whitton,' *Garden History* 14 (l986), p. 148.

26 BL Add. MS. 28726, fo. [34v]–35. In this letter Jersey refers to his 'Conjurer', another joke at Collinson's expense. Sir John Hill had written an article in the *Gentleman's Magazine* on *homunculi*, 'the secret operation of little Beings,' as Jersey calls it, and had attributed the piece to Collinson.

27 Of Switzer he wrote: 'he on't expect five hundred pound for a quarter of an hours thoughts.' Ibid., fo. 35.

28 BL Add. MS. 28727, fo. [42v]–43. A letter from John Hanbury to the Duke of Newcastle suggests that Collinson was an active Whig: 'all his Life long he has been Steady in your interest.' Add. MS. 32885, fo. 244.

29 Letter of H. J. Fox, 22 December 1754, Add. MS. 28727, fo. 32; letter to Duke of Newcastle, 25 February 1754/55, Add. MS. 33029, fo. 381.

30 Henrietta Pye, *A Short Account of the Principal Seats and Gardens in and about Twickenham* (London, 1760), p. 36.

31 Dr. John Fothergill, *Some Anecdotes of the Late Peter Collinson* (London, 1785), p. 13. The Pope quotation is from his 'Epilogue to the Satires. Dialogue II,' l. 67.

32 16 February 1747/48. Add. MS. 28727, fo. 5.

33 The Travels through England of Dr. Richard Pococke . . . 1750, 1751 and later years, Add. MS. 23001, fo. 36–37. In his 'Epistle to Burlington,' (1731) Pope asked that the new garden improvers restore 'Jones and Palladio to themselves,' but he also deplored those who 'turn Arcs of triumph to a Garden-gate.' Jones's gate is visible in a detail of a portrait of Anne of Denmark by Van Somer, reproduced in Roy Strong's *The Renaissance Garden in England* (London: Thames and Hudson, 1979), pl. 110.

34 Letter to Lord Lincoln, 20 June 1761, Linnean Soc., Collinson MSS. Small Book, fo. 178.

35 See John Dixon Hunt and Peter Willis, eds., *The Genius of the Place* (Cambridge, Mass.: M.I.T. Press, 1988), pp. 272–73.

36 Collinson letters of 16 May 1734 to Bedford and 24 January 1735 to John Bartram in *Forget Not Mee and My Garden: The Selected Letters of Peter Collinson, F.R.S. 1694–1768*, as yet an unpublished typescript ed. by Alan W. Armstrong, Jean O'Neill, and Elizabeth McLean, pp. 13 and 30. Collinson seems also to have suggested that Lord Bute join this scheme in 1745; See letter from Lord Bute of 7 March 1744/45, Add. MS. 28726, fo. [154v].

37 Letters of 16 May 1734 and 2 April 1759, Linnean Society, Collinson MSS., Small Book, fo. 112, 30.

38 Letter to Collinson, 17 December 1742, Add. MS. 28726, fo. [124v].

39 Letter of 28 December 1742, Add. MS. 28726, fo. 128.

40 Colen Campbell, *Vitruvius Britannicus* (London, 1725) III pl. 51–52. Letters in the Goodwood collection at the West Sussex Record Office show Richmond acquiring this land in the 1720s and 1730s.

41 Rudolf Wittkower, *Palladio and English Palladianism* (New York: Thames & Hudson, 1974), p. 178.

42 Campbell, *Vitruvius Britannicus*, III pl. 51–52.

43 Christopher Hussey believes that Burlington must have designed it, perhaps assisted by Kent and Giacomo Leoni, the architect also employed by Lord Petre. 'Goodwood House, Sussex II,' *Country Life* (16 July 1932), p. 69. Howard E. Stutchbury in *The Architecture of Colen Campbell* (Manchester: Manchester University Press, 1967), p. 62 says that the temple is 'probably' by Morris.

44 Collinson, like many eighteenth-century men of letters, continued to be interested in zoological curiosities. In some cases he was duped by freaks, but his interest in the migration of swallows was a legitimate scientific question. The great naturalist, Gilbert White (1720–93), remained puzzled by this question until the end of his life. Richmond remained interested in a wide range of natural history. Among the several accounts of natural curiosities he sent to Sir Hans Sloane is a piece on the earthquake of October 1734. BL Sloane MS. 4053, fo. 301, and Sloane MS. 4025, fo. 233–34.

45 J. Milles, 'Travels in England 1735–43,' Add. MS. 15776, fo. 245–46. It is not clear how trustworthy Milles's observations are. Although he writes of the Duke's having given up his menagerie, for example, a letter in the Goodwood papers (West Sussex Record Office, Goodwood 112) of 31 August 1742 discusses getting a possum from the Barbadoes.

46 West Sussex Record Office, Goodwood MS. 102, fo. 116.

47 Goodwood MS. 104, fo. 346 and MS. 110,

fo. 160.

48 Goodwood MS. 112, fo. 297. Although introduced about 1730, most of these specimens were killed off in the severe frosts of 1737/40. This may account for their being so expensive, as Richmond complains below. Richmond's specimen may have been one raised after that time. *Magnolia grandiflora* is said to have been introduced into England by the nurseryman, Christopher Gray, before 1719. His catalogue of 1737 refers to one growing at Sir Charles Wager's house in Parson's Green. See E. J. Willson, *West London Nursery Gardens* (London: Fulham and Hammersmith Historical Society, 1982), p. 19.

49 Goodwood MS. 208, fo. 799.

50 A note by Collinson in Miller's *Dictionary* records that the third Duke planted 1000 Cedars of Lebanon in 1761. See William Hagley Mason, *Goodwood, its House Park and Grounds* (London, 1839), p. 161. Among his memoranda Collinson also notes: 'In Spring 1742 Went with the Duke of Bedford to See Lord Petres Nurserys at Thorndon near Brent Wood in order to Purchase Plants after Lord Petre's Decease.' Linnean Society, Collinson MSS., Small Book, fo. 202.

51 Goodwood MS. 108, fo. 794.

52 See Mark Laird, 'Approaches to planting in the late eighteenth century: some imperfect ideas on the origins of the American Garden,' *Journal of Garden History* 11 (1991), p. 171, n. 31.

53 BL Add. MS. 28726, fo. 108.

54 Add. MS. 28726, fo. [122v–123v].

55 Add. MS. 28726, fo. [122v]–123. Richmond first refers to getting these acorns in a letter of 12 December (fo. 121). It may be that 'Nottingham' means 'Worksop.' There are detailed instructions in several of his letters about how trees are to be sent with the carrier, Bennett, from Southwark: at what times they are to be despatched and how packed.

56 Letter of 28 December 1742. Add. MS. 28726, fo. [127v].

57 William Hayley Mason, *Goodwood*, p. 164.

58 Letter of 17 December 1742, Add. MS. 28726, fo. 124.

59 Lindsay Fleming, 'England's Trees II—Deciduous Trees at Goodwood,' *Country Life* (9 April 1927), p. 576.

60 Ibid., p. 576. Evelyn refers to its commonness in Madrid in his manuscript notes for *Sylva*. Evelyn MSS., Christ Church Oxford, MS. 38, fo. 152–53.

61 Letters of 28 December 1742 and 16 February 1743, Add. MS. 28726, fo. 128, 131.

62 Letter of 27 June 1746, Add. MS. 28726, fo. 157.

63 Letter of 12 February 1747/48, Add. MS. 28727, fo. [4v].

64 Letter of 11 November 1747, Add. MS. 28727, fo. 14. On the letter Collinson writes, apparently in identifying *piorno*, 'the Silesia Pine from Pisa or Maritime Pine in Italy [*Pinus maritima calabrica* or *Pinus larico*] says Mr. Miller.'

65 Goodwood MS. 110, fo. 13.

66 Charles Lennox, eighth Duke of Richmond, *A Duke and His Friends* (London, 1911), p. 717.

67 Ibid., p. 442. Of the common euonymus (*Euonymus vulgaris*), Philip Miller wrote that it 'is seldom kept in Gardens, altho' it deserves a Place amongst Quarters of Trees.' Society of Gardeners, *Catalogus Plantarum*, p. 30.

68 See the detailed account of 7 October 1735 for planting 'The Flowers for the border under the South-East Wall.' West Sussex Record Office, Goodwood MS. 134.

69 Linnean Society, Collinson MSS. Small Book, fo. 52, 53. The third Duke also advised other gardeners. He writes of helping the Earl of Traquair to make 'the most complete Garden in the Kingdom (I'll except only the standard Thorndon).' Linnean Society, Collinson MSS. Small Book, fo. 91.

CHAPTER 7. PAINTING WITH LIVING PENCILS

1 *Twickenham 1600–1900 People and Places* (Twickenham: Borough of Twickenham Local History Society, 1981), Paper no. 47, p. 51. David Jacques gives a brief account of the group of planters and improvers associated with Peter Collinson in *Georgian Gardens: The Reign of Nature* (Portland, OR: Timber Press, 1984), pp. 65–66. As is apparent below, I disagree with his conclusion (on pp. 41–42) that Lord Petre's park layouts were 'passed by' by the work of Kent.

2 Given preliminary drawings and rough sketches accompanying Bourgignon's plans, it seems likely that Bourgignon's function was as a draughtsman to make working drawings. Peter Collinson makes clear that Petre was more than competent as a designer. See note 33 below and the appendix. Although these plans were never carried out completely, because of Lord Petre's premature death, there is considerable evidence that much of the tree-planting envisaged in them was completed. See Sir George Clutton and Colin Mackay, *Old Thorndon Hall, Essex: a History and Reconstruction of its Park and Garden*, Garden History Society, Occasional Paper no. 2 (1970), pp. 30–31.

3 It has also been suggested that Petre was involved in designing two other lost gardens: Buckenham House, Norfolk, and Jonathan Tyers's melancholy garden of reflection in Surrey called Denbies. The latter included a monument of Lord Petre in stucco by Roubiliac. See N. B. Penny, 'Macabre garden at Denbies and its monument,' *Garden History* 3 (1975), pp. 58–61. In 'Jonathan Tyers's Other Garden,' Brian Allen asserts there is no evidence to confirm that Petre had anything to do with either Denbies or Vauxhall; *Journal of Garden History* 1 (1981), p. 224. Nor is it likely that Petre had anything to do with the plan of South Weald in Essex for which Bourgignon did the finished design.

4 David Jacques also notes the early use of clumps at Blenheim (1709) and at Castle Howard (by 1727). See *Georgian Gardens*, p. 42.

5 Stephen Switzer, *The Practical Husbandman and Planter*, I part 3 (June), p. 22. Cf. Batty Langley's earlier recommendation that 'Ashes planted with Oaks, Chesnuts, etc. in Plumps, on the tops of little Hills in Parks, etc. have a very good Effect.' in *A Sure Method of Improving Estates* (1728), p. 85.

6 The catalogue of Petre's library is in the Essex County Record Office, D/DP Z4.

7 Batty Langley, *New Principles of Gardening* (London, 1728), pp. 181–83, 186.

8 Richard Bradley, *A Survey of the Ancient Husbandry and Gardening* (London, 1725), p. 359.

9 Joseph Spence, *Observations, Anecdotes, and Characters of Books and Men*, ed. James M. Osborn (Oxford: Clarendon Press, 1966), I:603, p. 250.

10 Christopher Hussey, *English Gardens 1700–1750* (London: Country Life, 1967), p. 80. The planting plan of part of the area south east of the house at Worksop is in the Essex Record Office, D/DP P. 150. It shows plainly the difference between Petre's large hand (the hand entirely used in D/DP P. 150[A]) and Bourgignon's careful finished hand. In 'Approaches to Planting in the late Eighteenth Century: Some Imperfect ideas on the Origins of the American Garden,' Mark Laird refers to the forecourt at Worksop as 'like the tiers of an ampitheatre.' He also notes that, later in James Meader's *The Planter's Guide* (London, 1779), the 'diagrams of plantations in six to seven graduated rows illustrate how the exotics which had been successfully introduced from eastern North America by John Bartram and Peter Collinson were incorporated into the stepped structure of the shrubbery by 1778.' *Journal of Garden History* 11 (1991), p. 155. This subject will receive further treatment in his forthcoming article, 'Ornamental Planting and Horticulture in English Pleasure Gardens 1700–1830' in *Landscape and Garden History: Issues—Approaches—Methods*, to be published by Dumbarton Oaks.

11 Mark Laird, *An Approach to the Conservation of Ornamental Planting in English Gardens 1730–1830* (University of York: M. A. Thesis in Conservation Studies, 1984), p. 50. Laird believes that planting of this density would have required subsequent thinning, a belief apparently confirmed by the plate in Russell and Price's *England Displayed* (1769). Petre's practice elsewhere at Worksop accords better with Philip Miller's recommendation that laurel 'is very proper to place in Clumps of Ever-greens, where it may be suffer'd to grow rude.' Miller, however, did not approve of using Swedish juniper; Society of Gardeners, *Catalogus Plantarum* (London, 1730), p. 44. I am extremely grateful to Mark Laird for his help with this part of the book.

12 Thomas Cooke, *Original Poems with Imitations* (London, 1742), p. 72. Cooke, who was abused by Pope in *The Dunciad*, also did an edition of Hesiod dedicated to Lord Petre, and mentions Petre's support of his edition of Virgil in a letter to Collinson of 28 November 1744. Linnean Society, Collinson MSS., Small Book, p. 2.

13 Laird, *An Approach*, p. 50. Even in its neces-

sarily restricted repertoire, Petre's list here is more interesting than those proposed a decade earlier by Bradley or Langley.

[14] Gray was a friend of both Philip Miller and Peter Collinson. Part of his extensive collection of plants came from Bishop Henry Compton's garden at Fulham after the latter's death in 1713. See E. J. Willson, *West London Nursery Gardens* (London: Fulham and Hammersmith Historical Society, 1982), chapter III.

[15] Cited as by Southcote in 1752 in Joseph Spence, *Anecdotes* I.1124, p. 424. Wooburn Farm was left to Petre's son by Southcote's widow. Osborn notes that Spence also studied colour effects: 'among his gardening papers is a list entitled "Shades of Green; deeper and deeper," ranging from weeping willow to sycamore.'

[16] Linnean Society, Collinson MSS. Large Book, p. 29.

[17] Petre's connection with Gisburn is unclear. The plan is signed 'P. Bourguignon' but its invention is probably, as at Thorndon and Worksop, Petre's work. Gisburn was owned by the Listers, a family to whom he was related. Jane Lister became the second wife of Petre's guardian, Sir Edward Southcote.

[18] Essex Record Office, D/DP P. 150.

[19] Linnean Society, Collinson MSS., Small Book, p. 202.

[20] 'The Travel Journal of Philip Yorke, 1744–63,' *Publication of the Bedfordshire Historical Record Society* 47 (1968), p. 128.

[21] BL Add. MS. 15800, fo. 22.

[22] Sarah Markham, *John Loveday of Caversham 1711–1789* (Salisbury: Michael Russell, 1984), p. 212.

[23] Written in Collinson's copy of Miller's *Gardeners Dictionary*, cited by Aylmer Bourke Lambert, *Transactions of the Linnean Society* 10 (1811), p. 275.

[24] Note on the last blank page of his copy of John Evelyn's *Sylva* (London, 1664), now in the Royal Forestry Society, Tring, Herts. Collinson, who seems to have been mistaken about the dates of introduction of a number of trees, believed that the cedar of Lebanon was a greater rarity at the time than in fact it was. It was not, however, used extensively until later in the century at Goodwood and by Capability Brown.

[25] London, *Arboretum*, I p. 55. Clutton and Mackay believe that Lord Petre's inspiration for tree-moving came from seeing Le Nôtre's practice at Versailles and the Bois de Boulogne. *Old Thorndon Hall*, p. 35. This copy of Miller's *Dictionary* is now in Aberystwyth.

[26] In fact the practice of moving mature trees occurs even earlier in the century. In 1722 Richard Bradley records the 'removal' of 'Lime-Hedges about Ten Foot high,' 'large Pear-Trees and Apple-Trees' and some 'Scotch Firr-Trees . . . near Thirty Foot high' in the garden of James Johnston (Secretary Johnston) in Twickenham. *The Monthly Register of Experiments and Observations in Husbandry and Gardening. For the Months of April and May, 1722* (London, 1724), p. 65. In *The Practical Husbandman and Planter* (1733 II part 2, p. 121) Stephen Switzer also affirms that

it is practicable to move mature trees of 10, 15 or even 20 years of age. And he notes that Pope's 'Man of Ross' (John Kyrle) also transplanted mature trees.

[27] Letter to Philip Southcote, 9 December 1752. Linnean Society, Collinson MSS. Large Book, p. 31.

[28] London, *Arboretum*, p. 84. The contemporary American poet, Brendan Galvin, celebrates a Bartram-like figure in the person of one 'Loranzo Newcomb' in his long poem *Wapanoag Traveler* (Baton Rouge: Louisiana State University Press, 1989), p. 28. In the ninth section, Newcomb, writing to a patron like Collinson says: 'but you must lift your / end of our burden by procuring me friends / who'll support my narrow searches.' Lord Petre and the Duke of Richmond were just such 'friends'.

[29] Switzer, *Practical Husbandman*, I part 1 (April), p. liv. Switzer had obviously advanced beyond the restricted repertoire of familiar domestic trees recommended fifteen years earlier in *Ichnographia Rustica*.

[30] Society of Gardeners, *Catalogus Plantarum* (London, 1730) sig. [cv].

[31] This and the following two quotations are from William Darlington, *Memorials of John Bartram and Humphry Marshall with Notices of their Botanical Contemporaries* (Philadelphia, 1849), p. 145. That Collinson appreciated all aspects of landscape design is evident in his concern with everything from the creation and draining of basins at Thorndon and Wanstead to the romantic landscape of fountains, trees, and cascades at 'Lonesome', the garden of his friend Jacobson at Leith Hill near Dorking. Linnean Society, Collinson MSS. Small Book, fo. 49, 216.

[32] Linnean Society, Collinson MSS. Large Note Book, p. 29.

[33] Ibid., p. 30.

[34] Pineapples had been grown much earlier, however. Another nurseryman gardener, Henry Telende, was cultivating pineapples at Sir Matthew Decker's in Richmond in 1719, and Peter Collinson records a John Warner of Rotherhithe who grew them before 1720. See Blanche Henrey, *No Ordinary Gardener, Thomas Knowlton* (London: British Museum (Natural History), 1986), p. 44. Henrey also notes that 'by 1730 pineapple stoves were to be found in almost every curious garden' in *British Botanical and Horticultural Literature* (London: Oxford University Press, 1975), II p. 478. See also Sandra Raphael's discussion of the domestication of the pineapple in *An Oak Spring Pomona* (Upperville, Va: Oak Spring Garden Library, 1990), pp. xxxii–xxxiii.

[35] The manuscript is now in the Sutro Library in San Francisco: f 580 P493h Sutro 16v. See Elizabeth P. McLean, 'An Eighteenth Century Herbarium at the Sutro Library,' *California State Library Foundation Bulletin* 6 (Jan. 1984), pp. 5–9.

[36] The chaos in taxonomy in the period makes it impossible to determine whether, as is the case in earlier editions of Miller's *Dictionary*, a number of identical species are being given different

names.

[37] Petre, *Hortus Siccus*, vol. XII, p. 7.

[38] This tree is also recorded in Collinson's garden and at Polehill long before that date.

[39] Petre, *Hortus Siccus*, vol. VIII, p. 10. This is probably *Haematoxylon campechianum*, introduced from the Caribbean in 1724.

[40] Darlington, *Memorials*, p. 157.

[41] Letter to Linnaeus in *A Selection of Correspondence of Linnaeus*, ed. Sir J. E. Smith, (London, 1821), I p. 9.

[42] Darlington, *Memorials*, p. 158.

[43] Letter to Linnaeus, 18 January 1744 in *A Selection of Correspondence of Linnaeus*, I p. 11.

[44] This is from a 'character' of Petre by Collinson written in a 'Catalogue of the Plants' at Thorndon Hall done by Philip Miller. See C. T. Kuypers, *Thorndon: Its History and Associations* (Brentwood Diocesan Magazine, 1930), p. 32.

[45] West Sussex Record Office, Goodwood MS. 112, fo. 297.

[46] Evelyn, *Sylva* (London, 1664). The note listing the trees is on a separate loose sheet of paper after the last page. It also includes on the reverse a list of trees that have died, among them such trees as beech, Spanish chestnut, and Virginian haw (*Viburnum prunifolium*). See also Clutton and Mackay, *Old Thorndon Hall*, p. 35. See also above n. 24.

[47] Evelyn, *Sylva*, p. 57. Although the larch was introduced into England in the early seventeenth century, new species were introduced in the eighteenth. Unknown to Collinson, it seems that the Duke of Atholl began cultivating the larch extensively in 1728. See L. J. F. Brimble, *Trees in Britain* (London: Macmillan, 1948), p. 82. The American larch (*Larix laricina*) quickly hybridized with the European larch to create *Larix pendula*.

[48] Batty Langley, *New Principles of Gardening* (London, 1728), p. 196. John Loveday of Caversham gives an interesting contemporary account of the making of a mount at Wentworth Woodhouse in 1735. In the gardens, he writes, 'are many fir-trees and a Mount of above 100 foot high perpendicular; but then great sums must be laid out to make this Mount anything Ornamental; at present 'tis a great dirty Hill, irregular and misshapen.' Sarah Markham, *John Loveday of Caversham 1711–1789* (Wilton: Michael Russell, 1984), p. 196.

[49] Richard Bradley, *A Survey of the Ancient Husbandry and Gardening* (London, 1725), p. 359.

CHAPTER 8. THE PRACTICAL PART OF GARDENING

[1] *Catalogus plantarum . . . A Catalogue of Trees, Shrubs, Plants and Flowers . . . By a Society of Gardeners* (London, 1730). Richard Bradley gives an account of an 'Academy for the Improvement of Gardening in Scotland' as well as of the founding of the English 'Company of Gardeners' in the reign of James I in his *A General Treatise of Husbandry and Gardening, For the Month of June*

(London, [1724]), I pp. 136–37.

2 James Lees-Milne, *Earls of Creation* (London: Hamish Hamilton, 1962), chapter 1, pp. 3–38.

3 *Catalogus plantarum*, sig. [b3].

4 Ibid., sig. [av].

5 Ibid., sig. [b3v].

6 Ibid., sig. [b3v].

7 Ibid., sig. [b3v]. Cf. Richard Bradley's objection to the 'strange Jargon sometimes in the Gardening Dialect' in *A Dictionary of Plants; Their Description and Use, with Their Culture and Management* (London, 1747), 'Introduction,' I sig. A3. Bradley's *Philosophical Account of the Works of Nature* (London, 1741), dedicated to John Boyle, takes its origin from Addison's appeal (in the *Spectator* no. 121) for what Bradley calls a 'useful Plan for Natural History' (sig. [b4]). Linnaeus's system was not, however, accepted without demur. The Earl of Bute wrote to Collinson that 'we shall have more *confusion with order* than we had formerly with *disorder*.' See *A Selection of the Correspondence of Linnaeus and Other Naturalists*, ed. Sir J. E. Smith (London, 1821), I p. 35.

8 *Catalogus Plantarum*, sig. [b3v]. The *Catalogus* had to content itself with using '*the most generally received Latin Name of each* Tree *and Shrub, by which it is called amongst the Modern Botanists*' (sig. c). Miller himself first adopted the Linnaean system in the tenth edition of *The Gardeners Kalendar* (1754), two years before adopting it in the seventh edition of the *Dictionary*.

9 *Catalogus*, sig. [bv].

10 See *The Sloane Herbarium*, rev. and ed. J. E. Dandy (London: British Museum (Natural History), 1958), pp. 211–15.

11 A. B. Lambert, 'Notes relating to botany, collected from the manuscripts of the late Peter Collinson,' *Transactions of the Linnean Society London* 10 (1811), p. 272.

12 Switzer, *Ichnographia Rustica* (London, 1718), I p. 70.

13 G. A. Agricola, *A Philosophical Treatise of Husbandry and Gardening . . . The whole Revised . . . by Richard Bradley* (London, 1721), p. 198. This work was also in the library of the Boyles at Marston. See *Catalogue of the Valuable and Extensive Library . . . of the Right. Hon. The Earl of Cork and Orrery*, sold at Christie's 21 November 1905.

14 Bradley, *Philosophical Treatise*, p. 246. This was not to become really noticeable until the 1730s with Lord Petre's estate at Thorndon Hall.

15 Ibid., sigs. [av] and a2.

16 Bradley, *A General Treatise* I p. 123. Among the proposals to cultivate gardening 'in a Philosophical Way', Bradley recommends both that a gardener 'should be instructed in the *Latin Tongue, Writing, Arithmetick, Mathematicks and Designing*,' and that 'he should, in the unbusy'd Times of his Practice, acquaint himself with the Rules and Terms of Botany' (ibid., p. 168). One of Bradley's correspondents, however, 'shun'd using any hard Words, because I think, in such a Business, the plainer a Man is, the better; and it is rather to Gardeners than Philosophers, that the drudging Parts of Planting belong.' See *A General Treatise* I p. 191.

17 Bradley, *Philosophical Treatise*, p. 261.

18 Bradley, *Dictionary of Plants* (London, 1747), I sig. [A2v].

19 Ibid., I sig. T.

20 Switzer, *The Practical Husbandman and Planter: or, Observations on the Ancient and Modern Husbandry, Planting, Gardening. . . By a private Society of Husbandmen and Planters* (London, 1733–34), I, part 3 (June), p. 45.

21 Bradley, *Dictionary*, I sig. [B5v]. The sycamore commonly used in Britain was *Acer pseudoplatanus*.

22 Bradley, *A General Treatise of Husbandry and Gardening . . . For the Months of August and September . . .* (London, 1724), III [part 3], p. 38. Morgam (or Margam) is in South Wales and is probably where Collinson saw the tree so used. Lord Mansell was one of the subscribers to John James's *The Theory and Practice of Gardening* (London, 1712).

23 See Blanche Henrey, *British Botanical and Horticultural Literature before 1800* (London: Oxford University Press, 1975), II p. 439.

24 Richard Pulteney, *Historical and Biographical Sketches of the Progress of Botany* (London, 1790) II pp. 132–33.

25 Ibid., III p. 129.

26 Published in 1741 and 1749 respectively. Martyn's first publication was a charming translation of a Latin poem on the sexes of plants, in which a retirement to the 'shady woods' such as Pope and Switzer both recommend leads to a comparison of the monoecious pine with the dioecious laurel and juniper. The poem was published in Patrick Blair's *Botanical Essays* (London, 1720), pp. 326–30.

27 G. C. Gorham, *A Memoir of John Martyn and Thomas Martyn* (London, 1830), p. 68. Unlike Pope and Switzer, however, Martyn (according to Gorham) was a supporter of the government (p. 74).

28 It was first advertised for sale by Christopher Gray in his 1755 catalogue. Martyn makes similar connections between Virgil's use of the elm and the ilex and John Evelyn's treatment of them in *Sylva*. It is not clear why Martyn rejected *Cupressus sempervirens* as Virgil's cypress.

29 Martyn himself had praised Miller's *Dictionary* on its first appearance in 1731, particularly Miller's attention to the size of shrubs and trees. Citing Miller's influential entry on wildernesses, Martyn said: 'Were the rules that Mr. Miller has laid down under this article widely pursued, we should reap a much greater satisfaction from this principal ornament of a fine garden.' Hazel Le Rougetel, *The Chelsea Gardener: Philip Miller 1691–1771* (London: Natural History Museum, 1990), p. 90.

30 *The Bucolicks of Virgil* (London, 1749), p. xvi.

31 Even in his translation of the *Pastorals*, Martyn describes the setting as 'a rural scene, a sort of fine Landscape, painted by a masterly hand,' words which suggest his sense of the landscape as a created thing with connections as much to painting as to botany. *The Bucolicks of Virgil* (London, 1749), p. xvi.

32 Pulteney, *Historical Sketches*, II p. 238.

33 David Neave, 'Lord Burlington's park and garden at Londesborough, Yorkshire,' *Garden History* 8 (1980), p. 75.

34 Knowlton may have acquired this tree through his connection with the famous botanist, William Sherard, who had been British Consul at Smyrna (Izmir). If so he would have had to have obtained seeds or seedlings before 1728, the year of Sherard's death. Elsewhere in the park throughout the 1730s he planted ash, elm, Scotch pine, spruce, hornbeam, and Dutch elm. See Neave, p. 75.

35 Chatsworth Correspondence 3/370, cited in Neave, p. 84.

36 'Lanesborough Park, a Poem' in *A Choice Collection of Poetry*, [ed.] Joseph Yarrow (York, 1728), II p. 119.

37 In the *Catalogus Plantarum* Philip Miller argued in favour of the introduction of exotics that many of the plants now commonly accepted as English, including 'Bread-Corn' (wheat) were at one time exotics.

38 Pulteney, *Historical Sketches*, II p. 276.

39 *A Selection of the correspondence of Linnaeus and Other Naturalists*, ed. Sir J. E. Smith (London, 1821), pp. 33, 31.

40 In *A Sure Method of Improving Estates* (London, 1728) Langley criticises Bradley's recommendations for oak-planting on the grounds of insufficient experimentation with different soils. Moreover, he comes close to accusing Bradley of plagiarising Evelyn on the elm. See pp. 3, 49.

41 Ibid., p. 110.

42 Bradley, *A Dictionary of Plants*, sig. [K5v].

43 Langley, *New Principles* (London, 1728), sig. [A2v]. Langley was no admirer of London and Wise and suggests that the 'thick Planting' of these earlier gardens may have been the result of the desire for 'greater Sales of their Plants.'

44 Langley, *A Sure Method*, p. 106.

45 Ibid., pp. 62, 48–49, 56.

46 Ibid., pp. 154, 155. In *New Principles* Langley recognises that the sycamore's tendency to attract flies makes it more suitable for coppices than for wildernesses close to the house (p. 135). Addison seems to have shared the common dislike of sycamores. In 1714 his cousin wrote to him from his estate at Bilton: 'You seem to dislike Sicamore, so non you shall have.' P. H. B. O. Smithers, *The Life of Joseph Addison* (Oxford: Oxford University Press, 1968), p. 309. Philip Miller, however, in the *Catalogus plantarum* claims that this tree 'when planted to make large Hedges in Wilderness-Work, affords a much beautifuller Prospect than when it grows to be a large Standard' (p. 4).

47 See Sir George Clutton and Colin Mackay, *Old Thorndon Hall, Essex: A History and Reconstruction of its Park and Garden*, Garden History Society, Occasional Paper no. 2 (1970), p. 38.

48 Langley, *A Sure Method*, pp. 156, 141, 123, 149. In *New Principles* (p. 131), Langley describes lindens as suitable both for hedges and espaliers because they are 'conformidable to any shape whatsoever.'

49 Langley, *New Principles*, pp. 129, 151, 152.

50 Langley, *A Sure Method*, pp. 159–60. It has been suggested that the 'concave' (a spiral in

a disused gravel pit) that Langley made for the Vernons at Twickenham Park was where Langley used these 'hedges of Hornbeam.' See A. C. B. Urwin, 'The Houses and Gardens of Twickenham Park 1227–1805,' *Borough of Twickenham Local History Society Paper* no. 54 (1984), p. 36.

51 Langley, *New Principles*, p. 152.

52 Bradley, *A General Treatise* (London [1724]), I p. 114. Bradley goes on to give instructions on how to construct a cooling water-cascade in such a house.

53 Langley, *New Principles*, sig. [A2v–A3].

54 Ibid., sig. [A3r–v].

55 See 'Scratch of the Grounds at Twitinham from the Earl of Straffords to Richmond Ferry and also the Grounds of Ham Octob: 1711' by John Erskine, eleventh Earl of Mar in *The History of Orleans House Twickenham* (London: Borough of Richmond upon Thames, 1984), p. 8.

56 Langley, *New Principles*, sig. [b3].

57 Langley, *Pomona* (London, 1729), sig. b.

58 Langley, *New Principles*, sig. [b2v].

59 Ibid., sig. b.

60 Langley, *Pomona*, sig. b.

61 Daniel Defoe, *A Tour Through the Whole Island of Great Britain*, ed. Pat Rogers (Harmondsworth: Penguin, 1971), p. 347.

62 Bradley, Dedication to *A General Treatise of Husbandry and Gardening* (London, 1722), I part 2, sig. [A2v]. Johnston's method was to plant the trees in a thick mud.

63 Langley, *New Principles*, sig. b.

64 Bradley, *A General Treatise* I p. 224. Bradley's correspondent is here echoing Addison's famous call for garden reform in *Spectator*, no. 414 (25 June 1712).

65 *Spectator* no. 37 (12 April 1711).

66 Langley, *New Principles*, sig. [bv]–b2.

67 Ibid., sig. b. Miller similarly recommends mixing almonds with '*Virginian Cherry Plumb* [presumably *Prunus serotina*] in Walks or Quarters.' *Catalogus*, p. 7.

68 Christ Church, Oxford, Evelyn MS. 45, p. 66.

69 Langley, *New Principles*, p. 196. Miller also recommends mixing 'several sorts of Roses ... with flowering Shrubs in small Wilderness Quarters.' *Catalogus*, p. 67.

70 Ibid., p. 152.

71 Ibid., p. 202.

72 Ibid., p. 155.

73 Ibid., pp. 202, 151, 163, 138.

74 Ibid., p. 168. Parsons Green was next to the famous and influential garden that Bishop Compton had created at Fulham. Peter Aram began his career there.

75 Ibid., pp. 131, 125, 149.

CHAPTER 9. GARDENERS

1 *The second volume of The Gardeners Dictionary* 2nd ed. (London, 1739). There is a marked difference between this list and the subscription list for John James's *The Theory and Practice of Gardening* (London, 1712) where all of the subscribers are at least 'Esq.' and most, like the Duke of Beaufort, Lord Bathurst, the Earl of Carlisle, the Earl of Pembroke, and the Earl of Jersey, were ennobled creators of gardens or about to be so.

2 Samuel Gilbert, *The Florists Vade-Mecum* (London, 1682), 'The Epistle,' sig. [A10v].

3 Penelope Hobhouse, 'The gardens of Newby Hall, North Yorkshire,' *Antiques*, 137 (June, 1990), p. 1385.

4 George Clarke, 'William Kent: Heresy in Stowe's Elysium,' in *Furor Hortensis*, ed. P. Willis (Edinburgh: Elysium Press, 1974), p. 51. In what follows I am much indebted to George Clarke's information.

5 George Clarke, unpublished paper delivered at the American Society for Eighteenth-Century Studies conference in Toronto in 1986.

6 John Ezard, 'The long climb back to glory,' *Weekend Guardian* (New Year 1989 [31 December 1988]), p. 4.

7 Like Lord Petre's early gardener, James Hunt, Hoyland was also a subscriber to Miller's 1731 *Gardeners Dictionary*.

8 See Gladys Scott Thomson, *Life in a Noble Household 1641–1700* (London: Jonathan Cape, 1937), pp. 239–61.

9 One of his successors at Cannons was Thomas Knowlton, who worked there in 1725 before going to Londesborough to work for Lord Burlington.

10 Bradley, *Survey of the Ancient Husbandry* (London, 1725) p. 360. Whitmill was himself a member of the London Society of Gardeners. See Henrey, *British Botanical and Horticultural Literature* (London: Oxford University Press, 1975), II pp. 340–41.

11 See Richard Pulteney, *Historical and biographical sketches of the progress of botany in England* (London, 1790), p. 188, and Henrey, *Botanical and Horticultural Literature* II p. 431, and Thomas Knowlton, pp. 91–96. Brewer's *Diary* was published in 1931. A manuscript note in the British Library copy of Pulteney cites information from Richardson's daughter Dorothy, that indicates that Brewer became head gardener for the Duke of Beaufort.

12 See Blanche Henrey, *Thomas Knowlton* (London: British Museum (Natural History), 1986), p. 232. On 4 September 1760 Henry Scott gave notice in the *Daily Advertiser* that he was 'leaving off his Business this Autumn' and intended 'to dispose of a large Quantity of Nursery Plants, viz. Forest Trees, Fruit Trees, Flowering Shrubs, and Evergreens; Cedars, several sorts, and curious shrubs' (p. 36). In *Observations, Anecdotes and Characters of Books and Men*, ed. J. M. Osborn (Oxford: Clarendon Press, 1966), Pope's friend Joseph Spence writes of Kent's work at Chiswick: 'Mr Scott has a drawing of the first thing done that way *there*' (I.1060, p. 405).

13 Langley was very critical of the common practice of turning out the gardeners who had created gardens and replacing them with cheaper labour, especially those 'Pretenders we have [in] great Numbers annually imported from Northern Parts.' See *Pomona* (London, 1729), sig. [b2v].

14 Langley, *A Sure Method of Improving Estates* (London, 1728), pp. 110, 126.

15 Ibid., p. 159. Wyat is also not in Desmond.

16 Langley, *New Principles of Gardening* (London, 1728), p. 151. In John Harvey's *Early Nurserymen* (Chichester: Phillimore, 1974) Appendix V is an abbreviated inventory of Mason's stock.

17 Greening, who was the son of Thomas Greening (1684–1757), the gardener to George II at Hampton Court, describes himself as 'Gardener to his Grace the Duke of Newcastle' in the subscription list to the second volume of Miller's *Dictionary* in 1741. He is identified in Desmond but does not appear in John Dixon Hunt's *William Kent, Landscape Garden Designer* (London: Zwemmer, 1987). Cf. the discussion of Kent's relation to the gardener at Rousham, David MacClary, below.

18 *Daily Advertiser*, 11 October 1760. Shiells's predecessor was a Mr. Moody who, Peter Collinson says, 'gave mee the Grand Tour' of Oatlands in 1735. Linnean Society, Collinson MSS. Small Book, fo.178.

19 See Harvey, *Early Nurserymen*, p. 87. Spence himself was supplied with chestnut trees by John Alston, a nurseryman near Chelsea College. See Harvey, p. 80.

20 Shenstone, *The Works in Verse and Prose* (London, 1764) I p. 110, lines 133–35.

21 In the advertisement to London and Wise's *The Compleat Gard'ner* (1699), John Evelyn wrote of them that 'they have a numerous Collection of the best Designs, and I perceive are able of themselves to Draw, and contrive others.'

22 Rose's apprentice may have been the grandfather of George London. See Robert H. Jeffers's Appendix, 'John Rose: (1619–1677)' to John Rose, *The English Vineyard Vindicated* [London, 1675] (Falls Village, Conn.: The Herb Grower Press, 1966), p. 24.

23 The warrant for payment to him (14 Oct., 1661) notes his responsibility for 'all of the orange trees and other trees and greens therein to be planted.' Jeffers, 'John Rose', pp. 14–15.

24 The firm was founded by Lewis Kennedy Sr. who was succeeded by his son. See Harvey, *Early Nurserymen*, pp. 84–85. Lee and Kennedy's catalogue was in Thomas Jefferson's possession, and Lee's largely a translation of Linnaeus's *Philosophia Botanica* (1751) *Introduction to Botany* (1760) was very popular.

25 Friday, 23 May 1760, p. 26.

26 Cited in E. J. Willson, *West London Nursery Gardens* (London: Fulham and Hammersmith Historical Society, 1983), p. 19. Gray is said to have published an untraced catalogue in 1740. Collinson also remembered John Parkinson of Lambeth (d. 1719) as a specialist in evergreens by 1712, but nothing else is known of him. See Harvey, *Early Nurserymen*, p. 86.

27 Advertisements for both appear frequently in the *Daily Advertiser* in 1743.

28 Quoted in John Harvey, *Early Nurserymen*, p. 87.

29 Francis Drake, *Eboracum: or the History and*

Antiquities of the City of York (London, 1736), p. 274.

30 See Desmond, *Dictionary* and Henrey, *Thomas Knowlton*, p. 74.

31 Henrey, *British Botanical and Horticultural Literature*, II pp. 336–39.

32 Fairchild's collection came largely from the labours of Mark Catesby in the Carolinas. Catesby worked for him and subsequently with Gray. See Henrey, *British Botanical and Horticultural Literature*, II pp. 275, 348–49.

33 Kenneth Woodbridge, 'William Kent's Gardening; The Rousham Letters,' *Apollo*, 100 (1974), p. 286. In what follows, I am also indebted to Hal Moggridge's article 'Notes on Kent's garden at Rousham,' *Journal of Garden History* 6 (1986), pp. 187–226.

34 Woodbridge, p. 286.

35 Woodbridge, p. 287.

36 Ibid., p. 290.

37 Walpole, 'On Modern Gardening' in *Anecdotes of Painting in England* (London, 1827) IV p. 269.

38 Joseph Spence, *Observations, Anecdotes and Characters of Men*, ed. James M. Osborn (Oxford: Clarendon Press, 1966), I.1136, p. 426.

39 Osborn MS. C 425, p. 35.

40 Spence, *Anecdotes*, I.1143, p. 427. Spence, quoting William Derham's *Physico-Theology* (1713), makes similar observations in I.1077.

41 White's letter for March 1739 reports MacClary 'levelling about the new pond and planting there 150 Scotch and Spruce firs from Faringdon.' (Woodbridge, 'William Kent's Gardening,' p. 287) A subsequent letter in 1741 refers to getting other evergreens from 'Mr. Williamson, the nurseryman' (Woodbridge, p. 288): presumably John Williamson, the successor to Robert Furber of Kensington.

42 Quoted in Mavis Batey, 'The Way to View Rousham by Kent's Gardener,' *Garden History* 11 (1983), p. 129.

43 Simon Pugh, *Garden-nature-language* (Manchester: Manchester University Press, 1988), pp. 78–79.

44 Woodbridge, 'William Kent's Gardening,' p. 287.

45 Ibid, p. 288.

46 Walpole, *Anecdotes of Painting in England*, IV pp. 265, 269.

47 Woodbridge, 'William Kent's Gardening,' p. 287.

48 Batey, 'The Way to View Rousham,' p. 129.

49 John Dixon Hunt, *William Kent*, p. 87.

50 See Harold Stutchbury, *The Architecture of Colen Campbell* (Cambridge, Mass.: Harvard University Press, 1967), pp. 64–65.

51 The records of the Aislabies are with the Vyner Papers in the West Yorkshire Record Office in Leeds. Most of the letters dealing with 1717 are in Vyner 5557.

52 Vyner 5557. Another letter in this file, of 1 June, tells Storzaker to deal with Fisher himself: 'If the Gardiner be too great to receive orders from you, he is too great for me: I scorn to send him such an order as you speak of . . . , you know your business too well sure, to suffer him

to domineer there.' Fisher does not appear in Desmond's *Dictionary*.

53 Edward S. Harwood, 'William Aislabie's garden at Hackfall,' *Journal of Garden History* 7 (1787), p. 325. Harwood modifies this position on p. 384. In what follows I am indebted to Harwood and to the pioneering work on Studley by W. T. C. Walker. Aislabie's early interest in gardens is indicated by his subscription to John James's *Theory and Practice of Gardening* (1712), one of the 'textbooks' of the 'French style'.

54 Harwood lists the 'Kentian' qualities of Aislabie's garden in 'William Aislabie's Garden at Hackfall,' pp. 328–32.

55 Peter Aram, 'Studley Park,' p. 19.

56 Letters of 18 April and 3 November 1718. Vyner 5557. A letter of 11 February 1720 records a number of payments for 'leading Stones from Galphay Moor to the Canall' (Vyner 5661).

57 Vyner 5560. Poaching of deer also remained a problem, and Lord Burlington's Keeper at Londesborough was asked to assist in dealing with it (Vyner 5557).

58 Vyner 5561, entries for 11 November 1717, 6 November 1718, and 19 November 1719. In 1710 Peter Aram's salary at Newby was £10. In 1750 Thomas Knowlton's at Londesborough was only approximately £22, though he would have earned extra money from other commissions.

59 Vyner 5561. There are also frequent payments for lime and ultimately one for a lime kiln on 16 March 1719. On 29 October 1719 William Hall is paid 5 guineas 'for a brass Cast for Canall pipe' and on 11 March 1720 William Plumer is paid £8 13s 0d for 'leading lead pipes to the Canall.'

60 Vyner 5557.

61 17 March 1719. (Vyner 5557).

62 Two accounts of 6 and 9 April 1724 refer to payments respectively to 'John Smith for 20 Furr Trees to Studley 2/13/4' and to 'Tho Jackson for 160 Furrs to Studley 6/8/4' (Vyner 5561).

63 4 April and 3 November, (Vyner 5561).

64 John Harvey in *Early Nurserymen* says that after 1729 Aislabie sent his regular orders to Telford of York, but a letter from Hallot on 5 Feb., 1738 shows that Perfect was still supplying elms to Studley. Hallot says of them that they have 'very fine tofts with the best roots of any that has come lately' (Vyner 5566).

65 Vyner 5619.(a) 286 Bundle A (Part 2)

66 Vyner 5566.

67 Vyner 288. The opposite page contains a list of men working on the estate including some 'att the Cascade Planting etc.'

68 Vyner 288. The accounts for 1723 show a bill on 5 December for £16 1s 3d for 'Mowers and Weeders for the Year' (Vyner 5561).

69 Letter of 11 December (Vyner 5566).

70 Letter of 19 February (Vyner 5566).

71 Vyner 5566.

72 Vyner 5566.

73 Richard Warner, *Tour* (1802), I p. 280. Cf. Philip Yorke's change of taste between 1744, when he first visited Studley Royal, and 1755. By the time of the later visit the water which he had formerly praised seemed 'ill-disposed' and

only beautiful where 'art had the least to do with it.' 'The Travel Journals of Philip Yorke,' *Publications of the Bedfordshire Historical Record Society* 47 (1968), pp. 149–50.

74 Harwood, 'William Aislabie's Garden,' p. 333.

75 Ibid. Harwood notes elsewhere, however (p. 380), that nowhere in the Aislabie records is the building called 'Fisher's Hall'.

CHAPTER 10. NATURE'S STILL IMPROV'D

1 The phrase 'Ornamental Farms' is used in the June, 1733 issue of Volume I of the *Practical Husbandman*. For much of what follows I am indebted to the pioneering article, 'The "Ferme Ornée": Philip Southcote and Wooburn Farm,' by R. W. King, published in *Garden History* 2:3 (1974), pp. 27–60, and to the subsequent replies and articles by David Jacques and James Sambrook in *Garden History* 3:2 (1975), pp. 3–6; 7:2 (1979), pp. 82–101; and 7:3, pp. 9–12.

2 Whately, *Observations on Modern Gardening* (London, 1770), p. 161.

3 Whately, *Observations*, pp. 181, 179.

4 *Present Taste in Planting* (London, 1767), p. 22. Facsimile, ed. John Harris (London: Oriel Press, 1970).

5 Whately, *Observations*, p. 181.

6 Whately, *Observations*, p. 180.

7 Spence, *Observations, Anecdotes, and Characters of Books and Men*, ed. James M. Osborn (Oxford: Clarendon Press, 1966), I.615, p. 255. It seems likely that through Pope Southcote came also to know Kent, though it is impossible to determine the extent of Kent's influence at Wooburn.

8 Spence, *Anecdotes*, I.603, p. 250.

9 *Lord Hervey and His Friends*, ed. G. S. H. Fox Strangways (London: John Murray, 1950), p. 118. The Duke of Norfolk was, of course, the owner of Worksop where Lord Petre was to make extensive planting plans in the late 1730s.

10 British Library, Add. MSS. 36056, fo. 108 and 36181, fo. 139.

11 Essex Record Office, MS. D/DP T351. MS. D/DP T356 records Southcote's marriage settlement with the Duchess. Other details of his early life are given in *An Apology for the Conduct of Mrs. Teresia Constantia Phillips*, a work in three volumes published in 1748–49 where Southcote's character is given under the name 'Tartufe.' See the notes by Paget Toynbee to Horace Walpole's notes on William Mason's *Satirical Poems* (Oxford: Clarendon, 1926), pp. 39–40.

12 An indenture between the ninth Lord Petre (to whom Wooburn passed) and his son and Sir William Bellingham in 1796 records the son as living at Wooburn possessed of $100\frac{1}{2}$ acres, the rest ($24\frac{1}{2}$ acres) being reserved to a Dominican priest called Short. (Essex Record Office D/DP T358). R. W. King believes it to have contained 116 acres in Southcote's time ('Philip Southcote and Wooburn Farm,' p. 31). David Jacques, replying to King, says that Whately's belief that

the estate contained 'an hundred and fifty acres' (*Observations on Modern Gardening*, p. 177) was evidence of Southcote's success in confusing the bounds. *Garden History*, 3:2 (1975), p. 5.

13 James Lees-Milne, *Earls of Creation* (London: Hamish Hamilton, 1962), p. 160.

14 *The Letters of Horace Walpole . . . Chronologically Arranged*, ed. Mrs. Paget Toynbee (Oxford: Clarendon Press, 1903) II p. 398.

15 Essex Record Office, D/DP 30/3/5.

16 Visit of 29 April 1757. BL Add. MS. 23001, fo. 35–36.

17 Yale University, Beinecke Library, Osborn MS. C 425, *Heads for Garden Letters*, p. 34. The views out of the walk and garden, on the other hand, are stressed by Henrietta Pye in her *A Short Account of the Principal Seats and Gardens about Twickenham* (London, 1760): 'Scarce a Spot in this Garden, but presents a different Landschape . . . Nature has indeed been particularly beautiful, in contributing to this Garden, its most striking Beauties; the Ground being very Hilly' (pp. 6–7).

18 BL Add. MS. 28727, fo. 2.

19 *London and Its Environs Described* (London, 1761), VI p. 361. The Earl of Portmore's estate, Hamm Court, separated Wooburn Farm from Oatlands, the estate of Spence's patron, Lord Lincoln.

20 George Mason, *An Essay on Design in Gardening* (London, 1795), p. 113.

21 *Anecdotes* I.1085, p. 413. In presenting an enlarged version of Spence's remarks on gardening, Osborn's edition unfortunately preserved the format of the inadequate nineteenth-century editions and distorted much of the overall sense of Spence's argument, especially in the document sometimes called *Tempe* or *Heads for Garden Letters*. Here, and in the chapter on Spence, I have included pasages omitted by him; otherwise I have followed his text.

22 *Observations*, I.606, 1130, pp. 252, 425. In I.1133, p. 425, Southcote quotes Pope's earlier observation about the obelisk.

23 *Anecdotes*, I.1130, 1132, p. 425.

24 *Anecdotes*, I.1130, p. 425.

25 See Spence's transcription of the 'Order of Planting after Mr. Southcote's Manner', reproduced in *Anecdotes*, I, facing p. 424.

26 Spence, *Anecdotes*, II pp. 649–50.

27 Batty Langley also provided a model of graduated planting in *New Principles of Gardening* (London, 1728), pp. 181–83. Nurserymen were also prompt to respond to this demand. A letter of 17 February 1732 from the Chiswick nurseryman, Henry Woodman, to the Steward of Gateshead Park in County Durham distinguishes the list of shrubs sent into lower and higher kinds. John Harvey, *Early Nurserymen* (Chichester: Phillimore, 1974), p. 181.

28 Spence, *Anecdotes*, I.1136, p. 426.

29 Osborn MS. C 425, p. 35.

30 Spence, *Anecdotes*, I.1143, p. 427. Spence, quoting William Derham's *Physico-Theology* (1713), makes similar observations in I.1077.

31 Linnean Society, Collinson MS., Large Book, p. 29.

32 Spence MSS., Box IX.

33 Spence, *Anecdotes*, I.1141, 1142, pp. 426–27.

34 Ibid., I.1128, p. 424. Mason *The English Garden* (1783) l. 522. Southcote's garden buildings are also outside the scope of this study. Although such buildings came to be a chief feature of what was later called an 'ornamented farm', gardens such as Shugborough that crammed a number of such buildings into a few acres were not in the spirit of what Southcote had initiated.

35 Quoted in James Sambrook, 'Wooburn Farm in the 1760's,' *Garden History* 7 (1979), p. 100.

36 Mason, *Satirical Poems* (Oxford: Clarendon Press 1926), p. 40. Dodsley also thought it 'too much ornamented for the simple plainness of a farm.' *London and Its Environs*, VI, 361.

37 Miles Hadfield, *A History of British Gardening* 3rd ed. (London: John Murray, 1979), p. 200.

38 Lincoln did not acquire Esher until after the death of his uncle, Henry Pelham, in 1754. Esher was, in any case, on the River Mole.

39 Letter of 28 April 1751. Newcastle Papers, University of Nottingham.

40 Spence, *Anecdotes*, I.1128, p. 424.

41 Ibid., I.1123, p. 423.

42 See John Harris's letter on this subject in *Garden History*, 7.3, (1979), p. 11.

CHAPTER 11. PROSPECTS AND THE NATURAL BEAUTIES

1 The reference to Chambers is printed in *Observations, Anecdotes, and Characters of Books and Men*, ed. James M. Osborn (Oxford: Clarendon Press, 1966) I.1098, p. 416. In the same place he also queries whether Vanbrugh or Bridgeman did not show some 'idea of the beauty of natural gardening' at Blenheim, a decade before Pope began his garden (I.1067, p. 407). The longer quotation is from Spence's 'Heads for Garden Letters' in Yale University, Beinecke Library, Spence Papers.

2 Notes for a lecture (Lecture 10) on the *Aeneid* in 1730 ('That it was a Political Poem') are in BL Add. MS. 17281, fo. 8–16.

3 *Joseph Spence: Letters from the Grand Tour*, ed. Slava Klima, (Montreal: McGill-Queen's University Press, 1975), pp. 114, 121, 132.

4 Spence, *Anecdotes* I.603, p. 250. When Addison was in Italy, on the other hand, it was the fact that these fields 'have been described by so many classic authors' that gave them their interest. *Remarks on Several Parts of Italy etc. In the Years 1701, 1702, 1703* ([London], 1769), p. 114.

5 Spence, *Anecdotes*, II p. 649.

6 Ibid., I.1124, p. 424.

7 Ibid., II pp. 649–50. Spence was also indebted to Henry Hoare for advice that 'the greens should be ranged together in large masses as the shades are in painting' (*Anecdotes* I.1105, p. 418). Although he admired the 'moderate prospects' of Stourhead and was plainly pleased with its classical *topoi* when he visited in 1765, his own garden relied increasingly upon borrowed landscape for its effects.

8 23 May 1752. Newcastle Papers, University of Nottingham.

9 Spence, *Letters from the Grand Tour*, pp. 329, 418, 228, 242.

10 Letter of 28 April 1751. Newcastle Papers, University of Nottingham. In the same letter, written a decade after their trip together, Spence observed that his first intention on that trip was to prevent Lord Lincoln from becoming entangled in a match with Lady Sophia Fermor. Lady Sophia was the daughter of Lady Pomfret, the close friend and correspondent of another great gardener, the Duchess of Somerset, who was a patroness of Switzer and a friend of Shenstone.

11 Leonard Welsted, *A Discourse to the Right Honourable Sir Robert Walpole . . . For Translating the Whole Works of Horace* (London, 1727), pp. 6–7.

12 Prefatory Note to 'Heads for Garden Letters,' Yale University, Beinecke Library, Spence Papers.

13 Maggie Keswick, *The Chinese Garden* (London: Academy Editions, 1978), p. 11.

14 Attiret's *Lettres édifiantes, écrites des missions* (1749) had been lent to Spence by Philip Southcote in 1751. His translation was published under the pseudonym of Sir Harry Beaumont. 'Yuen-ming-yuen, or the garden of gardens,' Spence wrote of the great Chinese imperial palace, begun in the early eighteenth century by the Emperor K'ang Hsi. Walpole misunderstood the appeal of Chinese gardens to Spence. Plainly it was their apparent wildness and grandeur, not the artifice of their buildings, that Spence admired. See 'On Modern Gardening,' *Anecdotes of Painting in England* (London, 1827), IV pp. 258–60.

15 David Jacques points out that Spence translated Attiret to resemble the *imitatio ruris* of Robert Castell's account of Pliny's gardens. *Georgian Gardens: The Reign of Nature* (Portland, OR: Timber Press, 1984) p. 46. Chambers, for his part, heartily disliked such gardens as the *ferme ornée*: 'a large green field, scattered over with a few straggling trees, and verged with a confused border of little shrubs and flowers.' See *A Dissertation on Oriental Gardening* (London, 1772), pp. v–vi.

16 Spence, *Anecdotes*, II p. 649. Spence would probably also have known the engravings of Matteo Ripa, see p. ●● above.

17 An extensive survey of Spence's gardens is given by R. W. King in *Garden History* 6.3 (1977), pp. 38–64; 7.3 (1978), pp. 29–48; and 8.2 (1979), pp. 45–65, 77–114. Also relevant is Peter Martin's 'Joseph Spence's Garden in Byfleet. Some New Descriptions,' *Journal of Garden History* 3, pp. 121–29, and E. Charles Nelson, 'Joseph Spence's Plan for An Irish Garden,' *Garden History* 15 (1987), pp. 12–18.

18 Unless otherwise noted, the Spence Papers cited below are those are in the Beinecke Library of Yale University. Most of the material relating to garden designs is in Boxes VIII and IX.

19 Letter of 2 August 1732. *Letters from the Grand Tour*, p. 114.

[20] Letter to Richard West, 28 September 1739. *Yale Edition of Horace Walpole's Correspondence*, ed. W.S. Lewis et al. (London and New Haven: Yale University Press,) XIII p. 181.

[21] Christ Church, Oxford. Evelyn MS. 38, fo. 208.

[22] Christ Church, Oxford. Upcott: Original Letters, Small Series, vol. I, fo. 28.

[23] In his letter to Wheeler, Spence commended Kent's staking out his 'grovettes' so that no three trees stood in a line. To that he added 'as a necessary rule . . . that in all smaller plantations one should never set above three or four trees of the same sort together.' *Anecdotes* II p. 649.

[24] Spence, *Tempe*, p. 59.

[25] Ibid., p. 52. Evelyn cites André Mollet's similar advice on perspective in the 1660s: that 'ground Works and Knolls neerest to the house, under the commanding Windows [;] such as are most remote from the eye in larger measure for an effect of perspective.' Christ Church, Oxford, Evelyn MS. 38, fo. 186.

[26] See above, p. 85.

[27] Richard Pococke refers to it as the latter in his account of the locality in his *Travels in England* (1757), BL Add. MS. 23001, fo. 34. Stephen Duck, the vicar of Byfleet, however, believed it to be Roman. In his poem *Caesar's Camp* (1755) a Druid prophesies the sort of British triumph over Roman values that was a commonplace of Augustanism.

[28] Letter to Reverend Robert Wheeler, 19 September 1751. *Anecdotes*, II p. 651.

[29] Spence MSS., Box VIII (Byfleet).

[30] Spence is quoting from Hutcheson's *Inquiry into the Original of our Ideas of Beauty*, a work published in 1725, just as the first rural landscapes were beginning to be created.

[31] Describing Spence's first designs for his garden, Peter Martin writes: 'His acres did not then comprise a *ferme ornée*, strictly speaking, though they would later; but the effects were similar.' *Journal of Garden History* 3, p. 122.

[32] Yale University, Beinecke Library, Spence Papers. Spence also wrote to Lord Lincoln on 12 August 1752: 'I hope you have either seen Matlock, or will see it, for it would be a Sin to miss it.' Newcastle Papers, University of Nottingham. The taste for what Addison called 'rude prospects of rocks rising above one another' (*Remarks on Italy*, p. 103) was, of course, well-established long before Spence's time. What is new is the desire to incorporate it in a landscape garden.

[33] There are three other undated plans that show the central opening getting larger and terraced round with tree plantations intersected by paths that go out to a perimeter walk.

[34] Spence had also made designs for laying out Dodsley's garden at Richmond in 1753. See R. W. King, 'Joseph Spence of Byfleet. Part III,' *Garden History* 8.2 (1979), p. 45.

[35] Shenstone had been reading Spence's *Polymetis* in 1748. Letter to Richard Jago, *The Letters of William Shenstone*, ed. Duncan Mallam (Minneapolis: University of Minnesota Press, 1939), p. 93.

[36] For an account of this visit, See 'Joseph Spence of Byfleet,' Part II, pp. 64–65.

[37] Walpole, 'On Modern Gardening,' *Anecdotes of Painting in England* (London, 1827), IV, 276. Letter to Richard Bentley, September 1753, *Horace Walpole's Correspondence*, ed. W.S. Lewis, (New Haven: Yale University Press, 1973), XXXV pp. 148–49.

CHAPTER 12. SMOOTHING OR BRUSHING THE ROBE OF NATURE

[1] Letter to Lady Luxborough, 30 August 1749, *The Letters of William Shenstone*, ed. Duncan Mallam (Minneapolis: University of Minnesota Press, 1939), p. 161.

[2] Richard Graves, *Recollections of Some Particulars in the Life of the late William Shenstone* (London, 1788), p. 49.

[3] Shenstone Manuscript, English Poetry Collection, Wellesley College.

[4] B L, Add. MS. 28964, fo. 6v, [12v].

[5] Thomson's association with Lord Lyttelton is dealt with extensively in John Dixon Hunt's *The Figure in the Landscape* (Baltimore: Johns Hopkins Press, 1976). Lyttelton included the inscriptions that he had composed for Hagley in his poetical works. He also celebrated Pope as the English Virgil.

[6] Shenstone, *Letters*, p. 41.

[7] At the entrance to Virgil's Grove, Shenstone placed the inscription: *P. Virgilio Maroni Lapis Iste Cum Luco Sacer Esto.*

[8] *Georgics*, I, Books 1, 2, ed. Richard F. Thomas (Cambridge: Cambridge University Press, 1988), p. 20.

[9] Graves, *Recollections*, p. 82. In 1747 Shenstone complained to Graves that doubtless Lord Lyttelton and James Thomson 'will lavish all their praises upon *nature*, reserving none for poor *art* and *me*.' *Letters*, p. 85. An account of Thomson's observations on the relation between art and nature at The Leasowes is given in Hunt and Willis, *The Genius of the Place*, p. 244. Shenstone's own opinion was that 'art should never be allowed to set foot in the province of nature, otherwise than clandestinely and by night' 'Unconnected Thoughts', *Works in Verse and Prose* (London, 1764), II p. 136.

[10] 'To the Honourable Mrs. Knight, at the Time she was laying out her Villa,' Shenstone Manuscript, English Poetry Collection, Wellesley College.

[11] Letter of 23 April. *Letters*, p. 143. The description of Barrels is from Graves, *Recollections*, p. 120. Lady Luxborough is said by the *OED* (2nd ed. 1989) to have been the first to use the term 'shrubbery'.

[12] Although this may prove a useful way of distinguishing between gardens that invoked an agricultural topos and those that did not, the verbal distinction was not rigorously observed. In his commentary on Virgil's use of the word *tempe* (in *Georgics* II l. 469), Peter Ramus remarks that in this word, by synechdoche, all felicitous places are included. *Georgica* (Paris, 1584), p. 203.

[13] *Poetical Works* (London, 1780), ll. 133–35, 289–93.

[14] *The Life and Poetical Works of James Woodhouse* (London: Leadenhall Press, 1896) ll. 22, 24. Spence encouraged Woodhouse by getting him the patronage of Mrs. Montagu.

[15] 'Hope', Shenstone Manuscript, English Poetry Collection, Wellesley College.

[16] Shenstone, *Works*, II pp. 381, 357–58, 370–71.

[17] Alexander Carlyle, *Autobiography* (Edinburgh: Blackwood, 1840) p. 369. Carlyle visited The Leasowes in 1758.

[18] *Four Topographical Letters* (Newcastle, 1757), pp. 58, 57. The British Library copy, G.15964 (1), has a manuscript note on the flyleaf identifying the author of this work as Resta Patching, a Quaker of London, whose death was reported in the *Publick Advertizer* on 21 May 1760. In a letter to Graves on 25 November 1758, Shenstone himself refers to reading 'Mr Patchen's "Topographical Letters" soon after they were published.' *Letters*, p. 357.

[19] Cited in John Riely, 'Shenstone's Walks.' *Apollo* 110 (1979), p. 203. Hull's original MS. of 'Shenstone's Walks' is at Yale University.

[20] Letter of 28 August. Shenstone, *Letters*, p. 117.

[21] Ibid., p. 51. Cf. Evelyn's proposal for the *Elysium Britannicum*, reprinted in *The Genius of the Place*, ed. P. Willis and J.D. Hunt (Cambridge, Mass.: M.I.T. Press, 1988), pp. 67–69.

[22] Shenstone, *Letters*, p. 51.

[23] This reflection occurs in a letter to Graves about the latter's proposal of an inscription to Shenstone. Shenstone was insistent that his interest in gardening be equally stressed with poetry and approves a text from *Georgics* II (493–94) to illustrate it. Letter of 3 October 1759. *Letters*, p. 375.

[24] 'The Leasowes' in Joseph Giles, *Miscellaneous Poems on Various Subjects* (London, 1771), pp. 2, 6.

[25] 'Perhaps a sullen and surly speculator may think such performances rather the sport than the business of human reason.' 'Life of Shenstone' in *Prefaces to the English Poets* (London, 1781) 10:4, pp. 6–7. Graves rebuked Johnson's ignorance of gardening: 'What leisure, or inclination, or opportunity, could such a man have to attend to or study the beauties of nature, and the pleasures of a country life.' Graves, *Recollections*, p. 109.

[26] Shenstone, *Letters*, p. 148.

[27] Shenstone, *Works*, II pp. 139–140, 342.

[28] Ibid., II p. 130.

[29] Shenstone, *Letters*, p. 141.

[30] Letter to Congreve, 1699, cited in Miles Hadfield, *Landscape with Trees* (London: Country Life, 1967), p. 93.

CHAPTER 13. NONE BUT REAL PROFESSORS

1 See D. D. C. Chambers, ' "Discovering in Wide Lantskip": *Paradise Lost* and the tradition of landscape description in the 17th century,' *Journal of Garden History* 5 (1985), pp. 15–31.

2 See John Harris, Stephen Orgel and Roy Strong, *The King's Arcadia* (London: Arts Council of Great Britain, 1973) and Roy Strong, *Henry Prince of Wales and England's Lost Renaissance* (London: Thames and Hudson, 1986).

3 An architrave from the Trajaneum at Pergamum (now in the Museum of London), sent back to Lord Arundel in the 1620s, was adopted by Van Dyck in one of his paintings and used by Inigo Jones both in the set for the masque *Albion's Triumph* and for the chapel of Somerset House. See David Howarth, *Lord Arundel and His Circle* (New Haven: Yale University Press, 1985), p. 82.

4 Cf. *Inigo Jones on Palladio, being the notes by Inigo Jones in the copy of I Quattro Libri dell Architettura di Andrea Palldio 1601* (Newcastle-upon-Tyne: Oriel Press, 1970) and Per Palme, *The Triumph of Peace: A Study of the Whitehall Banqueting House* (London: Thames & Hudson, 1957), passim.

5 In his introduction to *The Diary of John Evelyn*, E. S. De Beer states: 'To Arundel and the artists who worked for him Evelyn probably owed his lasting interest in the visual arts and a power of appreciating landscape such as rarely found expression among his older contemporaries.' (Oxford: Clarendon Press, 1955), I p. 5. Cf. D. D. C. Chambers, 'The Tomb in the Landscape: John Evelyn's Garden at Albury,' *Journal of Garden History*, I (1981), pp. 37–54, and Howarth, *Lord Arundel and His Circle*, pp. 214–18.

6 See *Ben Jonson's Conversations with Drummond of Hawthornden*, ed. R. F. Patterson (Glasgow: Blackie, 1924), p. 23.

7 Viz. the ambiguity of imperial iconography employed by Marvell in his 'Horatian Ode' where 'Caesar's head at last / Did through his [Cromwell's] laurels blast.'

8 Strong, *Henry Prince of Wales*, p. 107.

9 Second edition, 1623. On the side of the garden plan at p. 11 in chapter 5, the letter 'H' indicates 'Walkes set with great wood thicke' that lie outside the garden. I am grateful to Peter Goodchild for drawing my attention to this.

10 Sheffield University, Hartlib MSS. 67/22 and 25/6/4. I am indebted to Peter Goodchild for this reference from his article, ' "No Phantasticall Utopia, but a Reall Place." John Evelyn, John Beale and Backbury Hill, Herefordshire,' *Garden History* 19 (1991), pp. 105–27. I am also indebted to Erik de Jong for the information about Huygens.

11 George Mason, *An Essay on Design in Gardening* (London, 1768), pp. 22–23.

12 Switzer, *Ichnographia Rustica* (London, 1718), I p. xix.

13 Hannah More, *Letters*, ed. R. B. Johnson (London: John Lane, 1925).

14 Letter to Philip Southcote, 9 December 1752. Linnean Society, Collinson MSS. Large Book, p. 30.

15 Bernard Smith, *European Vision and the South Pacific 1768–1850* (Oxford: Clarendon Press, 1960), p. 4.

16 Brian Fried, *Translations* (London: Faber, 1981), a play about the 'renaming' of Ireland by nineteenth-century English cartographers and the obliteration of native names.

17 In his article, 'The Shaping of Angiosperm Taxonomy,' S. M. Walters elaborates the argument 'that the whole idea of genus and species is a natural product of European thought of the seventeenth and eighteenth centuries, based on Aristotelian logic.' *New Phytologist* 60 (1961), pp. 74–84.

18 Letter to Richard West, 28 September 1739. *Yale Edition of Horace Walpole's Correspondence*, ed. W. S. Lewis et al. (London and New Haven: Yale University Press) XIII p. 181.

19 Letter of 20 April 1754. *A Selection of the Correspondence of Linnaeus and Other Naturalists*, ed. Sir James E. Smith (London, 1821), I p. 31. In a letter of 10 April 1755, Collinson wrote: 'We have great numbers of Nobility and Gentry that know plants very well, but yet do not make botanic science their peculiar study.' Ibid., I p. 33.

20 Letter of 28 January 1660, Christ Church, Oxford, Evelyn MS. 39a, Epistle 161.

APPENDIX. THE MYSTERY OF 'SIEUR BOURGIGNION'

1 Essex Record Office D/DP.P.5, cited in Sir George Clutton and Colin Mackay, *Old Thorndon Hall, Essex: a History and Reconstruction of its Park and Garden*, Garden History Society, Occasional Paper, no. 2, pp. 28, 30. Clutton and Mackay mistake the phrase 'outrun the Constable' (in a letter from Petre's quondam guardian to his mother) to mean a nickname for Bourgignon, whereas in early eighteenth-century slang the phrase meant simply 'to outstrip one's resources.' Bourgignon's English career is noted in Andrew Wilton, *British Watercolours, 1750–1850* (Oxford: Phaidon, 1977), p. 12.

2 In fact the 1731 publication of the map credits the geographer brother with it.

3 In *Le Necrologe des Hommes Célèbres de France* (Paris, 1774).

4 This is from a 'character' of Petre by Collinson, said to have been written in a 'Catalogue of the Plants' at Thorndon Hall, done by Philip Miller. See Canon C. T. Kuypers, *Thorndon: Its History and Associations* (Brentwood Diocesan Magazine, 1930), p. 32.

5 Marcus Binney cites the map at Worksop as reading 'E. Petre inv. Peter Bourguinon delineavit,' but as Petre's initials were 'R. J.' it is equally possible that Bourgignon's Christian name is given in error. See 'Worksop Manor, Nottinghamshire—I', *Country Life* (15 March 1973), p. 681. The Gisburn plan, however, also records 'Designed by P. Bourguignon' (Yorkshire Archeological Society, MS. 918), though there the 'P' is suspiciously far away from the surname. Is it possible that Bourgignon, a professional chameleon, adopted the name 'Peter' as a joking reference to his employer?

6 Clutton and Mackay, *Old Thorndon Hall*, p. 30.

7 See James Britten, 'The Eighth Lord Petre,' *Dublin Review* 155 (1914), p. 310.

INDEX

fig. 1st

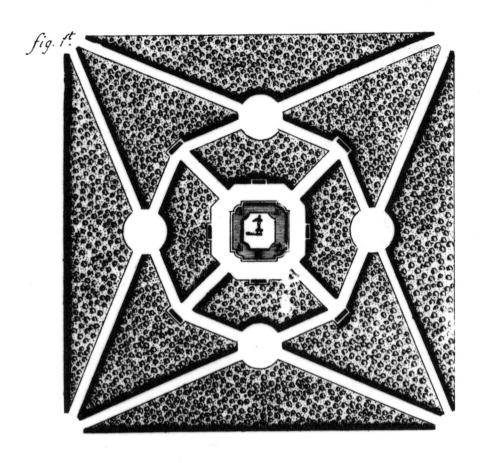

fig. 2^d

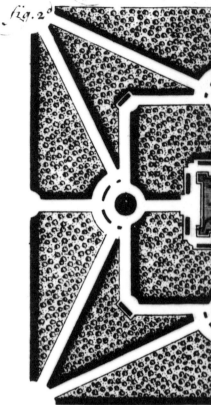

fig. 4^t

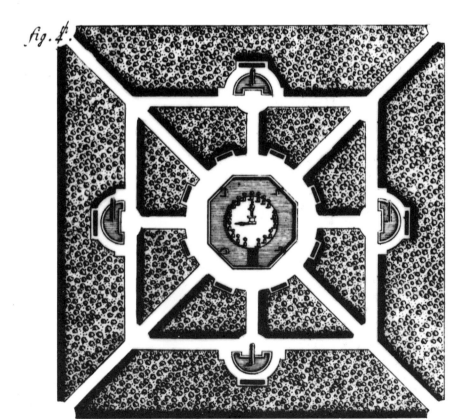

fig. 5th

Pl. 3. c .